Food Aid and International Agricultural Trade

A Study in Legal and Administrative Control

Robert L. Bard
University of Connecticut
Law School

Lexington Books
D.C. Heath and Company
Lexington, Massachusetts
Toronto   London

Contents

viii

List of Tables

List of Figures

Foreword

This book throws some different light on a much treated subject. It also compiles and analyzes for us as has not before been done the variety of organizational and legal instruments which bear on international issues in the international movement of agricultural products. It does more: a legal slant is provided us which suggests that, in the future, perhaps economic phenomena may have to be buttressed even more by jurisprudence in order to assure efficient but equitable trading processes. Therefore, while the treatise does not purport to add substantially to the existing literature with respect to the potential and dangers of food aid as an adjunct to economic development and commercial trade, it provides an interesting basis for speculation about the overall configuration of control mechanisms applied to agricultural product movement. These are, as an example of a particular use of law and law-related instruments, used to resolve intricate economic problems which have strong international implications.

The book is addressed to three principal audiences—national and international civil servants, responsible for the conduct of food aid operations, public and private personnel directly concerned with the augmentation and protection of international commercial agricultural trade and the wider group of scholars and policymakers interested in discovering more effective ways of achieving international economic order. For the first two groups, this book, by providing a comprehensive presentation and analysis of the wide array of specific legal-administrative devices currently and potentially available for the control of the delicate interrelationships of food aid and international trade fills the existing gap between existing economic analyses of these relationships and the day to day administrative decisions that must be made by officials charged with implementing food aid programs.

With respect to the utility of law oriented regulation of important international economic processes . . . food aid transactions are most specific to the point. As Professor Bard demonstrates, the history and current status of the international and national legal administrative infrastructure supporting food aid provides a pattern of the process whereby dangerous unilateral actions are gradually transformed into acceptable and useful channels. Domestic as well as international law becomes involved, and each forms the basis for action by the other. Noncoercive yet authoritative systems may be applied in many areas of international economic and commercial conduct where reluctance to cede national authority has made adoption of more traditional legal systems unacceptable.

Within the past fifty years, the progress of technology has made a literally world-wide world-state technically possible. Professor Toynbee, the English historian, has written extensively about this. We possess, as well, the organizational know-how for administering human affairs on a world-wide scale. On the economic plane, there is a number of concerns, especially private firms, which operate on a scale that extends to the entire habitable and traversable surface of the earth. Political life could be organized as well, but the will must be there to do so. This book suggests a route which man might take to approach solutions to some problems in a particular area—that of assisting international agricultural development through legal studies and operations.

One does not have to agree with all of Professor Bard's analysis to hold the opinion that he has treated a very important subject thoroughly and objectively. This is my position. As already mentioned, Bard has added the legal dimension which is a singular contribution to the literature. I would hope that he will pursue specifically the legal analysis of this subject in more detail in a future work. That and other works like it could help in bringing to fruition an international political life which is more organized—a hopeful condition for man's survival. With this optimistic note, let me compliment the author on a successful job and commend the work to the wide readership it deserves.

Jimmye S. Hillman
Head of the Department of
   Agricultural Economics
University of Arizona
   and
Past President
American Agricultural
   Economics Association

Preface

This book is concerned with those aspects of the economic and financial inter-relationships between food aid and international agricultural trade that may be affected through control methods fitting a broad definition of law. Heretofore, the little systematic work in this area has been by agricultural economists. This is understandable since charting relationships between food aid and commercial trade requires this discipline more than any other. But after baring the underlying economic dynamics of the principal varieties of food aid, the agricultural economist stops work at the point where his analyses of the impact of various food aid practices upon commercial trade must be translated into specific conduct rules and procedures for administering these rules. Usually, this task is undertaken by professional governmental administrators or to avoid the euphemism—bureaucrats—a highly respectable calling in my pantheon. It is here that an academic lawyer can make his contribution. The professional economist is uncomfortable with the nitty gritty of administering a complex rules systems, and the professional bureaucrat rarely has the time to reflect on the systems he is creating and operating.

Whether those directly involved with formulating, administering, and coping with the various devices now in effect to regulate relationships between food aid and international trade realize it or not—and I suspect they do not—they are participating in a legal system, though not necessarily one that most lawyers would recognize as such. Essentially, law is a set of norms designed to regulate future conduct in an important area in a consistent, predictable, effective, and equitable manner. Undoubtedly, the control systems operating on the food aid/commercial trade sphere significantly differ from those familiar to most lawyers. For the most part, the conduct directing standards are imprecise. There is not authoritative body empowered to interpret the norms and finally adjudicate disputes. Moreover, the norms are explicitly made nonbinding upon the subject parties. Yet, the system has been effective in regulating conduct, and that is the ultimate test for any legal system. Indeed, the success of the system largely flows from its essentially noncoercive nature, since under the existing international order, nations would refuse to accept binding restrictions upon their conduct in the politically sensitive areas of agricultural policy.

This study has two broad foci. The first is to establish a comprehensible working model of the economic and financial interrelationships between food aid and commercial agricultural trade and to describe the effect of various possible control devices upon these relationships. An effective analysis of the mechanisms for controlling the interaction of food aid and commercial sales relationships must proceed on at least five levels. These include (1) identifying the range of objectives attributable to a given food aid donor; (2) determining the extent to which these are internally consistent or conflicting; (3) establishing criteria for ranking or ordering these objectives; (4) measuring the degree to which various food aid transactions may achieve given objectives; and (5) evaluating the effectiveness of each potential legal/administrative control device in eliminating unwanted or undesirable side effects of uncontrolled food aid. The second purpose is to describe and analyze the standards and procedures now employed or seriously proposed to regulate the impact of food aid upon commercial agricultural trade.

This is a very difficult undertaking. Food aid transactions may take many different forms. And although control devices can be evaluated in terms of their efficiency in reaching given ends, there exists only a rudimentary framework for judging the relative desirability of the ends themselves. The analysis is further complicated by the lack of explicit explanation or expression by food aid administrators of the rules or policies which guide them in shaping various categories of food aid transactions. Therefore, any comprehensive attempt to evaluate existing practices must first create suitable conceptual and normative benchmarks which can be used to judge the wide array of food aid control techniques. For this purpose, it is first necessary to identify the goals of the food aid transaction and the interests might require protection. Although it may be relatively easy to develop food aid practices designed to achieve a particular objective, usually the decision-maker must satisfy a number of incompatible interests. Thus, a donor could find ways (1) to maximize protection and enhancement of its own commercial exports; (2) to maximize the economic benefit to the recipient; or (3) to afford the maximum protection of commercial interests of the donor's friends or allies; but it could not satisfy all three of these at once. The policy finally adopted will represent some kind of compromise among these objectives.

In order to evaluate any particular food aid practice in terms of the extent to which it achieves each of these goals, we must know the economic impact of both the food aid transaction and the control device upon all parties and interests likely to be affected thereby; know the objectives of the food aid donor with respect to these same groups; and have some basis for appraising these objectives. Although various aspects of food aid/commercial trade relationships have been closely examined by the international agency primarily responsible for the operation of existing international control machinery, they have not been in position to view the entire food aid/commercial sale picture with academic detachment. And the scattered scholarly work in this area has been limited in scope and ambition. Therefore, the economic and financial impact of various food aid transactions on each affected party has not been spelled out; the potential and actual objectives of the participants in the transactions have not been catalogued; nor has any serious attempt been made to evaluate alternate objectives. In these circumstances, the creation of appropriate conceptual tools for evaluating methods for controlling the relationship between food aid and commercial transactions not only is a prerequisite to a critique of these practices, but it is valuable in its own right. For once a workable framework is created, it may be used for the evaluation of a wide array of possible food aid forms and controls.

The central concern of this study is to develop the necessary structure to permit a thorough and accurate evaluation of the potential effectiveness of the various substantive rules and procedural devices that might be employed to facilitate the maximum use of food aid, consistent with the protection of other legitimate interests that would be threatened by unrestricted food aid. Because of the considerations outlined in the previous three paragraphs, it is necessary for this study to delve rather deeply into economic, political and administrative considerations. In doing so, I have tried to make maximum use of existing work in the relevant allied disciplines. Often, though, professional economists and political scientists have not developed the necessary tools for my purposes and I have had to fashion my own. Naturally, I feel more confident of those aspects of the work strictly centered on legal issues. This is the risk anyone venturing into interdisciplinary work must take. For the most part, I believe my use of other disciplines involves straightforward extrapolations of well-established principles and concepts. But no matter how far the work seems to stray from traditional legal considerations, it does so only because I have concluded that an adequate analysis of the legal aspects of the problem requires it.

Since this book is aimed at a number of audiences with somewhat conflicting interests, it presents difficult organizational problems. The attempt to describe the efficacy of alternate methods of moderating the relationships between food aid and commercial trade should be primarily of interest to students of international trade problems and those primarily interested in the efficacy of food aid as an adjunct to conventional foreign aid or as a partial solution to agricultural trade problems caused by chronic surplus production. Government officials, international civil servants, and private parties directly interested in agricultural trade will be mostly concerned with the efficiency of existing control devices and feasible alternatives to the less satisfactory practices. The organization best suited to a detailed analysis of food aid/commercial trade relationships will have the effect of dispersing specific criticisms and suggestions of various food aid control practices throughout the book. This feature makes it somewhat clumsy for people interested in particular aspects of food aid/commercial control problems. Simultaneously, the attempt to present an exhaustive treatment of current national and international attempts to control the impact of food aid on commercial trade may bog down the reader interested in the general utility and dangers of food aid.

The organization I chose for the book is designed to provide an orderly and comprehensive study of the problem from the scholar's viewpoint. At the same time, most of the individual segments can be read independently. As a part of the concluding chapter, I attempt to summarize my positions on many of the current operational problems in administering existing food aid machinery. Hopefully, this approach will make the book useful to the wide array of interests connected with food aid. Several important issues have not been explored in this book. Thus, based upon good authority, I have accepted the potential utility of food aid for humanitarian and developmental purposes. The potential impact of differently administered varieties of food aid on commercial trade is analyzed. But neither the underlying causes of agricultural disharmonies nor the best way of solving them are independently analyzed here. No comprehensive analysis of commercial trade practices in agricultural commodities is presented. Although food aid and commercially motivated price-cutting lie on a single continuum, I have limited my consideration of the latter to the extent required for a full understanding of the food aid aspects.

Hopefully, this study will contribute to a clearer understanding of the complex economic and political factors which have shaped United States food aid practices and which must be confronted in any bilateral or multilateral food aid program. Moreover, it is submitted that the evidence will demonstrate that the national and international authorities responsible for the shaping of food aid practices have done an extremely creditable job of reconciling large-scale use of agricultural products as a development tool with the commercial interests of exporting nations at all stages of economic development.

Part I: The Nature, Potential, and Threat of Food Aid

Much of the southern hemisphere demands sizeable financial assistance to achieve morally and politically acceptable rates of economic and social development. Indeed, many of these countries may require massive help to avoid widespread starvation within the next decade. Unfortunately, the steady reduction of the United States financial commitment to rapid economic development severely dampens the prospects for marshalling the large quantities of financial and economic resources from the developed world required for this purpose. In 1970, the United States foreign aid which reached nearly $4 billion annually during the peak of the Marshall Plan amounted to less than $2 billion, representing 0.31 percent of its Gross National Product, and placing it 12th among the 16 members of the Development Assistance Committee. In these circumstances, it is axiomatic that every potential source of economic assistance must be maximally exploited, particularly varieties likely to be available from the United States. Food aid, that is programs making agricultural products available to poor countries on less than commercial terms, may be one such source that can successfully withstand the effective insensitivity of many developed western nations to poverty outside their own borders (or even within them).

The Promise and Perils of Food Aid

Since the end of World War II, food aid programs, initially conducted on a bilateral basis, and recently expanded to include multilateral and international efforts, have provided more than $25 billion worth of agricultural products to economically needy countries to help combat hunger and malnutrition and to stimulate long-term economic development. Recently, the U.N.s World Food Program Intergovernmental Committee reviewed the role of food aid during the "second development decade." The Committee found that food aid had alleviated famine, improved the nourishment of vulnerable groups of the population and substantially contributed to the recipients' economic development. Based upon this finding and its predictions with respect to the needs of the world's poorer nations for the next decade, the Committee recommended that ". . . such food supplies as are in excess of commercial demand should be used to an increasing extent constructively to meet the unsatisfied needs of people in developing countries and in assisting in their economic and social development." (See the Committee's publication, 17/5 Food Aid and Related Issues Draft Report on Food Aid During the Second Development Decade.)

But as a substitute for conventional foreign aid, food aid suffers from one powerful drawback. Unless great care is taken, sizeable food aid transactions can severely disrupt commerical internal and international agricultural transactions (internationally and within the economy of the recipient). Therefore, if food aid is to play a significant role in economic development, means must be found to protect normal trade in agricultural products from the incursions almost certain to accompany unrestricted food aid programs. For this reason, it is essential that all parties concerned with development of agricultural trade understand how food aid transactions may affect ordinary commercial trade and how these effects may be controlled. In this book, we attempt to describe and evaluate alternate legal administrative techniques to control the impact of food aid. In the first part, we set out the economic and political factors that underlie food aid/commercial trade relationships. This includes (1) the factors promoting food aid programs; (2) the array and general operating characteristics of current programs; (3) the utility of food aid to donors and recipients; (4) the kind of threats to important economic interests posed by food aid; (5) the development of international attitudes towards these problems; and (6) the general dimensions and directions of the means that have been developed to deal with them.

1

Background to Food Aid Commercial Trade Problems

Ironically, the very factors facilitating the use of food aid as an escape from the current impasse between the demands and needs of the poor and the ability and desire of the rich to respond to these needs, are exactly those that render food aid a highly controversial, difficult and potentially dangerous undertaking. Both the danger and availability of food aid are a direct result of the chronic agricultural surpluses universally suffered by the agricultural sector of economically developed countries. In contrast to the developing nations' frantic efforts to achieve agricultural self-sufficiency, the more developed nations have experienced chronic agricultural overproduction.[1] Matters have been made worse by programs designed to maintain farmers' incomes which have the effect of encouraging continued production of commercially unsaleable agricultural products. The need to protect international agricultural trade from the depressive effects of these surpluses has engendered an extensive defensive network of international conventions and commodity agreements.[2]

The brilliant notion of giving or cheaply selling some of these burdensome agricultural products to poorer nations was conceived by the United States in the early 1950s as one way of disposing of the growing stocks of government-owned agricultural products being generated by the then existing price support policies. Everyone seemed to gain. American agriculture found a new outlet for its farm products. And even if food aid programs did nothing more than reduce existing surpluses, this alleviated pressure on domestic and international markets and helped blunt political hostility towards price support programs by reducing the costly and unseemly accumulation of agricultural products in government warehouses. Simultaneously, the availability of large amounts of free or low-priced food and fiber directly served United States foreign policy by providing the United States with the means to temporarily relieve hunger and promote the ultimate economic development of the have-not nations, thereby minimizing the threat to international order presented by countries threatened by immediate economic disaster. Of course, food aid also was supported by those who viewed the eradication of worldwide hunger and poverty as the direct concern and duty of the fortunate few.

These factors still operate. Despite significant progress in the United States and hopeful signs in some other nations, the agricultural plants of the western world exhibit strong tendencies towards overproduction. The situations in the European economic community and Japan are critical. And developing countries will continue to require food that they can neither produce themselves nor af-

3

ford to buy on commerical terms. Thus by meeting domestic needs of the donor, food aid recruits political support not generally available for other forms of humanitarian or foreign aid. In the United States, the strong support of food aid by farm-oriented Midwestern and Southern legislators sharply contrasts with their general antagonism towards foreign aid. But if agricultural products are in world surplus, the provision of low-priced products to potential commercial purchases can only worsen matters. If the supply of agricultural products already exceeds the demand for such products at financially remunerative prices, the transfer of large amounts of agricultural goods at cut-rate prices will be perceived as posing very serious threats to the existing markets of agricultural exporters unable or unwilling to finance food aid programs themselves.

Such programs present several distinct types of potential dangers to commercial markets. The developing countries have been and are likely to continue to be strong customers for commercial food and imports.[3] Therefore, the pursuit of bona fide assistance objectives may inadvertently cause serious damage to the world trade patterns in, or the price structures of, the commodities concerned. Or countries may use food aid programs solely to dump excess production, or even worse, use food aid transactions as a means to expand the giver's share of the recipient's commercial imports at the expense of nonfood aid giving agricultural exporters. Since most bilateral food aid programs are to some extent conceived and operate as a convenient method of surplus disposal, the uneasiness of other nations on this score is understandable. Programs administered by international organizations, such as the World Food Programme, are less suspect on these grounds. But unless sophisticated protective measures are employed, even international programs can have a deleterious impact upon commercial trade. And despite the clear short-run economic benefits of food aid, ill-considered programs may constitute a net detriment to the development needs of recipient countries.

Although all forms of economic assistance, particularly agricultural assistance, can be used as a weapon in international trade warfare, food aid is peculiarly suited for such purposes. These programs are founded upon the existence of surplus agricultural products or the capacity of a country to produce agricultural goods in excess of commercial demand, and are substantially fueled by a desire to benefit the donor's farm sector. Other forms of foreign aid, particularly aid tied to the donating country, may induce a nation to shift its purchase patterns to the detriment of third country exporters, or it may lead to the development by the recipient of productive capacities which could increase domestic food production and thus reduce their net food imports or even make them competitive exporters of economically related products. Food aid, though, is more dangerous since it focuses upon a single type of product already presenting severe international trade problems. Furthermore, the availability of cheap agricultural products from foreign sources anxious to maximize food aid shipments may induce hard-pressed developing countries to neglect development of their own agricultural potential. This could easily impede the recipient's long-term economic development or make it unduly dependent upon external sources for its vital food needs. Given the desires of the food aid donors' agricultural interests to maximize food aid shipments, food aid programs might be administered to tempt recipient countries to accept more food aid than is consistent with their development needs. Furthermore, the necessity of any country temporarily or permanently unable to meet its minimum domestic requirement to import food may cause it to accept food priced only slightly below commercial levels. And though the recipient might see such transactions as constituting food aid, third country exporters reasonably may perceive it as nothing more than thinly disguised dumping. Another drawback of food aid is that the relatively low financial and economic cost of food aid compared to the more flexible conventional forms of aid, may induce developed countries to substitute food aid for more developmentally useful, though costlier varieties of foreign aid.

The dangers to certain economic interests inherent in concessional sales of surplus agricultural products have drawn severe criticism from other commercial agricultural exporters upon existing United States agricultural aid programs. But do such interests merit protection? It may be argued that the commercial needs of developed countries deserve little consideration or protection compared to the needs of the usually poorer recipients. Or perhaps all nations, developed and developing, would be better off if the elaborate protective screens surrounding agricultural production and trade were dismantled forthwith. Undoubtedly, agricultural prices would be lowered and developing countries would benefit to the extent they import such products. But although in recent years some developing nations have been forced to convert from agricultural exporters to heavy importers of food products, this pattern is abnormal and dangerous. Normally, food importers tend to be the more industrialized nations, and lower food prices would tend to benefit the richer rather than the poorer nations. Moreover, it is highly unlikely that agricultural protection will be significantly reduced in the immediate future and to the extent food aid programs are needed at all, they are needed now. The highly important and complex controversies swirling about food aid have been aptly and succinctly stated by Otto Matzlae, the director of the Project Management Division of the World Food Programme.

Food aid has played an important, and in some ways perhaps a vital role in the world over the past few decades. Without it, it would have been impossible to provide millions of people with at least the bare necessities of life. Food surpluses therefore have served a good purpose and ought not to be regarded merely as a burden. But food aid is not a simple form of development aid. It is complicated by the fact that it requires adequate and long-term planning, while at the same time it deals with unplanned surpluses. Like any other form of development aid, it needs time to get under way. It is, however, beside the point to describe food aid, as has sometimes been done, as the worst form of development aid from the economic point of view. Surpluses do exist and will probably continue to do so; they must be put to the best possible use.

But it would be utopian to attempt to 'solve' the world food problem wholly or in large part through massive food aid, with the surplus countries not only continuing their surplus production but increasing it systematically to meet the growing demand in as many developing countries as possible. Such a system would certainly simplify some aspects of agricultural policy in the countries where production capacities are not being fully used, but the granting of food aid should be determined by the developing countries' interests rather than the interest of the donors. The interests of the developing countries evidently lie in an increase in their own food production as the only possible permanent solution. Consequently, the duration and extent of development aid in the form of food should only aid to tide over the period which must elapse before the developing countries are able to meet their total food requirements either from their own production or from commercial imports.[4]

Thus food aid may be criticized on two grounds: (1) its impact upon the economic development of the recipient; and (2) its effect upon international agricultural trade. It now appears that the furor over the utility of food aid as a development aid has largely subsided. Criticism and analysis of crudely administered food aid programs largely motivated and designed as pure surplus disposal operations have succeeded in eliminating most of the more objectionable features and have largely transformed most food aid programs into reasonably effective supplements and substitutes for conventional foreign aid. Moreover, strenuous efforts are being exerted to expand multilateral and international food aid programs, primarily designed to afford maximum benefits to the recipient, albeit with important shifts in emphasis and modes of administration. And, as we shall see, sophisticated and effective national and international control mechanisms have been developed to eliminate many of the adverse effects of large-scale food aid upon international agricultural trade.

International Controls of Food Aid

Until quite recently, the major controls upon food aid transactions have been self-imposed by the United States under pressure from other agricultural exporters. In addition, a rudimentary system of international controls have existed for some time, and it seems likely that from now on these, rather than national methods, will be playing the major role. This country, in both its roles as the principal donor and a major agricultural exporter, has acceded to a number of international arrangements designed to provide both substantive ground rules for the conduct of concessional transactions and a forum for resolution of disputes. The United States itself has established complex administrative practices and procedures for reconciling the inherently conflicting and competing interests operating in any food aid program conducted by an agricultural exporting nation. These procedures, in turn, have spawned a wondrously complex and sophisticated set of legal controls intended to cleanse food aid transactions of a wide range of unwanted and unnecessary interferences with vested commercial interests of the United States and other friendly powers. These arrangements are both important and interesting in their own right and have provided the model for other national and international programs based upon furnishing agricultural products on less than commercial terms.

Now, though, it appears that internationally conceived and administered controls will be playing an increasingly important role. International standards and dispute-resolving procedures have been in operation since the mid-fifties. By the mid-sixties, the international community had succeeded in controlling the worst features of bilateral food aid. But a few years later, concommitant shifts in the constitution of food aid programs and the technical, economic and legal structure of worldwide agricultural production and trade demanded strenuous new efforts to reformulate, modify and expand existing control mechanisms to meet the new situation. Throughout the 1950s and 1960s, the threat of food aid upon commercial international agricultural trade came from the United States and regulation of food aid transactions was achieved by preventing United States food aid practices from unduly injuring the trade of other agricultural exporters, most of whom were developed countries. A number of important events have drastically altered this picture. The sources of conventional foreign aid funds have begun to dry up as the needs of the developing nations continue to increase. Simultaneously, traditional grain exporters such as Canada, Australia, and Thailand have been encountering severe surplus problems compounded of the secular increase in agricultural productivity affecting all developed nations, and the recent dramatic improvement in wheat and rice production by traditional Asian food importers, and severe rice surplus problems in Japan. The new agricultural policies of the European Economic Community (EEC) have developed large internal agricultural surpluses, both in grains and dairy products, accompanied by import-export policies which shut off foreign imports while heavily subsidizing exports, in sharp competition with other noncommunity exporters.

In many respects, there now exists a situation very similar to that which propelled the United States into large-scale food aid programs during the early 1950s; the need for new sources of foreign assistance for developing nations combined with very large stocks of commercially unsaleable agriculture products. The response also has been similar, but with an important distinction. It is not the case of one single nation (the United States) acting upon very mixed developmental and selfish motives, and unilaterally transferring huge quantities of surplus products to poor countries. Rather, an increasing number of countries and international entities have become food aid dispensers. These new participants have acted both individually and collectively. The last two International Wheat Agreements included a Food Aid Convention which obligated certain Wheat Agreement members to provide developing countries with minimum amounts of food aid or its equivalent. More significantly, a new international organ, the World Food Programme has been permanently established to administer its own food aid program and to coordinate worldwide food aid efforts.

But if food aid is likely to remain relatively available, the reason for this availability must concern us. One of the prime forces behind the current increased interest in food aid is the deterioration of the agricultural sector in countries long suffering from agricultural imbalances and the spread of these problems to new countries and products. These surpluses have increased pressure on traditional agricultural exporters to protect their threatened commercial markets and can be expected to augment the ever-present temptation of food aid donors to seek ways of using food aid to improve their commercial export position. As this study should prove, the United States has conducted its food aid operations in accordance with sophisticated legal administrative practices and mechanisms which preclude blatant use of food aid to directly promote United States commercial exports. But the developed nations which for the first time pledged significant amounts of food aid activities under the Food Aid convention have only just begun to establish similar traditions or practices. And since many of these same countries include the United States' prime competitors for commercial agricultural export markets, this country has refused to tolerate a situation in which its self-denying food aid practices make it an easy victim for its competitors' predatory practices. Similar dangers faced those new food aid donors with extensive commercial agricultural exports who chose to play the game straight.

The current situation is that as more countries have surplus problems, they have begun significant food aid programs to help dispose of their surpluses and none of the new participants are superpowers. These factors change the requirements for control of the delicate relationship between food aid and commercial agricultural trade. In many ways, for countries feeling threatened by food aid transactions and for poorer nations seeking to gain maximum developmental benefit from food aid, the United States is an ideal food aid donor. As the leading opponent of communism and the prime seeker of a stable international order, the United States has been particularly sensitive to the complaints of allied and friendly agricultural exporters. It also possesses the political and administrative sophistication and resources necessary to conceive and implement an effective system of controls upon its food aid transactions. It was these factors that induced this country to modify its practices and to impose effective regulatory devices which met the needs of potentially affected third country exporters.

The introduction of many new food aid donors significantly changes the setting in which transactions will take place. Control problems are further complicated by introducing a much larger number of participants with varying needs and motivations. Also, the burden of formulating and administering effective controls falls upon nations both less sensitive to the needs of rival exporters and with reduced economic and political capacity for self-regulation. On the other hand, the rise of the World Food Programme as a significant source of food aid and a potential means for coordinating and directing efforts enhances the possibility of conducting food aid programs in conformity with the needs of the widest possible number of nations, both developed and developing.

These events already have produced strong international responses stimulated in large measure by the transformation of the United States into a potential victim of unrestricted food aid. The last two International Wheat Agreements have included guidelines for concessional transactions. More significantly, the United Nations' Food and Agriculture Organization has sharply modified the substantive rules and procedures of the control machinery operating under the aegis of the FAO Principles of Surplus Disposal. Existing standards and institutions were generated as a response of the major agricultural exporters to American practices. But with the United States transformed from the villain to a potential victim, this country has become far more cooperative in seeking new international restrictions. Indeed, it has insisted on measures to strengthen international control machinery.

Conceivably, the recent balance-of-trade difficulties of the United States might affect this country's attitudes towards food aid issues. Increasingly, the United States is asserting that the current rules of international trade unfairly discriminate against its interests. This is alleged to be particularly true with respect to agricultural trade. One effect of this attitude might be to induce the United States to reverse its previous cooperative attitudes towards food aid/ commercial trade relationships and revert to earlier practices in which food aid is used as an offensive weapon to expand commercial trade. So far, the United States' concern with its trade situation only has caused it to insist that its commercial trade protection practices be internationalized. But the next step might well be to reverse its cooperative and responsible food aid practices.

An Example—Control of Wheat Transactions

The subsequent analysis may be clarified by a brief presentation of the anatomy of a typical food aid transaction; sale of wheat by the United States to India on concessional terms. Due to current price support policies, United States domestic wheat prices usually are above the worldwide commercial price. Therefore, commercial wheat exports must be subsidized to the extent necessary to make United States wheat competitive with the exports of other nations. In terms of current international agreements and understandings, this would be considered neither as surplus disposal nor a food aid transaction. The sale of wheat to India in exchange for payment in Indian currency or for dollars payable over a forty-year period, however, would be deemed food aid. Such a transaction would have a discernible effect upon India's economy and finances, the United States farmer, the budget and balance-of-payments of the United States, and the opportunities for commercial sales of wheat, rice, and flour by all countries, including the United States, which normally export these products to India. The actual impact of such wheat transactions upon commercial trade patterns may be estimated by measuring the degree to which the trade patterns existing prior to the onset of large-scale concessional wheat sales to India have changed since the institution of the food aid. We will find trade patterns have changed, but that non-United States commercial exporters have suffered no net injury. Commercial markets lost in India have been replaced by increased sales to Europe and Japan.

In making concessional wheat sales to India, the United States might attempt to achieve any of several possible objectives. It might wish (1) to maximize the economic development of India; (2) to maximize the disposal of surplus wheat; (3) to protect or expand United States commercial exports to India; or (4) to accord the greatest degree of protection to the commercial wheat exports of Canada, Australia and Argentina. The actual policy followed will represent some compromise among these generally contradictory ends. An examination of the agreements accompanying wheat sales to India indicates that as a condition of receiving the wheat on concessional terms, India is required to purchase a certain amount of wheat on commercial terms with its own foreign exchange. The purchases may be made from any noncommunist country. At one time, concessional sales to certain countries provided that a portion of the mandatory commercial purchases must be from the United States.[5] Wheat sales agreements after 1959 have dropped this arrangement. Obviously, the impact upon United States' and other countries' commercial sales will be affected differently in accordance with the type of purchase requirement imposed on each case.

Gifts or concessional sales may affect agricultural commerce through their impact upon India's exports. In conducting food aid transactions, the United States always attempts to control exports by recipients directly attributable to the availability of underpriced food aid commodities. Generally, countries receiving food-aid financed products are prohibited from exporting the same commodity. Exports of economically related products also may be precluded or restricted. Thus, Pakistan was prohibited from exporting rice while she was receiving wheat under food aid. To determine the wisdom and efficacy of these controls, we must first gauge the impact of these particular restrictions on all affected parties and then evaluate them in terms of the possible objectives of the United States with respect to the recipient country and the third countries likely to be affected by increased rice exports. As we shall see, under certain circumstances, rice exports induced in part by concessionally priced wheat may make economic sense. At the same time, we must consider the effect of such exports upon United States rice exports and those of other countries, particularly poor countries such as Thailand.[a]

[a]Actually, only exports of ordinary grades of rice were prohibited. Exports of certain high-quality grades were permitted. If the recipient country traditionally exports the related product, exports are limited to the prefood aid level. In certain cases, increased exports are permitted at the cost of certain penalties.[6]

Food aid sales of other products to other countries carry similar kinds of restrictions and requirements albeit with important distinctions. These will be examined and analyzed in Part III with respect to all important food aid products. In all cases, the need for and effect of these restrictions flow from the economic and political factors discussed in Chapter 3.

The Reason for International Controls

As this book shall demonstrate, food aid has been subjected to a highly complex set of nationally and internationally administered controls. Moreover, it appears that nations participating in the food aid/commercial trade process have taken considerable pains to see that these controls work. At the same time, many nations heavily subsidize agricultural exports and domestic consumption of agricultural products. For example, it has been estimated that in 1970, the European Economic Community spent $900 million on export and consumption subsidies in a successful effort to reduce its stockpiles of wheat and dairy products, without attracting serious protests from competing exporters. But, until the United States upset the international applecart in the summer of 1971 only the most rudimentary efforts have been made to limit these practices through the kind of devices employed with respect to food aid. This disparity seems quite paradoxical since the food aid control system is designed to preclude just the kind of agricultural trade practices that go completely unregulated outside food aid, i.e., the transfer of agricultural products on less than commercial terms. I believe that the resolution of this paradox is essential to a thorough understanding of the food aid/commercial trade control system. Therefore, this contradiction should be borne in mind as one works through the complexities of the food aid/commercial trade problems. I shall return to this question in the concluding chapter, where, based on the insights gained from the study, I shall attempt to resolve the paradox.

Notes

1. *Food and Agriculture Organization, Commodity Review and Outlook: 1969-70*, 1970, Ch. 1; UN/FAO, *The Stabilization of International Trade in Grains* (FAO Commodity Policy Series, no. 20), 1970, Ch. 1; 1967, 1-29; E. Thorbecke and J.B. Condliffe, "The Pattern of World Trade in Foodstuffs: Past and Present," *Iowa State University Center for Agricultural and Economic Development, Food–One Tool in International Economic Development*, 177-218 (1962).

2. The following agreements purporting to control some aspect of trade in an agricultural commodity currently are in operation: the International Wheat

Agreement, the International Sugar Agreement, the International Olive Oil Agreement, the International Coffee Agreement, the GATT Long Agreement regarding Trade in Cotton Textiles, and the most recent arrangement concerning certain dairy products. Other agreements are under negotiation or consideration with respect to cocoa, peanuts, oil seeds, oils and fats, bananas, hard fibers, jute, kanef and allied fibers, rice, citrus fruits, rubber, and tea. Supra, ch. 4. A comprehensive discussion of the economic, political and legal implications of commodity agreements may be found in 28 *Law and Contemporary Problems*, 272-427 (1963), p. 3.

3. See, FAO Commodity Policy Series, no. 20, supra, chap. 1; UN/FAO, *Inter-agency Study of Multilateral Food Aid, Director General's Progress Report to CCP* (Committee on Commodity Problems, no. 67/13), 1967, Ch. II, p. 3.

4. *Need for Increased Future Resources* (World Food Programme Newsletter 6), January-February 1970, p. 8.

5. Agreement with Peru, Feb. 7, 1956, TIAS 3190, 6 UST 563 (1956). See Chapters 7, 8.

6. Supplementary Agreement with Pakistan, Dec. 26, 1967, TIAS 6422, Part II, Item IV-B, 18 UST 3275, 3277 (1969), p. 18.

2

Current and Conceivable Food Aid Programs

Food aid programs greatly vary both in their potential benefit to recipients and in their potential danger to commercial agricultural trade. In one sense, any food aid transaction presents the same kind of danger to commercial sales. The more food that is given away or sold on less than commercial terms—cash payable in convertible currencies—the narrower the potential commercial market for these products. Furthermore, given the nature of most existing agricultural price support systems, food sold considerably below market prices or on less than commercial terms may still yield a net positive return to the giver.[1] For purposes of analyzing the relative potential and danger of each kind of transaction, existing food aid programs can be divided along two continuums—sales versus gift and bilateral versus multilateral. Bilateral sales programs are the most controversial since in many cases it is very difficult to distinguish selfishly motivated surplus disposal operations from genuine aid activities. And since the United States has been the overwhelmingly predominant food aid donor, it is not surprising that its food aid program, particularly sales on concessional terms, have attracted the most criticism and have been subject to the most complex set of controls and restrictions. At the other extreme, international operations, such as the World Food Program are completely immune from selfish motives. Even so, international programs must exercise the same care to avoid undue disruption of commercial trade as is required for national programs.

Donations are less threatening than concessional sales since individual countries cannot derive much selfish benefit from giving food away. For this reason, bilateral donation programs have operated in a less hostile and more open atmosphere than other types of food aid programs. However, even with pure motives, donation programs do present some potential threat to commercial markets. And the threat increases as the thrust of programs shift from famine and disaster relief and combating malnutrition (particularly in children) to more developmentally oriented objectives. The danger becomes particularly acute when donations are made through market channels, thereby competing with commercial food sales rather than being directed to particular classes of people in limited locations.[2]

In one respect, concessional sales labeled as food aid may be more difficult to control than explicit export subsidies. The patent- self-centeredness of export subsidies make them relatively simple to identify, though very difficult to control.[a]

---

[a]To date, the only international standards applicable to export subsidies are found in Article XVI of the GATT. These require contracting parties maintaining subsidies, including any form of income or price support, which operate directly or indirectly to increase exports to notify the Secretariat in writing of the nature and extent of such subsidization.

Food aid programs, compounded of varying proportions of selfishly motivated surplus disposal efforts and altruistic economic assistance, require much more delicate treatment. If the benefit of food programs to developing nations is to be preserved, it is essential that efforts to protect legitimate commercial interests do not seriously undercut the potential benefits of food aid to worthy recipients. Methods must be found that will at once protect defensible commercial interests while permitting genuine aid efforts to continue and flourish. As we shall see, the diversity of interests affected by food aid and the wide ramifications of pressures exerted at any point in the international agricultural economy often make this a very difficult undertaking.

**Segregating Export Promotion from
Food Aid**

From the recipient's viewpoint, any action which reduces the price or payment terms of a commodity it wants is "food aid." This would include any general surplus disposal or export promotion transaction. At one time, certain United States programs seemed little more than export promotion. But the worst features of these programs have been eliminated. For the purposes of our analysis, we may concentrate on programs specifically designed to assist poorer countries. Presently, most of the potential cash markets for agricultural products still are concentrated in the developed world. It is towards these customers that agricultural exporters direct their export promotion efforts. The marginal reductions in price or terms available under current export promotion schemes are far too small to significantly increase purchases by food aid target countries. And current international practices and understandings preclude any general sharp departures from normal commercial terms. Therefore, under current practices, all efforts to provide economic aid via agricultural products generally will be conducted through specific programs limited to particular undeveloped countries and areas, and it is these which we will scrutinize.

Export Promotion

Although export promotion devices *per se* are not strictly relevant to the food aid problem, in fact, food aid may be viewed as an extension and exaggeration of export promotion schemes and at the margin may be indistinguishable from them. One such commercially oriented arrangement is the Export Credit Sales program of the United States Commodity Credit Corporation.[3] Here, credit is made available to finance exports of the United States farm products for credit periods of up to 36 months. However, current policy limits credit to 12 months for cotton and tobacco sales and 6 months for all other commodities. The Export-Import Bank extends credit and guarantees loans to facilitate agricultural exports, usually for periods of one year. The Canadian Export Development Corporation offers insurance against nonrepayment of credit for specified reasons on Canadian exports and a recently enacted program expands credit facilities for Canadian wheat and flour exports.[4] Australia offers similar facilities to its exporters.[5]

Barter. Under certain conditions, barter arrangements can be deemed a variety of food aid. A developing country is benefited if it is able to obtain part of its agricultural needs in exchange for goods it otherwise could not export commercially. It also gains if the food-producing country is willing to give more food per unit of the recipient's product than the market would yield. If the bartering is bilateral, the extent of profitable bartering arrangements is limited by the willingness of the food producer to accept the food recipient's products, the possibilities for commercial export of the product, and the size of the "price" discount the food grower will allow. But, if the food recipient's products can be sold to third countries, the range of beneficial barter arrangements can be extended. The degree of aid in every transaction will vary with the rate of exchange established between the traded products and the alternate markets for the product given up by the food recipient.

Of the major noncommunist agricultural exporters, only the United States has conducted extensive barter operations. Two types of programs are authorized. One falls under the same legislation—Public Law 480—which has provided the legal basis for all forms of the United States food aid over the past seventeen years.[6] The second and larger barter program is a function of the Commodity Credit Corporation.[7] From July 1, 1954, through December 31, 1970, exports under noncommercial barter programs totaled $1.7 billion.[8] Despite the possible benefits to developing countries, barter operations have been viewed by the United States and other exporting nations primary as surplus disposal operations rather than food aid.[9] As such, it has been heavily criticized by commentators and other countries.[10]

The barter program has undergone several metamorphases during its career. Technically, barter is a misnomer for American operations of this type since the only bartering is between a United States exporter and the federal government. The barter contractor delivers certain types of materials, goods, or services to the government and receives agricultural commodities for export at a favorable price. Originally, many of these exports were directed towards the commercial markets of the developed rather than undeveloped countries, and thus displaced potential commercial agricultural sales of other exporting nations.[11] The commodities accepted by the United States government were strategic materials for the government supplemental stockpile.[12] For Canada, at least, the United States stockpiling operations tended to offset some of the losses caused by additional United States wheat exports to Canadian markets fostered by the barter program. That is, the acceptance by the United States of such products as lead and zinc, in exchange for agricultural commodities like wheat tended to increase overall worldwide demand for lead and zinc, the latter representing, along with wheat, important Canadian exports.[13]

But since 1967, in response to sharp criticism, the barter program has been altered to minimize its adverse effect on other nations. First, a complex country-commodity system was established which barred sales of critical agricultural commodities to commercial markets of the United States and competing exporters.[14] In 1963, the government limited stockpiling operations and shifted emphasis towards procurement to be used outside the United States in furtherance of various government programs.[15] Paradoxically, it is not clear that Canada has benefited by this change in government policy. The reduction of the pressure on its wheat sales was counteracted by reduced United States government purchases of zinc and lead.

Most recently, barter deals for goods destined for the strategic stockpile were limited to cases in which the agricultural product involved is shipped to the country providing the materials.[16] This will ensure that barters will actually constitute food aid rather than surplus disposal. The preclusion of tricorner deals whereby an importer-exporter obtained raw materials from one country, exchanged it with the government for an agricultural product which was sold in a third country, should markedly reduce the possibilities for barter deals involving strategic materials. Only rarely will the same country simultaneously want United States agricultural products and be a source of strategic materials. Actually, this restriction represented a modification of a more drastic House provision which would have eliminated entirely barter deals for stratetic materials.[17]

The barter program is large and controversial, but its problems are easily separable from those of food aid. Although United States' commercial barter programs are substantial, for the moment, barter-food aid programs only have historical interests. Even those barter deals made with underdeveloped countries have stemmed from private initiative unrelated to any specific intent to assist the recipient country through this means.[18] However, it is possible that some of the countries recently commencing significant food aid operations may be tempted towards barter deals. If so, United States experience should provide a valuable guide for avoiding the dangers inherent in such programs.

Current Food Aid Programs

The remainder of this chapter will briefly describe all significant current programs involving agricultural products that could be deemed food aid. From July

1, 1954, to December 31, 1970, the United States supplied food and fiber on concessional terms valued at $19.6 billion[19] out of a world total of about $25 billion.[20] Moreover, some portion of the approximately 20 billion dollars spent by the United States in non-European countries for general economic aid has financed the purchase of agricultural products and significant amounts have been expended to meet food needs through development of the recipient's own agricultural capacity.[21] The magnitude of agricultural development aid is difficult to determine, although it certainly is much less than direct transfers of food and fiber.[b] But though the United States has consistently exhorted others to join the War on Hunger, the level of its own efforts have been closely tied to the size of its surplus holdings and the nation's overall fiscal position.

Products Supplied Under Food Aid

Food aid has been concentrated in cereals, fats and oils and dairy products, all products exported by developed countries which have been in surplus at one time or another. Wheat and now rice are chronic problems, and world trade in dairy products and butter oil are subject to sharp fluctuations. Many developing countries also export cereals; only Brazil exports significant quantities of fats and oils and no developing countries export dairy products. But developing countries have been unable to finance food aid programs with respect to the products they export. Certain significant food aid commodities—soya beans for example, and to some extent feed grains—have enjoyed relatively stable commercial markets. Skim milk and butter were not significant food aid commodities until the agricultural policies of the European Economic Community (EEC) resulted in severe overproduction of these commodities. Consequently, the EEC Council of Ministers pledged 120,000 tons of skim milk powder and 35,000 tons of butter oil to the World Food Program for 1970 and 1971. Similarly, Canada's current overproduction of eggs have induced it to contribute some portion of government purchased stocks to the World Food Program.

The United States Food Aid Programs. The dominance of the United States in bilateral food aid operations centers any investigation into the impact and control of food aid programs on United States' activities and practices. Since 1948, agricultural products have been supplied by the United States on concessional terms under several different programs.[22] For a time, the Mutual Security program financed sizeable transfers of these products.[23] Precursors of the current

---

[b]For example, in 1968, of the 3.3 billion dollars committed by the United States for foreign aid programs 1.2 billion was attributed to food aid and 2.1 billion was committed for non-food aid assistance.

Food for Peace program were established in 1953.[c] And 1954 saw the enactment of the Agricultural Trade and Development Act (P.L. 480), the cornerstone of current United States food efforts.[27] By the close of fiscal 1956, P.L. 480 had become the dominant source of agricultural commodities on concessional terms, and Mutual Security Act transfers had shrunk to insignificance.[d]

The current legislation, now entitled the Food for Peace Act of 1966, is a direct continuation of the original P.L. 480 legislation.[29] Under the Kennedy administration, the program acquired the name Food for Peace and President Johnson tried, with but indifferent success to rename it Food for Freedom.[30] With Richard Nixon, we reverted to Food for Peace. Though technically inaccurate, United States food aid still is widely called P.L. 480.

Forms of United States Food Aid. Currently, the Food for Peace program authorizes three major programs which could be considered food aid.[31] These are sales for local currency, sales on dollar credit and donations. Of these, the first and third clearly constitute food aid. The second, dollar credit sales, is harder to classify.

Sales Programs. The oldest form of United States food aid are sales for the currency of the recipient country. Normally, imported agricultural products, like

[c]In 1953, the Commodity Credit Corporation was authorized to transfer 1 million tons of wheat out of CCC stocks to Pakistan. Payment for the wheat and its transportation could be made from the CCC's annual appropriation.[24] The wheat was to be used to fight famine and as a reserve. Other provisions of the statute formed the basis of local currency practices under the subsequently enacted P.L. 480 program. Thus, local currency accruing under the program would be collected in a special account to be used to increase food production or for any other program of mutual benefit. Five percent was to be allocated for use by the United States in defraying its own expenses in Pakistan. In conformity with subsequent practice under P.L. 480, these funds could only be used by purchasing them with appropriated funds. The program was to be terminated by the President whenever he or Congress, by concurrent resolution, determined that no further assistance was necessary.

In the same year, Congress authorized an additional $100 million worth of any agricultural commodity within CCC stocks to be used for famine or emergency relief anywhere.[25] No restrictions applied to local currencies accruing under this authorization. The subsequent P.L. 480 program was further adumbrated in 1953 by the addition of section 350 to the Mutual Security Act. Under this provision, a minimum of $100 million and a maximum of $250 million of Mutual Security Funds was to be used to finance the sale of United States surplus agricultural products for local currencies. In these transactions, the President was to safeguard against displacement of commercial sales by the United States or other friendly countries. In these transactions, the President was to safeguard against displacement of commercial sales by the United States or other friendly countries, assure that the sales price was consistent with maximum world prices of like commodities, use private trade channels wherever possible, control transshipments of the commodities, and emphasize sales to underdeveloped and new market areas. The President was to obtain the recommendation of the Secretary of Agriculture in negotiating agreements. Local currencies generated by these transactions were to be used for a number of the same purposes subsequently authorized under P.L. 480.[26]

[d]In the calendar year 1956, United States agricultural exports under P.L. 480 totaled 890 million dollars. Exports under section 402 and 550 of the Mutual Security Act totaled 449 million dollars. In 1962, exports under the Mutual Security Act had dwindled to 35 million. In calendar 1970, P.L. 480 exports reached $1.178 million, and Mutual Security Act exports stood at $11 million.[28]

most other products, are sold for cash, payable in convertible currencies. But pursuant to Title I of P.L. 480, certain countries were permitted to pay for the products in their own currencies, at prices computed by converting the commercial price into the recipients' currency at a stipulated rate of exchange.[e] The local currencies received by the United States under these arrangements is deposited into special accounts, to be used by the United States or the recipient for specifically designated purposes.[33] Although some portion of these funds are, in effect, converted into hard currencies, the bulk of them are handled in ways that would ensure that the food aid recipient did not suffer a foreign exchange loss attributable to use of these funds.[34]

Now, though, sales for local currency are being phased out in favor of sales payable in dollars over the same long periods with low interest rates available under development loans made by the Agency for International Development (AID).[35] The Agency for International Development is authorized to make loans with a minimum interest rate of 1% for the first ten years and 2-1/2% thereafter.[36] Theoretically, no limit may be set on the terms of repayment, but in practice, the loans are made for no longer than 40 years with a 10-year grace period on the principal. Actually, 103(b) of the Food for Peace Act of 1966 authorizes a more complicated arrangement by which the payments made in local currencies may be converted to dollars, at the option of the United States, pursuant to a timetable analagous to an AID loan schedule.[37] This same section of the Act required that all sales be converted to dollar terms by December 31, 1971. The current practice is to make sales payable partially in cash in local currency and partially for convertible currencies repayable on AID terms.[38] Through calendar 1970, sales for local currencies have accounted for $12 billion of the $19.6 billion spent under P.L. 480 and sales in local currencies convertible to dollars on AID credit terms have totaled $1.1 billion.

Donations. Agricultural products also may be donated. Originally, donations under the P.L. 480 program were exclusively reserved for disaster relief and similar humanitarian activities on a case-by-case basis. They now may be used for economic development purposes and in certain countries are distributed through the same commercial channels used for Title I sales.[39]

Up to 1960, donations could be made only for meeting "famine or other urgent or extraordinary relief requirements."[40] Gradually, however, and without benefit of additional legislation, donations were expanded to include economic development projects.[41] In 1960, the Act was amended to authorize use of donated surplus products "to promote economic development in underdeveloped areas . . . ,"[42] and in 1963, donations for "community development" purposes were authorized.[43] In the comprehensive revisions of the P.L. 480 Act accomplished in 1966, the program was further expanded to provide donated food to combat malnutrition for "needy persons" and nonprofit school lunch

[e]Determination of the appropriate rate of exchange to be applied to the dollar value of the food aid commodities often is a complex and controversial process.[32]

and preschool feeding programs.[44] From 1954 through 1970, donations represented about 19% of the $19.6 billion worth of agricultural commodity aid offered by the United States. However, the proportion of donations has been increasing and in calendar 1970 donations represented nearly 17% of the total $958 million effort.[45]

Occasionally, donations have been used in lieu of Title I sales. At one time, political considerations dictated providing Afghanistan with free commodities which were destined to be sold through the recipient's normal commercial channels.[f] And donations have been used to supplement concessional sale transactions when funds for the latter prove insufficient. This seems to have been the case in India during the drought in 1966 and 1967.[g] Under these circumstances, donations may pose the same kinds of threats to normal commercial sales as do Title I sales. However, to the extent that donations bypass the local economic system and are made directly available to consumers with limited purchasing power, they are unlikely to interfere with significant commercial markets; they just facilitate additional consumption by the target groups that would not occur if food was available only on commercial terms. But this may not hold true if the donated commodities are generally distributed through usual market channels. The danger of United States gift transactions is heightened by the absence of the standard control features accompanying Title I sales. Under recent modifications, many of these gift transactions have been made subject to international controls.[48]

Dollar Credit Sales. At one time, so-called Title IV dollar credit sales were a clearly identifiable alternate form of food aid.[49] Sales were made under long-term supply contracts payable in dollars on credit terms. The terms, though, were considerably harder than those available under AID loans.[h] Although these transactions now are authorized by the same statutory provisions applicable to local currency and dollar convertible long-term local currency sales, they are conceived and handled as a separate program.[51] Theoretically, such sales are made only to semideveloped countries, but often they are made to very poor countries in combination with local currency sales.[i] Interest rates and payment

[f]From fiscal 1956 through 1965, Afghanistan received $28 million worth of donated commodities. However, it was not until 1966 that the first Title I sale of $890,000 was made. Even then, $9.3 million of donated commodities also were provided.[46]

[g]With respect to India, in fiscal 1964, Title I sales totaled $368 million and donations $17 million. In fiscal 1965, Title I reached 489 million and donations climbed to $27 million. In fiscal 1966, Title I sales reached $511 million and donations $35 million.[47]

[h]Under current legislation, the most favorable terms are twenty-year repayments with a two-year grace on principal and AID interest rates. Through canendar 1970, $900 million was spent under this program. However, these types of arrangements were only initiated in 1962 and have shown considerable growth. Thus, in calendar 1970, long-term sales accounted for $112 million of the total program of $958 million.[50]

[i]In calendar year 1966, Title IV agreements were signed with Iceland, Yugoslavia, Algeria, Congo, Ivory Coast, EACSO (Kenya, Uganda and Tanzania), Kenya, Liberia, Morocco, Sierra Leone, Afghanistan, Greece, Iran, Iraq, Israel, Jordan, U.A.R., Indonesia, Philippines, Bolivia, Brazil, Columbia, Equador, and Paraguay. Of those, Title I agreements were signed with Congo, Morocco, Israel, Jordan, U.A.R., and Bolivia.[52]

terms may vary from very soft (though still harder than AID terms) to nearly commercial levels.[53] As the terms harden, these transactions may become indistinguishable from export credit sales.

Products Supplied under Food for Peace. Up to 1966, United States food aid operations virtually were limited to so-called surplus commodities. These were defined by the relevant legislation as any privately or publicly owned agricultural commodities or products made in the United States which, at the time of export, were in excess of domestic requirements, adequate carry-over, and anticipated exports for dollars, as determined by the Secretary of Agriculture. Under these conditions, through December 31, 1970, the commodities supplied under the Food for Peace program were distributed as indicated by Table 2-1.[55]

One of the principal features of the 1966 revision of the Food for Peace Act was to unchain the program from exclusive dependence on surplus agricultural products.[56] Indeed, during that period, the rapidly diminishing stores of wheat and feed grain surpluses mandated some such action if the program was to be continued at its desired levels.[57] Actually, special arrangements had permitted the donation of certain nonsurplus goods, viz. animal fats, edible oils and dairy products.[58] But under the 1966 Act, all agricultural products are potentially available for use in the program, subject to a determination of availability by the Secretary of Agriculture. However, the removal of surplus-only restrictions is not terribly meaningful because "surplus" always has been an arbitrary designation, not related to any fundamental economic factors. The amounts and commodity complexion of the Food for Peace program actually depends upon such factors as the historical pattern of United States exports, alternate commercial opportunities, the level of subsidies for each product, and the needs of developing recipient countries.

Table 2-1
Distribution of Commodities under Food for Peace through December 31, 1970

Product	Value (Millions of Dollars)	Percentage of Program
Wheat and Wheat Products	9,824.2	50.1
Coarse Grains[a]	1,933.9	9.8
Rice	1,393.7	7.1
Fat and Oils	1,736.6	8.8
Dairy Products	1,628.8	8.3
Cotton	2,266.0	11.5
Tobacco and Cigarettes	566.4	2.8
Others[b]	230.3	0.1
	19,580.4	

[a]Includes corn, barley, grain sorghums, oats, rye, mixed feed grains, rye flour, cornmeal.
[b]Includes *inter alia* oilseeds and meal, meat and poultry, fruits and vegetables.

Procuring and Shipping Food Aid Commodities. Under all concessional food programs, commodities are made available to consumers in the importing country through the same international and domestic channels used for commercial imports. The only difference lies in the financial arrangements made by the two governments.[59] Sales are made pursuant to single- or multiple-year agreements specifying both the dollar value of each item and a formula for converting the dollar value into local currency. The agreements also divide the local currencies among the uses required or permitted by the statute.[60] The commodities provided under these agreements are procured, financed, and shipped by or through the Commodity Credit Corporation (CCC), the government corporation responsible for price support operations and various other domestic and international programs.[61] Actually, these commodities might originate from CCC stocks or from regular commercial sources, or they might represent acquisitions otherwise destined for purchase by the CCC.[62] The United States government ensures that exporters are paid in cash dollars and that the importing country need not pay with foreign exchange to finance the transaction—or at least may delay such payment for many years. Instead, the exporter may rely on the special terms granted by the United States government.

Administering Food for Peace. Given the extraordinary complexity of the factors underlying each major food aid decision, and the inherent vagueness of the statutory guidance, the character and orientation of the organizations administering the program assumes great importance. The history of the United States food aid programs has been marked by a constant struggle between the Department of State (including AID) and the Department of Agriculture for supremacy. The Secretary of Agriculture is responsible for those aspects of food aid likely to affect domestic agricultural interests; the Secretary of State has charge of the foreign relations aspects; and AID, an independently administered component of the State Department, subject to the foreign policy guidance of the Secretary of State, considers the economic impact of food aid transactions. The Secretary of Agriculture determines the types and quantities of particular commodities available for sale to particular countries.[63] State is delegated the function of negotiating and entering into sales agreements and resolving all foreign policy issues arising in the context of administering the program.[64] In the 1966 revisions of the Food for Peace legislation, the Secretary of Agriculture lost his long enjoyed statutory power to determine the countries eligible to receive commodities, thereby permitting the Secretary of State to exercise this function.[65] In practice, the Department of Agriculture takes the lead in making concessional sales and drafting the agreements, including special restrictions designed to protect the commercial exports of the United States. The State Department and AID comment upon the Agriculture proposals and generally try to ensure that the sales conform to our current trade and aid needs and policies.[66]

One deficiency of this sytem is the absence of established channels or focal point, short of the President, for resolving serious disagreements. In recent years, as food aid has become an increasingly important component of the United States economic assistance programs, pressure has mounted to shift the focus of power from the Department of Agriculture towards the State-AID complex. These efforts culminated in a draft Executive Order establishing a complicated system of administrative machinery, ultimately controlled by the Secretary of State.[67] But after an excruciating delay, President Johnson refused to sign the order and Agriculture retained all its former authority. This problem may be solved as part of the extensive reorganization of United States foreign aid efforts proposed by President Nixon. The new system would include a Coordinator of Development Assistance located in the Office of the President, who would be responsible for resolving interagency disputes over food aid as well as ensuring that all relevant issues involving food aid programs would be brought to the attention of policy makers at an appropriate time.

The agreement process begins with a request from a foreign government or private trade entity. It generally includes an explanation of the economic factors underlying the need and a list of specific commodities and quantities desired. The agricultural attache, officers of AID and other members of the United States Embassy formulate a recommendation. Both the request and the recommendation are then forwarded to Washington. The request and recommendation are reviewed by the United States Department of Agriculture, which formulates a proposal for consideration by an interagency staff committee. The proposal is analyzed, modified, and accepted or rejected by the Committee, which includes representatives from the Departments of Agriculture, State, Treasury, Defense, and Commerce, the Bureau of the Budget, and the Agency for International Development. This Committee, which is chaired by a representative of Agriculture, considers such factors as (1) the country's needs, economic status, and foreign exchange position; (2) the possible impact on dollar sales and other export programs; (3) effect on export markets of other supplying countries; and (4) the relationship of the proposal to the foreign aid program and the foreign policy of the United States. In the case of government-to-government proposals, the requesting country's internal and external financial position is analyzed to determine the most suitable program. Once agreement is reached within the United States government, the State Department is responsible for negotiating a sales agreement with the recipient. However, before commencing such negotiations, xthe Department consults with third countries likely to be concerned over the impact of the proposed transaction on their commercial exports, and with the Consultative Subcommittee on Surplus Disposal of the Committee on Commodity Problems of the United Nations Food and Agriculture Organization. We will discuss the functioning of the consultative subcommittee in great detail in Part III of this book. After the sales agreement is negotiated and signed, tenders are made to purchasing government or its purchasing agency by private grain exporters for given amounts of agricultural product of the class and type specified in the purchase authorization. If a tender is accepted, this is subject to an immediate price review at the Department of Agriculture. If the pricing arrangements are not disapproved, a sales contract is made and the assembly and delivery of the grain becomes the sole responsibility of the private grain firm.[68]

Stemming from the inherent conflicts of interest between Agriculture and State-AID, the program's course is characterized by constant tension between these groups. Naturally enough, during surplus periods, Agriculture is more interested in the welfare of the United States farmer than in finding the optimum level of food aid for the recipient. Thus, it will tend to favor policies designed to export maximum quantities of United States agricultural products. It also will exert strong pressures to include provisions likely to protect or enhance United States exports, such as mandatory commercial purchase requirements with maximum tying to the United States, and reexport restrictions geared to protect United States products.[69] Although the State Department often desires large food aid programs for political and economic development purposes, it is far more sensitive both to the needs of food aid recipients, and more importantly, friendly third country exporters of similar or related products. This bipolarity often erupts into disputes over the appropriate level and type of usual marketing requirements.[70]

All Food for Peace transactions are accompanied by government-to-government agreements. These agreements stipulate the terms of sale, the maximum dollar amount, and the approximate quantity of commodities to be purchased under the agreement, as well as quantities to be purchased commercially to meet so-called usual marketing requirements. A local currency sale agreement specifies the appropriate exchange rate and states what percent of local currencies received will be reserved for United States use and what part for use by the foreign country. A dollar credit sales agreement stipulates the payment period, interest rate, and schedule for repayment of the dollar credit. Agreements, except those with private trade entities, are negotiated on a government-to-government basis and include assurances that (1) the foreign country will protect usual marketings, i.e., established cash markets; (2) commodities will not be transshipped, i.e., sold to a third country without prior approval of the United States government; and (3) foreign currencies generated will be used for purposes approved by both governments.

Other National Programs

Even prior to the Food Aid Convention of 1967, which introduced a large number of countries into food aid operations, several other major agricultural exporting nations had been making bilateral food transfers, usually on an *ad hoc* basis.[71] Through the mid-sixties, these transactions have amounted to only about 1.5% of the value of P.L. 480 shipments. Canada and Australia have done the most, followed by France and West Germany; Canada's and Australia's contributions largely have been made to other Commonwealth countries under the Colombo plan. Commencing in 1966, both the absolute and relative amounts of non-United States contributions rose sharply. In 1965, non-United States food aid was valued at $32.8 million compared to the United States' contribution of $1,696.9 million; in 1966, the figures were $134.8 million against United States $1,615.9 million; and in 1967, $213.5 million compared to $1,578.0 million for the United States.

Until quite recently, almost all non-United States food aid was donated and in many cases, it included cash, debt relief, fertilizer, seed and other types of food production assistance.[72] This was in sharp contrast to the heavy sales orientation of United States programs. Given the small size of the transfers, the fact that they were donations rather than sales, and the substantial nonagricultural commodity components present, these programs did not seem to present serious threats to commercial transactions. And until the substantial modifications in international controls promulgated in 1969 and 1970, no effort had been made by the donors or other third country exports to institute any sort of control system, not to say one of the complexity employed by the United States and the World Food Program.

But beginning in the last years of the 1960s, events have sharply increased food aid activities by other developed agricultural-producing nations. Technological advances in agricultural production by Canada and Australia, increased industrialization by Japan, the dramatic expansion of grain production by the underdeveloped world and the high price supports established by the Common Agriculture Policy of the European Economic Community all have combined to produce severe surplus problems in these countries. The recent changes in the world agriculture picture are well illustrated by the redistribution of surplus stocks. In 1961, the United States held over 60% of the wheat stocks of the principal wheat exporters, and an even larger share of "surplus stocks." In 1970, its share in the aggregate carry-over is about 36 percent. By contrast, Canada which held only a quarter of these stocks in 1961, now, accounts for 40% of the 1970 carry-over, and Australia, whose stocks were negligible in 1961, holds about 15% of the total in 1970. EEC stocks climbed from 10% of the total in 1961 to 16% in 1969.[73] Canada has responded by broad changes in its agricultural policies and establishment of a food aid program administered by the Canadian International Development Agency. Over the past five years, the program has grown to a level between $70 and $80 million annually. In fiscal 1970-71, purchases of wheat, flour, and rapeseed, the major part of the food aid program, will total approximately $100 million. The EEC also has accelerated its food aid activities.

The European Economic Community

One unintended and largely unwanted result of the notorious Common Agriculture Policy of the European Economic Community may be to provide a new source of food aid, particularly food aid comprising the scarce, vital, high-protein commodities. Basically, the Common Agricultural Policy establishes a highly complex (and expensive) system of regulation of, and intervention in, domestic and international trade designed to protect and enhance the incomes of the inefficient agricultural producers within the community.[74] The domestic controls consist of price regulation through purchases and sales of specific commodities by intervention agencies, a system not dissimilar to that long employed by the United States Commodity Credit Corporation. Since the target price levels are higher (often substantially) than international prices, domestic markets and commercial exports are "protected" through a system of variable levies on imports, and export subsidies. One result of these policies has been the accumulation of large surpluses of grains and dairy products. Just before the 1969 harvest, EEC grain stocks reached a record level of over 14 million metric tons (compared to a million tons in 1955-56), and United States government officials estimate that the figure will reach 16.4 million tons in 1970. The dairy product situation was even worse. Through 1964, butter supply and demand were substantially in balance with stocks ranging between 50,000 and 60,000 tons. However, from 1965 the stocks grew steadily to the point where by January 1970 stocks had grown to over 40,000 tons with a projected increase to 1.9 million tons by 1974. Skim milk powder has followed a similar pattern with accumulations reaching a level of 500 million pounds at the beginning of 1969.[75] It is true that these stocks were drastically reduced in 1970. Grains stocks fell 10.3 million metric tons to 4.5 million, stocks of nonfat dry milk fell from 300,000 tons to 100,000 tons, and butter stocks were reduced by 50 percent to 213,000 tons within one year. The cost, though, was enormous. It is estimated that the EEC spent $900 million in the effort, which entailed export subsidies, subsidized prices for grain use as animal feed, subsidized domestic consumption and food aid.[76] These costs demonstrate that the basic structure of EEC agriculture remains badly imbalanced, and that the EEC situation will continue to present the paradigm food and commercial trade problem: high availability of food aid likely to be subordinated to the domestic agricultural problems of the donor.

World Food Program

Consistent with the current shift towards multilateral economic assistance, the World Food Program (WFP) has been established as a joint program of the United Nations and the Food and Agriculture Organization (FAO). Through April 30, 1971, the Program has committed resources totalling nearly 725 million to about 492 development projects in 83 countries. Of this total, $520 million was in commodities and $205 million in cash. A further $47 million in commodities was made available to the program in fulfillment of pledges under the Food Aid Convention.[77] This activity was established on a three-year experimental basis in 1962 under the joint direction of the United Nations and the Food and Agriculture Organization and in 1965 was given permanent status.[78] From 1963-65, the program operated on a budget of $94 million, made up of commodities, services, and cash. Of this amount, the United States contributed $40 million on commodities and $10 million for ocean freight and cash. When the Program was made permanent in 1965, a new target of $275 million was fixed for the period 1966-68, but pledges only totalled $225 million and only $189 million was actually made available. For 1969-70, the goal was reduced to $200 million which was exceeded by some $50 million. For 1971-72, the goal is $300 million and a figure of $400 million is being discussed for 1973/74.[79] For a variety of reasons the $300 million budget was not reached.

The Program was founded upon the theory that food could be used to relieve misery and finance development projects without displacing commercial sales. The underlying concept was to use the food as subsistence capital, or a wages fund, to finance labor-intensive projects such as rural public works, road buildings, minor irrigation, afforestation, and community development.[80] The additional food would be absorbed by the additional demand the new investment generated. Currently, 20% of WFP commitments go to special feeding projects to vulnerable groups such as infants, nursing mothers and school children, and the remainder to various types of development projects using food as a wages fund or as working capital. Generally, the latter schemes operate in the less monitized or subsistence areas of the economy, and are chosen in accordance with rigid standards designed to minimize adverse effects on commercial sales.

Not only has the size of the World Food Program been steadily increasing, but very serious consideration is being given to radical changes which would shift the locus of all food aid efforts from bilateral programs to an international basis, centered on the World Food Program. Such action not only would affect the efficacy of food aid as an adjunct to economic development, but also would have profound impact upon the relationships between food aid and commercial trade. Under its current philosophy, the project orientation of World Food Program activities are unlikely to interfere with commercial transactions. But as the ambitions and size of the Program expand towards greater emphasis on economic development rather than famine and nutritional relief, the potential threats to commercial markets increase.

Even without a radical reorientation of world food aid efforts, the World Food Program shows signs of moving in directions likely to raise trade problems. For one, there is interest in expanding the range of feasible projects by selling food for local currency and using the proceeds to pay wages. In addition, the WFP secretariate seems anxious to study the program approach, under which food aid is channeled through the normal commercial markets in support of the balance-of-payments during the whole period of a national plan. This, of course, would come very close to duplicating the techniques long used by the United States in its sales programs. Also, WFP has been moving towards larger projects, one of which, the establishment of a wheat reserve in Turkey, concerned other exporters. The WFP donated 400,000 metric tons of wheat at a total cost of $35 million to serve as a buffer against shortages in Turkey and neighboring countries and to enable the Turkish government to stabilize cereal prices. The specific problems raised by this type of project is discussed in Chapter 6. Both of these programs would raise many of the market displacement problems inherent in the United States' programs. At the same time, the multinational nature of the effort might blunt outside criticism, since those commercial exporters likely to be harmed also would be participants in the program. These problems also will be discussed in detail in Part III.

Food Aid Convention

Largely to cope with chronic wheat and grain surpluses, the world's major wheat exporters and importers have recently introduced a new type of food aid program along with the latest extension of the long-standing International Wheat Agreement (now called the Wheat Trade Convention). Entitled the Food Aid Convention, this program was introduced into the International Grains Agreements of 1967, and despite the sharp change in approach to wheat trade problems incorporated in the 1971 Wheat Agreement, the Food Aid Convention was retained. The Convention had three basic goals: an attempt by the United States to get other developed countries to share the burden of food aid to developing countries; to improve the prospects for commercial wheat trade by siphoning off surpluses to consumers unlikely to make commercial purchases; and to assist developing wheat exporters, principally Argentina, by directing that a fixed proportion of wheat purchased by nonwheat producing Food Aid Convention donors be purchased from developing countries.[81]

Under the 1971 Convention, nine nations, including the United States, the European Economic Community, Argentina, and Japan agreed to contribute annually for the next three years wheat and coarse grains (Japan is allowed to contribute rice) or their cash equivalent totalling 3,984,000 tons, valued at the rate of $1.73 per bushel.[82] It is expected that agricultural-producing countries would contribute cash. This represents a slight reduction from the commitments under the 1967 Convention which included twelve donors, pledging 4,259,000 metric tons of commodities. The United States share for both conventions remained at 1,890,000 tons, representing 42 percent of the first convention, and 48 percent of the second. Contributions may be made directly to the recipient countries, the method used by the United States, or through the World Food Program.

The Convention represents the efforts of the United States to shift some portion of its food aid burden to the other developed countries.[83] But the total pledges fall far short of the 10 million metric tons sought by the American negotiators of the Kennedy Round.[84] Moreover, the great bulk of the aid is not in addition to existing efforts, but only represents attribution of existing aid to the Convention. Among the signatories, only Japan seems to be increasing its net food aid levels.[85] Despite this, the United States at least, sees the Convention as a significant step towards its goal of spreading the foreign aid burden among all the developed nations. Moreover, this is the first time food aid has been included in an international commodity agreement.[86]

The conventions did introduce two potentially important innovations. The first is the requirement that a minimum percentage of the cash contributed be used for grain purchases from developing countries.[87] In the 1967 Convention, the requirement was 25 percent of the cash or the cash equivalent of 700,000 metric tons of grain. The percentage was increased to 35 percent in the 1971 Convention. This is important for the purposes of this book because the potential adverse impact of food aid upon the commercial possibilities of developing nations is one of the more serious side effects of food aid. This problem and the relationship of the Food Aid Convention to it will be discussed more fully in Part II. The second innovation is the introduction into the Wheat Agreements of provisions designed to protect commercial trade from the adverse effects of food aid.[88] This too will be fully discussed in Part II.

Notes

1. The principal statutory bases of United States price support programs may be found at 78 *Stat*. 182 (1964), 79 *Stat*. 1203 (1965), 7 U.S.C.A. §§601-04, 608, 611, 1281, 145 (a) (1971); 63 *Stat*. 1055 (1949) 7 U.S.C.A. §142 (1970); 7 CFR Parts 1481-1490.

2. At its forty-fourth session, the Committee on Commodity Problems of the UN Food and Agriculture Organization, for the first time, formally addressed itself to the problems inherent in gift programs. See CCP 69/28 (CL 53/4), 10 November 1969. Their findings and recommendations are discussed in Chapter 5.

3. *USDA/Economic Research Service, 12 Years of Achievement under Public Law 480*, at 15, 125-130 (1967) (hereinafter cited as *12 Years under P.L. 480*); 17 C.F.R. Parts 1488-90 (Jan. 1970).

4. *UN/FAO National Grain Policies* 70 (hereinafter cited as *National Grains Policies*); 1968-69 *Report of the Canadian Wheat Board* at 9-10. Since the newer program is primarily directed at the developing countries, it may be deemed a hybrid food aid-export promotion enterprise.

5. *National Grains Policies, supra*, 201, para. 39. But despite the obvious disparities, government export credit programs and food aid are lumped together for some purposes. The International Wheat Agreement, 1971, divides wheat sales into commercial and special transactions. Special transactions are defined

to include any sale under terms or conditions not conforming to strictly commercial practices. See International Wheat Agreement, 1971, Wheat Trade Convention, Art. 3. The Wheat Trade Convention also provides guidelines relating to "concessional" transactions, which are coextensive with "special" transactions. *Id.* at Art. 9. The reports and analyses of the International Wheat Council, the executive body created by the International Wheat Agreements, follows the same pattern. See *International Wheat Council, Review of the World Wheat Situation* 1969-70, at 29 (1970). However, recent United States reports on Public Law 480 operations include sales made with export credits with commercial dollar sales, e.g., Annual Report on Activities carried out under Public Law 480, as amended, during the period Jan. 1-Dec. 31, 1970, Tables 1-3. [hereinafter 19—Annual Report on P.L. 480]

6. 68 *Stat.* 459 (1954); 72 *Stat.* 1791 (1958); 82 *Stat.* 451 (1968); 7 *U.S.C.A.* §1692 (1970).

7. 15 *U.S.C.A.* §714C (a),(f) (1970).

8. *1970 Annual Report on P.L. 480, Tables 1, 31.* Beginning with the Annual P.L. 480 Report for 1968, barter operations which improve the United States balance-of-payments and which are conducted by the Commodity Credit Corporation, were not combined with barter deals conducted under the auspices of P.L. 480. In 1968, barter operations financed by P.L. 480 totalled only $3 million, and in 1969 and 1970 the figure dropped to zero.

9. According to the United States government, the primary objectives of the barter program are to increase exports of United States agricultural commodities and to improve the United States balance-of-payments position by financing offshore requirements of United States government agencies with agricultural exports in addition to cash sales. *1968 Annual Report on P.L. 480* at 14, 52-54.

10. University of Arizona Agricultural Experiment Station, *Policy for United States Agricultural Export Surplus Disposal* [Technical Bulletin 150] ; Wightman, *Food Aid and Development, International Conciliation,* no. 567, March 1968, p. 37.

11. *Technical Bulletin 150, supra* at 78. For example, in fiscal 1966, barter transactions with Europe, Japan and Australia amounted to $71,430,000. This represented 31.2% of total transactions; USDA/Economic Research Service, *12 Years under P.L. 480,* at table 10.

12. 68 *Stat.* 459 (1954); *Technical Bulletin 150, supra* at 45-47; *1966 Annual Report on P.L. 480* at 95-96.

13. *Technical Bulletin 150, supra* at 78-79.

14. *Id.* at 79; USDA/ERS *12 Years under P.L. 480* at 12. The regulations governing barter operations by the Commodity Credit Corporation are found in 7 C.F.R. Part 1495, 32 C.F.R.; 4.501-4.507; 30 Fed. Reg. 12002 (1965).

15. *1968 Annual Report on P.L. 480* at 39-41. U.S.D.A./ERS *12 Years under P.L. 480* at 12-13.

16. 82 *Stat.* 451 (1968), 7 U.S.C.A. § 1923 (1970).

17. *H. Conf. Rep.* 1642, 90th *Cong.* 2d sess. p. 5-6 (1968).

18. 1970 *Annual Report on P.L. 480*, tables 24-28.

19. 1970 *Annual Report on P.L. 480*, table 1.

20. *Toma, The Politics of Food for Peace* 38-39 (1967); *Organization for Economic Cooperation and Development, Food Aid–Its Role in Economic Development*, Ch. 2 (1963) [hereinafter cited as *OECD*].

21. Heady and Timmons, *Objectives, Achievements, and Hazards of the U.S. Food Aid and Agricultural Development Programs in Relation to Domestic Policy*; Iowa State Univ. Center for Agricultural and Economic Development, *Alternatives for Balancing World Food Production Needs* 195 (1967); Agency for International Development, *U.S. Overseas Loans and Grants*, Special Report Prepared for the House Committee on Foreign Affairs Committee 5 (1967); *The Foreign Assistance Program, Annual Report to the Congress Fiscal Year 1969*.

22. USDA/ERS *12 Years Under P.L. 480* at 14.

23. 67 *Stat.* 159 (1970); 68 *Stat* 843 (1954). From July 1, 1954, through December 31, 1970, the Mutual Security Act financed $2.2 billion in agricultural products, *1970 Annual Report on P.L. 480*, table 1.

24. 67 *Stat.* 80 (1953).

25. 67 *Stat.* 467 (1953).

26. 67 *Stat.* 159 (1953).

27. 68 *Stat.* 454 (1954); 7 U.S.C.A. §§ 1691-1736 (1970).

28. *1970 Annual Report* on P.L. 480, table 1.

29. The 1966 extension of the legislation authorizes that the Act may be cited as the "Food for Peace Act 1966." However, section 2 of P.L. 89-808 characterizes the 1966 revision as amendments to the Agricultural Trade Development and Assistance Act of 1954. 80 *Stat.* 1526 (1966). The Conference Report on the statute emphasizes the "Food for Peace" designation applied only to this particular act, while the "basic legislation remains entitled "Agricultural Trade Development and Assistance Act." H.R. Conf. Rep. No. 2304, 89th Cong., 2d Sess., 15, 112 (1966); 112 *Cong. Rec.* 24314 (1966).

30. In 1961, the basic Executive Order delegating functions under the Act, created a "Director of the Food for Peace Program." Exec. Order 10915, Jan. 24, 1961, Section 1; 25 F.R. 781 (1961). Subsequent Executive Orders pertaining to the program used the same title. See e.g., Exec. Order No. 11252, Oct. 23, 1965, 30 F.R. 13507 (1965). The amended program submitted by the Administration in 1966 was entitled "Food for Freedom" S. 2933, 89th Cong. 2d sess., 1966, p. 1. And the office in the Agency for International Development designated to coordinate food aid activities was named the "Food for Freedom Office."

31. Agricultural products also may be sold on concessional terms through private trade agreements. 80 *Stat.* 1532 (1966), 7 U.S.C.A. § 1717 (1970). Despite constant Congressional encouragement of this type of food aid, it has never assumed major proportions. In calendar year 1970, four agreements were signed totaling 6.5 million dollars in export market value. Since the inception of P.L.

480, there have been 13 private trade agreements with 12 private trade entities in 6 countries involving agricultural products valued at 825 million dollars. *1969 Annual Report on P.L. 480* at 15-16.

32. 80 *Stat*. 1526 (1966), 7 U.S.C.A. § 1701, 1703 (1970).

33. 80 *Stat*. 1528 (1966), 7 U.S.C.A. § 1704 (1970).

34. See *Technical Bulletin* 150 *supra*, at 42-45 (1962). *1970 Annual Report on P.L. 480* at 79-134.

35. 80 *Stat*. 1526 (1966); 7 U.S.C.A. §§ 1701, 1703(b) (1970). *1970 Annual Report on P.L. 480*, at 15-18.

36. 78 *Stat*. 1009, (1964) 22 U.S.C.A. § 2161 (1970).

37. 80 *Stat*. 1526 (1966), 7 U.S.C.A. § 1703(b) (1970).

38. See Agricultural Commodity Agreement between the United States and Pakistan, TIAS 6821, Aug. 3, 1967, 21 U.S.T. 375 (1971).

39. 80 *Stat*. 1534 (1970), 7 U.S.C.A. §§ 1721-25 (1970). Through December 31, 1970, donations totaled $3.8 billion. In calendar 1970, they totaled $255 million. *1970 Annual Report on P.L. 480*, table 1.

40. 68 *Stat*. 457 (1954); 70 *Stat*. 201 (1956).

41. *Wightman, supra* at 22; *Technical Bulletin 150, supra* at 47-50.

42. 74 *Stat*. 140 (1960).

43. 77 *Stat*. 390 (1963).

44. 80 *Stat*. 1534 (1966); 7 U.S.C.A. § 1721 (1970).

45. *1970 Annual Report on P.L. 480* at table 1.

46. *12 Years under P.L. 480*, at 100.

47. *Id*. at 103.

48. FAO Council Resolution 1/53, Annex (Nov. 1969); *Report of the CCP Working Group on CSD Functions to The Forty-Fourth Session of Committee on Commodity Problems* (CCP:69/13/1, CCP:FU/ CSD 69/116, at 6-8), July 15, 1969. See Ch. 5, 6.

49. Up to 1966, these sales were authorized by a separate title of the Act, Title IV. 73 *Stat*. 610 (1959).

50. 80 *Stat*. 1532 (1966), 7 U.S.C.A. § 1706(b) (1970); *1970 Annual Report on P.L. 480* at 15-19; 1970 *Annual Report on P.L. 480* at 16-17, table 1.

51. 80 *Stat*. 1526 (1966), 7 U.S.C.A. §§ 1701-10 (1970).

52. 1966 *Annual Report on P.L. 480*, Table 11 (1967).

53. *Hearings on the Food for Peace Program before the Senate Committee on Agriculture and Forestry*, 89th Cong., 2d sess., 472-80 (1966).

54. 68 *Stat*. 456 (1954), amended by 77 *Stat*. 390 (1963).

55. 1970 *Annual Report on P.L. 480*, Table 8.

56. 80 *Stat*. 1526, 1535-36 (1966), 7 U.S.C. §§ 1702, 1731 (1970).

57. *Hearings on the Food for Peace Program before the Senate Committee on Agriculture and Forestry*, 89th Cong., 2d sess., 22-24, 30-38 (1966).

58. 73 *Stat*. 609 (1959).

59. USDA/ERS, *Foreign Agricultural Report No. 65, P.L. 480 Concessional Sales*, Sept. 1970, 24-27.

60. See, e.g., Title I sales agreement with Guinea, May 22, 1963, TIAS 5349, Art. IV, Sec. (k), 14 U.S.T. 1006 (1964).

61. 62 *Stat*. 1070 (1948), 15 U.S.C.A. § 714(a)-(p) (1970).

62. See 7 C.F.R., subchap. C-Export Programs § § 1481-90, 1495 (1970).

63. 80 *Stat*. 1535 (1966), 7 U.S.C.A. § 1731 (1970).

64. Executive Order No. 10900, as amended, 26 F.R. 143 (1961).

65. In 1955, the Secretary of Agriculture was ceded the power to determine the nations with whom Food for Peace sales agreements were to be concluded. 69 *Stat*. 721 (1955). But after the 1966 revisions, the comparable section of the P.L. 480 Act, § 401, contains no such authority. 80 *Stat*. 1536 (1966), 7 U.S.C.A. §1731 (1970).

66. A report by the Comptroller General contains an excellent summary of the current administrative arrangements for conduct of concessional sales at pp. 3-6. General Accounting Office, *Report to Congress and Dept. of Agriculture, Review Precautions Taken to Protect Commercial Dollar Sales of Agricultural Commodities under P.L. 480* (Aug. 1966).

67. New York Times, 16 March 1967.

68. See USDA/ERS, *Foreign Agricultural Economic Report*, No. 65, *P.L. 480 Concessional Sales* 11-27 (Sept. 1970).

69. See Part III, Chapters 7-10.

70. *GAO Report, supra*, pp. 15-17. See also, National Planning Association, *Agricultural Surplus Disposal and Foreign Aid, A Study for the Special Committee to Study the Foreign Aid Programs*, 85 Cong. 1st sess. (1957).

71. Brief discussions of non-United States bilateral aid programs may be found in Wightman, *supra* pp. 45-48; and *OECD*, Food Aid–Its Role in Economic Development, pp. 34-40.

72. *Hearings on Extension of Public Law 480 Before The Senate Committee on Agriculture and Forestry*, 90th Cong. 2d sess., 182-85 (1968).

73. UN/FAO, *FAO Commodity Review and Outlook*, 1969-70, at 19-20 (1970).

74. Dam, *European Common Market in Agriculture*, 67 Col. L. Rev. (1967); USDA/ERS, Foreign Agricultural Economic Report No. 55, *The European Community's Common Agricultural Policy* (1969).

75. These figures were derived from a variety of sources. Authoritative data on the very dramatic doings surrounding the Common Agricultural Policy is widely reported and easily available from such publications as the U.S. Dept. of Agriculture's Foreign Agriculture, the EEC's publication, Statisque Agricole, and the International Wheat Council. Two of these sources might deserve special note: U.S.D.A./ERS, the European Community's Common Agriculture Policy–Implications for U.S. Trade, FAS Report No. 55, Oct. 1969; USDA/ERS, Foreign Agriculture, March 16, 1970, pp. 6-8.

76. USDA/FAS, *Foreign Agriculture*, Nov. 9, 1970, p. 7.

77. *World Food Program News*, May-June 1961.

78. The basic documents controlling the World Food Program are conveniently collected in UN/FAO, PL/WFP:BD 1, *World Food Program Basic Docu-*

ments (1966). Descriptions and analysis of the objectives and techniques of the Program may be found in the annual reports of the Executive Director on the World Food Program; UN/ECOSOC E 4538. *Multilateral Food Aid (1968)*; and Wightman, *Food Aid and Economic Development, International Conciliation* (March 1968, No. 567). Current activities of the Program may be followed through the UN/FAO bimonthly *World Food Programme News*.

79. A good, brief description and discussion of the World Food Program is Schlechty, *World Food Aid: In The Multilateral Manner, War on Hunger* Vol. V, no. 7 (U.S. Dept. of State, 1971).

80. FAO, *Uses of Agricultural Surpluses to Finance Economic Development in Under-developed Countries—A Pilot Study in India* (Commodity Policy Series No. 6 1955).

81. The operative provisions of latest version of the Wheat Agreement entered into force on July 1, 1971, for those countries ratifying it, and provisionally in force for those countries ratifying it provisionally. Russia has acceded to the Wheat Trade portion of the Agreement, but not the Food Aid Convention.

82. International Wheat Agreement, 1971, Food Aid Convention, Art. II.

83. *Senate Hearings, supra*, note 72 at 182-87.

84. Reply by the Executive Branch to Questions propounded by the Staff of the Ad Hoc Subcommittee on the International Grains Arrangement, Question 15, as printed in *Hearings before a Subcommittee of the Senate Committee on Foreign Relations Executive A*, 90th Cong., 2d sess. 27 (1968); 114 *Cong. Rec.* § 7117, June 12, 1968.

85. Reply by the Executive Branch, *supra*, at 27; 114 *Cong. Rec.* § 7121, June 21, 1968.

86. Reply by the Executive Branch, *supra*, at 27, 114 *Cong. Rec.* § 7128, June 21, 1968; 114 *Cong. Rec.* § 7194-95, June 13, 1968.

87. International Wheat Agreement 1971, Food Aid Convention 1971, Article II (7).

88. International Wheat Agreement 1971, Wheat Trade Convention, 1971, Article 9.

3 The Interrelationships of Food Aid and Commercial Trade

A basic assumption of this study is that food aid may affect commercial transactions which are the same or related to those given food aid. These relationships partially dictate the food aid strategies of national and international food aid givers. And these strategies may be implemented by a variety of administrative and legal devices, limited to some degree by existing international standards and domestic legislation. In this chapter, I shall try to build a model describing the interaction between various types of food aid programs and those economic and financial variables of prime concern to all parties significantly affected by large food aid programs. This will be followed by a brief review of the major factors shaping commercial trade in the principal food aid commodities. Then, I shall identify and evaluate the strategies available to food aid givers anxious to achieve particular commercial goals through their food aid programs. Subsequent chapters shall discuss the means of pursuing these strategies in light of existing or potential legal and economic constraints.

Potential Short-Run Impact of Food Aid

Food aid will affect both short and long term interests of donors, recipients, and third countries. The short term effects, though complex, may be clearly identified and fairly well analyzed. The longer run impacts, which cluster about the effect of food aid upon the economic policies of the donor and the recipient are inherently more difficult to predict.

The Efficiency of Food Aid as Foreign Assistance

Although this study is centered upon the economic impact of food aid upon the donor and third countries and the possible ways of controlling them, the utility of food aid as a tool for economic development is an important factor in considering the economic impact of food aid upon commercial trade and possible methods for controlling these effects. The more useful food is to developing recipients, the better the case for tolerance by developed countries for the damage such aid may do to their commercial interests. Therefore, we must briefly consider the relative benefits to the recipient of food aid sales versus all alternate forms of economic assistance.

35

Clearly, food aid can pose serious dangers to the recipient. These stem from the possible adverse effects upon the recipient's own economic development. Cheap imported food may lower internal agricultural policies sufficiently to discourage domestic producers. Also, the availability of a permanent source of inexpensive agricultural products via food aid may tempt the recipient to concentrate its development resources in the non-agricultural sectors of the economy, thus deflecting it from the most effective development strategy and chaining itself to permanent dependence upon imported food. By now, though, this lesson has been well learned, and most food aid donors and recipients have become sufficiently sophisticated to avoid these dangers. As stated in Chapter 1, the original universal condemnation of food aid by academic economists has abated in favor of the position that properly conducted food aid programs can be a useful adjunct to economic development.[1]

In foreign aid parlance, food aid may be characterized as a "doubly-tied aid"—tied as to source and tied as to product (at least class of product). Obviously, from the recipient's standpoint, any tying reduces the value of the assistance since it is denied the opportunity to purchase what it most needs at the lowest possible price. Thus, conventional foreign aid is more desirable than food aid since it may be used to finance a wide variety of products. Even if foreign aid is restricted to particular uses, it still may free foreign exchange for commercial food imports, if the foreign aid is used in lieu of the recipient's own resources, and if it deemed this to be the best way to allocate its own resources.[2]

There are some circumstances in which food aid might afford the recipient more flexibility than many other forms of foreign aid. If the food aid recipient otherwise would have been forced to use its own foreign exchange to import these products commercially, food aid will have the effect of providing the recipient with that much more foreign exchange which may be used at its total discretion. By contrast, most foreign aid has some strings attached. This assumes that foreign exchange is under government control, a likely assumption in developing countries.[3] As we shall subsequently demonstrate, food aid which permits the recipient to use foreign exchange normally earmarked for commercial food purchases for other purposes would violate the prime existing international norms for conducting food aid operations—minimum displacement of commercial sales. But, as we shall also demonstrate, such displacement is the rule, rather than the exception.[4] Also favoring food aid is the undeniable popularity of such assistance with potential aid givers compared to other possible "better" forms.[5] Moreover, food aid which results in increased food consumption by the recipient or lowers prices probably contributes to a more equitable income distribution in the recipient country than other forms of foreign aid. The lower income groups tend to spend a higher proportion of their income on food and any increased availability or decreased price for food helps them relatively more than higher income groups.[6]

Short-Run Economic Impact

Clearly, it is simpler to predict the short-run impact of food aid transactions than to envision the net effect of sizeable food aid transactions over a long period. Even here, the economic and financial consequences of concessional sales defy simple generalization. For one, food aid is perceived differently by each of the four principle affected groups—the aid giver, the recipient, the third country exporter, and third country importers. Moreover, the impact ultimately depends upon the status of certain key economic parameters in each affected country. Further complexities stem from the variation between the effects of food aid on private and governmental interests and the trade-offs between foreign exchange and domestic costs.

The Recipient

To the recipient, gifts or voluntary purchases of agricultural commodities on concessional terms either are foreign aid or relief. If in the absence of concessional sales, the country would have been content to consume less, the food aid transaction must be considered as international relief and humanitarian assistance. People are eating more and better than would otherwise be the case. The extent to which food aid constitutes foreign aid depends upon the specific terms upon which the sales are made and the amount of the commodity that would have been imported or grown without food aid. If such transactions replace commercial imports of the same commodities, the recipient has received a transfer of external resources, the magnitude of the transfer depending upon the difference between the commercial and concessional terms.[7] The "higher" the price for the food (nominal price, payment terms and the necessity to purchase minimum amounts of the product commercially) and the larger the portion payable in foreign exchange, the smaller is the aid component. If food aid commodities replace products that might have been grown domestically, the savings are either in local or foreign currencies, in accordance with the nature of the resources that would have been necessary to provide an equivalent quantity of the commodity. That is, increased domestic production may require inputs of labor, domestic subsidies, and imported fertilizers and machinery. This does not pass judgment on the long-term benefit to the recipient of increasing its investment in agriculture.

Perhaps the most important and most difficult consideration for the recipient is the effect of food aid upon the donor's total foreign aid commitment. The danger is that food aid will displace more conventional foreign aid. Dollar for dollar, untied conventional foreign aid is more useful than food aid, since foreign aid can be used to purchase food (or can free the recipient's own resources for food purchases) while food aid does not always permit purchase of nonfood products. But the relationship is not simple. The dollar value of food aid may sufficiently exceed the dollar reduction in foreign aid to render a net benefit to the recipient. Moreover, food aid seems to have more political appeal to donors, particularly for countries already committed to expensive domestic programs for purchasing agricultural surpluses or for removing land from production. In these cases, the net cost of food aid to the donor is significantly less than the market value of the product. Therefore, judgments upon the utility of food aid to each recipient may not be made *a priori* but depend upon the specifics of each situation.

This analysis does not depend upon resolution of the controversy over the impact of food aid on the recipient's economic development. Food aid may in fact facilitate, retard, or be neutral in its impact on economic development. The recipient's farm sector may be adversely affected, and a country could become unduly dependent on outside sources for its food supplies. But here we are looking at food aid from the recipient's viewpoint. And we must assume that any recipient voluntarily accepting commodities on this basis believes, correctly or not, that food aid constitutes a net benefit.

Third Country Agricultural Exporters

With respect to agricultural exporters other than the food aid giver, the effect of food aid ranges from relatively harmless to severely damaging. The effect in each case depends upon the product; the country to which it is sold; the measures taken by the food aid giver to mitigate adverse impact upon the commercial interests of third countries; and the existence and efficacy of efforts by the food aid-giving nation to better its own commercial position through the food aid transaction. As we shall see in the subsequent analysis of donor food aid practices, the conflicts between the desire of a food aid giver to assist its own commercial agricultural exports, to assist the development of recipient countries, and to protect the vital economic interests of third countries are extremely difficult to resolve.

Food aid may injure commercial exporters either through its effect on prices or volume or both. If both agricultural consumers and exporters were operating in a classical free market, this distinction would be meaningless since price and volume are functionally related. If supply is increased by X, price will drop by Y. If price is cut by Y, the volume sold would expand by the same X. But agricultural markets are controlled at both the producing and consuming end and seem to be becoming evermore so.[8] In addition, almost all food aid products are subject to a complex set of domestic controls. Also, international trade in wheat, the principal food aid commodity, has been subject to price and purchase and supply controls by the series of the International Wheat Agreements.[9] From the consumer end, agricultural commodities may not be freely imported in response to price and demand. For one, quotas may be established or high tariffs imposed to protect domestic production. And more importantly with respect to developing nations, the availability of foreign exchange will be strictly controlled in the service of optimizing available resources. Thus, poor nations are likely to limit the quantity of agricultural products that may be imported. Should minimum food needs be met through food aid, it is likely that no foreign exchange would be available to import additional food, no matter what the price or the nature of internal demand.

A second complicating factor is the existence of surpluses and the decision by major producers to maintain stockpiles rather than dump all excess production on the world markets. These stockpiles create a buffer between production and ultimate consumption. The transfer of a commodity from stocks to a consumer who otherwise would not have been able to purchase the product commercially should have no impact on normal export markets. But, the transfer from that same stockpile to a potential cash customer will reduce the total demand for the product without reducing the total supply in commercial channels. This should result in a price drop or reduction in commercial sales volume. On the other hand, if a product that otherwise would have been sold commercially is transferred to a consumer not otherwise able to purchase the product, world prices and volume for the same product should rise since some supply has been removed while demand for commercial products has remained constant. Finally, if products otherwise destined for commercial sale are given as food aid to a customer otherwise willing and able to purchase the product commercially, prices will not be affected, commercial exporters as a group will be unaffected, but the distribution of commercial markets among exports will change. Since the loss of a potential buyer has been matched by the removal of an equivalent supply, prices will be unchanged. But if the food aid recipient was a commercial customer of a country other than the donor, that country will suffer a temporary loss. But the donor itself has foregone a commercial opportunity somewhere, and thus increased market opportunities for other commercial sellers as a group. The country giving the food aid will suffer a loss to the extent that the price if any, received for the product transferred is less than that at which it could have been sold. In other words, a ton of wheat given to India can no longer be sold to Japan. Indeed, it was the hope that markets for United States agricultural commercial exports might be created in Europe if other exporters could be induced to divert food grains normally destined for European markets into food aid that partially underlay the United States effort to persuade the European Economic Community and other grain exporters to accede to the Food Aid Conventions.[10]

Under certain circumstances, food aid might benefit other exporting countries. Food aid may increase recipients' imports of other products, using the foreign exchange saved on agricultural purchases. Agricultural exporters which also export capital goods would seem to be potential beneficiaries of this process.

Thus, it has been suggested that food aid has permitted Australia to expand its wool sales to Asia. By the same token, countries like China that have been forced to purchase food with foreign exchange seem to have decreased other imports. And, of course, all exporting nations will benefit from the increased import capacity generated by the possible economic development resulting from well-managed food aid programs.

Concessional sales may injure third country exporters indirectly. Imports of certain commodities on subcommercial terms may facilitate the export of other commodities previously serving the same general purpose or lead to increased exports of products manufactured from the imported commodity, e.g., concessional wheat imports may facilitate rice exports; or soya bean oils may be consumed rather than domestically produced olive oil, which, in turn, is exported to the detriment of olive oil producers not receiving substitute oils on concession terms. The transformation of Food for Peace cotton into exported textiles is an everpresent headache. Also in semideveloped countries like Israel and Poland, feed grains can be used to increase the production of live stock and eggs, which either are exported or reduce imports of these products.[11] Obviously, these events would injure the commercial interests of third country exporters, either through reduced sales, lower prices, or both.[12] But the appropriateness of the transaction as a whole only can be evaluated in the broader context of world-wide responsibility for the well-being and development of the disadvantaged nations.

The Donor

The analysis of the impact of food aid transactions on the donor or concessional seller, will focus upon United States programs. However in the last few years EEC practice has assumed great importance. This may be justified on several counts. Most importantly, the United States is the country with the greatest interest in both surplus disposal, economic development and commercial exports. The interest in commercial exports includes its own foreign sales and those of other friendly or allied nations. Furthermore, until very recently, United States food aid programs both dwarfed all other bilateral programs, and had to be conducted consistently with a series of competing or only semicompatible interests. The multilateral World Food Program, the only other potentially significant food aid donor, is insulated from most of the problems faced by national donors, since it has no surplus disposal problems nor any interest in promoting commercial exports. The products at its disposal have no alternative uses and do not represent liabilities. They are simply assets to be used altruistically and efficiently.

Of the three major interest groups, viz., donor, recipient and third country exporter, the impact of food aid on the donor is the most equivocal and complex in any particular transaction. The net effect varies with the surplus status of the commodity involved, the existing policy towards surplus disposal, the potential of the recipient as a commercial customer, the type of domestic agricultural support and control system in effect, and the governmental or private status of the concerned party.[13] Under the United States Food for Peace program, private parties receive the same price and terms for commodities devoted to the program as they would for ordinary commercial exports. Therefore, concessional sales are a net addition to private income to the extent they do not displace commercial sales. In any event, private sellers are indifferent between Food for Peace and commercial sales; both yield them the same return.[14]

But Food for Peace transactions do affect both the national budget and the balance-of-payments. The government must pay the exporter the difference between the price and terms imposed upon the recipient and the current commercial market price.[15] The cost to the Treasury is measured by this amount less the amounts the government would have incurred in storage costs of soil bank payments absent the food aid transaction. Since the exporter receives cash payment in dollars at current world prices, donations, sales for the recipient's nonconvertible currencies, and sales payable over extended periods of time with low interest rates will require federal expenditures. The precise amount of the real burden will depend on the terms of the food aid transaction, the donating government's need for the local currencies received, and the type and status of existing farm subsidy programs.

Under current farm programs, the United States government is committed to large expenditures with respect to agricultural products whether or not the products are produced or used. Commodities eligible for price support must be purchased by the government whenever the market price falls below the minimum support level. Over the past twenty years, a changing variety of products has constantly been in government hands on this basis. In addition, the government pays farmers to keep large tracts of land out of production under a number of so-called "soil bank" programs. Thus, part of the cost of potential agricultural commodities affected by these programs has been prepaid.

If the commodity is not in or destined for government hands, the cost of using it for food aid is the price at which the commodity may be purchased and shipped less the production diversion payments otherwise payable.[16] If commodities under price support or soil bank programs are used for food aid purposes, the net cost to the government may be well below the "value" of the commodity to the recipient as measured by current world commercial prices. If the goods are already owned by the government or would have been purchased in the normal course of price support operations, the only additional cost of using the products for food aid would be the cost of shipping them to the recipient and under current United States practices, the recipient pays most of the freight charges unless the food is donated. Further-more, the government saves the cost of storing the commodities.[a]

The net budgetary impact of food aid on the United States depends upon the value of the payments and promises it receives from the recipient in exchange for the products transferred as food aid. Naturally, donated commodities yield nothing. Sales repayable in dollars on long-term credits ultimately will yield benefits, though measuring the current value of future receipts to a government is highly uncertain business. Moreover, current United States policy is to trans-mute all nondonated food aid to a dollar basis by December 31, 1971.[18] Even local currency sales may yield a variety of benefits to this country. Nowadays, an initial cash payment in dollars of at least 5% of the sale value is required "where practicable."[19] During 1970, agreements with seventeen of the twenty-one recipient countries have made such provision.[20] The P.L. 480 legislation authorizes, and to some extent requires that a portion of the local currencies received for food aid commodities be made available for the discharge of certain United States obligations incurred abroad, and that some portion be convertible into dollars.[21] According to one method of calculation, the dollar value of local currency receipts to the United States totaled 4.5 billion dollars through Decem-

[a]The Cargo Preference Act (Public Law 664, 83d Congress, which amended the Merchant Marine Act of 1936) requires that at least 50 percent of the quantity of all products exported under certain U.S. government programs be shipped on U.S. flag vessels to the extent that these vessels are available at fair and reasonable rates for commercial U.S. flag vessels. This requirement applies among other things, to concessional sales and donations under P.L. 480. Sales of fresh fruit and fruit products under Title I of P.L. 480 are exempt from this requirement as are shipments between foreign countries of commodities and defense articles purchased with foreign currencies generated by P.L. 480.

Most freight rates on U.S. flag vessels on some trade routes are higher than rates charged by other vessels on the same route. CCC reimburses the importer for all the amount by which the freight bill for the portion required to be carried in U.S. flag vessels exceeds the dollar equivalent of the freight bill for an equal quantity carried in foreign-flag vessels. This excess is commonly referred to as the "ocean freight differential." The existence and magnitude of this differential is subject to determination by CCC. If a trade route is served by companies which are members of a steamship conference, there is generally no differential since rates most often are identical. Except for the differential, the cost of transporting commodities must be paid by the importer. The importer—either a private firm, or in some countries, a government agency—pays this amount in cash or otherwise finances it on his own initiative.

Freight bills are usually payable in dollars or other hard currency and thus constitute a drain on the foreign exchange reserves of the recipient country. To partially alleviate this drain, the U.S. government, prior to FY 1970 (July 1, 1969), sometimes extended credit to the recipient government (not the importer) to offset the dollar cost of the portion carried in U.S. flag vessels. (Credit may also be extended to private trade entities under private trade agreements. This type of credit was not stopped on July 1, 1969.) This credit was extended only when the commodities involved were sold under a credit sales agreement or a convertible local currency credit sale. The amount of the credit was equal to the freight bill on the quantity carried on U.S. flag ships, minus the ocean freight differential—in other words, the cost of transporting the quantity actually carried on U.S. flag ships, but based on foreign-flag freight rates. The credit, when extended, was incorporated with the loan on the commodities and the same credit terms applied. The decision to cease financing freight costs was motivated by balance-of-payment considerations and a general attitude favoring hardening of food aid terms.[17]

ber 31, 1969.[22] Therefore, in figuring the net cost of food aid to the United States government, these receipts and claims also should be subtracted from the purchase and shipping costs of the food.

The impact of food aid on the balance-of-payments is computed somewhat differently. The foreign exchange loss from such transactions is caused by the displacement of commericial sales by food aid. Exports of agricultural commodities earn foreign exchange, and to the extent such sales are displaced by food aid, the balance-of-payments will suffer. But such losses must be balanced by the foreign exchange earned or saved in the food aid transaction. Payments made to American exporters and shippers with respect to the commodities used in the food aid programs do not affect the balance-of-payments since the dollars presumably stay home. But despite the widespread assertions that food aid has helped the balance-of-payments, the case is not a clear one.[23] Though difficult to calculate, food aid undoubtedly reduces commercial sales. Theoretically, food aid is supposed to be limited to transactions increasing net consumption of agricultural products, both as shall be demonstrated, any sizeable developmentally oriented food aid program must displace some commercial sales. For example, it has been alleged in Congressional debates that food aid has reduced commercial exports to India at the rate of .65 for every unit of food aid. Existing analysis of this problem is inconclusive, and perhaps impossible.[24] Given the complexity and volatility of international trade, it is impossible to know what would have happened if a given food aid transaction were not made. Moreover, it is very hard to know how much food a poor nation would buy if faced with starvation. The United States claims that it does not consider these kinds of purchases as part of normal commercial market opportunities. On the other side, as we shall see, there is evidence that eventually, food aid does lead to larger commercial exports.

EEC Practices

The European Economic Community (EEC) has made increasing use of food aid to relieve the pressure of agricultural surpluses developed by the Common Agricultural Policy. To date the Community has not yet developed systematic programs for the use of agricultural surpluses as food aid. Rather, it has sought opportunities for disposal on an *ad hoc* basis, sometimes as food aid and often—too often so far as the United States is concerned—as cut rate commercial sales. While the impact of the EEC's disposal practices is of the highest concern to other commercial exporters, until the EEC further institutionalizes its food aid programs, little will be gained by treatment of them here.

Third Country Interests. Third country exporters solely are interested in the effect of food aid on the commercial opportunities available to them at any given time. These may be affected by food aid in several ways. In the long run, if food aid leads to economic development and consequent expansion of commercial demand, they benefit. In the short run, their position depends both upon the displacement effect of food aid and the strategy followed by the donor in conducting its food operations. Third countries suffer in the following circumstances: food aid does not displace total commercial sales but the donor ties food aid to increased commercial purchases from it; food aid displaces commercial sales and the donor makes no provision for ensuring that third countries get an increased share of the remaining commercial market; food aid displaces total commercial sales and the donor requires that the recipient maintain the level of commercial purchases from the donor that might be anticipated in the absence of food aid.

Impact of Importing Third Countries. Although food aid does effect third country importers, the impact is spread so widely to render it unimportant as a factor to be considered by decision-makers in the food aid arena. The impact of a particular food aid transaction on third country agricultural importers depends upon the source of the food aid and the expected behavior of the recipient without food aid. If the food aid commodities come from a country which otherwise would not have marketed these products—that is, the food aid commodities came from surplus stockpiles, or retired acreage—and these commodities are transferred to a country which otherwise would not have purchased it, there is no impact upon third country importers. If the recipient would have purchased the commodity commercially, the food aid transaction removes demand from the market, thereby depressing prices to the benefit of third country importers. If the food aid commodities otherwise would have been put into commercial channels but the recipient would not have purchased them commercially, the effect is to remove supply from the market, raising world agricultural prices, to the detriment of food importers. If the recipient would have purchased the food commercially, there should be no effect on prices, since both supply and demand have been reduced by the same amount.

Here, most concern should be focused upon the impact of food aid upon developed nonagricultural countries. Undeveloped importing countries are interested in the price of agricultural imports, but their status as potential food aid recipients outweighs this interest. For developed importers, the impact of food aid is sufficiently diffuse and obscure and their general commitment to the economic development of the third world sufficiently strong to preclude strong opposition to food aid because of its potential for raising food prices. But, since food aid doesn't directly help them either, neither are they likely to be enthusiastic supporters.

Potential Long-Run Impact of Food Aid:
Economic Development, Market Development
and Preemption

In the long run, food aid may be compatible with commercial trade in agricultural products through the development of increased demand for the products of agricultural exporting nations. These new opportunities may be generally shared by all exporters or benefit just these nations able to establish a particular advantage in a product or area. Certainly, the United States' food aid program always has been billed as designed to and effective in expanding commercial export markets for United States agricultural products. This objective always has been and still is expressed in the declaration of policy and the substantive provisions of the Food for Peace legislation.[25]

Economic Development

Food aid accelerates the recipient's economic development, the argument goes, thereby providing the developing nations with additional foreign exchange to spend on imports—agricultural and nonagricultural.[26] Japan, Spain, Italy, Greece, Israel, and Taiwan invariably are cited as shining examples of countries which have come off the food aid dole to become good customers for United States (and others') agricultural products. Table 3-1 demonstrates the switch from food aid recipient to commercial purchase.[27] According to a study made by the United States Department of Agriculture, countries with per capita incomes over $600 per annum purchased an average of $7.88 worth of United States farm products per year; countries with a per capita income between $200 and $600 purchased $4.18 per person, while countries below $200 purchased only 30 cents worth per person. Since there are 825 million people in this last category, it is alleged that economic development holds vast potential for commercial sales.[28]

Moreover, food aid may well help develop new food tastes. Nations facing famine will accept (sometimes) new and unusual foods. Later, they may get to like them enough to become cash customers. Frequently cited cases are Japan, Taiwan, Korea, and Spain. Japan, formerly an exclusively rice-eating nation, received large amounts of P.L. 480 wheat in the postwar period. Now, it has become the largest single foreign commercial customer for United States wheat, purchasing 100 million bushels in fiscal 1971 plus large quantities of soya beans.[29] But by a similar process, Spain has become a large commercial buyer of soybean oil.

But economic development doesn't necessarily lead to increased commercial sales, particularly of wheat and rice. We have noted the existing doubts about the efficacy of food aid as a stimulant to economic development. Furthermore, as countries develop they will grow a much higher percentage of their food needs, thereby reducing their requirements for imported foodstuffs. Their food imports will tend to be high cost, high protein goods like meat, fish, and fruit, rather than the feedgrains that comprise most of their current diet. However, the demand for feedgrains should increase as developing countries increase livestock production. Given the considerable comparative advantage of highly developed western countries with temperate climates, such as the United States for the production of soy beans, nations which outgrow their need for food aid will continue to import soy bean oil, cake, and meat on commercial terms, rather than

Table 3-1
Transition of Food Aid Recipients to Commercial Purchasers

Country		Leading Dollar Markets for U.S. Agricultural Exports		Principal Countries of Destination for Government-Financed Agricultural Exports	
		Millions of $	Rank	Millions of $	Rank
Japan	1955	267	2	119	1
	1956	264	3	127	3
	1965	865	1	11	−
	1966	932	1	10	−
Philippines	1953	54	9	6	−
	1956	37	−	16	−
	1965	45	−	23	−
	1966	66	−	11	−
Spain	1955	11	−	83	4
	1956	13	−	153	2
	1965	148	8	9	−
	1966	183	8	7	−
Italy	1955	27	−	73	6
	1956	55	10	108	5
	1965	262	6	6	−
	1966	240	6	2	−
Israel	1955	7	−	38	−
	1956	6	−	42	−
	1965	38	−	45	9
	1966	51	−	35	8
U.A.R.	1955	12	−	22	−
	1956	14	−	35	−
	1965	15	−	83	4
	1966	76	12	62	5

attempt to grow these products domestically. Undoubtedly, the fear that developing nations ultimately might reduce their imports of United States agricultural products or compete with United States exports in third countries instigated the now discredited policy formerly advocated by Congress and implemented by the Department of Agriculture of severely limiting any type of economic assistance P.L. 480 or foreign aid likely to encourage production of commodities exported by the United States.[30] Both the Food for Peace Act of 1966 and the Foreign Assistance Act now clearly advocate maximum assistance and promotion of developing nations' agricultural capacity.[31] However, we might note that Congress, though conceding on food production, actually has strengthened the "legal" status of the policy discouraging production of nonfood agricultural products by adding specific language on this score.[32]

Future developments here are highly uncertain. At best, one can theorize that the creation of sizeable markets for commercial agricultural exports requires a pattern of economic development that will produce sufficient foreign exchange to pay for food imports without leading to total agricultural autarchy.[33] The shift away from wheat and rice imports may be compensated by increased sales of feed grains (for meat production) and soy beans. The final answer will depend in part upon the rate of increase in per capita income, the type of food tastes acquired by the inhabitants of the developing countries, and the capacity of the agricultural plant of potential exporters to meet future domestic requirements for high protein products, particularly meat and feed grains.

Market Development

In addition to the potential of food aid to improve the overall economic capacity of developing nations to import agricultural products commercially, food aid has been portrayed as an effective means to improve the relative market position of the food aid donor. This has been a continuous objective of the agricultural interests backing the United States Food for Peace programs.[34] Probably, the strongest efforts in this direction have been centered about the use of local currencies received under Title I sales to finance market development programs in developed countries.[35] These programs are in part financed by the foreign currencies received under sales for local currencies, in part by the dollars resulting from rights retained by the United States to convert a limited amount of local currencies to hard currency use in its market development activities, and in part by private groups participating in cooperative arrangements between the United States government and private trade and agricultural groups. These groups promote trade fairs and trade centers and marketing and utilization research.[36] Congress has gone to considerable lengths to ensure that adequate funds for market development were available by giving the Secretary of Agriculture direct control over a substantial percentage of local currencies generated by concessional sales for use in these programs.[37]

Strictly speaking though, any gains for American agriculture achieved through these means cannot be attributed to food aid. Although currencies generated by food aid well may have been used for market development, Congress could have as easily appropriated such funds directly. That is, the kind of market promotion activities involved here are available to any nation whether or not they engage in food aid operations. And although it appears that Administration proponents of food aid have been rather successful in connecting food aid with market development, the nexus is mostly attributable to successful press agentry.

Market Preemption

Food aid has been perceived by donors and worried competitors as effective means for establishing long-term commercial markets in recipient countries by permanently dislodging or discouraging other sources of supply. Thus, by supplying all imports of food at concessional prices until such time as the recipient becomes a cash customer, the donor could be in position to prevent entry of other food-selling countries.[38] In addition, this might serve to discourage local production, thus maintaining the recipient's dependence on food imports.[39] But practically speaking, once a country is capable of purchasing agricultural commodities on commercial terms, it is doubtful that given the highly competitive and flexible nature of international agriculture trade, no food aid donor could long prevent the entry of other countries into these markets. Moreover, the policy of discouraging local production has been reversed. Perhaps at a minimum, the continuous availability of food aid might prevent a country from moving too far towards total self-sufficiency where maintenance of some level of food imports made economic sense.[40]

The Impact of Food Aid on Domestic Agricultural Policies

In addition to the impact of food aid on commercial agricultural exports, the balance-of-payments and the federal budget, United States food aid programs are alleged to have impeded the development of sound domestic agricultural policy. Starting in the thirties, the United States and all other developed countries have suffered chronic surpluses of agricultural production (or where their production control policies have been effective, they maintain the capacity for excess production). That is, the economy was capable of producing more agricultural products than could be sold at prices offering an acceptable return to the producers—acceptable in terms of the comparable return being earned by labor and capital in other parts of the economy. Apparently, this phenomena is the direct result of technological advances outstripping expansion of demand for grains and fibers in an industry unable effectively to control its production levels.[41]

The most striking tangible result of this process was the accumulation by the United States of huge stockpiles of surplus products acquired through price support operations during periods of chronically low farm prices.[42] These stockpiles not only were costly to store but their size and rate of growth incited increasing criticism of the entire agricultural price support program. Moreover, their existence was believed to depress the commodity markets through the fear and expectation that eventually they would find their way into commercial channels.[43] Therefore, any program that could both permanently remove these commodities from the market and from United States government ownership was viewed as substantially helping United States agricultural interests. Burning them may have achieved the same end, but such a solution was morally and politically impossible in a hungry world. Therefore, the opportunity to reduce the stockpiles (and avoid the storage costs) by putting the food to what seemed excellent use—first the relief of hunger, and later, economic development—seemed heavenmade. Indeed, it is this lucky meld of parochial and humanitarian ends that has sustained this program at a high level for so long, particularly when compared to the vicissitudes of nonmilitary foreign aid.[44]

A good case may be made for the proposition that United States food aid programs have reduced domestic opposition to existing farm programs and the highly controlled agricultural trade that must result from national agricultural support policies that raise domestic prices above international levels. Until quite recently, agricultural economists have unanimously condemned these policies. And they have alleged that without the outlet provided by food aid, this country would have been forced to make fundamental changes in an essentially irrational farm policy. Moreover, the threat posed by large surplus stockpiles might have induced the removal of some of the formidable barricades laid across the path of international commerce in agricultural products. In other words, food aid may have served to deflect adverse public opinion aroused by the spectacle of useless commodity stockpiles, thereby impeding necessary reform.[45] And it has diminished the impetus for freer trade by recruiting both food aid recipients and producers as additional supporters of the existing system.[46]

But, there is another side to this argument. The relationships between domestic agriculture policy and food aid are most trenchantly and thoroughly analyzed in a study of food aid and economic development conducted by the Organization for Economic Cooperation and Development published in 1963. Unless noted otherwise, the discussion that follows is based on this work.[47] A country in which agricultural production is currently running ahead of commercial demand at home and abroad, giving rise to surplus stocks, can attempt to reduce its production, increase its commercial sales, destroy its surplus stocks or seek outlets through noncommercial channels. Reducing the level of agricultural production may be a solution in the long run, and as such, it is considered more fully later in this section. Experience has shown, however, that the obstacles to this course are very great and can only be overcome by a comprehensive policy applied over a period of years. In the meantime, the problem of dealing with excess production remains.

When surplus stocks come into being, it is likely that the possibilities for commercial sales at profitable prices have already been nearly exhausted. If in the past ten years, the United States had been forced to sell its surpluses of wheat and other products on the domestic market, the result would have been a catastrophic fall in prices; price guarantees to farmers would almost certainly have had to be reduced, with a consequent fall in farm incomes and adverse effect throughout the economy. Outlets on world markets also are limited, and if the United States had attempted to export its surpluses, it would have depressed world prices severely for its competitors and for itself. Not only has the United States government been unwilling to harm other exporters by dumping its wheat surpluses, it is doubtful whether it would have gained any benefit for itself in this way.

In the depression of the 1930s, various countries destroyed surplus stocks of foodstuffs in an attempt to relieve the market. Today, confronted with the spectacle of acute food needs of many underdeveloped countries, such a "solution" seems unlikely to be envisaged by governments or tolerated by public opinion; savings in storage costs not withstanding. The developments of recent years confirm the widespread desire to make more constructive use of existing surplus agricultural capacity.

There remains then, as an immediate solution, the recourse of diverting part of the supply to noncommercial channels. Within the country itself, there may well be possibilities for providing extra food for welfare purposes; the existence of such possibilities even within a country of high average standards of living has been demonstrated in the United States, where the present "food stamp" plan and previous arrangements are illustrations of what can be done. However, the possibilities are usually limited, and as high-protein foods are usually the most appropriate for such programs, it may be difficult to solve problems of surplus cereals in this way, that is, unless they can be used to raise output of the needed livestock products.

It therefore seems likely that in the short run, exports on a noncommercial basis may represent an important means of utilizing at least part of large surplus stocks. As we have already seen, the short-run cost of such programs to the government and private producers depends upon a number of factors distributed along several continuums. But so long as domestic supplies or potential production remains above effective demand, the cost of food aid in terms of opportunity costs (alternate productive uses of resources) will be quite low; in any case, it will be well below the value of the aid to the recipient.

Ultimately, it may be possible to match agricultural supply and demand. But past experience indicates this may not be easy or even possible in the face of resistance by entrenched agricultural interests with a powerful claim towards a fair share of the general prosperity.[48] Further, the constant spread of new technology makes possible increased agricultural output even with reduced inputs of labor and land, so that rising output may well be associated with even quite a rapid outflow of labor and land to other uses. It should also be borne in mind that in a hungry world there is considerable public opposition to measures for restricting production.

It seems probably that food aid programs, by providing a widely acceptable use for surplus production, and creating a climate of opinion favorable to high production, would reduce the incentive to make adjustments, even though these might be economically desirable. But the possibilities for using food aid to dispose of surpluses is limited. In practice, there is a finite amount which can be absorbed without damage to agriculture in the receiving countries or to world trade. Further, the financial cost to the donor country is also likely to keep such programs within bounds. And the resistance to food aid expenditures increases as soil bank programs succeed in replacing actual stored surpluses with nonproducing farm land.[49]

Moreover, it is not entirely clear that food aid programs monopolize resources that could be used more productively elsewhere. If serious shortages of industrial labor existed, pinning down sizeable numbers of workers in submarginal agricultural pursuits would constitute a serious economic waste. But, if opportunities in industry were limited, particularly for unskilled or semiskilled labor, no immediate loss would occur. Capital might be tied down that could be better used elsewhere. But again actual economic loss depends upon available alternatives and land is a notoriously inflexible factor of production. It is probable that the existence of food aid programs and the consequent higher level of agricultural output may lead to a higher demand by agriculture for inputs from other sectors than would otherwise be the case, but the size of this extra demand and the nature of its consequences for the economy as a whole seem impossible to assess without detailed study of individual circumstances. And, of course, farm land could not be readily transferable to other uses.

Therefore, the proposition that food aid inevitably has an adverse effect on the donor's economy through its inhibiting effect on agricultural policy reform may not be uncritically accepted. Despite food aid programs, in the United States at least, there has been substantial movements towards more flexible farm policies.[50] Both grain surpluses and the farm population have been drastically reduced. More rapid acceleration of the farm exodus may not be wise policy in light of current urban problems. Furthermore, even if effective food aid only may be obtained at the price of slight dislocations in the economies of the developed world, this may not be too high a price for the rich to pay for their "privilege" of coexisting with so much hunger and poverty.

The Actual Impact of Food Aid on Commercial Transactions

Granting the great uncertainties in making precise estimates of the impact of food aid on donors and recipients, each seems to benefit to some degree; if not immediately and financially, then in the longer run and with respect to noneconomic interests. But for third country exporters, the immediate threat to current markets would seem to outweigh any potential long-run benefits that might flow from accelerated economic development of the recipient countries. Therefore, it is not entirely surprising that from the outset the only large bilateral food aid program—the United States' Food for Peace—would appear highly suspect to other exporting nations. At various times, it has been charged that this program affords the United States an unfair advantage in the competition for international sales and unduly interferences with the legitimate trade interests of other exporters.[51] Also, it has been alleged that the Food for Peace program conflicts with our support of free trade and opposition to bilateralism.[52]

The Norms for International Agricultural Trade

In part, this type of criticism implies that the norm for international trade in agricultural commodities is the free markets of the ninteenth century. Clearly, this cannot be so. Every major agricultural exporter exercises varying levels of controls over its domestic farm production and international trading. Major commodities such as wheat, coffee, cotton and sugar are subject to international agreements designed to avoid classical competition. In fact, the international system of free trade in agricultural commodities of the nineteenth century broke down long ago, and has been replaced by a series of controlled and separate markets with widely diverging prices, linked precariously by a succession of international commodity agreements.[53] World agricultural trade has been pushed even further towards neomercantilism by the agricultural policies of the European Common Market, featuring high domestic supports protected by variable levies on imports and accompanied by highly subsidized export policies designed to move the surpluses generated by high internal prices.[54]

Since Food for Peace has been concentrated on commodities in actual or potential world surplus, it is very difficult to separate the impact of the surpluses *per se* from that of programs designed to deal with the surpluses. Admittedly, the world price of products involved in food aid programs dropped 25% during the seven-year period following the onset of the first United States agricultural disposal programs.[55] But prices probably would have dropped even more had the United States dumped all its surpluses on the world market.[56] Of course, prices might have dropped less if the United States had stored all its surplus. The path it took compromised between bearing the entire brunt alone, and shifting it all to the rest of the world. Therefore, in the absence of clear international agreements or standards for the behavior of each surplus country, it is not possible to attribute the price decline to United States food aid programs. Food aid was a response to an existing problem; it did not create the surplus problem itself.

Current Status of Agricultural Grain Trade[57]

Wheat, coarse grains, rice and cotton are the commodities that are heavily represented in food aid transactions and in which food aid transactions constitute an important factor in world trade patterns. The figures in Table 3-2 with respect to United States food aid and world trade in 1968 are representative of the current world situation.

The world grain picture has radically changed in the past twenty years with respect to trading practices and policies and the supply/demand situation. Between the prewar period and the late 1950s, the developed countries accomplished a complete reversal of their historical position as a net importing area for grains. They became the world's residual supplier of some ten million tons annually, and during most of the sixties their net exports averaged 25 million tons. (See Table 1, FAO Commodity Study #20). This reflected a combination of factors, but primarily the stimulus given to their production in the immediate postwar period of food shortages, the price and income support provided by national policies, the progress in production techniques, and the growing use of food aid as part of the general economic assistance given to developing countries. Con-

Table 3-2

Commercial and Concessional Transactions in 1968

Commodity	World Exports[a] (Millions of Dollars)	Food for Peace Sales[b] (Millions of Dollars)	Food for Peace Sales as a Percentage of Total Exports
Wheat and Flour	3.414	543.3	15.9
Coarse Grains	2,241	77.7	3.5
Rice	1,025.4	155.5	14.4
Fats and Oils	2,898	113.9	4.6
Cotton	2,259	108.3	4.8

[a]UN/FAO, *FAO Commodity Review and Outlook*, 1969-70, Tables 4, 5, 6, 14, 31.

[b]Annual Report on P.L. 480 for 1968, 1969, Table 33. (In order to convert the P.L. 480 figures which are on a fiscal year basis to a calendar year basis, the figures for fiscal 68 and 69 were averaged.)

sumption of grains as food in developed countries has been more or less station-
ary since 1950. By contrast, developing countries—a source of large exportable
supplies of grains prior to World War II—showed until very recently an increasing
overall dependence on grain imports. This affected especially Asia and Africa,
where domestic production lagged behind the rise in demand caused by population growth and the improving living standards. A marked reversal also occurred
in the trade position of the centrally planned economies. These changes were
most pronounced in wheat, but similar changes, though on a smaller scale, occurred for coarse grains.

Associated with these changing trade positions has been a massive expansion
in the volume of international trade. World exports of wheat and coarse grains
have more than doubled from an average of 40 million tons in 1949/50-1953/54
to about 95 million tons in recent years. The peak year, both for coarse grains
and wheat, was reached in 1965/66, when total trade in grains amounted to 106
million tons. Since then, wheat exports have fallen markedly and a moderate
decline occurred in coarse grains exports, although 1969/70 brought a limited
recovery. However, of the 25 million metric ton increase in both wheat and food
grain exports, 15 million tons of the wheat increase was in food aid, while only
1.32 million metric tons of the feedgrain increase is in food aid.

The main shifts in the direction and structure of world trade occurred in
wheat. Trade between the developed exporting countries and the traditional importers of western Europe has shrunk and ceased to be the largest commercial
sector. Japan has emerged as a new large commercial market, accounting for 10%
of world trade in 1968/69, and 9% in 1969/70, and for an even larger share of
commercial trade. Another new sector of commercial trade has developed with
the centrally planned economies of eastern Europe and China (Mainland). The
purchases of China and eastern Europe together now constitute almost 20% of
world trade and there have been large purchases periodically by the U.S.S.R.
Commercial imports into developing countries have also grown rapidly, particularly in recent years. They accounted for almost 33% of world trade in
1968/69, compared to 20% ten years earlier. Shipments under special terms, initiated a temporary measure of United States surplus disposal, rapidly became a
permanent form of food aid to meet the growing requirements of the developing
regions. The number of food aid donors in grains steadily increased and was further extended by the Food Aid Convention in 1968.

The pressure exerted on international prices by the mounting surplus supplies
and excess productive capacity gave rise to additional government aids to exports, especially larger subsidies and special credit facilities from some exporting
countries, and there was an intensification of import restrictions by some importing countries. The number of the countries exporting wheat and flour since
1949 and their relative importance has changed. The four principal exporters,
Australia, Argentina, Canada and the United States, were joined in the mid-1950s
by France and the U.S.S.R. and together now account for about 90% of world

trade. Among the smaller exporters, some, like Turkey, Tunisia and Morocco, have become net importers in recent years, while others (e.g., Bulgaria and Romania) have succeeded in exporting increasing quantities or, like Mexico and Spain, have emerged as new exporters following successful efforts to attain self-sufficiency.

The two decades witnessed wide fluctuations in world wheat stocks. The rapid transformation of the world wheat situation in the early 1950s from one of acute shortages to one of burdensome surpluses, followed a series of bumper crops in exporting countries, particularly in North America. Combined carryover stocks of five major exporters (the United States, Canada, Australia, Argentina and the EEC) jumped from 18 million tons at the beginning of 1952/53 to three times this level (54 million tons) by the end of 1955/56 (see Table 2, FAO Commodity Study #20). They were concentrated in the United States and Canada, but affected the whole grains situation. At this level, stocks amounted to roughly twice the current volume of world trade. This fundamental imbalance between supply and demand continued throughout the 1950s. In both importing and exporting countries, national support measures and technological progress caused a steady increase in yields and hence in production. At the same time, total consumption of wheat for food in developed countries did not increase despite population growth.

Various programs were devised to dispose of the surplus production, but only the United States took action to curtail output. With production limited by United States acreage controls, and exports stimulated by food aid programs and the growth of commercial demand from centrally planned countries, world trade expanded to around 50 million tons a year and stocks fell substantially in the early 1960s. By the middle of the decade, the main exporters' carryover stocks had reached a level which the International Wheat Council described as "a state

Table 3-3

Closing Stocks of Wheat in Five Principal Exporting Countries in Selected Years[a]

	United States 30 June million tons	Canada 31 July	EEC[b] 30 June	Australia 30 Nov.	Argentina 30 Nov.	Total Five Countries
1951/52	7.0	5.9	4.0	0.5	0.2	17.6
1955/56	28.1	15.8	6.5	2.3	1.2	53.9
1960/61	38.4	16.5	6.5	0.7	0.8	62.9
1965/66	14.6	11.4	6.8	0.6	0.2	33.6
1969/70	24.0	27.5	6.5[c]	8.0[c]	1.0[c]	67.0[c]

[a]UN/FAO, *FAO Commodity Policy Study No. 20, The Stabilization of International Trade in Grains* 4 (1940).

[b]1969/70 = 31 July

[c]Provisional

of approximate, if precarious, equilibrium." Indeed, United States wheat stocks temporarily fell below the minimum desirable level.

In the past two years, there has been another abrupt turnabout in the world grains situation, and in patterns of trade. Net exports of wheat from developed countries dropped steeply to little more than 20 million tons in 1968/69, compared to an average of almost 30 million tons in the six preceding years. The sharpest fall was in net exports to centrally planned countries reflecting the changed trade position of the U.S.S.R. and eastern Europe. Net shipments to developing countries were also much lower in 1968/69 than in the previous year, although still somewhat above the longer-run average. One cause of this recent development has been the change in world supply and demand patterns. The rapid growth of international trade in wheat in recent years, though partly reflecting transient factors, encouraged exporters to gear themselves to an expanding market. The higher minimum prices for wheat stipulated in the International Grains Arrangement (IGA) in 1967 provided an additional incentive, and production rose in several exporting countries. At the same time, several important deficit countries achieved dramatic increases in grain production—India and Pakistan in particular—due partly to better weather, and partly to the success of high-yielding varieties. Larger investments in agriculture brought bumper crops also in the U.S.S.R. and eastern Europe, with the U.S.S.R. rejoining the ranks of the world's exporters. Thus, while crops expanded in several exporting countries, world imports during 1968/69, the first year of the new IGA, dropped to 45 million tons.

The other cause lies with national grain policies, and their determining influence on production patterns. National agricultural policies in many developed countries originate in the measures introduced in the 1920s and 1930s to protect farmers from the violent price fluctuations of that period. Production incentive programs were extended after the war in order to assist agricultural recovery and meet the postwar food shortages. Since 1952, when the immediate and most acute scarcities were overcome, national policies have been modified and refined to make them more responsive to the market situation. The need for a conscious management of supplies at international levels has also become somewhat more widely accepted, principally among exporting countries, but this has not been generally reflected in national policies. Several importing countries, and particularly developing countries where grains are a basic item in the food economy and balance-of-payments, have continued to encourage grain production with the aim of reducing their reliance on imports, irrespective of the world supply position. Most developed exporting countries still operate policies which are not capable of adjusting production quickly to changes in the world market situation. This inflexibility in national policies, and the other factors mentioned above, led to the renewed accumulation of surplus stocks in 1969—only three years after the equilibrium reached in 1966.

The main difference between the present stock situation and that of the early

1960s lies in the distribution of surplus stocks. Whereas in 1961 the U.S.A. held over 60% of the main exporters' carryover stocks of wheat, and an even larger share of surplus stocks, its share in the aggregate carryover is expected to be only one-third in 1970. Canada, on the other hand, which held only a quarter of these stocks in 1961, accounts for approximately 40% of the 1970 carryover, and Australia whose stocks were negligible in 1961 will probably hold about 15% of the total in 1970. Although it is difficult to define precisely the surplus element in wheat stocks, it can be approximately estimated that over two-thirds of the present surplus are in the hands of Canada and Australia. Argentina has only a very small carryover, and stocks in the EEC, though still above normal levels, are somewhat lower than in 1969. The wider geographical distribution of stocks is an important destabilizing factor in the present world wheat situation. A similar, though less pronounced, shift has taken place in coarse grains; whereas the United States accounted for 86% of exporters' stocks in 1961, this share has declined to about 68% in 1970.

The Impact of Food Aid on Wheat

Food aid undoubtedly has been given to countries that, faced with severe food shortages, would have used scarce foreign exchange to purchase food rather than starve. Hopefully, these are not the kind of commercial sales food exporters are anxious to make. At the same time, food aid may have deprived agricultural nations with export opportunities vital to their economic well-being. Table 3-4 attempts to present the data relevant to the impact of food aid on commercial wheat and flour markets.

The figures presented in Table 3-4 support the conclusion that food aid has filled import needs that otherwise would have been satisfied through commercial imports. In the period 1949/50-1953/54, the developing nations imported 9.4 million metric tons of wheat and flour. These imports were divided among the major wheat exporting nations as follows: United States—36%; Canada—23%; Australia—17%; Argentina—14%; EEC countries—2%. During the period 1966/69-1968/69, the developing nations imported 23.70 million metric tons, shared as follows: United States—57%; Canada—6%; Australia—11%; Argentina—6%; EEC—9%. In 1969/70, the developing countries imported 23.35 million metric tons, divided as follows: U.S.—51%; Canada—6%; Australia—10%; Argentina—6%; EEC—19%. But of the 23.70 metric tons of wheat and flour imported by the developing nations in the period 1966/67—1968/69, 10.26 m.m.t. or 43% represented food aid, and of the 23.35 m.m.t. imported by developing countries in 1969/70, 10.23 m.m.t. or 45% was food aid.

Although food aid has drastically changed the wheat trade patterns in the developing countries, it does not seem to have injured the overall position of most commercial wheat exporters. The most dramatic changes involved Canada and the United States. In 1949/50-1953/54, Canada had 23% of the market in the developing countries, in 1966/67-1968/69, their share dropped to 6%, and remained at 6% in 1969/70. By contrast, the United States' share of the developing countries' market increased from 36% in 1949/50-1953/54 to 57% in 1966/67 and 51% in 1969/70. From 1949/50-1969/70, Australia's share of this same market dropped from 17% to 10%. Argentina suffered a sharp drop from 14% to 6% but most of this was attributable to reduced availabilities of exportable wheat.[58] The sharpest increase in sales to developing countries was achieved by the EEC, whose share of this market rose from 2% in 1949/50-1953/54 to 9% in 1966/67-1968/69, and then to 19% in 1969/70. Most importantly, the EEC increased both its share of the total sales and its share of commercial exports. By contrast, almost all United States gains are attributable to food aid. Thus, during the period 1949-1970, United States *commercial* exports to the developing countries rose only from 3.4 m.m.t. to 4.34 m.m.t., while the EEC's commercial exports went from 0.2 m.m.t. to 3.11 m.m.t. a 15 fold increase. Canada's exports to developed countries also decreased; from 3.4 m.m.t. to 1.35 m.m.t., but this was more than overcome by an increase in commercial exports to socialist countries from 0 to 3.64 m.m.t. in 1969/70. Australia increased its exports to all three markets, and the EEC exports increased even more dramatically. Thus, in 1949/50-1953/54 the EEC's market shares of the developed, socialist and developing markets were 3%, 0% and 2% respectively, in 1969/70 the percentages were 11%, 11%, and 19%. But as we have previously noted much of this increase was heavily subsidized, and the result of the huge internal surpluses generated by their Common Agricultural Policy.[59]

The picture looks quite differently, if we focus solely upon commercial markets. Here, the past twenty years has witnessed a wide redistribution of commercial wheat markets. The developing countries have increased their commercial wheat imports from 9.4 m.m.t. to 13.12 m.m.t., and overall, the United States share of total commercial sales has declined from 36% to 33%, and Canada's from 31% to 20%. Australia's share has increased from 11% to 18%; the EEC's has increased from 3% to 15% and the USSR's from 3% to 14%. Argentina's share has dropped from 8% to 4%. Thus, the losses suffered by Canada have been to Australia, the EEC and Russia. The United States has lost a comparable amount. The United States and the EEC have greatly increased their share of all exports to developing countries, but while the United States' share of *commercial* exports to developing countries has remained constant, the EEC has increased its share from 2% to 24%. Canada's share of commercial exports to developing nations has declined from 23% to 4% but it cannot blame these losses on food aid. Rather, Canada's and the United States' share has been eaten away by the EEC which has increased its share from 2% to 24%. Again, much of this gain is attributable to very aggressive EEC export subsidy programs. Australia and Argentina have maintained an even keel in their commercial exports to developing countries. But Canada has been well compensated for losses in com-

Table 3-4
Patterns of World Wheat Exports (in millions of metric tons)

Period / Exporter-Destination	1949/50–1953/54 (average annual level)		1966/67–1968/69 (average annual level)			1969/70		
	Volume of Exports	Percentage Share of Market	Volume of Exports	Percentage Share of Market	Percentage Share of Commercial Market	Volume of Exports	Percentage Share of Market	Percentage Share of Commercial Market
United States	7.3	36	19.11	38	29	16.48	33	22
a. Developed Countries	5.9	37	4.80	32	32	4.59	32	32
b. Socialist Countries	–	–	0.74	1	9	0.01	0	0
c. Developing Countries	3.4	36	13.57	57	38	11.9	51	33
Commercial	3.4	36	5.09			4.34		
Food Aid	[a]	[a]	8.48			7.56		
Canada	8.0	31	10.87	22	28	8.85	18	20
a. Developed Countries	5.8	36	4.98	34	34	3.86	27	27
b. Socialist Countries	–	–	4.30	37	54	3.64	29	29
c. Developing Countries	3.4	23	1.59	6	12	1.35	6	4
Commercial	3.4	23	0.79			.47		
Food Aid	[a]	[a]	0.80			.86		
Australia	2.8	11	6.40	13	17	7.25	14	18
a. Developed Countries	1.2	7	1.88	13	13	2.33	16	16
b. Socialist Countries	–	–	1.97	17	25	2.54	21	21
c. Developing Countries	1.6	17	2.55	11	15	2.38	10	17
Commercial	1.6	17	2.37			2.17		
Food Aid	[a]	[a]	.18			0.21		
European Economic Community	0.7	3	3.53	7	10	7.13	14	15
a. Developed Countries	0.5	3	0.75	5	5	1.54	11	11
b. Socialist Countries	–	–	0.65	1	8	1.38	11	11
c. Developing Countries	0.1	2	2.13	9	15	4.21	19	24
Commercial	0.2	2	2.67			.11		
Food Aid	[a]	[a]	.06			.30		
Argentina	2.0	8	2.38	5	7	2.00	4	5
a. Developed Countries	0.7	4	0.75	5	5	0.52	4	4
b. Socialist Countries	–	–	0.09	–	1	–	–	–
c. Developing Countries	1.3	14	1.54	6	1	1.49	6	11

Commercial	1.3	14	1.54			.49		
Food Aid	[a]	[a]	–			0		
USSR			4.86			5.89		
a. Developed Countries	0.9	3	0.38	9	1	0.75	12	14
b. Socialist Countries[c]	0.9	6	3.74[d]	2	3	4.83[b]	5	5
c. Developing Countries	–	–	0.74	34	0	0.31	39	39
Commercial	–	–	–	3	0	.01	1	–
Food Aid	[a]	[a]	0.74			30		
Others	1.7	6	3.06			2.32		
a. Developed Countries	1.0	6	1.23	6	8	0.78	5	6
b. Socialist Countries	0.1	100	.25	8	8	0.03	5	5
c. Developing Countries	0.6	6	1.58	2	3	1.51	0	0
Commercial	0.6	6	1.58	7	12	1.51	6	11
Food Aid	[a]	[a]	–			0		
Total Commercial	25.5	100	36.11			39.69		
Total Wheat Exports	25.5		50.21	100	100	99.92	100	100
Developed Countries	16.0	63	14.77	30	41	14.37	29	36
Socialist Countries	0.1	0	11.74	24	22	12.37	25	31
Developing Countries	9.4	37	23.70	46	N.A.	23.35	46	N.A.
Commercial	9.4	37	13.44	N.A.	37	13.12		33
Food Aid	0	0	10.26	N.A.		10.23		

Notes

[a] No food aid during this period.

[b] Exports were on non-commercial terms.

[c] Excluding exports to Mainland China and Eastern Europe.

[d] Non-commercial.

mercial sales to the developing world by gains in exports to the socialist countries. Here, Canada's exports rose from zero in 1949/50-1953/54 to 3.64 m.m.t. in 1969/70, representing 29% of this market. Australia and the EEC also have done well in the socialist countries. Their sales to this market have increased from zero to 2.54 m.m.t. and 1.32 m.m.t., respectively.

The Organization for Economic Cooperation and Development (OECD) reaches similar conclusions. Its study of the role of food aid in economic development concludes that although the United States through special export programs has greatly increased its wheat exports and its share in total wheat trade, other exporters cannot be said to have lost sales as compared to the prewar period. Australia is exporting more on a commercial basis to Asian countries, and Canada has expanded markets in Japan and Europe. And although Argentina has lost its near-monopoly of the Brazilian wheat market, this seems to have resulted from lack of exportable products rather than preemption by the United States. Furthermore, it seems that most concessional sales have met needs that otherwise would have remained unfulfilled.[60]

The Impact of Food Aid on World
Coarse Grain Trade

Feedgrains show a similar though less dramatic pattern. The development and structure of international trade in coarse grains has differed from that of wheat, although there have been several common characteristics. Exports grew fast until the mid-sixties but, in contrast to wheat, concessional sales have played only a minor role. The expansion has reflected almost entirely the growing commercial sales for livestock feeding in economically advanced countries. It has taken place in spite of a very strong upward trend in coarse grain production in western Europe, the main importing region. Until the mid-sixties, western Europe was the fastest growing market for coarse grains, but this role has more recently been taken over by Japan. About a quarter of world imports are now going to Japan, compared to only 6% ten years ago. As requirements rose, importers came to rely increasingly on the United States as a source of supply. During most of the sixties, over half of the coarse grain exports originated in the United States, compared to only one-third in the early fifties. More recently, reflecting a falloff in markets and increasing competition from other sources, the United States share has fallen below 50 percent. Trade in coarse grains still flows mainly between developed countries but developing countries as a group, traditionally the source of a significant portion of total supplies, have expanded their sales in recent years. By 1968/69, they contributed over one-quarter of world exports compared to about 20% in the early sixties. In addition to Argentina, the largest exporters in this group, Thailand, Mexico and Brazil have established themselves as regular exporters of sizeable quantities of corn, and a number of other developing countries also participate in this trade. The accumulation of excessive stocks since the early 1950s has been a characteristic shared by world coarse grain markets and basically for the same reasons as for wheat. But it has caused few international problems, since almost 90% of the stocks were held in the United States where they accounted for a much smaller share of total domestic consumption and trade than wheat stocks. During the nine-year period 1952 to 1961, stocks of coarse grains in the main exporting countries—United States, Canada, EEC, Australia and Argentina—rose from about 27 million metric tons to a peak of 88 million tons, but had been reduced to about 50 million tons by 1966.

Table 3-5
Closing Stocks of Coarse Grains in Five Principal Exporting Countries in Selected Years[a]

	United States 30 June	Canada 31 July	FEC[b] 30 June	Australia 30 Nov.	Argentina 30 Nov.	Total Five Countries
1951/52	18.4	3.6	...	–	0.4	...
1955/56	39.6	4.6	3.3	–	0.5	48.0
1960/61	77.2	4.5	5.4	0.1	0.5	87.7
1965/66	38.6	4.5	4.9	0.6	0.1	48.7
1969/70[c]	45.8	9.0	6.0	1.7	2.1	64.6

Coarse Grains = Barley, Oats, Maize (Corn), Sorghum, Rye
[a]UN/FAO, FAO Commodity Policy Study No. 20, *The Stabilization of International Trade in Grain*
[b]Provisional
[c]1969/70 = 31 July

It seems clear that food aid has not distorted coarse grain trade patterns. In the preconcessional sale period, 1949/1950-1953/54, the United States net exports of feedgrains to all countries (corn, grain, sorghums, oats) totaled 3.13 m.m.t., representing 33% of total net exports of this commodity. During the same period, the export share of Canada was 24%, Argentina's 15% and U.S.S.R. 9%. In the period, 1959/1960-1963/1964, net feedgrain exports for the United States totaled 13.231 m.m.t., representing 56% of net exports. Canada's share was 2%, Argentina's 15% and U.S.S.R. 27%. Of the 10-m.m.t. increase in United States exports, 2.64 m.m.t. represent concessional sales. In 1969/70, world feedgrain exports climbed to 38.39 m.m.t. The United States took 50% of the market, Argentina 17%, the EEC 9%, Canada and Thailand had 4% and South Africa 3%. Of the United States' total exports of 19.04 m.m.t., 1.32 m.m.t. was food aid.[61]

Rice.[62] The impact of food aid upon rice markets is difficult to determine. Largely, this is a function of the extreme volatility of the rice situation, making it difficult to precisely identify the causes of the changes. The pattern of world trade over the past ten years is presented in Table 3-6. Transient factors produced a slight increase in rice trade during 1970.

The first half of the sixties was marked by relative stability, during which export supplies and trade gradually rose and world prices were remarkably steady. A combination of factors including government regulation of exports, restriction on imports to save foreign exchange, and the availability of ample supplies of alternative cereals, mainly wheat on concessional terms, had cloaked the latent unstable elements in the world rice economy in these years. The instability came to the surface in full force with the wide-scale crop failures of 1965 and 1966 in many rice countries and the consequent emergence of an acute world shortage of rice. Heightened import demand resulted in a scramble for available rice when the main exporting countries could not increase their export supplies to the extent required. The volume of world trade shrank and prices increased steeply nearly reaching the high levels that had prevailed during the Korean war.

Now, once again, the picture has changed radically as production has significantly increased, particularly in importing countries in the closing years of the past decade, and scarcity conditions have been replaced by easy supply situation. A huge surplus of rice has accumulated in one major rice-producing developed country, namely Japan. Rice prices have declined to the lowest levels of the past decade and a half and export earnings from rice in the developing countries have been drastically reduced. Japan and several exporting countries have now adopted policies to reduce rice area and diversify agriculture.

The volatility witnessed in recent years emanates from certain basic economic and technical conditions governing rice production and trade. The subsistence character of a very large part of the world rice supply, the inelastic nature of demand for rice, and a very small proportion (less than four percent) of world production entering international trade—all these factors render rice prices and trade susceptible to violent changes. This uncertainty, and particularly its repercussions on international trade, affects developing countries the most.

Rice is not only the principal source of foreign exchange for several developing countries, especially in the Far East, it is also a big import item in trade balances of a number of others. Moreover, in many developing countries, rice is the key crop on which plans of agricultural and economic development hinge. Consequently, the growth and stability of entire economies as far apart as Madagascar, Ceylon, Korea and Guyana are vitally linked to the prospects for rice. Instability in prices, uncertainty of export outlets, and insecurity in obtaining import requirements virtually reduce the exercise of forward planning to a gamble for many developing countries.

The pattern of rice trade has undergone marked changes in recent years. The most striking of these is the considerably reduced importance of exports from the Far East—the world's largest rice producing region. Exports from the Far East declined from 3.7 million tons in 1959-63 to 1.9 million tons in 1969. This

Table 3-6
Pattern of World Rice Exports[a]

	1959-63 Average	1967	1968	1969
Exports	Thousand Metric Tons (milled)			
World Total	6,364	6,944	6,321	6,508
Developed countries	1,234	2,245	2,351	2,593
United States	957	1,848	1,898	1,918
Japan	–	–	–	328
Developing Countries	4,185	3,369	2,972	3,080
Far East	3,705	2,559	1,872	1,912
Burma	1,685	540	346	541
Thailand	1,309	1,482	1,068	1,023
Vietnam, Rep. of	299	–	–	–
Near East	222	434	560	742
U.A.R.	220	430	558	730
Latin America	214	383	456	357
Africa	44	54	83	69
Centrally planned countries	945	1,330	998	835
China (Mainland)	872	1,192	928	712
Imports	Thousand Metric Tons (milled)			
World Total	6,149	6,829	6,423	6,346
Developed countries	813	1,135	1,041	813
EEC	278	259	323	278
Japan	196	489	264	52
Developing countries	4,699	5,024	4,838	4,966
Far East	3,472	3,683	3,430	3,445
India	451	453	446	487
Pakistan	257	149	35	30
Ceylon	477	376	338	274
Indonesia	1,006	347	707	605
Malaysia	425	390	309	315
Philippines	90	290	–	–
Korea, Rep. of	24	118	216	750
Vietnam, Rep. of	12	765	678	326
Near East	342	351	367	385
Latin America	338	358	367	410
Africa	502	567	594	656
Centrally planned countries	637	670	544	567
U.S.S.R. & E. Europe	605	645	511	562

[a]FAO, *Celes* vol. 4, no. 2 at 17 (March-April 1971).

has been mainly due to a steep decline in Burmese exports—from 1.7 million tons in 1959-63 to 541,000 tons in 1969—and a shift in the position of Vietnam from a net exporter to a net importer since 1964. This shift has significantly affected the pattern of world trade, for the former exports and the large import needs in recent years of Vietnam add up to one million tons—or about one-sixth of the total world exports.

The rise of the United States as the world's leading rice exporter since 1967 is another notable recent development. From less than one million tons in 1959-63, the United States exports increased to 1.8 million tons in 1967 and 1.9 million tons in 1969. The increase in the United States exports virtually filled the gap created by the steep decline in the Burmese exports and the reversal in the trade position of Vietnam. But a considerable part of the United States exports is channelled to Vietnam on concessional sales.

Another striking trade shift in recent years is illustrated by Japan, which until recently was a large rice importer. From an average import of over one million tons in 1952-56, Japanese purchases were reduced to only 196,000 tons in 1959-63 as a result of rising domestic production. However, following a leveling off in the output, imports into Japan increased again to 940,000 tons in 1965. Since then, domestic production has resumed an upward trend, while consumption has steadily decreased. As a result, Japan is no longer an importer, but instead has now accumulated a huge surplus stock (estimated to reach 7.3 million tons by March 1971) from which some quantities are shipped to other countries on concessional terms. This reversal in Japan's trade position is likely to remain an important factor in the future pattern of world rice trade.

All these shifts in the pattern of trade, when analyzed in terms of economic regions, reveal two broad changes. First, rice exports from the developing countries as a group have declined by about 33% over the past decade, and their share in the world exports has been cut from 66% in 1959-63 to only 45% in 1969. On the other hand, the developed countries raised their share from 19% to 40% in the same period. Second, imports into developing countries showed a small increase during the sixties, while developed countries slightly reduced their purchases. The overall increase in imports into developing countries, however, conceals important shifts in import requirements of individual countries, and partly reflects the exceptional requirements of Vietnam which may not continue indefinitely. On the other hand, the decrease in the imports into developed countries is mainly attributable to the virtual cessation of imports into Japan, which seem likely to be a more permanent feature.

While these shifts are part of a dynamic situation, several recent developments have heightened the uncertainty for world rice trade and prices. First is the buildup of sizeable rice stocks in recent years in several exporting countries. The most massive accumulation has been in Japan since 1968 and now the stock of the old rice crop alone in that country exceeds the level of annual world rice exports.

With their domestic prices well above the current world prices, exports from some countries, such as the EEC, the United States, Spain, Argentina, etc. are now aided by subsidies. The prima facies objective of the policy of subsidizing rice exports is to enable the rice exporters of the producing countries to sell at the ruling world prices. It could be argued that such subsidized sales—so long as they do not undercut ruling prices—do not constitute unfair competition to other exporting countries. However, the need to resort to subsidies basically arises from high domestic prices, which, particularly when there are no effective controls on production, act as an incentive to produce more. Generally, a part of such higher production is ultimately sought to be sold internationally and such an increase in the quantity supplied in world markets tends to depress prices, especially when demand is not rising or may be declining. Another important recent development, which is likely to affect the prospects of rice trade and prices significantly in the medium-term future, is the development of the high-yield varieties of rice. These new varieties offer an important opportunity for accelerating the rate of growth of production in several developing countries. The increased returns from these varieties, together with attractive prices, have encouraged farmers in many countries to devote more area and use more fertilizers for rice production. These developments have raised hopes in several developing countries to increase food production at a much faster rate than they achieved in the past.

Since the onset of the war in Southeast Asia, food aid has been an important factor in rice trade. During the early years of the sixties, United States rice exports on concessional terms (i.e., under P.L. 480) varied from a high of 663,000 tons to a low of 418,000 tons. By the end of the decade, these exports have increased to nearly a million tons, representing more than half of total United States rice exports. Moreover, with the emergence of huge surplus stocks, Japan has also become an important source of concessional rice supplies, amounting to about one-half a million tons a year. As a result, concessional transactions now form roughly one-quarter of the total world rice exports. While such exports have helped the importing developing countries to finance their rice imports without any undue burden on their balance-of-payments position, the increasing role of concessional sales from developed countries has created problems for some developing exporting countries, such as Thailand, especially as they are not in a position to offer similar easy terms for their exports.

Therefore, Thailand and other developing rice-exporting countries, believe that these problems are being exacerbated by increased competition from developed exporters who sold rice on concessional terms, including long-term credits or subsidized commercial sales. They have suggested that the main aim of food aid in rice should be to alleviate the suffering caused by natural catastrophies; but where it was necessary for a country to supply its surplus rice for other reasons, that country should first consult and receive the approval of the rice-exporting countries whose interests might be adversely affected by such aid; and when exporting rice in the course of normal commercial trade, developed countries should refrain from granting export subsidies, particularly as they put developing export countries at a disadvantage. Under present international rules, countries supplying rice on concessional sales are required to notify and consult with rice-exporting countries likely to be harmed by such transactions. But, after consultations, food aid suppliers are not obligated to change their plans in the face of third country complaints, and this is likely to be the case for the foreseeable future.[63] Developing importing countries suggested that the rice situation might be improved by using more rice in international food aid programs, such as the Food Aid Convention. Japan, a developed country, has been given the right to use its mounting rice surpluses to fulfill its obligations under the Food Aid Convention. Conceivably, this could serve as a precedent for purchasing rice from other developing countries.

Establishing Norms for Food Aid-Induced
Damage to Commercial Trade

The foregoing analysis indicates that food aid has affected international commercial trade, particularly in rice, and particularly with respect to the trade of developing exporters. Little can be said in support of food aid-induced injuries to developing countries. But the issue is more complex with respect to developed exporters. Here, the appropriateness of trade losses attributable to food aid depends in large part upon one's view of the proper relationship between the rich and poor nations. That total commercial exports of third countries have risen despite food aid does not preclude the likelihood that without concessional sales, the increase would have been greater. Moreover, the availability of low-price farm products from the United States and other developed exporters may well have lowered world prices to the benefit of exporters and the detriment of importers.

One particularly difficult problem in assessing the impact of food aid on international agricultural trade is the evaluation of the benefits derived by donors from food aid transactions. The more a donor directly benefits from food aid, the greater the basis for complaint by third country exporters. Since 56% of the imports of developing countries is food aid, proper evaluation of the value received by the food aid donor is essential to a fair judgment of the legitimacy of various food aid practices. Unfortunately, such evaluations are very difficult to make, particularly on a general basis. As has been demonstrated earlier in this chapter, the impact of each food aid transaction varies with the donor (or even with the particular food aid program of the donor), the product, the level of the donor's surplus stocks, prevailing international commercial market conditions, and the readiness of the recipient to make commercial purchases without food aid. Certainly, few general rules can be induced, and each case must be judged according to the facts relevant to it.

For analytic convenience, we can divide the effect of food aid upon commercial imports into one of three rough categories. Total effective demand and therefore demand for commercial imports may be expanded through the economic development of food aid recipients or shifts in tastes towards products produced by the food aid donors; the percentage of total agricultural products supplied by the donor to a particular country will increase at the expense of other commercial exporters; or concessional sales may be kept sufficiently below the anticipated level of import needs to permit considerable opportunity for commercial sales, both by the donor and other exporters. Clearly, an increase in total demand for commercial agricultural products would benefit everyone. The second possibility, diversion of agricultural exports to the donor, is the phenomenon most feared by third country exporters and the impetus for international countermeasures. The impact of food aid on third countries is measured solely by their loss of potential commercial sales. The degree to which the aid donor shares in these losses is really irrelevant since each country, theoretically, is concerned with its own injuries rather than the donor's gains. But certainly injured third countries will be particularly incensed if they suffer while the donor arranges to maintain or increase its own commercial sales.

The problems relevant to the effect of food aid on the recipient's desire for commercial products and the possibility that food aid may be tied to acceptance of abnormal amounts of the donor's own commercially priced agricultural products may be handled by familiar and relatively straightforward techniques. But even if such predatory practices are eschewed, the level, *per se*, of food aid granted to each recipient remains a key factor in determining the impact of such programs on world commercial sales. Therefore, determination of an appropriate food aid level in each case becomes one of the crucial decisions for all parties likely to be affected by food aid transactions. Unfortunately, establishing the proper mix of commercial and concessional sales to a particular country presents extreme theoretical difficulties, demanding problem-solving techniques either not available or not as yet politically or administratively functional. This problem is intimately connected with that of imposing conditions on food aid that have the effect of preempting the commercial markets in countries receiving concessional products might be designed solely for the benefit of the donor or else be shaped to assist all commercial exporters.

Optimum Food Aid Commercial Policies
for Each Affected Party

The conduct of a food aid donor with respect to food aid obviously depends in part upon the impact of various food aid strategies and policies upon the needs and desires of all parties likely to be affected. Therefore, before seeking an optimizing food aid strategy for any donor, it will be necessary to determine optimum food aid strategies from the viewpoint of each interested participant in the transactions.

Maximum Benefit to the Food Aid Recipient. The position of the recipient needs little further explication. Assuming it is capable of determining its own best interests, all recipients favor food aid policies entailing the fewest possible restrictions. Any limitation on the level of food aid or positive requirements with respect to commercial purchases can do it no good and might make it more difficult to optimize the utility of the food aid. This would occur if the recipient either received less food aid than it could use effectively or, in order to be eligible for food aid, it was induced to import more agricultural products than was consistent with its long-run economic well-being and development.[64]

Maximum Benefits to Selfish Donor Country Interests. In analyzing the financial and economic benefits and burdens of food aid to the donor, one must look at the transactions from the separate viewpoint of each segment of the economy. Maximization strategies vary sharply for each of the affected parties and may vary with the length of the time perspective. The totality of a donor's interests must be divided between those of the private and public sectors. Public sector interests may be further divided into concern for the impact of food aid on the national budget and the effect upon the balance-of-payments.

Usually, the donor's agricultural producers and exporters should prefer the largest possible food aid shipments to each country. This is the case in all countries, such as the United States, where private sellers receive the same price for food aid as they would for commercial exports; for them the two types of transactions are equally desirable. Therefore, the larger the total figure, the greater their economic gain. Moreover, private interests should have no desire to increase the level of commercial purchases imposed upon the recipient. This follows from the fact that as the price decreases the country will purchase more food, and food aid is by definition cheaper than commercial imports. Any attempt to force the recipient to increase its commercial purchases must result in a smaller quantity of total purchases. Of course, given any level of commercial imports, the agricultural producer wants to get as much of that market as possible. Therefore, his optimum position would be to press both for a maximum food aid program and for arrangements assuring the maximum share of the remaining commercial sales possibilities.

In keeping with this theory, United States agricultural producers have consistently supported both food aid programs and maximum expansion of commercial exports.[65] Furthermore, as demonstrated earlier in this chapter increased concessional sales now should not impair opportunities for commercial sales when food aid is reduced or withdrawn. Indeed, all current theories hold that concessional sales should enhance the possibilities for future commercial sales. More importantly, even if food aid were used as leverage to obtain current commercial sales, an abnormal share of these markets probably could not be maintained after the termination of the food aid. Therefore, the private producer/exporter should opt for maximum food aid now but be prepared to compete for commercial sales on an even footing with others when food aid is withdrawn.

Public Sector Interests. Besides the impact on the recipient, the donor government has three concerns: (1) the budgetary cost of food aid; (2) the impact on the balance-of-payments; and (3) the effect on the exports and economics of other exporting countries. The budgetary cost of food aid solely depends upon the size of the program and the amount and form of the financial compensation the donor receives from the recipient. In this regard, the impact is not affected by the extent to which food aid displaces commercial sales, or the degree to which food aid is used to increase such sales. Increases in the prices charged for concessional sales are the only direct means for reducing the budgetary impact of food aid since this would narrow the gap between the cost to the government of the products and the receipts from them. Conceivably, if food aid-eligible countries are forced to make more commercial purchases, they may have less need or financial ability to purchase food aid commodities, thereby saving money for the donor. Of course, such savings only will materialize if the donor is prepared to reduce its total food aid program; that is, savings in one country will not be lost through expanding the program elsewhere.

Commercial sales do have a very direct effect on the donor's balance-of-payments. True, the balance-of-payments is not affected by increases in the level of food aid *per se*, since the payments to domestic producers of food aid commodities stay in the country. But to the extent that food aid transactions displace potential commercial sales, the balance-of-payments is injured through the loss of anticipated foreign exchange earnings.[66] Actually, the damage is not measured simply by the value of the lost commercial sales but by the difference between the potential foreign exchange earnings of the foregone commercial sales and the foreign exchange value of the payment, if any, received for the food aid. If, as seems to be the case with the United States, food aid transactions produce some foreign exchange for the donor but less than a comparable commercial sale, an equilibrium trade-off rate may be reached whereby a given amount of concessional sales may compensate for a smaller amount of commercial sale losses.

The impact on the balance-of-payments also depends upon the policies followed by the donor in administering the program. As we have seen, concessional transactions which do not impair commercial sales have a positive impact on the balance-of-payments to the extent of the foreign exchange earned by them. Even if commercial sales are displaced, the net effect depends upon the rate of displacement. Conceivably, if high additionality is achieved and consumption of the concessional product in the recipient country is increased sharply, the value of lost commercial sales might be less than the value of the hard currency earned by the concessional sales. In this regard, policies designed to assist the donors balance-of-payments would coincide with those of third country exporters—commercial sales displacement should be minimized. But the food aid donor's commercial sales also may be protected by requiring food aid recipients to maintain given levels of such purchases from the donor, even if it means reducing those of other nations. This is called tying. Under these circumstances, the donor would earn foreign exchange from the concessional sales without fear of counterbalancing losses in commercial sales. Third countries, though, would be victimized. The frequency and legitimacy of tying has been under continued international scrutiny.[67]

United States Strategy. The United States position as both a major agricultural exporter, in fact, the largest agricultural exporter, and the economic and political leader of the western bloc severely complicates the formulation of effective food aid policy. The United States not only wants to protect existing commercial sales—its own and that of friendly third country exporters, particularly developing exporters—but it also attempted to seek ways to use food aid to expand its commercial sales—either through inducing general increases in the buying capacity and desires of developing countries or on occasion through more predatory tactics.

As a major agricultural exporter, the United States, or at least certain segments of its economic-political structure, shares the fears of third countries that gifts and concessional sales of agricultural products will preempt commercial sales to the same markets. In recent years, agricultural exports have been making an increasingly important contribution to the United States balance-of-payments, rendering these transactions particularly sensitive in the current era of chronic balance-of-payments difficulties.[68] And though to private agricultural producers and exporters, food aid and commercial sales are interchangeable, the impact on the federal budget and the balance-of-payments is quite another matter. Even the domestic producer/exporters would much prefer not depending for their markets on inherently unstable government aid programs.

Consequently, in administering its food aid programs, the United States is pulled in four directions. It must simultaneously strive to maximize the effectiveness of food aid as a political, humanitarian, and developmental tool; to protect its own commercial exports; to recognize and respond to the essential commercial interests of other nations as expressed through international agreements and bilateral representations; and to cope with internal pressures demanding that the food aid program be used as a lever to expand United States commercial exports. The policy choices are further complicated by the piebald character of the program's supporters—partly agricultural forces anxious to dispose of surpluses and to augment commercial sales of United States agricultural products and partly groups interested in the humanitarian, political or economic developmental goals achievable through food aid.[69] Over time, the disposition of forces pulling in each direction tends to shift depending upon the particular economic and political position, direction and interests of the nation at large. At the moment, it is abundantly clear the winds are blowing strongly in protectionist and export-expanding directions, and the forces of economic development are in disarray, if not headlong retreat.

The Graduation System. The graduation concept comes closest to expressing a rationale for United States food aid policy. According to this formulation,

United States food aid policy is designed to move an underdeveloped country from destitution to the status of a cash customer of agricultural products— preferably American. This concept charts the gradual evolution of Food for Peace sales from outright donations to commercial sales. In between are food for work, soft-currency sales, government-to-government dollar credit sales, private trade agreements, and combinations of concessional and commercial sales. Along the way, the terms of dollar credit sales are hardened until they approach commercial levels. When a country finishes the course and "graduates" to purchasing entirely through private channels on commercial terms, the theory "has been proved."[70]

Certainly, many countries have changed from food aid recipients to commercial purchasers of United States agricultural products. Most of Western Europe, Japan, Spain and Taiwan fit this description.[71] But whether the shift from gifts to commercial sales proves anything about the ability of food aid to create commercial markets is questionable. Certainly, it does not prove that food aid always or usually results in expanded commercial markets for United States agricultural products. If these countries have become commercial customers, it is largely due to their economic development, which may have been helped or hindered by food aid. It does appear, though, that shifts in taste towards products exported by the United States, such as soybean oil and wheat, may have resulted in part from the large gifts of these products made by the United States in the postwar years.

Actually, the phenomenon described by the graduation theory is nothing more than a reflection of the standard aid cycle. Donations are given to meet emergencies and for limited development programs. If the United States decides to increase food aid, it shifts to concessional sales for which larger appropriations are available. If and as the country develops, total aid is reduced and the terms of concessional sales are hardened. Finally, general aid is cut off, but dollar credit sales of agricultural products on nearly commercial terms are continued for some time.[72] Thus, the program envisioned by the graduation theory has been implemented in many countries, but the implication that the theory has somehow created the conditions necessary for the shift from concessional to commercial sales may be highly misleading. Economic development cannot be accomplished solely by the advance scheduling of the liquidation of food aid.[73]

The graduation theory has been skeptically received by competing agricultural exporters. They have questioned both its efficacy for protecting normal commercial trade and even its existence. That is they doubt whether the United States really does stop food aid when a country achieves a given degree of economic development. The United States concedes that in the absence of food aid, countries might well purchase food commercially so that in a sense food aid does reduce commercial sales. But it has argued that "purchases born of desperation are not something any country would like to see happen."[74] While third country exporters accept this in principle, some exporters have been concerned that countries will gear their economies to regular supplies of concessional foodstuffs, with the risk of permanent dependence. Also, the continuance of food aid programs to countries like Iceland, Israel, Poland and Yugoslavia has been interrupted as evidence that the United States does not always terminate food to self-supporting countries. However, there are good political reasons for continuing food aid to these relatively developed countries. Although United States' policy in this regard may be uneven, the record supports the United States' determination to phase out food aid as a nation develops. For example, in calendar 1970, only four agreements permitted any local currency payments (Vietnam, Pakistan, Korea, and Ghana).

Post Food Aid Expansion of Commercial Markets. In Chapter 8, we shall demonstrate that for the recipient, attempts to require a food aid recipient to maintain given levels of commercial imports results, in the short run, in an economically inferior solution for the recipient.[75] But neither will such a requirement materially help the donor to increase its commercial sales to food aid recipients after the termination of food aid. Under the United States so-called "graduation theory," concessional food sales are to be phased out and shifted to a commercial basis in the foreseeable future. But the level of commercial sales in countries receiving concessional commodities is not relevant to the donor's ability to establish markets for these products upon the termination of concessional sales. Since one country's agricultural commodities are largely interchangeable with the same commodity of all other producers of that product and international agricultural trade is organized to permit very rapid switches from one exporting country to another. Thus, any commercial foothold gained through use of food aid leverage cannot be maintained without such leverage if the transactions at issue run counter to the economic logic of the situation at the time each sale is made. Similarly, given a minimum commercial infrastructure, a nation can gain new markets very quickly if economic conditions so warrant. And since most large-scale food aid transactions are conducted through practically the same channels as commercial sales, the existence of the market mechanisms necessary for future commercial transactions will be there without regard to the mix of commercial and concessional sales at any particular time. This is not to say that a gradual increase in commercial sales, replacing steadily diminishing concessional sales would not be sound policy. This might be ideal for the recipient. But logically, this kind of pattern should flow from decisions based upon the recipient's food and foreign aid needs. Also, a decision to reduce food aid in order to reduce the donor's total sales may be rational from the donor's viewpoint. But there is no basic to believe that steady reductions in food aid, accompanied by rising mandatory purchase requirements as a condition of food aid, assures that commercial purchases from the donor will continue after when food aid is ended.

Can An Optimum Strategy be Found?

The foregoing analysis should demonstrate that it is exceedingly difficult to determine an optimum strategy respecting food aid and commercial import levels for food aid recipient countries. Such a strategy must attempt to achieve as many of the goals of the program at the smallest possible cost to the Treasury and the most favorable impact on the balance-of-payments. The potential gains would include the foreign assistance and humanitarian components of food aid and the benefit to the donor's agricultural sector. The potential losses are the cost to the Treasury and the net loss of foreign exchange through foregone commercial sales. The larger the commercial component of any donor's total agricultural commodity sales to a given country, the more favorable the impact on the balance-of-payments and the less the necessity for subsidizing food aid transactions with government funds. But the smaller the concessional component, the less the recipient benefits. And as the concessional component is reduced, the lower the total purchases of imported agricultural commodities by each potential food aid recipient since sales on concessional terms, through their substitution and income effects, tend to increase total agricultural purchases. Thus, if we assume that the level of concessional sales to each country is computed in terms of its needs for imported food, its balance-of-payment position, and the impact on its agricultural sector's growth, every attempt to substitute commercial for concessional sales runs counter to the program's fundamental purposes and is tantamount to a reduction of the food aid program. Assuming, reasonably, that if the recipient nations were not poor, developed countries could not justify these kinds of transactions at least not to the same degree it can be argued that injured exporters are being forced to make some sacrifice in order that the developing countries may receive cut-rate commodities. They may be deemed third party victims or passive participants in the food aid process.

For rich countries, at least, the degree of assistance they render to the developing nations through suffering some market diminution may well be argued to amount to no more than their duty. As the OECD has observed, highly developed exporters "would presumably not wish to profit from having the underdeveloped countries forced into making commercial imports they cannot afford."[76] Certainly, explicit understanding among all donor nations regarding the level and nature of foreign aid would be a far superior method of dividing the foreign aid burden. And with respect to large aid recipients such as India, Brazil, Pakistan and Turkey, foreign aid, including food aid, has been put on a multilateral footing through the use of consortiums or "aid clubs."[77] Shifting the bulk of economic aid to a multilateral agency, such as the United Nations, would accomplish the same end. But general agreements in this regard neither exist nor seem likely to be achieved within the foreseeable future.[78] Admittedly, the case for protection is much stronger if the injured exporting nation is itself underdeveloped or semideveloped, such as Thailand, Burma and Argentina. Things get more complicated if the affected country is itself a recipient of either food aid or foreign aid, such as Egypt or Mexico.[79] Clearly, food aid induced injuries to commercial exports of developing countries are indefensible and United States practice in these cases has been to conduct its food aid to afford the maximum market protection to underdeveloped exporters.[80]

If the impact on third country exporters is ignored, high levels of food aid conditioned upon maintaining given levels of commercial imports from the donor would seem the best solution. This approach would satisfy foreign aid objectives by providing appropriate amounts of food aid, would satisfy the agricultural interests by increasing demand for their products, and would provide maximum benefit to the balance-of-payments by preserving commercial sales while obtaining additional foreign exchange through concessional sales. The sufferers would be the budget and third country exporters. The balance between the desire to minimize total federal expenditures and the goals of food aid programs only may be made in terms of the relative benefits of alternate public and private uses for these federal funds. The interests of third country exporters are far more difficult to qualify. How does one balance Canada's irritation with United States food aid policies against the benefits to the recipients and the donor? Of course, the dilemma may be resolved, in part, if budget restraints limit the food aid program to levels which still permit adequate commercial markets for third country exporters. And with respect to United States programs, the sensibilities and interests of third countries have been protected by the elimination of out-and-out predatory tactics such as requiring food aid recipients to make large commercial purchases from the donor. The international community is now seeking ways to increase these safeguards while the United States insists that they be applied to all donors. These matters will be discussed in detail in Parts II and III of this book.

Notes

1. For general analyses of the relationship of food aid to economic development, see University of Arizona Agricultural Experiment Station, *Policy for United States Agricultural Export Surplus Disposal, Technical Bulletin 150* Ch. V (1962) [hereinafter *Technical Bulletin 150*] ; Wightman, *Food Aid and Economic Development*, 68-70 (1962) [hereinafter Wightman] ; *International Conciliation*, no. 567, generally and 56-72 (March 1968); Iowa State University Center for Agricultural and Economic Development, *Alternatives for Balancing World Food Production Needs* (1967), and, *Food—One Tool in International Economic Development* (1962).

Until the end of the 1960s food aid was subject to severe criticisms by most academic economists. See *Statement of Prof. T. Schultz, Hearings on War on Hunger before the House Committee on Agriculture*, 89th Cong., 2d sess., ser. W, at 156-60 (1966); testimony of AID Administrator David Bell, *Hearings on Food for Peace before the Senate Committee on Agriculture and Forestry*, 89th Cong., 2d sess., at 351, 354 (1966); statement of Sec. of Agriculture Freeman, id. at 32, 34-35; *UN/FAO World Food Program Studies* no. 5, at 5-9 (1965); Schultz, *U.S. Malinvestments in Food for the World*, in Iowa State University *Alternatives for Balancing World Food Production Needs* 224 (1967); Heady and Timmons, *Objectives, Achievements and Hazards of the U.S. Food Aid and Agricultural Development Programs in Relation to Domestic Policy*, id. at 186, 188-91; Ginor, *Uses of Agricultural Surpluses* (Bank of Israel, Jerusalem) (1963); OECD, Food Aid–Its Role in Economic Development 45-47; Wightman, *Food Aid and Economic Development, International Conciliation*, 41-43 (March 1968). But these attitudes have changed. While recognizing the potential dangers of food aid, the official position of the U.N. and its agencies concerned with economic development have accepted food aid as part of the development armory. See UN/ECOSOC, E14538, *Multilateral Food Aid, Programme of Studies Called For in General Assembly Resolution 2096 (XX)* (12 June 1968); UN/FAO, CCP 67/13, *Interagency Study of Multilateral Food Aid, Director-General's Progress Report to the Committee on Commodity Problems* (4 Oct. 1967); World Food Program, WFP IGC 17/5, *Food Aid and Related Issues During the Second Development Decade. – Report of the Intergovernmental Committee of the World Food Programme in Response to Resolution 2462 (XXIII)* (9 March 1970).

2. This well may have been the case with Pakistan during fiscal 1967. In that year, Pakistan, a major foreign aid recipient, increased its imports of wheat from Canada and Australia from 89 thousand metric tons in fiscal 66 to 904 thousand metric tons. *International Wheat Council, Review of the World Wheat Situation* 1965/66 App. II, at 93 (1966); *International Wheat Council Review of the World Wheat Situation* 1966/67, App. II, at 83 (1967). Since Australia's total food aid in fiscal 1967 only totaled 150 thousand metric tons, and Pakistan imported 698 thousand metric tons of wheat and flour, clearly much of Pakistan's increased imports were on commercial terms. Id. at 35, 83.

3. Hoffman, *The Economics of Surplus Disposal*, 5 *Australian Journal of Economics* 41 (1961) [hereinafter Hoffman].

4. See Chapter 4.

5. Wightman, at 54; Organization of Economic and Cooperative Development, *Food Aid–Its Role in Economic Development* 18-19 [hereinafter OECD].

6. Hoffman, at 37-38.

7. OECD, at 52.

8. For an excellent recent analysis of the agricultural policies of major producers, see Malmgren and Schlechty, *Rationalizing World Agricultural Trade*, 4 *Journal of World Trade Law* 515 (1970).

9. The most recent International Wheat Agreement (1971-74) has deleted minimum and maximum price provisions and supply obligations, principally because the exporting countries could not agree upon the method for setting prices.

10. For a full discussion of the International Wheat Agreements see Chapter 4.

11. The means available to control these effects are discussed in Chapter 9.

12. OECD, supra, note 5 at 52. *Technical Bulletin* 150, supra note 1 at 72.

13. A good brief analysis of these relations may be found in UN/ECOSDC/ E14538, *Report of the Secretary General on Multilateral Food Aid*, at 36-40 (1968).

14. The producer and exporter receive the same price for commodities destined for Food for Peace uses as they do for any other export sale. This is true both for surplus and nonsurplus transactions. This may be illustrated with wheat which, because of the two-price system, is the most complicated. Through the so-called certificate system, farmers receive a cash subsidy for that portion of their production deemed to be their aliquot share of the wheat required for domestic consumption. 79 *Stat.* 1203-06 (1965), U.S.C.A. §§ 1379c(a)-(e) 1445a (1970). All other production must be sold at prevailing market prices or to the Commodity Credit Corporation at the support price, which is considerably lower than the price available for "domestic" production. Id. In 1970/71, wheat for domestic consumption (within acreage allotments) was supported at $2.00 per bushel and the CCC buying price for other wheat, including wheat for export, was $1.25 per bushel. In February 1971, the market price for No. 2 Hard Winter Wheat (f.o.b. Gulf ports) was $1.73. *International Wheat Council*, 1970 *World Wheat Statistics*, Tables 16, 20 (1971).

Although the present policy is to maintain the export price of United States wheat at international levels, sometimes slight adjustments are needed to make United States wheat competitive at those prices. This is accomplished through a system of export certificates, under which the CCC subsidizes exports if the United States price is higher than world prices and taxes them to the extent they are lower. 7 U.S.C.A. §§ 1379(a)-(d) (1970).

15. Ibid.

16. The Department of Agriculture's analysis and computation of the relative costs to the United States of acreage diversion versus Food for Peace sales may be found at *Hearings on Food for Freedom Program and Commodity Reserves before the Senate Committee on Agriculture and Forestry*, 89th Cong., 2d sess., 499-501 (1966) [hereinafter *1966 Senate Hearings*]. For a detailed discussion and analysis of the costs of food aid to the United States, see also *Extension of Public Law 480, Hearings before the Senate Committee on Agriculture and Forestry*, 90th Cong., 2d sess., 107-23 (1968) [hereinafter *1968 Senate Hearings*].

17. USDA/ERS, *Foreign Agricultural Economic Report No. 65, P.L. 480 Concessional Sales*, 16-17 (1971).

18. 80 *Stat.* 1526 (1966), 7 U.S.C.A. § 1703(b) (1970); *Annual Report on P.L. 480 for 1970* at 3, 15-18 (1971) [hereinafter 1970 Annual Report]. See Chapter 2.

19. 80 *Stat.* 1528 (1966), 7 U.S.C.A. § 1703(k) (1970).

20. *Annual Report* on *P.L. 480* for 1969 at 18 (1970).

21. 80 *Stat.* 1528-31 (1966), 7 U.S.C.A. §§ 1703(m), 1704(a)-(e), (g), (j), (1970).

22. 1969 *Annual Report*, table 12; 1970 *Annual Report* at 24, 25, 79-134, tables 13-16.

23. Remarks of Representative Poage (Chairman of the House Agriculture Committee), 114 Conn. Rec. H. 3721 (Daily ed.). See also 114 *Cong. Rec.* H. 3721-22, 3724-25, 3725-26, 3728-29 (Daily ed. May 24, 1968); *1968 Senate Hearings*, supra note 16, at 146-51.

24. Statement of Dr. Don Pearlberg, Hearings on War on Hunger before the House Committee on Agriculture, 89th Cong., 2d sess., ser. W, 114-15 [hereinafter 1966 *House Hearings*].

25. Sections 2, 101(c), 68 *Stat.* 455, 456 (1954); §§ 2, 103(f), 107(a), 80 *Stat.* 1526, 1527, 1532 (1966); 7 U.S.C.A. § 1691 (1967); H.R. Rep. No. 1776, 83rd Cong., 2d sess., 5-7 (1964); *H.R. Rep.* No. 754, 85th Cong., 1st sess., 58 (1961); *National Planning Association, Managing Farm Surpluses*, 1 (Pamphlet No. 117, 1962).

26. There is a very extensive literature on the impact of Food for Peace on economic development. See Iowa State University Center for Agricultural and Economic Development, *Alternatives for Balancing World Food Production Needs* (1967); Eicher and Witt, *Agriculture in Economic Development* (1964); testimony of Drs. Max Millikan, Don Pearlberg, Roger Revelle, and Theodore Schultz, *Hearings on War on Hunger before the House Committee on Agriculture*, 89th Cong., 2d sess., ser. W, 25-38, 53-68, 109-26, 156-32; O'Hagan and Lenti, *Some Economic and Policy Considerations of Food Aid*, FAO Monthly Bulletin of Agricultural Economics Statistics, vol. 17, no. 2 Feb. 1968.

27. *H.R. Rep.* 1297, 90th Cong., 2d sess., tables 1A, 2B (1968). See also 1968 Senate Hearings, supra, note 16 at 149-50 for a comparable analysis.

28. 1968 Senate Hearings, supra, note 16 at 150.

29. FAS/USDA, *Spotlight on Japan, Billion Dollar Market for U.S. Farm Exports*, Foreign Agriculture, Aug. 31, 1970 at 3; FAO/USDA, World Agricultural Production and Trade, Aug. 1970 at 21-25.

30. Statement of T. Schultz, *1966 House Hearings*, supra, note 35, at 166-67. *S. Rep.* 2478, 85th Cong., 2d sess., 5 (1958). Actually, the policy of impeding potential sources of competition with U.S. agricultural exports never appeared in the legislation itself. Section 104(e) of the old P.L. 480 Law did contain a restriction on the use of Cooley Loans to finance the production of agricultural commodities to be marketed in competition with United States' goods. 71 *Stat.* 345 (1957). The Foreign Assistance Act also contains certain general restrictions against promoting activities that might have adverse effects on the United States economy. 75 *Stat.* 426, 427 (1961), 22 U.S.C.A. §§ 2161(b) (6). 2171(a) (1970). But, despite the lack of explicit legislative direction until very recently, the executive followed a very restrictive policy regarding production of certain agricultural products, and almost any type of assistance to cotton production was tabu.

31. Sections 103(a) requires the President, in administering the Food for

Peace program to take into account the potential recipients efforts to meet their own food needs. 80 *Stat.* 1526 (1966), 7 U.S.C.A. § 1703(a) (1970). See also Section 104(f), 109; 80 *Stat.* 1530, 1533 (1966), 7 U.S.C.A. § 1704(f), 1709 (1970). The 1966 Foreign Assistance Act added a provision supporting research programs to increase food production. 80 *Stat.* 797 (1966), 22 U.S.C.A. § 2171(e) (1970). Foreign Assistance Act of 1967 goes even further. Section 207(c) of the Act now requires that: "In furnishing development assistance under this chapter the President shall place appropriate emphasis on ... programs directed at enabling a country to meet the food needs of its people from its own resources, including the furnishing of technical knowledge and of resources necessary to increase agricultural productivity; assistance for improved storage, transportation, marketing, and credit facilities (including provision for foreign currency loans to small farmers), cooperatives, water conservation programs, and adaptive research programs; and technological advice ... " 81 *Stat.* 445, 22 U.S.C.A. 2167 (1970).

32. Section 103(i) of the Food for Peace Act of 1966 states that the President shall promote progress toward assurance of an adequate food supply by encouraging countries with which agreements are made to give higher emphasis to the production of food crops than to the production of such nonfood crops as are in world surplus. 80 *Stat.* 1528 (1967), 7 U.S.C.A. § 1703(i) (1970). Section 109(a) (1) makes the same point by making this a factor that the President must consider before entering into agreements with developing countries for the sale of United States agricultural commodities. 80 *Stat.* 1533 (1967), 7 U.S.C.A. § 1703(a)(1) (1970). According to the House Report, these restrictions were aimed at discouraging production of cotton and tobacco—products still in great surplus in the United States *H. Rep.* 1358, 89th Cong., 2d sess., 40 (1966).

The cotton problem has been a major headache for many years. At the end of 1965, the Commodity Credit Corporation owned $1.1 billion worth of cotton. *Statistical Abstract of the United States–1966*, table 930, at 636 (1967). The tobacco problem is of more recent origin; in 1965 CCC had no inventory of tobacco, but during that year purchased or made loans for $850 million worth. Id. The philosophy of this type of restriction has been challenged by an eminent expert; Prof. Schultz has stated that the United States should assist underdeveloped countries to produce any products congenial to their natural agricultural resources, including products like rice, cotton, and wheat for export as well as domestic consumption. *1966 House Hearings*, supra, note 24, at 158.

33. According to then AID Administrator David Bell, the United States' goal was to establish in the underdeveloped countries agricultural self-sufficiency or the capacity to earn sufficient foreign exchange to import food commercially. Another expert, Roger Revelle, believes that, with certain exceptions, the long-term effects of our programs will be to eliminate the market for United States agricultural products. *1966 House Hearings*, supra, note 24, at 32. Certain representatives of farm interests agree with this analysis. *1966 Senate Hearings*, supra note 16, at 90.

34. *Report by Sen. Hubert Humphrey on the P.L. 480 Program to the Senate Committee on Agriculture and Forestry*, 85th Cong., 2d sess. (1964); *1966 House Hearings*, supra, note 24 at 477-513; *H.R. Rep.*, 1558, 89th Cong., 2d sess., 40-41 (1966).

35. Section 104(b) (1), 80 *Stat.* 1529 (1967); 7 U.S.C.A. § 1704(b)(1) (1970).

36. 1970 *Annual Report* on P.L. 480, at 82-93.

37. This has been an area of prime Congressional concern for some time. See *H.R. Rep.* No. 1939, 85th Cong., 2d sess., 38-39, 46-47 (1958); *S. Rep.* No. 1357, 85th Cong., 2d sess., 5-7 (1958); *Hearings before the House Committee on Agriculture*, 86th Cong., 2d sess., ser. FFF, 134-142 (1960); *1966 Senate Hearings*, supra, note 16, at 367-398, *H.R. Rep.* 1939, 85th Cong., 2d sess., p. 12 (1958). This provision was slightly strengthened and certainly lengthened in the 1966 Act. 80 *Stat.* 1529 (1966), 7 U.S.C.A. § 1794(b) (1970). The Administrations' bill would have eliminated the requirement for a fixed 5% minimum of generated local currencies to be set aside for this purpose. S. 2933, 89th Cong., 2d sess., 304(b) (1) (1966). By contrast, the Senate would have required, as a prerequisite to the Secretary of Agriculture releasing any local currencies allocated to him in excess of his needs, prior submission to both Congressional Agriculture Committees and the absence of a veto by either of these bodies. *S. Rep.* 1527, 89th Cong., 2d sess., 37 (1966). Following the pattern established for other attempts by the Senate to include this type of requirement, the Conference Committee removed the veto power, but retained the obligation of prior submission. *Conf. Rep.* H.R. 2075, 89th Cong., 2d sess., 17 (1966). *Annual Report* on P.L. 480 for 1967, at 8-9.

38. *Operational and Administrative Problems of Food Aid*, p. 8-9 (UN/FAO, No. 4, 1965); UN/FAO, *The Demand for Food, and Conditions Governing Food Aid during Development*, pp. 21, 22-46, 61-65 (No. 1, 1965).

39. Senator Ellender implied this possibility when he suggested that stimulation of the agricultural capacity of less developed nations may hurt U.S. exports in the long run. *1966 Senate Hearings*, supra, note 16 at 90 (1966). But at the same Hearings, the representative of the National Farmers Organization opined that economic development will make such countries even better customers for U.S. products. Id. at 121.

40. See also discussion of the United States' "graduation theory" at page 70, infra.

41. Heady, Haroldsen, Mayer, Tweeten, Roots of the Farm Problem, ch. 1 (1965); National Advisory Commission on Food and Fiber, Food and Fiber for the Future, 49-58 (1967); Heady, *Agricultural Problems and Policies of Developed Countries*, ch. 1 (1966); Wightman, supra, note 1 at 32-33.

42. As of June 30, 1953, the Commodity Credit Corporation owned agricultural commodities valued at $3.3 billion. At the close of fiscal 1955, the figure was $6.7 billion; 1958, $6.3 billion; 1963, $7.3 billion; 1964, $7.1 billion; 1965, $6.4 billion; 1966, $5.3 billion. During the same approximate period, the food aid accounted for $17.9 billion of commodities that otherwise would have been added to CCC stocks. 1967 *Annual Report* on P.L. 480, Table 1.

43. National Planning Association, *Agricultural Surplus Disposal and Foreign Aid*, 1 (1957), printed for use of *Special Committee to Study the Foreign Aid Program*, 85th Cong., 1st sess. (1967).

44. Toma, *The Politics of Food for Peace*, 39-45 (1967); *H.R. Rep.* 1958, 89th Cong., 2d sess., 9-11 (1966); Remarks of Sen. McGovern, 111 *Cong. Rec.* 14000 (1965).

45. *UN/FAO, The Impact of Food Aid on Donor and Other Food Exporting Countries*, 23-24 (No. 2, 1965). It was this possibility that made the Farm Bureau question the overall value of P.L. 480, *Hearings before the Subcommittee on Foreign Agricultural Operations of the House Committee on Agriculture*, 88th Cong., 2d sess., ser. LL, pp. 83-89 (1964). Interestingly, the Bureau has altered this stand with respect to the 1966 Act. *1966 Senate Hearings*, supra, note 16. For another approach that implicitly condemns the surplus disposal program on the same grounds but recommends more rather than less government action, see Conference on Economic Progress, *Food and Freedom*, 18-19. See also Swerling, *Current Issues in Commodity Policy, in Essays in International Finance* 41 (1962).

46. Witt, *Trade and Agricultural Policy*, 331 *Annals of the American Academy of Political Science* 1, 17 (1960).

47. *OECD*, supra, note 5, at 53-57.

48. Johnson, *Government and Agriculture: Is Agriculture a Special Case*, 1 *Journal of Law and Economics* 122, 131-134 (1965).

49. See *S. Rep.* 1527, 89th Cong. 2d sess., 8-10 (1966); *H.R. Rep.* 1558, 89th Cong. 2d sess., 7-9 (1966); Statement of Leon Kyserling, *1966 House Hearings*, supra, note 24 at 43-45.

50. See Wilcox, *Implications of Recent Changes in United States Farm Price Support Policies*, 49 *J. Farm. Econ.*, 1032 (1967); Schnittker, *Farm Policy—Today's Direction*, 48 *J. Farm Econ.*, 1091 (1966); UN/ECOSOC/E 4538 *Report of the Secretary General on Multilateral Food Aid* 34-36 (June 1968). *S. Rep.* No. 1527, 89th Cong., 2d sess., 9-10 (1966); Report of the National Advisory Commission on Food and Fiber, Food and Fiber for the Future, 49-52 (1967). Heady, *Agricultural Problems and Policies of Developed Countries*, Ch. 1 (1966). See, e.g., Testimony of Leon Kyersing, *1966 House Hearings*, supra, note 24, at 406-19 (1966).

51. *National Planning Association Report*, supra, note 43, at 12-13, 21-23; *UN/FAO, Food Aid and Other Forms of Utilization of Agricultural Surpluses*, 15 (Commodity Policy Series, 1964); *Technical Bulletin 150*, supra, note 1, at ch. VI; Hamilton and Drummond, *Wheat Surpluses and Their Impact on Canada-United States Relations*, ch. 3 (1959); *1966 Senate Hearings*, supra, note 16, at 193, 238-240.

52. Secretary of Agriculture Benson, in an Executive Communication supporting the 1957 extension of the Act, characterized the program as a temporary measure to dispose of farm surpluses that would not be made a permanent part

of our foreign trade program since it was inconsistent with U.S. opposition to bilateral trading. Letter to the President of the Senate, Feb. 2, 1957. See also, *H.R. Rep.* No. 432, 85th Cong., 1st session., 1-3, 10 (1957).

53. E. Thornbecke and J. Condliffe, *The Pattern of World Trade in Foodstuffs: Past and Present*, Iowa State University Center for Agricultural and Economic Adjustment, *Food—One Tool in International Economic Development* 209-10 (1962).

54. See Chap. 2.

55. *Technical Bulletin* 150, supra, note 1, at 72-75. Since 1959, the world prices of wheat and feedgrains have regained some of this loss. International Wheat Council, *World Wheat Statistics*, 1971, tables 16-23 (1971), UN/FAO, The Stabilization of International Trade in Grains, Ch. 1 (Commodity Policy Series 20, 1970).

56. *Wightman*, supra, note 1, at 41.

57. Unless otherwise indicated, much of the analysis of the status and causes of the current status of world grain trade is a slight reformulation of the analysis and language of a recent authoritative study of international trade in grains by the Food and Agriculture Organization conducted in the Basic Foodstuffs Service of the Commodities and Trade Division, with the assistance of Mr. Claude Hudson, formerly of the Canadian Department of Agriculture and Executive Secretary of the International Wheat Council from 1960-62, and of Mr. T. Josling of the London School of Economics. It is published as UN/FAO, *FAO Commodity Policy Study 20, The Stabilization of International Trade in Grains* Ch. 1 (1970). The subsequent analysis of the impact of food aid upon grain trade is entirely the author's.

58. UN/FAO *FAO Commodity Review and Outlook*, 1969-70, at 17-21 (1970).

59. See Chapter 2.

60. *OECD*, supra, note 5 at 50-51.

61. International Wheat Council, *Review of the World Grains Situation*, 1969/70, at 43-47 (Nov. 1970).

62. The analysis of the structure of world rice markets is largely based on an excellent article in FAO, *Ceres* vol. 4, no. 2, pp. 15-17 (March-April 1971).

63. See discussion of consultative procedures under the FAO control system in Chapter 6.

64. See Chapters 7, 8.

65. *1968 Senate Hearings*, supra, note 16 at 46-48, 58-60, 75-77, 86, 91-92, 104-106.

66. 114 *Cong. Rec.* H 3721-22, 3724-25, 3728-29 (Daily Ed. May 24, 1968), USDA/ERS, *12 Years Achievement under Public Law 480* at 3; *Extension of Public Law 480, Hearings before the Senate Committee on Agriculture and Forestry*. 90th Cong., 2d sess., at 146-51 (1968).

67. See Chapter 7, infra.

68. President's Science Advisory Committee, *The World Food Problem*, tables 2-4 and 2-19 at 145, 167 (1967). *1968 Senate Hearings*, supra, note 16, at 145-51.

69. *H.R. Rep.* No. 1776, 83rd Cong., 2d sess., 5-7 (1954); *H.R. Rep.* No. 432, 85th Cong., 1st sess., 10-12 (1957); *H.R. Rep.*, No. 754, 87th Cong., 1st sess., 58 (1961). See statement of David Bell, Administrator of the Agency for International Development, *Hearings before the Subcommittee on Foreign Agricultural Operations of the House Committee on Agriculture*, 88th Cong., 2d sess., ser. LL, at 138, 145 (1964). Furthermore, in the memorandum accompanying Executive Order 10915 and in the whereas clause of that order, the Food for Peace program was described as offering "a unique opportunity for the United States to promote the interests of peace in a significant way . . . " 26 F.R. 781 (Jan. 26, 1961).

70. *H.R. Rep.* No. 1297, 90th Cong., 2d sess., 3; *1968 Senate Hearings*, supra, note 16, at 145-52.

71. See text at note 30, supra.

72. In calendar year 1966, Title IV dollar credit agreements were signed with Iceland, Yugoslavia, Greece, and Israel, all countries receiving little or no other foreign aid from the United States. *Annual Report on Activities Carried Out under P.L. 480 During the Period of Jan. 1-Dec. 31, 1966*, table 11 (1967).

73. Apparently, Congress has made some effort to do just that. In 1966, P.L. 480 was amended to require the President to take steps "to assure a progressive transition from sales for foreign currencies to sales for dollars . . . " 80 *Stat.* 1576 (1966), 7 U.S.C.A. § 1703(b) (1970). The transition is to be completed by Dec. 31, 1971. Id. The legislation is accompanied by history indicating that sales for dollars means cash dollars. *H.R. Rep.* No. 1558, 89th Cong., 2d sess., 37-38 (1966).

74. UN/FAO, CCP/CSD/65/8, Statement on P.L. 480 *Consultation Procedures by Jerome Jacobson, Deputy Assistant Secretary of State for Economic Affairs* (16 February 1965).

75. See Chapter 8.

76. *OECD*, supra, note 5 at 51.

77. W. Friedmann, G. Kalmanoff & R. Meagher, *International Financial Aid*, 135-51 (1966); *1968 Senate Hearings*, supra, note 16, at 174-80.

78. For a recent, critical view of efforts to implement this approach, see S. Rubin, *The Conscience of the Rich Nations* (1966). See also Chapter 10.

79. *Technical Bulletin 150*, supra, note 1, at 71, 76-83.

80. See Chapter 5 for a further discussion of the impact of food aid on developing agricultural exporters. See also Ch. 4, text and notes at N 13, 14 for the history of the United States' problems with Egypt's cotton marketings.

Part II: National and International Legal Framework for Food Aid Transactions

Part II of this book will present the legal basis for all effective control systems designed to modulate the relationships between food aid and commercial agricultural trade. For the most part, these controls are imposed through a variety of semiintegrated international and domestic systems. Although there is no single international body exercising jurisdiction over all the relevant transactions, most of the legal regimes do respond to actions taken elsewhere in the international community by major food aid donors. Moreover, there seems to be signs of movement towards a more integrated international response to the food aid/commercial problems.

The first chapter of Part II will deal with existing substantive international and domestic legislation applicable to food aid/commercial trade problems, other than the system based upon the principles of surplus disposal of the Food and Agriculture Organization. These include the International Wheat Agreement, the International Sugar Agreement, the General Agreement on Tariffs and Trade (GATT), and the domestic legislation and administrative practices of major food donors.

4

National and Multilateral Food Aid / Trade Controls

This chapter will trace the general development of international law and machinery as a means of modulating the relationships between food aid and commercial trade. Although the relationships between food aid and commercial trade now are subject to some legal control, the current strong trend towards expanding, diversifying, and internationalizing food aid programs has demanded much more sophisticated and comprehensive legal concepts and institutions than those employed during the past fifteen years. So long as the United States was the sole significant food aid donor and there seemed to be some reasonable chance that a sufficient quantity of conventional foreign aid would be made available to meet the anticipated needs of the developing world, it sufficed to employ a rudimentary international legal order, primarily designed to cope with the most flagrant food aid practices through voluntary cooperation and consultation and to rely upon the United States to unilaterally control its own food aid practices. But increased participation in food aid programs by other nations, the spread of excess agricultural productive capacity to new nations (EEC) and products (dairy products), and the rapid development of the World Food Program as a significant source of, and potential promotion and coordinating agency for, food aid activities, requires a considerably more sophisticated system of substantive standards and authoritative adjudication. The legal responses to many aspects of this problem have taken the form of general guidelines or have been concentrated upon the use of nonbinding consultation and information guidelines.

General Characteristics of Controls
on Food Aid

Legal and administrative controls of food aid developed out of the same basic set of economic and political factors that stimulated the United States to begin large-scale food aid programs in the early 1950s. On the one hand, food aid met demands by poorer nations for agricultural products they could neither produce themselves nor wanted to purchase with scarce foreign currencies earmarked for basic economic development. On the other, the imbalance in developed nations between agricultural productive capacity and effective demand (desire backed by purchasing power) for those products supersensitized every nation with exportable agricultural products to food aid transactions, which could well displace

85

desperately sought commercial export sales. Thus, from the outset, the world community has insisted upon the development of legal and administrative devices which could prevent serious disruption of commercial trade in agricultural products while preserving the potential benefits of food aid to developing countries as a source of external assistance and to develop agricultural nations as a method of removing excess production from commercial markets.

These pressures have engendered a series of international and national responses. While the United States completely dominated food aid activities, the most significant controls were those developed by the United States for use in its own food aid activities. Simultaneously, various international institutions developed a roughly similar parallel set of controls over those transactions within their jurisdiction. The most ambitious of these are the principles of surplus disposal formulated and implemented by the United Nations Food and Agriculture Organization. Theoretically, many aspects of food aid/commercial trade problems fall within the jurisdiction of the General Agreements on Tariffs and Trade (GATT). And though GATT has taken some action in this area, it has never been effective in the agricultural sphere. International commodity agreements covering products likely to be included in food aid transactions—the International Wheat and Sugar Agreements—have attempted to deal with those aspects of food aid most relevant to the objectives of the agreement. Also as new nations or national groups such as Canada, Australia, and the European Economic Community begin to mount significant food aid programs, they also are developing their own set of food aid controls.

The General Operation of International Controls

International controls over food aid have taken a rather special form. Although some substantive international law does apply to food aid transactions, these are exceptional. Rather than providing a specific set of positive rules and regulations and an authoritative institution to interpret and apply these rules to specific cases, the approach has been to establish certain general standards and establish procedures where nations or institutions contemplating food aid transactions must consult interests likely to be adversely affected thereby and individual nations who deem themselves aggrieved by particular transactions are provided a forum to air their complaints. This situation largely stems from the general reluctance of some key countries to submit their food aid and agricultural trade practices to binding international controls which might restrict their flexibility in shaping domestic policies in the economically and politically sensitive agricultural sector. Instead, the world community's attempts to modulate the relationships between surplus disposal, food aid programs and international commercial trade have taken the form of relatively informal consultations rather than the formulation of substantive norms applicable by judicial bodies. An essential feature of the system is that the requirements for advance or subsequent notification with respect to those transactions covered by the system do not oblige the food aid donor to heed complaints of individual nations, or those of the international institution responsible for administering the system.

Over the past 15 years, the Consultative Subcommittee on Surplus Disposal (CSD)—a subcommittee of the FAO'S Committee on Commodity Problems—has played an increasingly important and useful role in implementing and facilitating the consultative process. The recent widening and internationalization of food aid has led to the expansion of the information gathering and consultative functions of the CSD, and certain other specialized international bodies responsible for the impact of food aid on commercial activities, and has induced the adoption of specific provisions regarding the means to be employed to protect commercial markets of affected third parties. Even so, great pains have been taken to ensure that the freedom of aid donors to reject complaints raised against them remains unimpaired.

Scope of International Controls. Theoretically, any international agricultural transactions made on other than strict commercial terms or subject to some form of subsidy might be subject to FAO controls, the General Agreement on Tariffs and Trade and/or particular commodity agreements. Some parts of these agreements attempt to control disposals of commodity surpluses and others cover export subsidies in all their varied forms. Our interest is with any transaction in which a developing country obtains commodities at lower than market cost or on less than commercial terms for the specific purpose of relieving hunger or malnutrition or to assist its economic development. In the past, such transactions involved so-called surplus commodities. More recently, countries have adjusted their production to provide commodities for food aid programs.

One of the difficulties in determining whether any particular agricultural transaction is subject to international control is the variation in terminology and orientation of the several relevant law sources with respect to food aid. "Food aid" itself is nowhere defined explicitly, although through a series of encircling maneuvers a common usage seems to have developed: to wit; food aid consists of transfers of agricultural products to more-or-less poor countries at prices or on terms not generally available to other purchasers. Thus, a country granting a subsidy of all exports of a particular product would not be giving food aid, since all customers are paying the same price. And even if the subsidy is not generally granted, noncommercial food sales only qualify as food aid if transacted with developing countries for the purpose of overcoming some of the economic and human problems suffered by such countries.

To a considerable degree, all these control devices cross-pollinate each other. But the approaches and language are sufficiently different to produce puzzling and annoying gaps and contradictions. The current interest in multilateralizing food aid efforts (and other forms of foreign aid) and the rapid expansion of the World Food Program may result in centralization of both the provision of food aid and the regulation of food aid problems. For the present though, the control system developed by the United States independently of the FAO is still the most important regulatory force. Therefore, our discussion of legal control devices will be bicentric; it will be organized around both the FAO and United States systems. To accomplish this, the discussion will commence with a discussion of the principal features and general approach of the United States system. This will be followed by a presentation of the controls imposed through multilateral efforts other than those of the FAO. This will include EEC measures, the International Wheat Agreement, the International Sugar Agreement, and the GATT. The chapter will conclude with an extensive analysis of the substantive standards and administrative machinery developed under FAO aegis. Detailed discussions of the particular legal administrative devices employed by the United States and the FAO will be deferred to Part III of this book.

United States Control System

Notwithstanding the trend towards increasing international involvement and effectiveness, the bulk of the applicable legal controls of food aid/commercial trade relationships remain those imposed by the United States—partially in response to international pressure and partially in attempts to further its own commercial interests.

Although the legislation underlying United States food aid programs has been influenced to some degree by the FAO Principles, the relevant enactments are overwhelmingly concerned with the protection and promotion of United States commercial exports. Strict enforcement of the statutes would require food aid practices in violation of the norms developed through the FAO Principles. However, the actual administration of United States food aid has demonstrated greater sensitivity to the interests of third country exporters than a literal reading of the statutes would indicate. For the most part, the practice has been to attempt to protect existing United States commercial markets. There has been no serious attempts to use food aid to increase United States commercial sales at the expense of other exporters. Certain practices though, ostensibly designed to protect legitimate commercial interests have been severely criticized by other countries as unfair use of food and to increase the donor's commercial sales. This section will briefly discuss the basic statutory structure of the United States food aid program. Analysis of the methods used by this country to implement these enactments will be deferred to Part III which covers the specific legal/administrative tools available to control food aid/commercial trade relationships.

The Statutory Framework

The principal statutory expressions with respect to protection of commercial markets are sections 103(c), 103(n) and 103(o) of the P.L. 480 Legislation. Section 103(c) requires the President to take reasonable precautions to safeguard usual marketings of the United States.[1] This language or its equivalent appears somewhere in all agreements covering concessional sales (Sales Agreements).[2] The statute has been interpreted by the Administration to require that the administrators of food aid programs make a genuine effort to see that concessional sales do not displace the usual dollar sales by the United States of the same, similar or related products but result in sales additional to usual dollar transactions.[3] Section 103(n) of the Act requires the President to take maximum precautions to assure that sales for dollars on credit sales do not displace potential dollar cash sales of agricultural commodities. This provision seems designed to preclude the Administration from equating sales on long-term dollar credit with much more highly favored cash dollar sales.[4]

Arguably, these provisions may be said to be consistent with the basic requirement of the basic international food aid conduct code—FAO Principles of Surplus Disposal. But in reality they may well be incompatible with the spirit of the Principles. In theory, the Principles require that concessional sales only should be made under circumstances where the concessionally priced goods lead to additional consumption. If consumption is additional, then protection of normal United States commercial markets would preserve the status quo ante and third country exporters would not be injured. But as we have demonstrated, the large food aid transactions that form the bulk of the United States Food for Peace program do, and if they are to serve their economic development purpose, must, displace commercial sales to some considerable extent. Under these circumstances, attempts to ensure that food aid does not deprive the United States of commercial sales must result in the reduction of commercial sale opportunities for third country exporters. In other words, if food aid substitutes for some commercial purchases, total commercial sale possibilities to the food aid recipient will be reduced. Therefore, if the United States succeeds in maintaining commercial exports at the level that would have prevailed absent food aid, the entire burden of the food aid induced market shrinkage must be borne by other commercial exporting nations. Clearly, this is not what the framers of the FAO Principles contemplated.

Examination of United States food aid practices indicates that the statutory language is not taken to its logical conclusion. With respect to section 103(c), the United States representative to the Consultative Subcommittee on Surplus Disposal, the organ responsible for administering the FAO Principles, has stressed the words "reasonable" and "unduly." The implication being that the United States does not require absolute protection of American markets.[5] However, the representative also suggested that the use of the term "maximum precautions" in section 103(n) implies the necessity for stronger protective action than required by section 103(c) which only speaks of "reasonable precautions to safeguard usual marketings."[6] These provisions are given as the justification for the highly controversial practice of tied usual marketing requirements. These are arrangements whereby recipients of United States food aid are required to make minimum commercial purchases of the same or related commodities from the United States. The merits of this position will be analyzed as part of a general discussion of usual marketing requirements and tying in Chapters 7 and 8.

Sensitivity to the Interests of
Third Countries

Although at one time the United States seems to have been deliberately insensitive to the impact of its concessional sales programs on other exporters, this attitude had been sharply modified in the direction of international responsibility and cooperation. The United States subscribes to the FAO Principles, and the impact of these obligations is partially reflected in the P.L. 480 legislation. Originally, the Act just called for the protection of the usual marketing of the United States.[7] Partially in response to complaints from other exporting countries, this section was amended to require the President "to assure that sales [under this Act] will not unduly disrupt world prices of agricultural commodities or normal patterns of commercial trade with friendly countries."[8] For this purpose, "friendly countries" are defined in Section 103(d) of the Act.[9] The barter provisions of the statute contain similar protective language.[10] The Report of the Senate Agriculture Committee on the 1966 Act seems to imply that this language obliges the Administration to give primacy to the protection of United States exports at the expense, if necessary, of the interests of other exporting countries.[11] But this interpretation of the statute has not been adopted by the Administration—at least not openly. Evidence for this attitude is supplied by the language of the form agreements employed by the United States with respect to all concessional sales, which indicates that the United States does not take a parochial view of its duty to protect normal patterns of commercial trade. Here, no distinction is made between protection of United States and other countries' exports.[12] This is not to say that certain United States practices are beyond reproach. But, as we shall see, these seem to be isolated instances, not stemming from wholesale adoption of the devil take the hindmost attitude suggested by the Senate report.

However, despite genuine Administration desire to give due regard to the interests of friendly exporters, efforts to protect markets of other nations frequently draw sharp Congressional criticism. Cotton, a chronically surplus commodity in the United States, has been quite troublesome in this respect, particularly when the country being protected was Egypt.[13] In at least one instance, a small country has decided to take self-help measures to protect its cotton exports. Mexico once made imports of motor vehicle parts, which mainly originated in the United States, contingent upon successful exports of cotton threatened by United States concessional sales.[14]

Interpretation, application and enforcement of provisions designed to protect commercial trade cause great difficulties, often leading to squabbles within the United States Executive Branch between the Department of Agriculture, the Agency for International Development (AID), and the Department of State. As a rule, AID, which is interested in maximizing the developing countries' foreign exchange earnings, takes the most liberal view. The Department of Agriculture may be counted upon to support maximum United States trade protection. And State wobbles, depending upon which other exporting country might be affected. By now, though, a case law has been developed which narrows the issues to manageable dimensions.

Although the cited statutes provide an important basis for a responsible attitude towards food aid/commercial trade issues, the chief contribution of the United States has been its desire to protect its own commercial agricultural exports and its sensitivity to the interests and complaints of other exporting nations. These attitudes have been evinced by the conditions included in the food aid agreements contracted by the United States and in its willingness to consult with other nations in accordance with the substantive and administrative guidelines promulgated by the FAO. Detailed consideration of the wide variety of control devices employed by the United States in its food aid transactions to discharge its statutory (and international) obligations towards commercial trade will be deferred to Chapters 7, 8, and 9.

Food Aid Policies of the European
Economic Community

Although still dwarfed by United States bilateral food aid programs and outsized by the World Food Program, the European Economic Community, considered both as a separate entity and as the collection of activities of its member nations, is becoming an important factor in food and commercial trade problems. Its importance derives from both the absolute magnitude of its food aid activities and commercial trade in agricultural products, and the nature of its current agricultural policies. The EEC's infamous Common Agricultural Policy tends to develop large surpluses in wheat, the traditional lynch pin of food aid activities and problems, and dairy products, another bête noir of developed agricultural economies. The latter is an important source of desperately needed proteins that has not yet been widely available as food aid. The EEC's attitude towards international efforts to cope with food aid programs is unsettled. While recognizing the importance of international controls over certain aspects of food aid, it is very jealous of its autonomy over domestic agricultural policies.[15] However both the EEC and all its member nations subscribe to the FAO Principles and are active members of the subcommittee on Surplus Disposal.

As noted in Chapter 2, both individual members of the EEC, and the Community as a separate entity, engage in food aid transactions. For the most part, the EEC as a community has attempted to control only Community food aid programs. The programs of both individual EEC members and Community activities are subject to relevant international standards and requirements. Although the Community has become increasingly concerned with the impact of its food aid transactions upon commercial trade, it has not yet developed the kind of sophisticated devices employed by the United States to control food aid/commercial trade relationships, although it is moving in that direction. From the outset of its programs in 1968, the Community has included general provisions in its food aid agreements stipulating that the implementation of the food aid agreement should not harm the existing conditions of international production and trade. Also, recipient countries were barred from reexporting the food aid products or products similar thereto for six months after the last food aid delivery.[16]

During 1970, the Community's executive body undertook a case-by-case analysis of its food aid transactions to determine the effect of food aid upon commercial imports from the Community and other exporters. Its tentative conclusion was that international cooperation was essential to avoid any deterioration of commercial transactions stemming from food aid actions. Based on these findings, the Community stated that it "firmly" intends to continue to stipulate in its food aid agreements that recipients must take the necessary steps to ensure that food aid supplements and does not substitute for normal commercial purchases.[17]

Controls Exercised under
Commodity Agreements

Food aid transactions are subject to some extent to controls by two commodity agreements, the International Wheat Agreement of 1971 and the International Sugar Agreement.

International Wheat Agreement. The International Wheat Agreement which became effective on July 1, 1971, is the successor to the International Grains Arrangement of 1967, and is the latest of a series of wheat agreements dating back to 1949. It consists of two parts—the Wheat Trade Convention, 1971, and the Food Aid Convention, 1971. According to Article 1 of the Convention, the objective of the Wheat Trade Convention is:

a. To further international cooperation in connection with world wheat problems, recognizing the relationship of the trade in wheat to the economic stability of markets for other agricultural products;

b. To promote the expansion of the international trade in wheat and wheat flour and to secure the freest possible flow of this trade in the interests of both exporting and importing members, and thus contribute to the development of countries, the economies of which depend on commercial sales of wheat;

c. To contribute to the fullest extent possible to the stability of the international wheat market in the interests of both importing and exporting members; and

d. To provide a framework, . . . for the negotiation of provisions relating to the prices of wheat and to the rights and obligations of members in respect of international trade in wheat.[18]

It should be noted that the change in the title of the Agreements from the "International Grains Arrangement" back to the "International Wheat Agreement—the name used for wheat agreements from 1949 to 1967—reflected the inability of the world's major grain traders to conclude an agreement covering all food grains. Also the 1971 Agreement abandoned its previous efforts to stabilize wheat prices by setting minimum and maximum prices and establishing purchase and sale quotas for members of the Agreement.[19]

The Wheat Trade Convention component of the Wheat Agreement deals with food aid in two contexts. The first is an attempt to distinguish commercial transactions from noncommercial ones through detailed definition. Actually, now that the Convention has abandoned the effort to stabilize prices and trade patterns through direct controls, this distinction has little direct impact on wheat trade. But it still is important. The categorization of nonstandard transactions is central to the control scheme being developed by the FAO. And the most powerful members of the Wheat Agreement also are members of the Committee on Commodity Problems, the focus of FAO activity with respect to food aid controls. Therefore, the interpretation by these nations of both the Wheat Agreement and the rules established by the FAO are likely to coincide.

To qualify as a commercial transaction, a wheat purchase must meet two tests. It must conform to the usual commercial practices in international trade and not fall into any of the categories of special transactions as defined by Article 3(2). Article 3(2) defines "special transactions" as follows.

a. Sales on credit in which, as a result of government intervention, the interest rate, period of payment, or other related terms do not conform to the commercial rates, periods or terms prevailing in the world market;

b. Sales in which the funds for the purchase of wheat are obtained under a loan from the Government of the exporting member tied to the purchase of wheat;

c. Sales for currency of the importing member which is not transferable or convertible into currency or goods for use in the exporting member;

d. Sales under trade agreements with special payments arrangements which include clearing accounts for settling credit balances bilaterally through the exchange of goods, except where the exporting member and the importing member concerned agree that the sale shall be regarded as commercial;

e. Barter transactions:
  i. which result from the intervention of governments where wheat is exchanged at other than prevailing world prices, or
  ii. which involve sponsorship under a government purchase programme, except where the purchase of wheat results from a barter transaction in which the country of final destination was not named in the original barter contract;
f. A gift of wheat or a purchase of wheat out of a monetary grant by the exporting member made for that specific purpose;
g. Any other categories of transactions, as the Council may prescribe, that include features introduced by the Government of a member concerned which do not conform to usual commercial practices.

As we shall see, this list of special transactions differs in many respects from the layout developed by the FAO to guide it in carrying out its functions under the guidelines for surplus disposal. Moreover, the term "special transaction" is unique to the Wheat Trade Convention. The FAO Principles refers to "commercial sales," "suplus disposal" and "concessional sales." The Food Aid Convention refers to "food aid."

Actually, "Special Transactions" represents an explicit cop-out by the parties to the Convention from the task of unequivocably identifying commercial sales, surplus disposal activities and food aid. Most of the negotiators of the International Wheat Agreement of 1971 wanted to remove the ambiguities from the existing definitions of commercial transactions. The European Economic Community urged the adoption of the scheme developed by the FAO Committee on Commodity Problems.[20] A second group wanted to eliminate the definition of commercial transactions. Some developing countries feared that any new definition would be likely to widen the range of special transactions, subject to international controls thereby harming countries anxious to maximize their food aid imports. The most serious objections were raised by Argentina, an important wheat exporter lacking the resources to make any significant concessions on wheat sales. It has been waging a long, lonely battle in every available forum to label as concessional all wheat sale arrangements according credits of more than six months. Since the United States deemed the three-year credits granted by the Commodity Credit Corporation as commercial, Argentina's position would require sharp changes in current attitudes towards the identification of concessional transactions. Argentina, despite assurances to the contrary, also feared that the failure to identify certain transactions as "special" might "legitimize" these transactions and that any definition established for the Wheat Agreement would be applied elsewhere as well. In the end, the parties abandoned the effort to rationalize Article 3 and retained the old wording.

Guidelines Relating to Concessional Transactions

The Wheat Trade Convention also attempted to regulate concessional transactions through the establishment of Guidelines in Article 9 of the Convention.[21] These played a crucial role in curbing certain aspects of food aid wheat transactions. It still has some importance in this respect, but many of the protections to commercial trade imposed by the Wheat Agreements have now been incorporated in the FAO Principles of Surplus Disposal. In a real sense, the Guidelines of the Wheat Agreements foreshadowed later actions with respect to all food aid products by the FAO. The Guidelines were included in the 1967 Grains Arrangement to control the conduct of countries that would be providing food aid for the first time pursuant to the Food Aid Convention. Under the Food Aid Convention, the exporting members of the Wheat Agreement agreed to share some of the food aid burden previously borne by the United States. The United States, in particular, wished to ensure that these countries were held to the same standards for protecting the interests of third party exporters, which now included the United States itself, that the United States had accepted with respect to its food aid programs.

These provisions closely follow the FAO Principles of Surplus Disposal and United States legislation. Briefly stated, these standards require Wheat Trade Convention members "to conduct any concessional transactions in wheat in such a way as to avoid harmful interference with normal patterns of production and trade," and to "undertake appropriate measures to ensure that concessional transactions are additional to commercial sales which could reasonably be anticipated in the absence of such transactions."[22] Many of the negotiating countries favored incorporating the FAO principles, *per se*, into the Guidelines. This action was opposed on several grounds. Argentina again feared that such action would somehow sanctify certain dubious credit transactions. The developing countries were afraid that the FAO might change its principles in ways which would impede their access to wheat food aid. The EEC was divided. Certain members favored the incorporation, but France objected to certain aspects of the consultative procedures developed by FAO. Under FAO practices, third party consultations must take place prior to negotiations with the potential recipient. France believed these consultations should proceed along with negotiations with the recipient. The United States, as the major food donor, shared France's concern that the consultative process not unduly complicate food aid transactions, but distinguished "conversations" which could accompany consultations with "negotiations" which must await the completion of consultations.

To ensure additionality, the Guidelines also authorized the use of the device long employed by the United States for this purpose—usual marketing requirements (UMR's). Thus, Article 9 (2) of the Wheat Trade Convention, 1971 states that measures to achieve additionality shall be consistent with the Principles of Surplus Disposal and Guiding Lines recommended by the FAO and may provide that a specified level of commercial imports of wheat, agreed with the recipient country, be maintained on a global basis by that country. In establishing or adjusting this level, Article 9(2) requires particular attention to the commercial import levels in a representative period and to the economic circumstances of the recipient country, including in particular, its balance-of-payments situation. Some of the negotiators tried and failed to make usual marketing requirements mandatory rather than optional as provided by Article 24 of the 1967 Wheat Trade Convention. The setting of minimum commercial purchase requirements accords with United States practice although, as we shall see, this country sometimes limits some or all of these purchases to the United States. Furthermore, countries anticipating concessional sales are directed to undertake the maximum possible prior consultations with exporting member countries likely to be affected by such transactions. This also accords with current United States practices and FAO requirements. A key concept here is that commercial purchases must be made on a "global" basis. At one time, the United States restricted a portion of the required commercial purchases to the United States. Since tied purchases are not a global basis, this would constitute a violation of Article 9(1). The issue was avoided when the United States stopped tying wheat requirements in 1959. (Though it did continue tying with respect to other commodities.) However, it is possible that the pressure of its balance-of-payments deficits may induce the United States to resume tying wheat purchase requirements, with all the problems this would entail.

The accession of the Soviet Union to the Wheat Agreement further complicates matters.[23] Invariably, the bilateral agreements controlling United States concessional sales have limited required commercial purchases to "free world" sources[24] or "countries friendly to the United States."[25] "Free world sources" is a well-worn euphemism for non-Communist bloc nations. "Friendly nations" are defined by the P.L. 480 statute to exclude Communist countries and other assorted current bogey men.[26] The definition employed in recent sales agreements is somewhat less precise; to wit, "friendly nations" are countries deemed by the United States as friendly to it.[27] Obviously, such limitations are inconsistent with the Article 9(2) requirement that mandatory commercial purchases be on a global basis—particularly with Russia, an adherent to the Wheat Trade Convention, 1971.

But recognizing communist bloc countries as eligible sources for meeting minimum commercial wheat purchases imposed upon concessional sale recipients in accordance with the Guidelines would be (at least until very recently) extremely embarrassing for the United States executive branch. We have noted that originally United States practice in concessional sales transactions was to tie commercial wheat purchase requirements in whole or in part to the United States.[28] As a result of international pressure, this policy has now been altered, albeit not without sharp domestic criticism, to permit these requirements to be met by purchases from "free world sources" or "friendly nations."[29] Untying the purchase requirements from the United States and permitting them to be met from Communist sources would have drawn very sharp congressional and public reaction. (Perhaps this is no longer quite as true.) It may be that the United States accepted the concept of global UMR's in 1967, when the Guidelines were first incorporated into the Wheat Agreements, because no communist bloc countries signed the 1967 Wheat Trade Convention. With Russia's accession to the 1971 Wheat Trade Convention, this is no longer the case. So far, no one has raised this issue and perhaps they won't.

Recent modifications to the FAO Principles of Surplus Disposal now require that global minimum commercial purchase requirements must be included in most food aid transactions. However, the FAO ducked the tying issue. Therefore, the stronger language of the Wheat Trade Guidelines may become important if the United States attempts to again tie wheat commercial purchase requirements. Also, Clause 3 of Article 9 of the Wheat Trade Convention has been included in the FAO control system for some time. It obliges members making concessional sales to "consult with exporting members whose commercial sales might be affected by such transactions, to the maximum possible extent before such arrangements are concluded with recipient countries." Indeed, as shall appear, this is the heart and soul of the FAO control system.

Although the Guideline Relating to Concessional Transactions does not formally adopt the FAO Principles, it does incorporate their substance and much of their language. To the extent the Guidelines venture beyond the Principles, they usually follow current United States practices. The incorporation of current United States practices in an international agreement should have a threefold effect: it ratifies present United States actions; it forces other nations to follow the same procedures; and it makes it difficult for the United States to change its current practices (like using untied UMRs for wheat). Previously, this country has experimented with a number of devices designed to protect commercial sales, including variations of a highly parochial cast. Now, though, it will be more difficult to revert to such narrowly conceived practices. These practices will be analyzed in Chapters 7, 8, and 9.

As do the Principles of Surplus Disposal, the Guidelines admonish member countries to conduct concessional transactions to avoid harmful interference with normal patterns of production and international commercial trade. More specifically, the member countries are to "undertake appropriate measures to ensure that concessional transactions are additional to commercial sales which could reasonably be anticipated in the absence of such transactions." Thus, the Wheat Trade Convention seems to demand 100% additionality in contrast to the FAO Principles, which strongly emphasize but do not absolutely require that every concessional transaction result in the additional consumption of an equivalent quantity of the product involved. But we may assume that the Guidelines really do incorporate the more flexible standards of the Principles—if for no other reason than that a strict nondisplacement standard is unachievable. Moreover, as stated above, the objective of adding the Guidelines to the Grain Arrangement was to apply the United States' standards to other countries' concessional sales and United States practices have followed the flexible FAO approach.

The Food Aid Convention

As discussed in Chapter 2, the International Grains Arrangement 1967 added a new dimension to the International Wheat Agreements by coupling a Food Aid Convention to the traditional Wheat Trade Convention. And despite the sharp change in approach to wheat trade problems adopted by the 1971 Wheat Agreement, (removal of minimum price and purchase requirements) the Food Aid Convention was retained.

In addition to shifting some of the United States' food aid burden to other developed countries, the Convention was designed to act as an indirect method of protecting commercial wheat export markets. This would be achieved in two ways. Grain surpluses would be removed from commercial markets and directed towards consumers in developing countries unlikely to make commercial purchases. And by specifying the terms upon which food aid could be offered under the Convention, it would become more difficult to disguise commercial transactions as food aid.

Eligibility for participation and the required accessions to effectuate the Convention take the same form in both the 1967 and 1971 Food Aid Conventions. The Convention may be accepted by three groups of countries. The first includes those countries which negotiated the International Wheat Agreement of 1971. These include Argentina, Australia, Canada, Finland, Japan, Sweden, Switzerland, the United States, the EEC and its member nations. This group does not include Denmark, Norway, and the United Kingdom which had acceded to the 1967 Convention.[30] The apparent reason for this discrepancy is that these countries all are applying for membership in the EEC and are understandably reluctant to commit themselves to giving food aid until their status viz-a-viz the EEC had been settled. The first group includes both grain exporters and nonexporters. Argentina, Australia, Canada, the EEC, and the United States are major grain exporters. Finland, Japan, Sweden and Switzerland export little or no grain. The second eligible group includes all countries which had signed the 1967 Food Aid Convention, provided that their contribution is at least equal to that which they had agreed to make in the Food Aid Convention 1967.[31] Finally, any other member of the United Nations or its specialized agencies may join upon the approval of the Food Aid Committee. The Food Aid Committee is the executive organ of the Convention and consists of the contributing members and of all other countries that become parties to the Convention.[32] However, all signatories to the Food Aid Convention 1971 also must ratify the Wheat Trade Convention 1971.[33] The Food Aid Convention will enter into force when ratified by the negotiating countries, and the EEC and its member nations, provided that the Wheat Trade Convention 1971 has taken effect.[34] Thus, at a minimum, the membership of the Food Aid Convention would account for 84% of total world wheat and wheat flour exports.[35]

The structure of the Food Aid Convention is designed to provide the maximum possible assistance to the commercial exports of the donating members. The Convention requires that all contributions of grains under the program must come from participating countries.[36] Officially, contributions must be made in wheat, coarse grains (corn, oats, barley, sorghum), or in cash.[37] Japan, though, was conceded the right to make part of its contribution in rice. In the 1971 convention, a minimum of 35% of the cash contributions, or that part of the contributions required to purchase 200,000 metric tons of grain must be used to purchase grains produced in member developing countries.[38] The comparable figure in the 1967 convention was 25%. In fact, the only participant in the Convention able to meet these conditions is Argentina. Thus, for a pledged contribution of 23,000 metric tons, Argentina gets the inside track on 200,000 or more metric tons of purchases by nongrain-producing member countries.[39] Undoubtedly, Argentina would reply that if they are getting a good deal, it is small recompense for the damage done her commercial exports by fifteen years of massive United States food aid sales to her traditional markets.

The 1971 Convention stipulates three types of transactions for the supply of food aid. These terms are soft enough to remove any question over whether the transactions are truly food aid or disguished commercial sales. Food may be sold for the currency of the importing country which is not transferable and not convertible into currency or goods and services for use by the donating country. Under exceptional circumstances, 10% of the currencies are exempt from these requirements.[40] Local currency sales under the United States Food for Peace program do not seem to meet this requirement since most of these transactions would result in more than 10% of the foreign currencies collected by the United States available for reuse by the United States.[41] Therefore, the United States has been meeting its obligations under the 1967 Convention through their Title II grant program, which meets the requirements of the second category of food aid transactions authorized by the Convention.

The second type of food aid are gifts of grain or a monetary grant to be used to purchase grain for the importing country.[42] Only convention members are eligible sources for grain supplied in this manner. Finally, the 1971 Convention revises the 1968 version to authorize sales made on credit terms with payment over twenty years or more and with interest at rates below commercial rates in world markets. The credit sales agreement may provide for cash payment of up to 15% of the principal upon delivery of the grain.[43] Apparently, the third category was added to correspond to the 1966 changes in United States Food Aid Programs. Under the Food for Peace Act, local currency sales are to be replaced by dollar credit and local currency convertible sales by the end of 1971. The provision of the Convention which permits the collection of up to 15% of the purchase price upon delivery of the grain also was induced to conform with United States practice. Section 103(k) of the Food for Peace Act requires a minimum cash payment of 5% of the purchase price in all dollar and local currency convertible transactions.[44] However, according to the text of the Convention, it is understood that food aid shall be supplied to the maximum extent possible under straight local currency sales and grants.

In addition to the provisions of the Food Aid Convention itself, food aid transactions in wheat, under the Convention are subject to the previously discussed Guidelines Relating to Concessional Transactions established by Article 9 of the Wheat Trade Convention. And the Guidelines incorporated much of the FAO Principles of Surplus Disposal. All members of the Food Aid Convention must subscribe to the Wheat Trade Convention and there is no doubt that food aid transactions under the terms specified by Article II(5) of the Food Aid Convention are concessional transactions under any definition of that elusive term. Indeed, one of the principal purposes of adding the Guidelines to the Wheat Trade Convention was to cover transactions under the Food Aid Convention. By its terms, the Guidelines apply only to wheat transactions, while the Food Aid Convention includes coarse grains and unofficially permits rice transactions. But since the bulk of food aid transactions under the Convention will be in wheat, this discrepancy has only limited practical import.

The administrative organ of the Food Aid Convention—the Food Aid Committee—is endowed with limited supervisory powers. The Committee is authorized to receive reports from member countries on the amount, content, channelling and terms of their food aid contributions under the Convention, and to "examine" the way in which the obligations undertaken under the food aid program have been fulfilled. The Committee also is to keep under review the purchase of grains financed by cash contributions, particularly with respect to the obligation to purchase minimum amounts of grain from developing countries. In addition, the Committee is to exchange information on a regular basis regarding the impact of the activities taken under the Convention, particularly with respect to its effect upon food production in recipient countries.[45] Finally, the Committee has the power to admit new nations as members of the Convention and to impose conditions upon such entrance.[46] Unlike the FAO Committee on Surplus Disposal, the Food Aid Committee may not require member nations to consult with it prior to engaging in food aid transactions under the Convention.

It is difficult to assess the impact of the Food Aid Convention upon the level of food aid or world wheat and grain trade. There is evidence that the Food Aid Convention was partly intended to unburden world grain markets of surpluses arising from the imbalance between supply and demand. This might have worked if the contributions under the Convention had been large enough to constitute a net addition to existing bilateral food aid programs. But this was not the case. Under the 1967 Convention, the food aid obligations totalled 4.3 million metric tons of food grains per year—mostly, but not entirely, wheat and under the 1971 Convention, 3.97 m.m.t. Total food aid wheat shipments by Convention members in 1969/70 are estimated at 14.8 m.m.t., compared to average food aid wheat shipments of 14.0 m.m.t. in 1966/67-1968/69. Thus, it seems quite likely that contributions under the Conventions represent no net addition to the food aid level that would have prevailed without the Convention. The same may be said about the efficacy of fixing the terms upon which transactions under the Convention may be made. While the Convention ensures that a minimum amount of food aid will be conducted upon terms that clearly distinguish these transactions from commercial sales, thereby ensuring that food aid isn't being used as a form of disguised price cutting, the total transactions covered by the Convention represent less than a third of total concessional sales, thus leaving wide opportunity for possible questionable practices in food aid transactions not covered by the Convention.

Still, the Convention could serve as the core of an effective system of food aid controls for the products included in the Convention. If the food-giving and food-receiving nations are ready to take effective steps to minimize the potential adverse effects of food aid upon commercial trade, they could substantially increase the proportion of their total food aid program that is handled under the Food Aid Convention. The result would be that most food aid would be conducted upon terms that are likely to preclude attempts to disguise price cutting as food aid. Moreover, increased use of the Convention could get around the seemingly insolvable problem of defining commercial sales. Unlike the FAO Principles which speaks of "surplus disposal" and "sales or grants on concessional terms," and Article 3 of the Wheat Trade Convention which uses the terms "commercial purchases and special transactions," the Food Aid Convention refers only to "food aid," and stipulates terms for these transactions that unmistakedly distinguish them from commercial sales. Conceivably, as the proportion of total food aid transactions conducted under the Convention increase, and assuming the stipulations regarding the terms of these transactions continue along the present lines, a clear demarcation of food aid and nonfood aid concessional transactions in wheat will emerge—those conducted under the Convention are food aid; other transactions not conforming to normal commercial practice would be deemed commercial transactions at below commercial prices or terms.

International Sugar Agreement 1968. The International Sugar Agreement 1968 also attempts to control disruptive food aid transactions in that commodity. Article 43 of the Agreement requires that all agreements providing for donations of sugar by an exporting member, other than those made through United Nations assistance programs must include conditions designed to protect commercial transactions. These conditions are to include requirements for prior consultations and adequate safeguards to normal trade patterns (Article 43(3)). All donations of sugar are to be promptly reported to the Council of the Sugar Agreement by the donor member country and any member which deemed the donations as actually or potentially prejudicial to its interest may request the Council to examine the matter (Article 43(4)).

*Efficacy of Controlling Food Aid
Commercial Trade Problems through
Commodity Agreements*

Commodity agreements have distinct strengths and weaknesses as effective in-struments for the control of food aid/commercial trade relations. In this regard, we are speaking of those commodity arrangements which impose direct controls on imports, exports, and/or prices such as the International Coffee Agreement. At the other extreme are Commodity Agreements largely relying upon consulta-tions between producers and/or consumers. The now lapsed Sultana (Raisin) Agreement fits this description. The Wheat Trade Convention stands somewhere between these two. In those situations where the dangers of unrestricted trade have induced the interested trading nations to restrict their freedom of action sufficiently to effectively control international markets, it is likely that they may be sufficiently motivated and organized to control food aid and concession-al sales as well. Even if some of the members of the basic commodity agreement ordinarily would not agree to effective food aid controls, their interest in main-taining the basic agreement may be strong enough to induce them to accept food aid controls as the price of continued loyalty of these countries desiring effective controls. Another consideration is that the administrative machinery developed for the main agreement may be available for effective policing of the food aid controls.

The disadvantages of controlling food aid through commodity agreements principally flow from the necessarily narrow focus of any such agreements. All commodity agreements in force or contemplated apply to but a single product, where effective food aid control requires taking account of transactions in a number of allied commodities. In some situations, one product is under a com-modity agreement while a closely allied one is not. This is the situation with wheat and feedgrains, and frustration with this arrangement led to the abortive efforts during the Kennedy Round negotiations to encompass all grains under a single agreement. Potential recipients of food aid are likely to be prejudiced by commodity-based control schemes. In many cases, developing recipients are not major commercial traders in the commodity. Thus, either they will not be mem-bers of commodity agreements, or if they are members, they may have limited voting power. Under these conditions, the food aid needs of the recipients are likely to be sacrificed to the commercial interests of the large trading nations. There is a more fundamental objection to using commodity agreements as the focus for food aid control. It absolutely precludes any chance of developing ef-fective measures to maximize the utility of food aid as an instrument of eco-nomic development and humanitarian relief. It also renders it difficult to devise equitable means of sharing the role of food aid donor among the developing countries, whether such sharing takes the form of providing food aid, cash, or merely accepting some injury to a nation's commercial sales as a result of food aid transactions. Although the picture is still quite fuzzy, there does seem to be a trend towards increased internationalization of food aid programs and controls, and any shift towards increased emphasis on commodity agreement based controls would be a retrograde step.

Of course, all this does not preclude use of commodity agreements as an adjunct to international controls. That is, the basic decisions regarding the total amounts, kinds, directions, and operating methods of food aid could be determined internationally, with the commodity agreements serving to develop those aspects of food aid problems peculiar to their respective commodities, and serving to take responsibility for the daily administration of food aid programs and possibly to adjudicate disputes. To a considerable extent, this is the case with respect to the International Wheat Agreements. The Guidelines Relating to Concessional Transactions of the Wheat Trade Convention, 1971, require its members to undertake appropriate measures to ensure that concessional transactions are additional to commercial sales which could reasonably be expected without such transactions, and that such measures be consistent with the FAO Principles of Surplus Disposal. Moreover, the Wheat Trade Convention guidelines follow the procedures established by the FAO Committee on Surplus Disposal for consultation with potentially affected third countries prior to concluding concessional export transactions with recipient countries. The Food Aid Convention goes beyond the FAO Principles by limiting the terms upon which food aid may be given under the said Convention.

The Role of the GATT and other International Organizations

In addition to the instrumentalities discussed so far, there are some other international organizations which play some role in the food aid/trade picture.

The GATT. In theory, food aid/commercial trade problems fall within the general ambit of the General Agreement on Tariffs and Trade (GATT). In the postwar period, GATT has emerged as the central international trade institution with plenary jurisdiction over agricultural as well as industrial trade.[47] Thus, Article XVI of the GATT requires contracting parties maintaining subsidies, including any form of income or price support, which operate directly or indirectly to increase exports, to notify the other GATT members of the nature and extent of the subsidization. Direct subsidization of exports or a particular product would not meet our definition of food aid. However, Article XVI has been interpreted to include a number of arrangements which could be deemed food aid. These include government export credits and credit guarantees on less than market terms.

GATT's position on surplus disposal affects food aid transactions. Under the

Resolution of 4 March 1955 on Disposal of Surpluses, GATT parties have agreed to give at least 45 days notice of its intention to liquidate a substantial quantity of surplus stocks and to consult with and sympathetically consider the views of any party which considers itself injured by such a transaction.[48] Food aid operations could well be included within some transactions covered by these procedures. Australia has notified donations made in fulfillment of its obligations under the Food Aid Convention and the United States has notified a wide range of food aid activities. But not all surplus disposal constitutes food aid. In any case, coverage of a food aid transaction by GATT does not subject it to any specific restriction or requirement, other than the duty to notify potentially affected GATT members and consult with them if required.

Commencing in 1967, GATT has been considering strengthening its controls over government assistance for agricultural exports. At the 24th Session of the GATT membership, some governments supported the creation of machinery that would expand existing rules applicable to surplus disposal to include transactions involving agricultural supplies intentionally produced for food aid purposes. Some members also were interested in export sales described as commercial but those prices or terms fell well below market levels. During the discussion of these matters, comments generally focused on the need for more adequate reporting and effective safeguards. At the twenty-fifth session held in November 1968, GATT requested its Agriculture Committee to consider changes in the existing procedures for notification and consultations and the discharge of other responsibilities of GATT members with respect to surplus disposals.

The Adequacy of GATT in the Agricultural Sphere. Although the recent efforts to upgrade GATT's performance with respect to agricultural problems may change the picture somewhat, based on its performance so far, one must conclude that GATT has failed to exercise effective control over agricultural trade. Effective protection of domestic agriculture not only is on the average higher than in any other sector of the international economy, but there is substantial evidence indicating that the rate of protection is increasing.[49] Universally, the protection against imports is necessitated by domestic price support programs which increases the domestic price above prevailing world levels. Simultaneously, the high domestic prices induce countries to subsidize exports in order to meet world competition. One reaction to this situation has been the establishment of alternate partial control systems through commodity agreements and the FAO. And though those responsible for the administration of these alternate control mechanisms are very sensitive towards avoiding encroachment on GATT jurisdiction and avoiding overlapping and duplication, constant pressure is exerted by some agricultural exporters to enlarge commodity agreement and FAO jurisdiction at GATT's expense. These problems will be analyzed in greater detail in our discussion of FAO administered controls.

Other Intergovernmental Machinery

The problems of agricultural surpluses and methods for dealing with them, and concern with maximizing the effectiveness of food aid in economic development fall within the jurisdiction of other intergovernmental institutions. Problems of the effects of surpluses on the markets; the search for methods of stabilizing commodity markets; the study of methods of utilization of surpluses outside normal commercial channels and related matters—all these have come to the attention of bodies concerned with international trade in general and with respect to individual commodities. The five main worldwide agencies involved are the FAO, United Nations, the World Food Program, GATT, and more recently the United Nations Conference on Trade and Development (UNCTAD). The principal regional bodies are the OECD, the EEC and the Organization of American States (OAS); and of the many commodity groups outside those established by FAO, the International Wheat Council, the International Cotton Advisory Committee and the International Coffee Organization should be mentioned.

Although the policy aspects of agricultural surplus problems and food aid matters are the concern of the Council and the Conference of FAO, it is the Committee on Commodity Problems and its subsidiary body the Consultative Subcommittee on Surplus Disposal which carry out the major responsibilities in this respect. As for the United Nations, it was the General Assembly which took the initiative for promoting certain studies on the utilization of surpluses, among them the request to FAO for a study on World Food Reserves and on National Reserves. The General Assembly also initiated studies carried out largely within the FAO which led to the establishment of the World Food Program. Currently, the UN and the FAO have completed a study on the possibilities for and implications of an expanded multilateral food aid program.[50]

The Organization for Economic Cooperation and Development. The Organization for Economic Cooperation and Development (OECD) provides another forum for discussion of agricultural production and trade policies that may affect food aid practices. The OECD is principally designed to coordinate the efforts of the developed nations to assist the economic growth of the have-not countries. It grew out of the Organization of European Economic Cooperation (OEEC), which was established in 1947 to distribute United States economic aid to 17 European member countries. OECD expanded its activities to all major economic fields in later years, including the annual examination of different aspects of the agricultural policies of the member countries. It now has 20 members including the United States and Canada. Under the OEEC, a number of commodity groups had met frequently to discuss market conditions and developments, in particular for butter and whole and skim milk powder, and in some cases, recommendations were adopted to remedy threatening or existing market disturbances. The Agriculture Committee of the OECD not only continued this work but also extended its activities to the search for both short-term and longer-term solutions to disturbances on the international commodity markets, and to the study of international commodity arrangements. Particular stress is also placed on the agricultural problems of developing countries and regions, and the role that food aid may play in economic development.

During their annual meeting in November 1962, the Ministers of Agriculture of the OECD countries approved a report on the role of food in economic development and adopted a statement which mentioned the desirability of adjustments in agricultural production; the taking into account of international trade responsibilities; the avoidance of stimulating uneconomic production; and the stabilization of international markets. Emphasis was placed on the contribution which food aid might provide to developing countries; the risks involved with regard to the level of domestic production and to third countries; and finally, the obvious necessity to coordinate food programs with other aid programs. Special attention was given to the danger that food aid may reduce the incentive for donor countries to make adjustments in their own agriculture.[51]

The net impact of the OECD on food aid/commercial trade problems is difficult to assess. Its membership includes the major agricultural exporting nations who have committed themselves to assist less developed countries. The character of its membership makes it an ideal body for consideration of food aid related problems—since both the problems and economic potential of food aid are likely to receive sympathetic and expert attention. So far, its most concrete contribution to these problems has been the publication of an excellent study of the role of food aid in economic development.[52] It does not administer any food aid problems nor has it attempted to assert formal jurisdiction over food aid problems and disputes. Its future would seem to lie as another forum for discussion of basic economic development issues and as a source of authoritative studies of various aspects of the problem.

Private Organizations. The International Federation of Agricultural Producers (IFAP) is a nongovernmental organization of 46 members from 32 countries with Category A consultative status in the United Nations and in FAO. It is an active observer-participant on the FAO Committee on Surplus Disposal. The purpose of IFAP is to promote the well-being of all who obtain their livelihood from the land and to assure to them the maintenance of adequate and stable remuneration. It considers that to achieve this objective the assistance and support of national governments will be required. It realizes, however, that such national government programs may have serious international repercussions and has constantly urged international cooperative programs. It has, in particular, supported the negotiation of international commodity agreements, and it has recommended international cooperative action to solve the problems arising out of the anomaly of hunger in the midst of plenty. The IFAP advocates that agricultural production, especially of food, in both the developed and developing countries, should be geared to the satisfaction of human needs and not merely to the effective demand of the commercial market. This would involve the production of large supplies of surplus food in the developed countries and their movement on special terms to underdeveloped countries where population growth has been outrunning current production capacity.

Notes

1. 80 *Stat.* 1526 (1966), 7 U.S.C.A. § 1703 (6) 1970).

2. The language in the Standard Form Sales Agreement that has been in use since spring 1967 is found in Pt. 1, Art. III-A. It states that "the two Governments shall take maximum precautions to assure that sales of agricultural commodities pursuant to (the) agreement will not displace usual marketings of the exporting country in these commodities . . ." e.g., Agricultural Commodities Agreement with Afghanistan, July 19, 1967, TIAS 6322, 18 U.S.T. 1766, 1769 (1968).

3. *General Accounting Office, Report to Congress and Department of Agriculture "Review Precautions Taken to Protect Commercial Dollar Sales of Agricultural Commodities under P.L. 480,"* at 3. (Aug. 1966).

4. Wightman, *Food Aid and Economic Development, International Conciliation*, no. 567, March 1968 at 38.

5. UN/FAO, CCP 69/13/3, (CCP/CSD/69/51). *Report on Tied Sales*, Annex A (17 July 1969).

6. Since Section 103(b) of the Food for Peace Act requires that by December 31, 1971, all concessional sales be made on a dollar-to-dollar convertible basis, the "stronger" language of 103(n) will soon apply to all concessional sales.

7. 68 *Stat.* 455. (1954); 72 *Stat.* 1790 (1958).

8. 80 *Stat.* 1526, 7 U.S.C.A. 1703(c) (1970); *University of Arizona, Agricultural Experiment Station, Policy for United States Agricultural Export Surplus Disposal, Technical Bulletin* 150, at 78. (1962).

9. 80 *Stat.* 1527 (1966), 7 U.S.C.A. 1703(a) (1970).

10. 68 *Stat.* 459 (1954), 72 *Stat.* 1791, 82 *Stat.* 451 (1968), 7 U.S.C.A. 1692 (1970).

11. *S. Rep.* no. 1527, 89th Cong., 2nd sess., 14 (1966).

12. Art. III-A, Pt. I of the Standard Sales Agreement of April 20, 1967 states "The two Governments shall take maximum precautions to assure that sales of agricultural commodities pursuant to this agreement will not displace usual marketings of the (United States) in these commodities or unduly disrupt world price of agricultural commodities or normal patterns of commercial trade with countries the Government of the exporting considers to be friendly to it. . . ."

13. *Cong. Rep.* no. 683, 85th Cong. 1st sess. 29 (1957); *S. Rep.* 85th Cong. 2d sess., 9 (1958). This was translated into law in 1958 via a provision requiring the "extra long staple cotton shall be made available in the same manner as upland cotton is in surplus supply, and no discriminatory or other conditions shall be imposed which will prevent or tend to interfere with their sale or availability for sale under the Act. . . ." 72 *Stat.* 1792. This enactment was never accorded a Code number, perhaps implying that the codifers shared the author's doubts with respect to the enforceability of this kind of provision. Obviously, the Administration will and must take the position that in pursuing the program they will not discriminate against any produce but will make all decisions within the discretion and limitations imposed by the Act. Therefore, it is difficult to see how Congress could force the Administration to sell any specified commodity. Events seem to bear this out. No noticeable increase in the level of government financed exports can be discerned. Government-financed exports of cotton in 1958 were worth $288.1 million. Statistical Abstract of the United States, 1962, #902, at 648. In the years 1959-64, the figures were, in millions of dollars, $258.6, 155.9, 227.7, 230.3, 173.6.

14. *Technical Bulletin 150*, supra note 8, at 81.

15. A report of the EEC to an organ of the Food and Agriculture Organization is prefaced "(T)he Subcommittee on Surplus Disposal (CSD) is certainly not the appropriate framework within which the Community should accept discussion of its food aid program." UN/FAO, CCP/CSD/71/16, *Food Aid Policy of the European Economic Community* (12 Feb. 1971), p. 22.

16. In fact, in many cases, this might constitute a more stringent restriction than that imposed by the United States, which limits such exports only during the year during which food aid deliveries are to be made. See Chapter 9. In practice, this feature has little importance, since the United States programs usually are continually renewed, thereby keeping export restrictions always in effect.

17. Ibid.

18. For a brief history of the Wheat Agreements up to 1967, see *International Wheat Council, Review of the World Wheat Situation* 1966-67, 64-65 (1967) (hereinafter cited as *66/67 Wheat Review*).

19. The performance of the International Grains Arrangement of 1967 is analyzed in FAO/UN, FAO Community Policy studies #20, *The Stabilization of International Trade in Grains*, Ch. 4 (1970).

20. See Chapter 6.

21. This provision was first introduced into the Wheat Agreements by Article 24 of the Wheat Trade Convention of the International Grains Arrangement, 1971. The term "concessional transaction" is not defined anywhere in the Wheat Agreement. Undoubtedly, "concessional transactions" are closely related to "special transactions," but more precise definitions are unavailable. The same nations that unsuccessfully tried to clarify the definition of commercial transactions in the context of Art. 3 of the Wheat Trade Convention also attempted

again unsuccessfully to conform the Guidelines of the Wheat Trade Convention to the FAO Principles.

22. International Wheat Agreement, 1971, Wheat Trade Convention Articles (9)(1), 9(2).

23. After failing to accede to the International Grains Arrangement of 1967, the USSR renewed its association with Wheat Agreements by acceding to the Wheat Trade Convention of the International Wheat Agreement, 1971 on May 25, 1971.

24. E.g., Agricultural Commodities Agreement with Ryukyu Islands Dec. 23, 1965 (1966), TIAS 5927, 16 U.S.T. 1932, 1938 (1966).

25. E.g., Agricultural Commodities Agreement with Chile, July 27, 1965 (1966), TIAS 5898, 16 U.S.T. 1725 (1966).

26. 80 *Stat.* 1527 (1966), 7 U.S.C.A. § 1703 (d) (1970).

27. E.g., Agreement with Tunisia, March 12, 1967, TIAS 6323, 18 U.S.T. 1777, 1783-84 (1968).

28. Agricultural Commodities Agreement with Italy, May 23, 1955, TIAS 3249 6 UST, 1122 (1956); Agricultural Commodities Agreement with Israel, Nov. 7, 1957, TIAS 3945, 8 UST 2205, 2210, (1958). Agricultural Commodities Agreement with Ecuador, June 30, 1968, TIAS 4105, 9 UST 1192, 1198 (1960).

29. Agricultural Commodities Agreement with Tunisia, Mar. 17, 1967, TIAS 6323, 18 UST 1777, 1783 (1968), Agricultural Commodities Agreement with India, Feb. 20, 1967, TIAS 6221, 18 UST 217, 223 (1968), *General* Accounting Office, Report to Congress and Department of Agriculture, Review Precautions taken to Protect Commercial Dollar Sales of Agricultural Commodities under P.L. 480, 17-18 (Aug. 1966).

30. International Wheat Agreement 1971, Food Aid Convention 1971 Art. VI(I).

31. Id. at Article VI(2).

32. Art. III, VIII(2). The Food Aid Committee may impose conditions upon accession of these nations.

33. Art. VII.

34. Art. X.

35. Forty-two m.m.t. of the fifty million total wheat exports in 1969/70. *International Wheat Council, Review of the World Grains Situation* 1969/70, Appendix Table II (Nov. 1970).

36. Art. II(6).

37. Art. II(1).

38. Art. II(7).

39. Art. II(2).

40. Art. II(5)(2).

41. According to United States figures, over 25% of the foreign currencies received by the United States under P.L. 480 programs was devoted to U.S. uses. 1969 Annual Report on P.L. 480, Table 13 (1970).

110

42. Article II(5)(b).

43. 80 *Stat.* 1526, 1528 (1966), 7 U.S.C. §§1703(b), 1703(k).

44. 80 *Stat.* 1528 (1966), 7 U.S.C.A. 1703 CK (1970).

45. Art. III.

46. Id. at Art. VIII(2).

47. Dam, *The GATT, Law and International Economic Organization*, Ch. 2. (University of Chicago Press, 1970).

48. General Agreement on Tariffs and Trade, *Basic Instruments and Selected Documents, Third Supplement*, 51 (Geneva, June 1955).

49. Id. at 257.

50. UN/FAO, CCP/CSD/68/44, *Role of Sub-Committee (CSD) in Light of Current and Prospective Developments in Agricultural Surpluses and Food Aid* (26 July 1968).

51. FAO/UN, (CP/CSD/62/27). *Changing Attitudes Towards Agricultural Surpluses*, 13 (12 April 1963).

52. *OECD, Food Aid–Its Role in Economic Development* (1963).

5 The FAO Principles of Surplus Disposal

This chapter will focus upon food aid/commercial trade control systems developed and administered by the Food and Agriculture Organization (FAO) of the United Nations. To fully understand the nature of the FAO's rather unique approach to international economic regulation, it is necessary to understand something of the political structure of the FAO, and its relationship to other relevant international entities.[1] The FAO, first of the permanent specialized agencies of the United Nations to be founded after World War II, came into formal being in October 1945 with the signing of its constitution at a conference held in Quebec. The immediate factor leading to its foundation was the Conference on Food and Agriculture convened at the request of President Franklin D. Roosevelt at Hot Springs, Virginia, in 1943.

The ideas underlying foundation of the new organization came from two sources. The first was the International Institute of Agriculture (IIA) founded in Rome in 1905, whose functions FAO took over soon after its first conference. The IIA was designed to protect farmers against the effects of sudden slumps and gluts, principally through analysis and dissemination of information about market trends and agricultural statistics. Second was the League of Nations, which in the period immediately before World War II had been interested in problems of nutrition and their relationship to health. Both the IIA and the League, however, had been principally concerned with the more advanced countries, whereas in the foundation of the FAO, several of the new and so-called underdeveloped countries took great interest and played an active part.

Since its inception, a number of proposals have been made to broaden the powers of the FAO over various aspects of agricultural problems. The first was for the creation of a World Food Board with almost plenary authority over all aspects of international agricultural problems. The Board would have performed the following functions:

1. To stabilize prices of agricultural commodities on the world markets, including provision of the necessary funds for stabilizing operations.
2. To establish a world food reserve adequate for any emergency that might arise through failure of crops in any part of the world.
3. To provide funds for financing the disposal of surplus agricultural products on special terms to countries where the need for them is most urgent.
4. To cooperate with organizations concerned with international credits for industrial and agricultural development, and with trade and commodity

policy, in order that their common ends might be more quickly and effectively achieved.

For the purpose of stabilizing prices, the World Food Board, operating through its commodity committees, was to be given powers to hold stocks of each of the most important commodities, and to release or add to these stocks with a view to counteracting excessive market fluctuations.

Partly because of United States opposition, which reflected, among others things, awareness of congressional objections to international control of American food reserves, fear of compromising domestic freedom of action on price supports and other matters, dissatisfaction with the financial implications of the proposal, and the growing American interest in the contemplated International Trade Organization, the commission discarded the plan for a World Food Board in favor of a proposed World Food Council. The council was not to be a separate operating agency, but an integral part of the FAO with responsibility for consultation, review, and some types of action between the annual sessions of the FAO Conference. It was to examine current developments in intergovernmental commodity arrangements, particularly as they affected adequacy of the food supply, the use of food reserves, famine relief, and special food programs for the undernourished; to promote consistency and coordination of national and international agricultural commodity policies; to initiate study and investigation of critical agricultural commodity situations; and to advise on such emergency measures as would affect the export and import of supplies required under national programs of agricultural production. A World Food Council along these lines, although a comedown from the World Food Board, still seemed to impair freedom of action in the politically sensitive area of agricultural policy. The third session of the FAO Conference in 1947, therefore, established instead the FAO Council to act as the main FAO organ on world food questions in the intervals between sessions of the conference.[2]

The governing power of the FAO is exercised by the FAO Conference.[3] The Conference is composed of all member nations and associate members with each member nation having one vote.[4] It meets once every two years to determine policies and approve the budget for the next two years.[5] The Conference may submit to member nations conventions and agreements concerning questions relating to food and agriculture.[6] The Conference also may make recommendations to member nations and associate members concerning questions relating to food and agriculture, "for considerations by them with a view to implementation by national action." In addition, the Conference may make recommendations to any international organization regarding any matter pertaining to the purposes of the Organization.[7] General matters are decided by majority vote, while important issues require a two-thirds vote.[8] Budget approval requires only a majority vote, but admitting new members,[9] recommending actions to member nations and associates,[10] and proposing international conventions and agreements, all require a two-thirds vote.[11] The FAO Council consisting of thirty-four member nations with one vote each is elected by the Conference, for three-year terms with one-third of the positions filled each year.[12]

The FAO Constitution provides for the establishment of five Committees to assist the Council in its work. These are the Program Committee, the Finance Committee, the Committee on Commodity Problems, the Committee on Fisheries, and the Committee on Constitutional and Legal Matters.[13] The Committee on Commodity Problems is of most interest to our study of food aid/commercial trade problems. It is composed of thirty-four member nations, elected by the Council for two-year terms. The Council is specifically required to ensure a Committee membership balanced between importing and exporting countries and continuity of experience in the problems encompassed by the Committee.[14] The responsibilities of the Committee on Commodity Problems are to:

a. keep under review commodity problems of an international character affecting production, trade, distribution, consumption and related economic matters;
b. prepare a factual and interpretative survey of the world commodity situation, which may be made available directly to Member Nations;
c. report and submit suggestions to the Council on policy issues arising out of its deliberations. The reports of the Committee and its subsidiary bodies shall be made available to Member Nations for their information.[15]

The Committee may also establish subcommittees, subsidiary working parties or commodity study groups. The FAO Council may include in the membership of such subcommittees or subsidiary working parties member nations and associate members that are not members of the Committee on Commodity Problems. It also may admit to membership of commodity study groups which are neither members nor associate members of the FAO but are members of the United Nations.[16]

Food Aid Control by the FAO

The Food and Agriculture Organization of the United Nations has formulated general substantive standards to curb the most dangerous aspects of large-scale uncontrolled surplus disposal. It also has established an investigative and consultative body—The Consultative Subcommittee on Surplus Disposal (CSD) to administer these standards.[17] The continued requirements of the developing nations for food aid, the spread of agricultural surpluses and surplus disposal efforts to additional developed nations, and the growth of multilateral and international food aid efforts through the Food Aid Convention and the World Food Program strongly imply the necessity for international concern and action. Given the generally successful performance of the FAO control system and the increasing size and importance of the UN/FAO World Food Program, coupled with the consistent weakness of the GATT in agricultural matters and the inherent limitations of commodity agreements as effective control instruments, the FAO seems to be the appropriate place to center world community efforts for the control of food aid/commercial trade conflicts. However, if the FAO is to continue its effectiveness, it must respond to the quite different circumstances now prevailing.

These circumstances relate both to the nature of the surplus situation in agricultural commodities, and to the extent and type of food aid transactions today. Through most of its life, the FAO has been concerned with the disposal of surplus agricultural commodities deriving from fortuitously or accidentally produced excesses of production over domestic demand and/or commercial export, such commodities being disposed of as food aid. For much of this period, food aid programs were bilateral and engaged in by the country which had the largest surpluses in the generally accepted sense (i.e., the United States), or by agricultural exporting countries responding to special requests for emergency assistance. Over the last few years, however, three lines of development can be identified which strongly effect many aspects of world production and trade in agriculture products, including, of course, food aid. First, there is the increasing relevance of food aid contributions derived explicitly or implicitly from the planned production of agricultural commodities for aid purposes. Second, there is the increasing and continuing involvement (primarily multilateral) of countries whose commodity contributions derive from what might be regarded as a normal production pattern. Third, there is the availability of commodities shipped on terms which are neither purely commercial nor purely concessional or the export of which commodities are facilitated by subsidies or other forms of government intervention.

The Legal Order Established By the Principles

The key to understanding the legal order originally sought by the Principles and Guidelines is their focus on "surplus disposal." This is emphasized by the body established to administer the Principles—the Consultative Subcommittee on Surplus Disposal (CSD), which is an adjunct of the FAO Committee on Commodity Problems. Originally, the central concern of the FAO Principles and Guiding Lines was the generation and disposition of the agricultural surpluses of the developed countries. The Principles were established by the major agricultural producers in order to develop and implement policies and programs to avoid the production of surpluses and to minimize the damage to international trade being inflicted by uncontrolled disposal policies of the nations burdened with agricultural commodities which could not be sold through normal commercial channels and on normal commercial terms. Although the concept of making surplus commodities available to developing countries on concessional terms was embodied in the Principles, the prime objective of such transactions was to direct surpluses to consumers who would not ordinarily be able to purchase them on commercial terms, rather than run the risk of dumping these products into normal commercial channels with the concomittant risk of severe reductions in the net proceeds to commercial exporters. Since the promulgation of the Principles closely coincided with the decision of the United States to use surplus agricultural products to assist the economic development of the less developed world, the focus of the Principles was rapidly widened to include active concern with food aid activities substantially motivated by their potential for assisting economic development, including programs employing nonsurplus agricultural products or products deliberately produced for use as food aid.

The end point of this progression was reached when countries deliberately expanded their production in order to provide food aid. Up to 1966, the United States' Food for Peace Program was limited to surplus products.[18] Thereafter, food aid could be provided with any agricultural commodities the Secretary of Agriculture deems to be available for such purpose after considering productive capacity, domestic requirements, farm and consumer price levels, commercial exports and adequate carryover.[19] An important effect of these changes is that potential disruption of commercial trade attributable to concessional transactions must be weighed against the interests of undeveloped beneficiaries of low-priced agricultural commodities.

Despite recent shifts towards increasing concern with food aid rather than surplus disposal, the surplus-oriented origin of the Principles has permanently shaped their formal structure and to some degree their implementation. And although the factors leading to surpluses and effective and useful means of using actual and potential surpluses are interrelated, simultaneous administration of appropriate control machinery for both badly overburdens the relatively tiny group charged with the implementation of the Principles. The result is that though the Subcommittee's jurisdiction over the broader problems of surplus creation is formally recognized, little is done in this regard.[20] The little that is done will not be analyzed in this study which assumes the existence of agricultural commodities available for food aid, and is concerned solely with means to make the food aid available with minimum adverse trade impact.

The three basic concepts established by the Principles and Guidelines also focus upon surplus disposal:

1. The solution to problems of agricultural surplus disposal should be sought, wherever possible, through efforts to increase consumption rather than through measures to restrict supplies.
2. Member governments which have excess stocks of agricultural products should dispose of such products in an orderly manner so as to avoid any undue pressure resulting in sharp falls of prices on world markets, particularly when prices of agricultural products are generally low.

3. Where surpluses are disposed of under special terms, there should be an undertaking from both importing and exporting countries that such arrangements will be made without harmful interference with normal patterns of production and international trade.

A second important shift in the food aid international order is the move away from the nearly exclusive concern with United States practices which marked international food aid control efforts up to the late sixties. The general language and form of the documents not withstanding, the relevant international and bilateral arrangements relevant to surplus disposal and food aid were aimed at the United States.[21] Although other nations have surplus problems, until the last five years none had the desire, or financial capacity to purchase and store for long periods large quantitites of concessional sales on any significant scale. Originally, the giant United States holdings of government-owned agricultural products targeted that country for special concern by other agricultural exporters. Moreover, even when government-owned commodity stockpiles were reduced in response to acreage diversion policies, the foreign aid interests of the United States induced it to use concessional transactions in food and fibers as a development tool through concessional sales. The situation has drastically changed now that other nations (Canada, Australia, the EEC) and international organizations (the World Food Program) are becoming significant food aid donors under programs whereby food aid is given via bulk transfers of commodities through commercial channels. Moreover, the United States has been amenable to international consultation with respect to its food aid practices. Other countries for a variety of reasons—good and bad—are unlikely to be quite as cooperative.

The Noncoercive Nature of the FAO
Control System

The FAO's approach to food aid/commercial trade problems sharply departs from domestic legal models. Such systems are characterized by a set of conduct-directing norms which are interpreted and applied by an authoritative judicial body. The basis of the FAO control system is a set of often vague general substantive standards—the Principles and Guidelines for Surplus Disposal which have been accepted by most of world's agricultural trading nations. As of February 1, 1972, 48 countries have agreed to adhere to the FAO Principles on Surplus Disposal.[22] But in most important respects, these standards are too general to be self-executing. Indeed, they are so vague that they could not be applied by an adjudicative body operating within the usual limits of such institutions.

The only aspect of the system that is binding on the adhering members is the duty to notify and consult with nations likely to be affected by generally enumerated categories of noncommercial agricultural transactions. There is no requirement that the nations proposing these transactions modify their plans in response to criticisms and suggestions of the nations consulted. Therefore, the chief impact of the Principles flows from voluntary acceptance of criticisms raised by other nations of particular programs or transactions in the course of consultations required by the Principles for certain kinds of noncommercial sales.

Along with the Principles, the FAO established the Consultative Subcommittee on Surplus Disposal (CSD) to serve as "a forum for the discussion of matters coming within the purview of the Principles and the Guiding Lines."[23] Membership on the CSD is open to all FAO member nations who wish to take an active part in its activities. As of June 30, 1971, the CSD included 46 member nations (including the European Economic Community), 18 member nations and 7 observer organizations,[24] including some Member and observer Nations which have not subscribed to the Principles.[25]

In line with the FAO's general policy of avoiding the establishment of institutions empowered to make authoritative rules binding on the members, the CSD may only provide a forum for consultations and recommend actions. To underscore the noncoercive nature of CSD activities, the Subcommittee reports to the Committee on Commodity Problems and not to the nations adhering to the Principles. The actual impact of this organizational nicety should not be exaggerated. Since the members of the Committee on Commodity Problems all are government representatives, recommendations of the CSD really are being made to governments.

Technically, the FAO Principles apply to all transactions meeting the definitions of the Principles, whether or not the matter is brought before the Subcommittee. Practically though, the effectiveness of the FAO substantive standards depends upon the extent transactions raising potential conflicts with the Principles and Guidelines are subject to notification and consultation procedures of the CSD. If the transactions lie beyond CSD jurisdiction, there is no forum clearly authorized to hear complaints based upon violations of the Principles. Conceivably, the Principles may have some impact apart from consultations. This could occur if a transaction so blatantly violated the Principles that injured parties could protest through normal diplomatic channels, or some instrumentality of the FAO. The Principles also have direct impact where they have been incorporated into commodity agreements or they have become part of the standard practice of food aid donors. As previously noted, this has occurred to some extent with respect to the International Wheat Agreement and in United States food aid legislation and its administration of food aid programs.

The Ambit of The FAO Principles

Consistent with their original surplus orientation, the FAO Principles and Guiding Lines seek both to prevent the creation of agricultural surpluses and to provide standards for disposal of such surpluses as are produced. Roughly speaking, the Principles focus upon surplus disposal and the Guiding Lines upon surplus accumulation. Consistent with the limits of this study, our interest mainly lies with the Principles.

First, we shall try to identify the class of transactions to which the Principles apply. Actually, this issue has become somewhat moot. To the extent that the real impact of the FAO Principles depends upon the amenability of particular transactions to the jurisdiction of the CSD, it is no longer necessary to attempt to establish the classes of transactions subject to the Principles by textual analysis of its terms and definitions. Recent actions by the FAO Council have clarified the CSD's jurisdiction by establishing a detailed list of transactions subject to CSD procedure. But, as we have noted, the potential effect of the Principles is not completely congruent with the jurisdiction of the CSD. Moreover, the jurisdiction of the CSD is subject to change, and the basis of change is likely to stem from evidence that expanded jurisdiction is necessary in order to fully implement the basic objectives embodied in the Principles.

Under a strict interpretation of its terms, the FAO Principles apply solely to surplus disposal—not food aid. And there has never been any doubt about the relevance of the FAO Principles to both food aid and nonfood aid surplus disposal transactions. At the same time, with the encouragement given to it by the parent Committee on Commodity Problems to regard its terms of reference with flexibility, the CSD has taken jurisdiction over those food aid transfers which are not categorized as having arisen from surpluses, including transfers made possible by production planned to meet food aid needs. The only cases challenging CSD jurisdiction involved certain export sales claimed by certain countries as deriving from the existence of abnormal stocks and assisted by special or concessional terms through government intervention. Other countries declined to accept the thesis that these sales would come within the terms of reference of the CSD, using the argument-amongst others—that such sales involve trade practices and commercial transactions which appropriately would come under the purview of the GATT.

The Guiding Lines attempt to establish some basic precepts for the prevention of surplus accumulations.[26] Since the Consultative Subcommittee believes that these matters are the prime concern of the Committee on Commodity Problems, the Guding Lines have played no direct role in the operative FAO control system. Nevertheless, their substance has in the past influenced discussions on specific disposal problems or policies, and they may now have greater relevance in the context of national programs and policies embracing deliberate production for food aid purposes.

Surplus. The CCP Working Party which structured the CSD deliberately refrained from attempting to define surplus commodities. It appeared to them that the different attitudes taken by governments in identifying their respective commodity stocks as surplus precluded arriving at a generally acceptable and precise definition based upon objective criteria. Similarly, it is difficult to agree upon which export transactions are surplus disposal. Some governments, may officially identify a particular operation as surplus disposal. But what may appear to be a long-term oversupply of a particular commodity in a certain country is not necessarily regarded by that country as a surplus; while a temporary hump in supplies which might be expected to clear itself in the normal course of trade may sometimes attract government assistance in its disposal and become the subject of discussion by member governments. Most attention, therefore, tends to be focused on the surplus disposal programs of those countries which are required by their own legislation to declare a surplus in certain circumstances. Outstanding examples of such programs were those of the United States, where until 1966, sales, gifts and barter transactions made under Public Law 480, or agricultural supplies provided under mutual security aid, are restricted to those commodities declared by the Secretary of Agriculture to be in surplus.

In practice, it has not been proven necessary to find a universally acceptable definition of surplus. The implementation of the FAO Principles through the CSD, has been focused upon the terms of disposal of food commodities rather than upon the nature of the supply situation. That is, the concern has been with how agricultural products are sold or disposed of—not with the origin of the supplies. In its latest review of its operations, the CSD reaffirmed its early conclusions that further definition of surplus was unnecessary.[27]

Surplus Disposal. Surplus disposal also was left undefined by the Principles. But in 1958, the CSD found that the lack of a formal definition impeded its work since in practice it could not reach a working concept of surplus disposal based on common sense factors. Therefore, it had no clear indication of the type of transaction which can be regarded as a surplus disposal operation and which should therefore fall within its terms of reference. Conceivably, some governments engaging in special export transactions may have been unclear as to where the limits of the Subcommittee's work were drawn, and therefore were in doubt as to the types of disposal matters that should be brought before the Subcommittee. Some countries believed that certain important transactions were not being handled in accordance with the Principles. Thus, Resolution No. 6/57 adopted at the Ninth Session of the FAO Conference, expressed the concern that transactions were being made with commodities which, though not set aside as surplus stocks, have become surplus in the originating countries as the result of national support policies, and are then disposed of in international markets, often on a subsidized basis, thereby displacing commercial trade and depressing price levels.

To remedy this situation, in 1959 the FAO adopted the following definition of surplus disposal to guide the CSD in determining which transactions fall within its province.

Surplus disposal of an agricultural commodity in international trade is an export operation (other than a sale covered by an international commodity agreement) arising from the existence or expectation of abnormal stocks, and made possible by the grant of special or concessional terms through government intervention.[28]

However, it is understood that government payments designed to facilitate international sales do not necessarily convert exports into surplus disposals.[29] This exception is designed to exclude domestic agricultural price support policies followed by many of the world's leading agricultural producers, including the United States and the European Economic Community, which tend to raise the domestic price of certain products above the world level, and therefore sometimes require subsidies to bring the export price down to the world market level.[30] Thus, when the CCP adopted the expanded definition of surplus disposal at its 30th session in 1958, it attempted to clarify its position through the following observation

In the practical interpretation of the definition of surplus disposal . . . , the committee understood that an export operation should not be considered a surplus disposal merely because there was an element of subsidy to bridge the gap between the domestic and export price, but because there was the existence of expectation of abnormal stocks and because harmful interference with normal patterns of trade might be caused as a consequence of the terms granted and/or the quantities and rates of movement of commodities concerned . . .[31]

Further protection was given exporters by the understanding that the initiative for bringing matters to the CSD lay with the exporter, rather than possibly injured third parties.

For the same reasons, the crucial concept of concessional sales also was left largely undefined. Even though the control of concessional sales is the Principles' prime objective and the bulk of the Principles and Guidelines are devoted to various aspects of concessional sales, the closest either document comes to a definition is a footnoted remark explaining that "(c) concessions in terms may relate to prices or to other conditions of sale or payment."[32] However, the lack of definition of concessional sales is no longer a problem. As shall appear in the subsequent discussion of the jurisdiction of the CSD, this problem has been finessed by establishing categories of transactions subject to the FAO-imposed standards and procedures, based upon objective factors. In fact, the Principles' sole concern is with concessional transactions. On the one hand, such transactions are accepted and encouraged as the optimum strategy to cope with the technologically advanced world's proclivity to create more agricultural commodities that can be sold at prices affording a politically acceptable income to the producers. On the other, concessional sales are subjected to a complex though general set of restrictions and limitations with regard to the destination and form of such transactions.

Despite the exclusive textual surplus disposal orientation of the Principles, they have been applied to nonsurplus food aid transactions. Therefore, when the United States broadened its Food for Peace activities to permit the use of nonsurplus products, the CSD continued to treat these transactions as falling within CSD jurisdiction.[33] Concern with nonsurplus food aid was one of the principle stimulants to the recent reexamination and reformulation of the FAO's role and operations in food aid matters. The net effect is that the CSD has applied the Principles to any transaction involving agricultural commodities that in form and intent are designed to assist a particular developing country and that threaten commercial markets. Long-term export subsidy programs directly linked to domestic agricultural policies and not designed to yield short-run benefits on an *ad hoc* basis are excluded. Moreover, the CSD is barred from considering the domestic agricultural policies which may breed surpluses. These fall within the jurisdiction of the CSD's parent, the Committee on Commodity Problems. Thus, surplus disposal activities not featuring significant food aid possibilities are left to GATT and the FAO Committee on Commodity Programs, and nonsurplus food aid is included within CSD jurisdiction if there is a substantial possibility of market disruption. That is, the FAO control system focuses upon how agricultural products are sold or disposed of and the potential dangers of such transactions to commercial markets—not with how or why the supplies arose, in the first instance.

The Impact of FAO Principles on Food Aid/Commercial Trade Problems

The Principles of Surplus Disposal include "General Principles" which relate to surplus disposal problems and "Principles Governing Sales on Concessional Terms." The latter are of direct relevance to our study. They will be examined in terms of the goals they seek to achieve rather than in sequential order.

Although nowhere explicitly stated in so many words, one crucial result of the substantive and jurisdictional matrix formed by the Principles of Surplus Disposal (including the scope of CSD jurisdiction) and the International Wheat Agreement is to divide international trade in agricultural commodities into two spheres—the developed and underdeveloped world—each with its own set of ground rules. Concessional sales, whether from surplus stocks or not, are to be limited to the underdeveloped world. Here, the high elasticity of demand for food affords maximum opportunity for increased consumption, thereby minimizing the danger of displacing commercial sales. Transactions with the developed world, with its low elasticity of demand for agricultural products, are to be conducted solely on commercial terms. Moreover, the Principles recognize that the relative benefit of concessional sales to underdeveloped recipients may justify some possible damage to the commercial exports of the better developed exporting countries. This does not preclude the possibility of commercial sales to the underdeveloped world. Indeed, both the United States' Food for Peace program and those of countries newly entering the field emphasize preservation if not expansion of such transactions in the underdeveloped areas. With respect to the United States, concern with commercial sales to food aid recipients is built into the enabling legislation as well as the individual sales agreements.[34]

Legitimizing Concessional Sales

The acceptance of concessional sales to the underdeveloped world as the prime method of surplus control is perhaps the most important feature of the FAO Principles. The first General Principle holds that increased consumption rather than supply restriction is the preferred solution to surplus problems. And, according to the FAO Committee on Commodity Problems, the best prospects for moving substantial amounts of surplus agricultural commodities into additional consumption are sales on concessional terms, or grants in aid of development, to the world's poor nations.[35] This proposition would seem consistent with the widely held theory that consumers at low-income levels exhibit a high income and price elasticity of demand for food, particularly the demand for the high-starch, low-protein type of products currently in world surplus.[36] That is, for those consumers with low incomes, either a decrease in price or an increase in income will result in significant increases in their demand for food, while for those higher on the income scale, these same events will result in little increase in the overall demand for food. Actually, for low-value products like wheat, increases of available income to people above the poverty line usually will decrease consumption through substitution of more expensive foods like meat, fruit and vegetables.[37]

The enthronement of concessional transfers of surplus agricultural products to underdeveloped countries as the preferred solution to agricultural overproduction must be viewed as a compromise between more drastic and perhaps more effective approaches. Supply control or reduction of domestic subsidies would be a more forthright and effective solution. But no consensus could be achieved in favor of this proposition. Undoubtedly, most of the world's major agricultural producers would have preferred the United States to continue its policy of storing all domestic surpluses, thereby permitting other nations to follow their own expansionist agricultural policies without fear of significant disruption of international markets. But the United States simply was unwilling indefinitely to sit on its surplus mountains.[38] Thus, authorizing and encouraging the transfer of surplus products to the poor nations, nations unlikely to provide significant commercial markets, while barring all cut-rate sales to the traditional cash markets in the developed countries, seemed the best attainable compromise. And, as the requirements for food in the poor nations accelerated, this policy, originally designed to protect the economic interests of the agricultural exporting nations, acquired a new, enhanced value as an effective means to relieve international distress, and ultimately as a potential tool for economic development by the havenots. Over the past decade, the United States and certain other countries have succeeded in limiting agricultural production. But intensive efforts to establish international limitations on domestic agricultural subsidies have failed. The most recent attempt centered around the International Grains Arrangement in 1967.[39]

Additionality and Interference with
Normal Trade Patterns

To ensure that concessional transactions are barred from traditional commercial export markets, the third General Principle requires that in conducting surplus transactions, both the importing and exporting countries undertake that "such arrangements will be made without harmful interference with normal patterns of production and international trade."[40] And harmful interference will be minimized if concessional sales and gifts are made to such places and through such means that will maximize the possibilities of absorbing the commodities through additional consumption;[41] that is, consumption which would not have taken place in the absence of concessional sales.[42] This phenomenon is generally termed "additionality." The preferred method for achieving additionality is alleged to be concessional sales to developing countries which do not harmfully interfere with normal patterns of production and international trade. The theory is that if properly managed, concessional food sales will lead to economic development, which will, *inter alia*, result in increased purchasing power to be used, in part, to buy more food.[43] Obviously, this approach legitimizes current United States strategy to use food aid as a development tool. Not surprisingly, since it is a creature of the FAO, the World Food Program relies on the same theory to justify its activities.[44]

But, as the FAO itself recognized, it may not be possible to always ensure that the concessional sales will result in additional consumption and thereby not upset commercial sales. Indeed, in most cases, it may not be desirable, since an important purpose of any sizeable food aid transaction is to conserve a developing country's scarce foreign exchange reserves by relieving it of the burden of purchasing its food imports on normal commercial terms. Additionality may be an appropriate goal for small projects in which food is being used to accomplish other development purposes—such as using food to pay workers and building an irrigation system. But it is entirely inappropriate for the large program-type sales which typify the United States Food for Peace program. Nevertheless, the FAO believes it valuable as "a continuing reminder to surplus exporting and recipient countries of their joint responsibilities to avoid harm to the normal patterns of trade and production."[45] Perhaps it would be more realistic to interpret General

Principle 3 to preclude unnecessary interference with normal patterns of production and international trade.

Food Aid and Economic Development. A basic assumption of the FAO Principles is that food aid will accelerate the recipient's economic development, which will in turn, increase the effective demand for commercial food imports. Unfortunately, the impact of food aid on the recipients' overall and agricultural development is among the most controversial aspects of food aid. Even if concessional sales did retard the recipient's economic development, such sales, on balance, might still be the best way of disposing of agricultural surpluses; best, that is, from the viewpoint of agricultural exporting nations. But clearly, no world body such as the FAO could endorse openly a procedure found harmful to its poorer members.

But the long controversy over the effect of food aid upon the recipient's economic development seems to be over—at least as far as the major international development institutions are concerned. While the dangers of uncontrolled food aid are recognized, it is now accepted that well-conceived and well-managed food aid programs can aid development. And with the increasing international impoverishment—economic, political and moral—of the United States, development-minded institutions can no longer afford the luxury of rejecting any available aid form.[46]

Normal Patterns of Production and Trade

But what are normal patterns of production and trade? And what constitutes harmful rather than nonharmful interference therewith? The FAO, it seems, concluded that it could not devise a satisfactory definition of these terms. That is, it did not think it could provide definitions sufficiently precise to form the basis of legally enforceable standards of conduct. Definitions of normal trade patterns based solely on historical base periods were rejected as inconsistent with the purposes of the Principles. They did not allow for the change and growth that forms a vital part of international trade. Moreover, applying rates of change based on past performance was impractical because of the volatility characterizing trade in several of the key commodities.[47] Harmful interference also is an imprecise, value-laden characterization. Clearly, unless surplus products sold on concessional terms were used to meet demands that either would not have existed, or if existing, would not have been met with commercial imports, some interference with trade patterns must result from any gift or concessional sale.[48]

The persistence and acceleration of government-sponsored export programs since 1954 exacerbate the problem by making it increasingly difficult to identify normal trade patterns, that is, the pattern that would appear absent the distorting efforts of massive government interference. In the United States, and the

EEC for example, the government may assist in the export of all price-supported commodities. Examples in some other countries would indicate a similar situation. There is also the distortion to trade patterns occasioned by import quotas, special exchange rates, multiple pricing, currency allotment or preference systems, local currency settlements and other devices which are usually a concomitant of price support and surplus disposal systems. Thus, while it is becoming increasingly difficult to determine normal trade in some agricultural products, it is equally difficult to assess the extent to which food aid, *per se*, interferes with normal patterns of production and trade.

A Balancing Approach to Additionality

Since perfect additionality could not be attained and no alternate single standard was available, the FAO opted for a balancing technique to be applied on a case-by-case basis. Under this formulation, a number of factors are to be considered within general guidelines purportedly designed to provide some insight into the method of performing the required juggling act. In this regime, additionality would be the preeminent but not exclusive touchstone.[49] To the extent that sales of the commodities supplied on special terms may constitute some danger of displacement of commercial sales of identical or related commodities, that danger is to be assessed in light of "all the relevant factors," particularly the following ones.

a. the exporter's share in the region's imports of the commodity concerned during a representative base period, due allowance being made for factors which lessen the significance of such historical comparisons;
b. whether the exports on special terms are likely to form so small (or large) a share of the region's imports of the commodity that the effect of special terms on such trade is likely to be of minor (or major) significance;
c. the degree of importance of trade in the commodity to the economy of the exporter concerned, to the economies of competing exporters of the commodity concerned and of closely related commodities and to the importing region's economy;
d. the character and extent of the concession offered and their probable effect on (i) the region's usual total imports of the commodity concerned and related commodities, (ii) the exporters' share of the region's imports of the commodity concerned, and (iii) the interference with implementation of treaties or agreements which deal with world trade in these commodities;
e. the degree to which commercial market prices are, or are likely to be, affected in the importing region and in world trade;
f. the degree, if any, to which effects of the kind mentioned under (d) and (e) above are likley to affect the stability, or desirable expansion, of production and trade of the commodity concerned and of closely related commodities in both exporting and importing countries.[50]

Clearly, all these factors are pertinent to a determination of the degree of harmful interference with normal trade or production patterns attributable to any particular gift or concessional sale. Equally clearly, no precise standards have been provided by which participants and interested parties may definitiely judge all such transactions—either a *priori* or *post hoc*.

The CSD, in its 1958 review of the adequacy of the Principles and Guiding Lines, attempted to remedy this. The Subcommittee recommended that in considering that harmful interference with normal patterns of trade might be caused by such export operations, the nature of the terms and/or the quantities and rates of movement of the commodities should be regarded as of primary importance.[51] This appears to be an attempt by the Subcommittee to narrow the considerations to be used in evaluating individual transactions to those most susceptible to quantification and which ultimately can be developed into consistent conduct norms. The Subcommittee's judgment seems sound. The terms concessional transactions and the quantities of commodities involved certainly are crucial issues. Moreover, it should be possible to develop norms in these areas which can serve as effective guides to conduct and form the basis for principled decisions in individual cases. Of course, by focusing upon but one of the six categories of considerations established in the Principles, the Subcommittee may unduly narrow the issues. But if this occurs, the blame should not fall upon those who must administer the Principles. The problem stems from the inability of the FAO decision-makers to reach agreement on the complex and sensitive issues implicit in reaching workable decisions in the agricultural surplus and food aid/commercial trade areas.

Although the FAO Principles specify a wide variety of criteria that are relevant to determining the degree of disruption that will be accepted in food aid transactions, in practice, the two most important aspects are the world trade situation with respect to the commodities concerned, and the economic and financial situation of the recipient. However, Principle 4 (2)(c) authorizes consideration of the degree of importance of trade in the commodity to the economy of the exporter. In one of the few instances where this issue has been critical, the FAO has indicated that low prices for an important export item will not be deemed sufficient justification for a transaction that disrupts normal trade patterns. New Zealand, which usually supplies most of Peru's dairy products, agreed to sell Peru dairy products on concessional terms without including the protections for the trade of third countries usually required for such transactions. In response to FAO criticisms, New Zealand justified its behavior on the basis of the generally depressed world dairy market and its great dependence upon dairy exports. Although it was conceded that the dairy situation was indeed difficult, the concept that market stringencies justified the failure to take the usual steps required to protect normal trade patterns was vigorously rejected. Certainly, this position is correct. The very existence of food aid is largely the result of difficult agricultural trade markets. To accept this as a reason for departing from the FAO Principles undercuts the entire purpose of the FAO control scheme, which is designed to establish methods to benefit developing countries while protecting third country exporters' markets; markets which are assumed to exhibit serious weaknesses.

The FAO has tried to strengthen the concept of noninterference with normal trade patterns by requiring the insertion of appropriate language in concessional sale agreements. In its review of its operations in 1958, the Committee on Surplus Disposal recommended that all countries include in their written agreements covering food aid transactions, a specific provision that it was the intention of the parties that the transaction would not interfere with normal patterns of production and trade of other FAO member countries subscribing to the Principles. And in cases where no such provision can be made because the advantages of the transaction to the recipient are deemed to outweigh other considerations, the parties would be required to bring their reasons for excluding the provision to the Subcommittee. The Subcommittee believed that it would stand as a constant reminder of the obligations undertaken by the adherents to the FAO Principles.[52]

It is difficult to see that much would be gained through this means. At least there is little to be gained now. Countries who would be bound by this regulation would in any case be obliged to consult with other member nations and the Committee on Surplus Disposal. And transactions which seemed to unduly interfere with commercial trade patterns would have to be justified. Those nations not generally disposed to cooperate with the CSD are not likely to be any more willing to comply with this kind of requirement. Perhaps when it was first suggested, in 1958, the Subcommittee was less sure of its jurisdiction and this was seen as a way of effectively clarifying it. As we shall see in subsequent chapters, the United States does regularly include language with respect to impact on normal trade patterns. Also, as previously noted, the EEC has included such provisions in its food aid agreements.

Related Commodities

The Principles apply to possible displacement of identical or *related* (emphasis added) commodities.[53] In forwarding its recommendations to the FAO Conference, the Committee on Commodity Problem Working Committee which drafted the Principles, interpreted related commodities as covering those commodities likely to be substituted for the food aid commodity. These would need to be judged on the merits of each case, with special reference to established trade patterns of the countries concerned. The term is used in the context of the danger that concessional supplies would displace commercial imports of identical or related commodities (Principle 4(2)); or where the intended beneficiary is cautioned to prevent the export of supplies of the same or related commodities which might be freed as a result of the country's imports on special terms (Principle 7(2)). Identification of related commodities which may be affected by concessional sales often involves very complex judgments based upon relevant economic and technical factors in each case. The treatment of the most important commodity relationships will be discussed in greater detail as part of an analysis of the restrictions imposed by food aid donors in their food aid agreements.[54] Generally speaking, the CCP Working Committee's approach to the problem is the only feasible one, since it is impossible to prescribe in advance rules for deciding how to treat intercommodity relationships for every potential food aid transaction. Actually, the Subcommittee has done relatively little with this problem, leaving it to be handled by exporting countries case by case.

Prohibited Transactions

In some cases, the Principles do attempt to supply clear answers with respect to certain potential uses of food aid. Thus, not permitted are concessional sales designed to generate additional foreign exchange for the recipient through direct or indirect subsidization of related agricultural exports. Conceivably, a large surplus holder like the United States which is precluded by its size and position from disposing of surpluses through reducing prices, could, in effect, use an underdeveloped country as its sales agent for surplus products. Initially, the United States would sell the commodity to an underdeveloped country on terms sufficiently favorable to permit resale to third countries at competitive or below competitive prices but which still afford the "retailer" a good profit. These profits could then be used for economic development like any other form of foreign aid. But, the Principles direct the intended beneficiary country to make every effort to prevent the resales or transshipments of the same or similar products.[55] Moreover, the recipient is enjoined to prevent exports "of supplies of the same or related commodities" which might be freed for sale abroad as a result of the country's imports on special terms.[56] Under these circumstances, a country may not directly or indirectly sell to others the food it receives on concessional terms.

Although it may seem incontrovertible that these restrictions are dictated by the concept of additionality, a more imaginative analysis of the underlying relevant concepts might justify under certain circumstances, exports of products related to concessional sale products. Thus, it may be argued that the additional consumption need not necessarily occur in the recipient country. That is, if direct or indirect transshipment to a third country results in a net increase in total consumption of the product involved without adverse effects on the price structure, the ends of additionality will be served. In practice, direct transshipments are universally banned. But exports of commodities "freed" for sale abroad by imports at concessional rates are sometimes permitted. Detailed statement and critique of the response of the United States to this problem is discussed in considerable detail in Chapter 9.

The Relationship of the Principles
to Developing Countries

Any acceptable international system for the control of food aid/commercial trade relationships must protect the access of developing countries to food aid necessary for their well-being and economic growth. Given the FAO's general commitment to assisting the world's poor, we should reasonably expect that any control system it devises and administers would be scrupulous in this regard. As we shall see, both the Principles and Guidelines and the practices of the CSD show sensitivity to these aspects of food aid. But it also must be recognized that the initial impetus and driving force behind FAO activities in this sphere has been provided by developed Western agricultural exporters.[57] This is evidenced by the establishment of the CSD as a Subcommittee of the Committee on Commodity Problems (CCP). The CCP is recognized as the voice of the major agricultural exporting nations. Although the CCP is concerned with tropical, as well as temperate products, food aid and surplus disposal problems exclusively are concerned with temperate products since tropical exporters are almost entirely small, poor nations without the resources to engage in food aid or other surplus disposal actions. Moreover, the language of the Principles is strongly oriented towards export problems—indeed, food aid is nowhere explicitly mentioned. To some extent, the situation is complicated by the fact that some developing countries are also major agricultural exporters of temperate products. Argentina, Thailand and Burma are traditional exporters and Taiwan and Korea are beginning to join them.

Up to now, except for those developing countries which export products likely to be included in food aid transactions, the prime interest of the developing countries in the FAO control system is to ensure that efforts to protect commercial sales do not reduce the size of or complicate the receipt of food aid. However, developing countries which do export food aid affected commodities are among the most anxious to protect commercial trade from damage by food aid. Argentina, Thailand, Burma, Mexico and Peru fit this category. Such countries lack the resources to assist their exports through food aid or heavy export subsidies and are therefore most anxious to protect their exports from the food aid transactions of their wealthier competitors. Protection of the domestic agricultural markets of food and recipients also is cited as a necessary objective of international controls.

This aspect of the FAO's approach to food aid/commercial trade problems is well-illustrated by the problems involved in interpreting Article 5 of the Principles. Instinctively, one would assume that in evaluating each food aid transaction, the needs of and benefits to the recipient would be balanced against both the absolute level of potential damage to third parties and the ability of the affected nations to bear such injury. Although this reading can, and should be extracted from the general language and purport of the Principles, the specific language seems unduly oriented towards the protection rather than benefit side of the equation. Actually, this is not surprising considering that the Principles largely are the work of and reflect the views of the trade-directed rather than aid-oriented Committee on Commodity Problems. Despite this bias, the Principles contain sufficient explicit provisions which, combined with the general commitment of the FAO to economic development, permit interpretations giving due regard to the developmental interests of food aid recipients.[58] Persuasive evidence of the weight to be given to the benefits obtained by food aid recipients is supplied by a recent report on multilateral food aid rendered by the Director General of the Food and Agriculture Organization to that agency's Committee on Commodity Problems.[59]

Granted, the language and form of the Principles do not easily yield this interpretation and other less enlightened positions might be possible. However, the policy preferred reading is at least as good as any alternative, and certainly, it is the most consistent with current FAO and world community opinion. Besides, as shall appear subsequently, the United States in its administration of Food for Peace, does seem to take very seriously the relative economic position of potentially affected developing third countries.

Emergency Relief. The Principles also include some innocuous considerations pertaining to concessional sales or grants for relief purposes. In such cases, account is to be taken of the "character, extent, and urgency" of the emergency, "the effect of the emergency on the stricken country's ability to pay," and "the volume of relief and the character and extent of the concessions offered, and their probable effect on the total commercial imports of the stricken country and on trade of competing exporters."[60] Relief programs have not been considered a serious problem, and even if they were, it would be very difficult to oppose them solely because they might harm commercial interests. In fact, the CSD did examine the impact of these programs in 1959 and again in 1968. In both cases, it concluded that these transactions had little effect on commercial trade, though in "isolated instances," the food found its way into commercial channels. Under the revised procedures established in 1970, these transactions are to be reported to the CSD *ex post facto.*

Notes

1. A current set of the fundamental documents governing the Food and Agricultural Organization are printed by the FAO in *Basic Texts of the Food and Agriculture Organization of the United Nations* (FAO 1970).

2. Asher, et al., *The United Nations and Promotion of the General Welfare*, 220-32, Brookings Institution, 1957.

3. FAO Constitution, Art. IV.

4. Id., Art. III. (1).

5. Id., Art. III. (6).

6. Id., Art. XIV. (1), (2).

7. Id., Art. IV.

8. Id., Art. III. (8).

9. Id., Art. III. (2).

10. Id., Art. IV. (3).

11. Id., Art. XIV. (1).

12. FAO Constitution, Art. V (1), General Rules of the Organization, Rule XXII (1).

13. FAO Constitution, Art. V (6).

14. General Rules of the Organization, Rule XXIX (1).

15. Id. at Rule XXIX (6).

16. Id. at Rule XXIX (9).

17. The Principles of Surplus Disposal and the Consultative Sub-Committee on Surplus Disposal were the ultimate outgrowth of a Resolution of the Seventh Conference of the FAO (November-December 1953), directing the Committee on Commodity Problems of the FAO to prepare appropriate procedures for handling surplus commodity transaction. FAO, Resolution No: 14 (53), *Disposal of Agricultural Surpluses, Principles Recommended by FAO*, 10-11 (1963) (hereinafter cited as *FAO Principles*). The *Principles* were reviewed and reaffirmed in 1959. Resolution No. 11159, id. at 19-22.

18. 73 *Stat.* 610 (1954).

19. 80 *Stat.* 1535 (1966), 7 U.S.C.A. § 1731 (1970).

20. For an excellent discussion of the original development of the FAO Principles, see FAO/UN, CCP/CSD/58/7, *Report on Consultative Machinery and Procedures* (21 April 1958) and FAO/UN, CCP/CSD/59/23, *Report on The Operation and Adequacy of The FAO Principles of Surplus Disposal and Guiding Lines* (22 May 1959).

21. It has been asserted by certain government officials that neither the Principles of Surplus Disposal nor the relevant provisions of the International Wheat Agreements control what the United States does in its Title I agreements. Memorandum from Howard Gabbert of the Food for Peace Division of the Agency for International Development, dated Oct. 31, 1969 (available in author's files). This clearly is untrue with respect to the International, and only accurate with respect to the FAO Principles if "control" means binding legal obligation. But as shall appear in the text, the FAO Principles function as an effective restraint despite their "nonbinding" nature.

22. The adhering nations are:

Argentina	Germany, Fed. Rep. of	Khmer "Republic"	Panama
Australia	Ghana	Laos	South Africa

Austria	Greece	Lebanon	Spain
Belgium	Guinea	Libya	Sweden
Brazil	India	Malaysia	Switzerland
Burma	Indonesia	Mexico	Thailand
Canada	Iran	Netherlands	Tunisia
Ceylon	Ireland	New Zealand	Turkey
Costa Rica	Israel	Nicaragua	United Kingdom
Denmark	Italy	Nigeria	United States
Finland	Japan	Norway	Uruguay
France	Jordan	Pakistan	Yugoslavia

23. UN/FAO, *Disposal of Agricultural Surpluses—Principles Recommended by FAO*, 17 (reprinted 1967) (hereinafter, FAO Principles).

24. *The CSD has the following membership: Member Countries (46)*

Argentina	Ghana	New Zealand
Australia	Greece	Nigeria
Austria	Guatemala	Pakistan
Belgium	India	Panama
Bolivia	Indonesia	Paraguay
Brazil	Iraq	Peru
Burma	Ireland	Spain
Canada	Israel	Sweden
Ceylon	Italy	Switzerland
Costa Rica	Jamaica	Thailand
Cuba	Japan	Turkey
Denmark	Jordan	United Arab Republic
Ecuador	Lebanon	United Kingdom
France	Malawi	United States
Germany, Fed.	Mexico	Uruguay
Rep. of	The Netherlands	

European Economic Community

Observer Countries (18)

Chile	Iran	Philippines
Colombia	Korea	Portugal
Dominican Republic	Laos	Saudi Arabia
El Salvador	Libya	Tunisia
Finland	Malta	Viet-Nam
Honduras	Norway	Yugoslavia

International Organizations

International Bank for Reconstruction and Development
International Cotton Advisory Committee
International Federation of Agricultural Producers

Internation Monetary Fund
Organization for Economic Cooperation and Development
Organization of American States
United Nations–Economic Commission for Latin America

25. Members of the CSD which haven't subscribed to the FAO Principles include Ecuador, Iraq, Jamaica, Malawi, Paraguay, Peru, the Philippines, and the United Arab Nations. Observer nations in the same category include Chile, Colombia, Dominican Republic, El Salvador, Guatemala, Honduras, Korea, Malta, Portugal, Saudi Arabia, and South Viet-Nam.

26. *FAO Principles* 8.

27. FAO/UN, CCP/CSD/68/44, *Role of Sub-Committee CSD in Light of Current and Prospective Developments in Agricultural Surpluses and Food Aid* 22 (28 July 1968) (hereinafter, Role of CSD).

28. *FAO Principles* 19 (1963).

29. Id. at 20.

30. *Report of the National Committee on Food and Fibre for the Future* at 71-80 (1967): *Report of the President's Science Advisory Committee, The World Food Problem*, 142-43, 148-56 (1967).

31. Id. at 20.

32. Id. at 15.

33. UN/FAO, CCP/CSD/68/44, *Role of CSD, 20*.

34. Commercial sales to developing countries is discussed in Chapter 3.

35. Id. at 15-16; *Organization of Economic and Cooperative Development, Food Aid–Its Role in Economic Development 49* (1963).

36. USDA/FAS, *Report No. 35, World Food Situation* 2-4 (1967); Brown, *The World Food Population Problem: An Overview*, collected in Iowa State University Center for Agricultural and Economic Development, *Alternatives for Balancing World Food Population Needs*, Ch. 1 (1967).

37. Heady, *Agricultural Problems and Policies of Developed Countries* 10-12 (1966).

38. Hamilton & Drummond, *Wheat Surpluses and Their Impact on Canadian-United States Relations*, Ch. IV (1959). *Hearings on Commodity Inventories of the Commodity Credit Corporation before the Senate Committee on Agriculture and Forestry*, 83rd Cong., 1st sess., 65 (1953); *Hearings on Report of Sec. of Agriculture Benson on Policies and Programme of the Department of Agriculture before Senate Committee on Agriculture and Forestry*, 83rd Cong., 1st sess., 8 (1953), H.R. Rep. No. 1776, *Agricultural Trade Development and Assistance Act of 1954*, 83rd Cong., 2d sess., 10 (1954).

39. FAO, 1967 *Commodity Review* 196-97 (1967); Dam, *The European Common Market in Agriculture*, 67 Col. L. Rev. 209, 259-60 (1967).

40. *FAO Principles*, at 3.

41. Id. at 3, 5, 9, 15.

42. Id. at 3-4.

43. *FAO Principles* Pt. 1 (1), 6(1) (a).

44. *FAO, Report on the World Food Program by the Executive Director*, 10 (1965).

45. FAO/UN, CCP/CSD/59/23, *Report on the Operation and Adequacy of the FAO Principles of Surplus Disposal and Guiding Lines* 14-15 (22 May 1959).

46. See Chapter 3, note 6.

47. *FAO Principles*, at 12-13.

48. Id. at 4-5.

49. Id. at 3-5, 12-14.

50. Id. at 4-5.

51. Id. at 19-22.

52. FAO/UN, CCP/CSD/88/7. *Report on Consultative Machinery and Procedures 6-7, 10* (21 April 1958).

53. *FAO Principles*, Principle 4 (2) at 4.

54. See Chapter 9.

55. *FAO Principles*, Pt. I (1) 7 (1) at 6.

56. Id. at Pt. I, 7 (2) at 6.

57. Resolution 14 (53), Seventh Session of 1953 Conference of the FAO Principles, as reprinted in *FAO Principles* at 9-11.

58. The value of food aid to recipient countries is implicitly recognized in paragraphs 5 and 6 (B) of the Principles. Paragraph 5 requires that "in weighing the advantages to countries benefiting from special disposal measures against the possible harm done to other countries, account must be taken of the relationship of possible sacrifices to the economic capacity of the countries concerned, and in particular of the effects of such sacrifices on their rates of development. *FAO Principles*, at 14. Standing alone, the admonition to consider the impact of concessional sales on the economic development of affected third countries is somewhat confusing. On one level, the language seems solely oriented towards the protection of developing exporting countries such as Argentina, Thailand, Burma, and the United Arab Republic, without regard to the identity and needs of potential recipients. Furthermore, it is not quite clear if the "countries benefiting from special disposal measures" refers solely to the developing recipients, or includes the countries making the sales or gifts as well. But paragraph 6 (1) (b) of the Principles, dealing with sales on concessional terms or grants in aid of development, clearly recognizes the interests of recipient countries. According to this provision, the dangers of damage to commercial sales that might result from the export of the commodities supplied on special terms in aid of development programs must be weighed against the advantages resulting from such programs to the receiving country and to the world at large. *FAO Principles*, at 5. Thus, balancing of benefits and costs is made a vital part of the decision-making process. And read together with the prior language, we may detect an intention to place the burden on those best able to bear it. Thus, benefits to recipients are to be compared with the harm to commercial interests, but the relative eco-

nomic position of the affected parties plays an important role in the final weighing.

59. FAO/CCP 67/13, *Director General's Progress Report to CCP on the Inter-Agency Study of Multilateral Food Aid* Paras. 128, 130 (4 Oct. 1967).

60. *FAO Principles*, at 6.

The Consultative Subcommittee on Surplus Disposal

In large measure, the real import of the FAO Principles only may be determined through examination of the functioning of the body specifically created to implement them—the Consultative Subcommittee on Surplus Disposal (CSD). Of course, the same may be said about any set of conduct-directing norms, viz., the law system they create only has meaning in terms of the way they are applied. But in the case of the FAO Principles, the implementation process is peculiarly crucial. The Principles are deliberately vague and general, and are but infrequently modified. More importantly, the FAO control system is based upon the concept of the consultation rather than upon legally binding rulings or adjudications. And the CSD is the focus of these consultations.

Operation of the CSD

This chapter will study the operational structure of the CSD. The emphasis here will be upon the procedures employed by the Subcommittee rather than upon the substantive conduct norms that were evolved from CSD operations. The broader import of the FAO Principles have been discussed in Chapter 5. Major substantive problems confronting the relationships between food aid and commercial trade and the means being used and considered to handle them will be taken up in Part III. Given the nonprescriptive nature of the FAO control system, substantive and procedural matters cannot easily be separated. Usually, the crucial question is whether a transaction falls within CSD jurisdiction and is thereby subject to the consultative procedures applicable to transactions within the cognizance of the CSD. However, I believe a rough division between substance and procedure is necessary for purposes of clear exposition of these very complex matters.

History of CSD Functioning

The history of the CSD is a progression from rudimentary efforts to cope with the most egregious aspects of the United States surplus disposal activities to far more sophisticated modalities for confronting the changed circumstances of today. Since its inception, the CSD has been gradually developing procedures and substantive norms, initially, in response to United States practices and most recently to deal with the implications for food aid and agricultural trade of the drying up of conventional foreign aid and the spread of agricultural surpluses to developed countries other than the United States. These events have instigated a concommitant development by new nations of substantial bilateral food aid programs and their participation in multilateral (Food Aid Convention) and international food aid programming (World Food Program). The history of the CSD also is marked by a gradual shift from largely passive and rudimentary control techniques to active investigation of important aspects of food aid/commercial trade problems and increased insistence on adherence to the basic objectives of the Principles and Guidelines. Now, the CSD and the international approach to food aid problems its activities represent has reached a watershed. The changes in the jurisdictional and substantive structure of the CSD adopted by the FAO at its Fifty-third (1970) and Fifty-fifth Sessions (1971) could well be the basis for the FAO, through the medium of the CSD, moving towards a central and influential role in shaping food aid policies over the next decade.

The work of the CSD may be roughly divided into three phases. The first phase of the Committee's activities, 1954-1957, commenced with the adoption of the FAO Principles and Guidelines, and the establishment of the CSD as the instrument for their implementation. the CSD was given the following assignment, it being understood that the CSD was to make recommendations to the Committee on Commodity Problems, but not to governments:

1. to keep under review developments in the disposal of agricultural surpluses, and to assist FAO Member Nations in developing suitable means of surplus disposal;
2. to provide a forum for the discussion of proposals, programs, policies or transactions of Member Governments for the disposal of agricultural surpluses in the light of the principles recommended by the Seventh Conference Session and in the Report of the CCP Working Party on Surplus Disposal, and to promote the observance of these principles;
3. to report periodically to the CCP, it being understood that copies of its reports and summary records of its proceedings, including any conclusions, should be circulated to FAO Member Nations as soon as possible.[1]

During this initial period, the Committee functioned as a forum for hearing grievances and developing surplus disposal proposals. For the most part, the CSD's efforts were devoted to seeking accommodation between the United States, with its Public Law 480 program for massive surplus disposal, and the competing exporting countries; to developing a practical interpretation of the FAO Principles; and to establishing a basis for consultations. At the same time, much thought was given to and action was taken in respect of surplus disposal measures. Working groups on butter and dried skim milk as well as on national reserves were set up. This was a period during which third countries were looking closely at the various disposal methods of the United States, with particular in-

terest in sales for local currency. It was also one during which triangular transactions, barter deals, and Commodity Credit Corporation (CCC) sales—involving
United States surpluses—were of major importance.[2]

The second phase 1956-68 saw the Committee begin to raise its sights beyond
the narrow interest of developed agricultural exporters in protecting their markets against the incursions of subcommercial transactions. During this period,
the CSD reviewed the Principles and the effectiveness of the procedures of the
Subcommittee. In addition to the previously discussed attempt to find an acceptable definition of "surplus disposal," the Committee offered recommendations for strengthening and protecting its consultative procedures.

With certain important exceptions and additions, the CSD's recommendations
were adopted by its parent, the Committee on Commodity Problems and, ultimately, the Conference of the FAO. In reaffirming the utility of the Principles
and implicitly endorsing the CSD's recommendations, the FAO Council, for the
first time endorsed the use of food aid as an important adjunct to economic
development, albeit with due admonition that these transactions be made without harmful interference with normal patterns of trade.[3]

The peculiar legal status of the FAO Principles makes it difficult to precisely
determine the formal status of this set of CSD recommendations. Juridically, the
Principles lie somewhere between an international agreement and a recommendation. In 1959, as a result of action taken by the CCP and endorsed by the previous session of the FAO Conference, a report on the operation and adequacy of
the FAO Principles and Guiding Lines, prepared by the Consultative Subcommittee on Surplus Disposal, was presented to the Tenth Session of the Conference.[4]
In accordance with standard procedures with respect to the Principles, these
recommendations, together with the CCP's comments on them, were circulated
to Member Governments of FAO with a request for their cooperation. The Conference of the FAO then reaffirmed "the usefulness and validity of the FAO
Principles and Guiding Lines, taking cognizance of the review undertaken by the
Committee on Commodity Problems through its Consultative Subcommittee on
Surplus Disposal.

During the last nine years of the second phase of its activities, the CSD undertook a series of studies of some of the important and vexing aspects of food
aid/commercial trade practices and problems. Much of this work was inspired by
the change in United States food aid policies which for the first time permitted
food aid transactions with nonsurplus products, and to altered domestic agricultural control policies to include production for food aid in calculating agricultural production levels.[5] In this regard, the Committee developed outlines for
studies in depth of the utilization of agricultural surpluses for economic development in Japan and Pakistan. These studies ultimately were completed in 1958
and 1961 by the FAO in cooperation with the UN Economic Commission for
Asia and the Far East (ECAFE).

A major effort of the CSD in this period was the so-called "Changing Attitudes Study," which raises most of the basic food aid/commercial trade problems. Discussion and analysis of these issues is spread throughout this book. In addition, the CSD submitted a series of routine reports to the CCP. It set up working groups on case studies of a variety of issues, on "Grey Area" transactions, on United States Title IV and Private Trade Agreements, and on "Tied Sales" provisions in P.L. 480 Agreements. Also, the Subcommittee improved and extended consultative procedures for both the United States programs and the World Food Program. These reports will be analyzed in the context of subsequent discussion of the problem areas covered by the reports.

In the last years of the second phase, the future of FAO-administered food aid controls were foreshadowed by its work regarding the World Food Program. First, the CSD did the spade work which led to the establishment of the UN/ FAO World Food Program, the first multilateral food aid agency. These efforts included the establishment of rules and procedures to ensure that WFP project proposals were submitted to the CSD's consultative machinery. These actions strongly influenced the comprehensive study of its operations by the CSD which was completed in 1968.[6] The changes in FAO standards and procedures stimulated by this report moved the CSD into its next and current phase. These matters are the subject of the next major section of this study.

The Effectiveness of the CSD

By 1968, the CSD had matured into an effective institution for fulfilling the role assigned to it. However, by that time, the food aid and world agriculture picture had drastically changed. Over the past ten years, the importance of food aid with respect to agricultural surplus problems and economic development seemed to be gradually declining as a result of (1) significant progress towards agricultural self-sufficiency by the major food aid recipients; (2) the success of the United States in developing domestic agricultural policies which controlled the creation of new agricultural surpluses; and (3) the effectiveness of bilateral and international efforts to protect third countries from unwarranted injuries to their commercial trade. But as the United States was solving its agricultural problems, surpluses began to arise in new countries and new products. This was due in part to the spread of improved technology to other developed nations, accompanied by the same sort of overproduction that had plagued the United States for so long. Also, the Common Agricultural Policy gradually adopted by the EEC commencing in 1965 stimulated the rapid creation of European surpluses, which in turn led to vigorous efforts to dispose of these surpluses through food aid and export subsidies. These events in the commercial agricultural trade picture were accompanied by an increasing reluctance of the developed nations, particularly the United States, to provide sufficient quantities of conventional foreign aid to adequately meet the needs of the developing nations. Therefore, with commercial overproduction of agricultural commodities accompanied by an increased pressure to find alternate forms of foreign aid, food aid was again seen as an attractive method of relieving the pressures of agricultural surpluses on commercial markets while serving as a source of development capital for the economically backward nations.

However, though the basic economic factors leading to the rise of food aid in the fifties and late sixties were similar, important features of the food aid picture had changed. The United States no longer was the sole significant actual and potential source of surpluses and food aid. Canada, Australia, Japan, and the European Economic Community had joined the United States in this regard. Moreover, the International Grain Arrangement of 1967 had established a multilateral food aid program centered upon wheat and the UN/FAO World Food Program was growing in size and ambition. For these reasons, the FAO decided that it was necessary to study its role and functioning with respect to the new conditions.[7] The study was completed in 1968 and consisted of an evaluation of the performance of the Subcommittee to that point and recommendations of changes necessary to adequately cope with the new situation facing it. These recommendations are presented and analyzed in Chapter 8. But first, it is necessary, following the format of the CSD's report, to evaluate the performance of the CSD under the conditions prevailing prior to the above cited changes.

Operating Procedures of the CSD

Through most of its history, the heart of the CSD's functions were the bilateral and multilateral consultations conducted under its aegis. Although these consultations are not clearly required by the FAO Principles themselves, the FAO has made consultations mandatory through a quasiinterpretative process.[8]

The Obligation to Consult. Although consultations form the essence of the FAO control system, until 1970, the obligation of countries accepting the FAO Principles to consult within the format provided by the Consultative Subcommittee on surplus disposals remained somewhat ambiguous. Item (2) of the terms of reference of the CSD authorizes the Subcommittee to provide a forum for the discussion of proposals, programs, policies or transactions of Member Governments for the disposal of agricultural surpluses in the light of the principles recommended by the Seventh Conference Session and in the Report of the CCP Working Party on Surplus Disposal, and to promote the observance of these principles. In 1958, the CSD reviewed its operations and recommended, *inter alia* that there should be agreement in principle for consultation on a bilateral basis between countries exporting surpluses and interested third party countries before arrangements are concluded with recipient countries. It also recommended consultations during the currency of a food aid program. Importing countries would be expected to consult with interested exporting countries if requested to do so.[9]

The Committee on Commodity Problems accepted the report with certain reservations. However, some national delegations, particularly France, maintained that the FAO Principles as originally formulated and accepted by member governments did not include any explicit requirements for consultations before making final arrangements for surplus transactions.[10] The CSD's recommendations, together with the CCP's comments, were circulated to the member governments of the FAO with a request "for their cooperation." Although the FAO Conference subsequently took "cognizance" of the CSD's Report and proceeded to reaffirm the "usefulness and validity of the FAO Principles and Guiding Lines," the Conference never explicitly resolved the controversy over the extent of member's consultative obligations.[11] Here again, the predominance and cooperative attitude of the United States permitted the FAO to duck a difficult issue. The United States agreed to prior consultations in general accordance with the CSD's recommendations. Other countries interpreted the FAO requirements as they saw fit. So long as the only significant programs were those of the United States, the failure of other countries to fully notify and consult under the FAO rules could be ignored. With the reduction of United States predominance, these aberrations have taken on increased importance and the recent modifications of the FAO system have attempted to remedy the situation.

What May be Discussed within the CSD. The principal topics discussed within the Consultative Subcommittee includes the methods of disposals, suitable means for utilizing surpluses, government policies or legislation, and individual transactions. Although the machinery of the CSD has been available since 1954 for the discussion of all concessional exports, the vast scale of United States disposals under Public Law 480 in recent years, coupled with the fact that it is one of the few countries that declare "official" surpluses, has naturally resulted in the Subcommittee's spending a high proportion of its time considering, in retrospect, United States food aid programs. Relatively little attention has been given to disposals by countries other than the United States of commodities which, although not officially classed as surplus, may have been exported on concessional terms. Furthermore, despite the fact that the United States has dropped from its P.L. 480 legislation the requirement (effective 1 January 1967) that a commodity had to be declared in surplus before it could be supplied as food aid, it continues to treat these supplies as coming within the competence of the CSD. This was in line with the CSD's declaration that such supplies would still need to be examined in the light of the FAO Principles of Surplus Disposal.

Recently, the food aid programs of other countries have come under increased CSD scrutiny. For some time Canada has been supplying the Subcommittee with notifications of particular transactions and general information on its food aid allocations. Other countries are increasing their reporting.[12] In the quarter ending in October 1971, Australia, Belgium, Canada, the EEC, West Germany, Japan, the Netherlands, and of course, the United States reported transactions. In addition, Canada, Denmark, Finland, West Germany, Ireland, Japan, the Netherlands, and New Zealand, Sweden, the United Kingdom, the United States, and the EEC reported budget allocations and commitments for food aid programs. Apparently, France, though a major wheat producer, never reported a food aid transaction or a budget allocation.[13]

Most consultations refer to individual transactions or programs. Individual transactions, though, represent a final stage of a policy or program. Thus, there is a role for international cooperation at earlier stages, when surplus policies and programs are being shaped. Given national sensitivities to interference by international bodies in domestic matters, it isn't surprising that member governments have been reluctant to have prospective national legislation brought before the CSD for open debate and criticism. Therefore, the Subcommittee's activities in this field have tended to be limited to discussion on the interpretation and implementation of legislation and to retrospective examination of the terms of individual programs and transactions. However, it is also true that CSD may represent an appropriate international interest in the nature and direction of legislation and other governmental action affecting food aid and commercial trade problems, and governments may well find it useful to use the collective experience of the Subcommittee as a measuring rod for the probable effect of policy proposals on other countries. When these actions involve administrative changes in existing programs it would be useful to inform and consult the Subcommittee.

Form and Timing of Consultations

Consultations pursuant to CSD procedures either may be bilateral or multilateral. Multilateral consultations present peculiar difficulties. Concededly it may be awkward for the details of a transaction to be disclosed in a multilateral forum before provisional agreement has been reached between the parties to the transaction. On the other hand, it has been recognized that consultations held after the agreement has been substantially negotiated may preclude any modification that might be sought by third parties. While this has led, especially in the case of individual transactions, to a preference for bilateral consultations, there were other considerations which favored a multilateral approach. In practice, it was found difficult for a government exporting surplus commodities to be aware of all possible third party interests in a given transaction.

Thus the CSD, in 1958, set up additional procedures to strengthen consultations with a view to ensuring observance of the Principles. These procedures included the previously discussed working definition of "surplus disposal"; an agreement in principle for bilateral consultations between surplus supplying countries and third party countries; and the protection of marginal interests of other countries through the CSD. In addition to the definition of surplus disposal, the CSD recommended the following:

2. There should be agreement in principle for consultation on a bilateral basis between countries exporting surpluses and interested third party countries before arrangements are concluded with recipient countries and also during the currency of a programme. Importing countries would be expected to consult with interested exporting countries if requested to do so.
3. The Chairman of the Subcommittee should also be consulted because of possible marginal interests of other member countries.
4. The Subcommittee should act as a forum to which third party countries might subsequently refer specific complaints if they did not consider that their views had received sufficient consideration, or if there had been no bilateral consultations.
5. Written agreements should include specific provision that it was the intention of the parties thereto that sales of surpluses should not interfere with normal patterns of production and trade of FAO member countries subscribing to the Principles of Surplus Disposal. In cases where no such provision can be made because, for instance, the advantages of the transaction to the economy of the receiving country are deemed to outweigh other considerations, it should be the responsibility of the parties concerned to bring before the Subcommittee their reasons for the exclusion of the provision.
6. Wherever possible, member governments should inform the Subcommittee in advance of proposed changes in policy on surplus disposal.[14]

With one important exception, the FAO adopted these recommendations. But the Council of the FAO refused to accept the CSD's recommendation (and that of the Committee on Commodity Problems) that recipient countries should be required to consult with affected third country exporters of the CSD. This is a good illustration of the exporter attitude of the CSD and its parent, the CCP, which is overcome to some extent by the broader orientation of the FAO Council. In addition, the Committee on Commodity Problems, itself, softened the requirements of paragraph 2 of the CSD's recommendations relating to the timing of consultations. The CCP "realized" that it may not always be practicable for countries to consult with interested third countries and the CSD prior to the completion of a food aid transaction. As previously noted, some delegations to the CCP went further, maintaining that the original FAO Principles did not contain any general provision requiring such prior consultation. The CCP compromised by permitting countries, in certain circumstances, to complete the transaction and discuss the arrangement with third countries at the earliest possible time.[15]

The controversy over the proper timing of consultations on transactions within the CSD's jurisdiction is still unresolved. The official position of the CSD is that normally consultations are to precede finalization of a food aid transaction. For some time, the United States followed a different approach that permitted some negotiations with food aid recipients before completing the consultation process. After long and intense pressure from most other exporters, the United States gave some ground. Its current position is that although formal negotiations may not be begun until the consultations are completed, "conversations" may precede or accompany consultations, but "negotiations" must follow consultations. France insists that consultations should accompany negotiations. As we shall see, this attitude severely complicated the recent efforts of the FAO to adopt new rules with respect to protecting commercial imports.

If the entire CSD apparatus is to have any meaning, consultations must come soon enough to permit changes in the terms of the transactions in response to legitimate objections of affected third countries. At the same time, potential food aid donors and recipients must engage in very extensive and specific exploration of possible food aid transactions before there can be any basis for consultations with outside interested parties. All that can be said (or, perhaps need be said) is that consultations must take place at a point in the negotiations where the parties have sufficiently defined the transactions to expose potential dangers to third parties, but have not gone so far as to preclude changes in response to potential objections. Often problems regarding the timing of negotiations arise when food aid commitments are made at high political levels by passing the normal channels for such transactions—the President of France promises the King of Morocco X amount of wheat. Where the food aid is handled through normal procedures, there is considerably less difficulty in accomplishing effective consultations with other interested governments.

United States Practice. The United States and the EEC have proceeded furthest in formalizing their procedures for notification and consultation under the FAO rules. Given the predominant size and extent of experience of the United States with food aid, United States practice has provided the working norm for other nations and except for certain changes required by the new procedures adopted pursuant to the CSD's 1968 recommendations, these will continue to provide the model for CSD consultations. We shall first present the United States system in detail, followed by a brief discussion of the recently adopted practices of the EEC. The policy of the United States is to consult, as a matter of course, third countries having a significant record of sales to the receiving country of the commodity in question and to consult other third countries only if they specifically ask to be consulted. Canada, Australia, and Argentina have asked to be consulted on all sales of wheat; Rhodesia, on all sales of tobacco; and New Zealand, on all sales of dairy products, under P.L. 480, regardless of whether or not the sale is to a country in which these countries have markets, and the United States has agreed to do so. Among countries frequently consulted are Greece, Turkey, and Rhodesia on tobacco sales; Peru, Egypt, Sudan, Uganda, and Tanganyika on sales of cotton (Colombia is also becoming an exporter of upland cotton and was consulted for the first time recently on a proposed sale to Ecuador); the Netherlands, Denmark, New Zealand and Argentina on dairy products and fats and oils; Ceylon on fats and oils; and Thailand, Burma, and Viet Nam on rice. In the case of Public Law 480 operations, the United States has initiated bilateral consultations on individual proposals usually in Washington, although some take place at the national capitals of the importing countries (e.g., Thailand, Burma, Ceylon). The usual procedure in Washington is to complete the consultations within a two-week period, beginning with the dispatch of written notification of food aid proposals to representatives of interested countries. Any objections are to be raised within the first week in order to permit further consultations.

For the United States, its consultation implies something more than merely informing a third country of its intentions. But it is not synonymous with obtaining the agreement of third countries. Consultation gives a third country an opportunity to make its views known on a particular proposal, but not to veto that proposal. According to the United States, if a third country objects to a particular proposal and can make a good case that the proposal program seems likely to displace its sales to the receiving country, it is willing to consider modifying the proposal either by reducing the P.L. 480 amount or increasing the standard requirement to maintain a minimum level of commercial purchases (usual marketing requirement) or both. For example, a recent United States food aid wheat sale to Ceylon did not include a usual marketing requirement (UMR). After objection by Argentina a usual marketing requirement of 50,000 metric tons of wheat flour equivalent was imposed. In very exceptional cases, the United States has decided to withdraw a proposal because it was convinced by the evidence submitted by third countries that any program at all would have been incompatible with our commitment to protect normal commercial sales. But in all cases, the final decision on a particular proposal rests with the United States; it is not subject to the agreement of third countries. If the United States is satisfied that a third country's objections to a proposal are not well founded, it will proceed with the proposal in spite of these objections.

Following bilateral consultations, the United States has provided to the CSD Secretary a Notice of Impending Agreement for circulation to Members and Observers at least 48 hours in advance of the signing of the agreement. This gives countries with marginal interests some warning; it also provides all CSD representatives with essential information on the agreement, such as the kind of program, the types of commodities, the quantities involved and their value as well as the provisions for usual marketing requirements and "tied sales" if relevant. These transactions may be discussed at the monthly meetings of the Subcommittee, although by the time of the meeting the transaction will have been completed.

Combining the notifications and consultations with negotiation of a complex food aid agreement can be quite tricky. For the bilateral consultations and the CSD discussions to be meaningful, the details of the transaction must be at hand. But unless there exists some history of prior transactions of the same type, some of the terms of most interest to the CSD members can only be determined *after* negotiations. The donor country may be able to tell the CSD what terms it will try to impose, but the recipient may not accept them as offered. This becomes particularly important with respect to usual marketing requirements, which are now required in all food aid transactions. In order to determine if the FAO requirements are being met, the members must know the level of the UMR. But, in many cases, particularly where there is little prior experience, the UMR will be the subject of intense negotiation between the donor and the recipient. Once again, the shift away from complete United States predominance in food aid will have its effect. With one country involved in almost all the transactions, the terms, in many cases, become routine and predictable, thereby permitting the United States to provide all the necessary information before entering into formal negotiations. The more countries giving food aid, the greater the need for real negotiations between donor and recipient, and the more difficult it becomes to comply with the requirements of consultation before negotiation. This may have been one reason why the question of establishing a time frame for consultation caused so much difficulty during the 1968 revamping of CSD procedures.

EEC Practice. Except for usual marketing requirements, which cannot be discussed with food aid recipients before consultation with third countries, EEC members (and the EEC as a unit where food aid is given on a community basis), will notify and consult with other countries, under FAO procedures after the details of the transaction have been negotiated with the recipient. This includes, *inter alia*, the nature of the commodity, the quantity and the date and means of delivery. At the conclusion of this negotiation, concerned third country exporters will be notified of the details which have been agreed upon by the two parties. This notification will include the proposed usual marketing requirements which will not be discussed with the recipient until consultations with third countries are completed.

These procedures reflect the EEC's position that consultations with third countries under FAO procedures may be delayed until the basic forms of the transaction, except for usual marketing requirements, have been negotiated with the recipient. These procedures contradict the position of the United States and other CSD members that consultations on all aspects of a proposed food aid transaction must precede extensive negotiations between the donor and the recipient on these matters. There seems little possibility of reconciling these differences in the near future. But, as indicated above, it is difficult to choose between these views, and so long as donating nations are responsive to the legitimate complaint of third countries, either method will work.[16]

World Food Program Practices. The details of World Food Program (WFP) proposals which are furnished by the WFP Secretariat to the CSD Secretary are summarized and circulated to the CSD Members and Observers. Any objections are to be made within 10 working days to the Secretary who in turn cables WFP as to the outcome of the consultations. Since establishing these arrangements with the WFP, the Subcommittee has provided some working criteria to guide the

WFP where their projects include proposals to sell commodities in recipient countries.

Even with respect to specific transactions, the scope of consultations may be controversial. Countries generally are more willing to discuss pending food aid transactions bilaterally rather than discuss them before the semipublic CSD. This is particularly true where trade information likely to benefit competitors may be involved. However, there is no clear distinction between the matters which may be discussed before the CSD and those reserved for bilateral consultation. Some countries have attempted to distinguish between matters of principle which are appropriate for CSD discussion and the facts and details of particular transactions which need only be discussed bilaterally.

In practice, it is very difficult to draw such a line. Many factual matters are directly relevant to decide if particular transactions comply with the Principles. This would include the size of the transaction, the terms of payment, and now, the level and form of the usual marketing requirement. (Usual marketing requirements, the prime food aid/commercial trade control service are the subject of Chapter 8.) Conceivably, it could be argued that since the CSD has no decision-making or adjudicative powers as such, it may not even discuss the applicability of the FAO Principles to pending transactions. Under this theory, the sole requirement of the FAO system is to provide sufficient advance notice of pending food aid transactions to potentially affected third countries and to bilaterally consult with countries voicing objections. But even without decision-making powers, the CSD has been ceded the power to measure individual transactions against the Principles. It is this process which permits the growth of general standards by a consensus process. Without this power, no way would exist to translate the vaguely worded Principles and Guiding Lines into effective conduct rules.

Adequacy of Notification Procedures. The 1968 CSD report was satisfied with existing CSD notification and consultation procedures. These were primarily derived from experience with individual transactions by the United States and the World Food Program. However, the Subcommittee believed that with some minor adjustments these would work equally well with respect to sizeable concessional transfers by other countries. Moreover, according to the Subcommittee, these procedures would permit the CSD to extend the range of transactions it considers, if governments agree to do so. The Subcommittee took note of the fact that concessional transactions under the Food Aid Convention would be subject to consultative procedures. Since at the time of its report negotiations for renewing the Food Aid Convention were under way, the Subcommittee deemed it inappropriate to express any opinion on the possible role of the CSD in relation to that arrangement. It did point out, though, its belief that consultations on food aid and surplus disposal activities would be everywhere facilitated by the adoption of both a common terminology and uniform consultation procedures.

We have already discussed the difficulties in reaching accord on a definition of concessional transactions under the International Wheat Agreements. But these difficulties need not impede agreement regarding the procedures to be employed on those transactions which are subject to consultation. Actually, all this is a bit premature. To this date, no machinery has been established for conducting consultations under the International Wheat Agreement and the Food Aid Convention.

Administrative Capacity of The CSD. Given the unique status of the CSD as the only international institution permanently concerned with surplus disposal and food aid/commercial trade problems, it is manned by a skeleton crew. The FAO provides two resident economists for the Washington office with back-up from FAO headquarters in Rome. Member governments are represented on the Subcommittee by personnel drawn from the various Embassies and the Missions in Washington, who are necessarily heavily occupied in their normal duties and who, in any case, are liable to be moved to other posts. The experience which they have gained is then lost to the Subcommittee. In the early days of the Subcommittee, members were called upon to spare only a day or two each month for meetings. In the past, this devotion of time together with the services provided by a small secretariat sufficed to cope with the matters before the Subcommittee. More recently, there has been an increasing call on members' time to serve on working parties and drafting groups. This seems likely to continue for some time. Regular meetings of the entire Subcommittee are held monthly, with *ad hoc* working groups established whenever specific problems cannot be resolved in the general meeting. Without exception, for representatives to the CSD, this post is only a sideline to their main responsibilities. Under these conditions, the CSD has been forced to limit itself to one working party at a time.

Relationship to Other Bodies. Because of its particular location in the FAO organizational structure, the CSD does not have natural links to other bodies concerned with food aid/commercial trade problems. As a subcommittee of the Committee on Commodity Problems within the FAO, the CSD is somewhat handicapped in obtaining direct representation on other organizations interested in the same or related problems. These include the Executive Committee of the Food Aid Convention, GATT, the OECD, etc. Although the Subcommittee's 1968 Report recommended that the CSD should have a formal link with these bodies, no direct action was taken by the FAO on the matter. Actually, the FAO probably lacks jurisdiction to unilaterally implement this kind of action. The bodies themselves would have to accept CSD membership. The fact that CSD really doesn't represent anybody—it reports only to the CCP—could make these bodies a bit reluctant to establish formal links. Informal arrangements would serve the purpose of keeping the CSD abreast of developments elsewhere, but it wouldn't permit it to present a viewpoint on pending matters.

The CSD's Decision-Making Powers. The exclusively consultative nature of the CSD has been heavily stressed. This position was most recently reaffirmed by the Committee on Commodity Problems in adopting the latest changes in the CSD operating procedures.[17] Strictly speaking, these limitations should preclude the Subcommittee from taking any action as a body. In practice, though, it has proven difficult to avoid taking positions. One of the prime functions of the Subcommittee is to discuss transactions or practices in terms of their compliance with the FAO Principles. Often, a concensus is reached among the members with respect to a particular issue. The question then is whether any formalization of this concensus should be made. On occasions, members have challenged the power of the Committee to do anything which smacks of decision-making. The issue is still unresolved. Certain members believed that since the CSD had to report to the CCP in Rome, there should be some way to achieve an orderly conclusion of extensive discussions. This could take the form of conclusions. Others thought the Chairman should refrain from trying to establish a formal set of conclusions. A compromise position was that the Chairman should sum up the discussion, including "conclusions" reached by Subcommittee members. And there the matter rests. My legal colleagues probably would enjoy trying to determine how one describes the concensuses reached by a nondecision-making body which examines particular transactions in terms of given standards.

Recent Modifications of CSD Operations

After thoroughly examining its operations through 1968, a working committee of the Committee on Surplus Disposal found that the CSD has operated over the years as an effective, purposeful and responsible body, largely fulfilling, within the context of the demands made upon it, the role mapped out in 1954. Put this way, I would agree with that evaluation. But the key words are "within the context of the demands made upon it." For most of the CSD's existence, these "demands" have boiled down to ensuring that the United States food aid practices did not unduly threaten the export markets of major agricultural producers. For the most part, this has been accomplished. After some initial resistance from the U.S. Congress and the Department of Agriculture, the United States has fully complied with the reporting and consultation requirements of the CSD system.[18] And, as we shall see in Part III, over the past ten years, the United States has developed sophisticated and effective control devices to avoid many of the potential dangers of food aid to legitimate trade interests.[19] The record with respect to food and surplus disposal activities of other countries has been much more spotty. Non-United States fund aid activities have accelerated under the pressure of increased surplus problems and it was often difficult to determine the extent to which member nations were observing the FAO Principles and the consultative reporting obligations stemming from these Principles. As long as the size of non-United States programs remained small these did not undermine the overall effectiveness of the CSD system. Now, however the situation has changed drastically. Surpluses have spread to new countries and new products. And food aid is being considered as a permanent and important source of development resources. Under these circumstances, there are grounds to fear that competition among exporters might lead to food aid and other special transactions being used as an incentive to promote commercial exports and obliterate the distinction which had thus far been maintained between food aid and commercial trade, with adverse effects on both. Therefore, controlling United States programs is no longer sufficient. Moreover, the United States is unlikely to continue exercising its exemplary self-control unless its agricultural competitors are compelled to show similar restraint.

Recognizing the need for substantial improvement and reformation in the operation of the CSD, the FAO has made a thorough investigation of the functioning of the CSD and has adopted significant philosophical and procedural changes. Part III, *inter alia*, will attempt to identify major weaknesses in the FAO control system and to evaluate the impact of the newly adopted practices and procedures. The remainder of this chapter will concentrate on structural problems. Discussion of specific problem areas, such as tying, quasicommercial transactions, and measures to assure additionality will be deferred to Part III.

The Modification Process. The interrelationships of the various operating components of the FAO involve subtle problems of authority and jurisdiction. Therefore, before discussing the substance of the changes adopted, it would be useful to outline the process by which these changes were adopted. The process was initiated by a report dated July 26, 1968, to the Committee on Commodity Problems by the CSD on *The Role of Subcommittee (CSD) in Light of Current and Prospective Developments in Agricultural Surpluses and Food Aid.*[20] The Report identified three large questions which required decisions by the FAO. The first relates to the future role of the CSD with respect to food aid. More particularly, should the CSD serve as the central point for information on all varieties of food aid. The second issue concerns the scope of reporting and consultation requirements under the FAO Principles, including the role of the CSD. More specifically, the issue is:

what commodities and what types of transaction are to be reported; how often and by what means is reporting to take place; to what extent, in particular, does acceptance of a reporting requirement signify acceptance of a consultation requirement also.[21]

The third, and in the view of the CSD Working Party, the most fundamental issue, was to define the CSD's authority with respect to so-called "extra commercial" transactions. Throughout its history, there has been disagreement among members of the CSD over the scope of FAO jurisdiction regarding certain export transactions which allegedly arose from the existence of abnormal stocks and were assisted by special or concessional terms through government intervention. Some countries deem these to be within CSD jurisdiction, while others do not recognize a need to notify or engage in consultations through the CSD on the export transactions under discussion. In their view, these transactions are not "surplus disposals" as defined, and involve trade practices (export aids) which appropriately would come under the purview of the GATT. Under these circumstance, the working party believed that:

A decision is required as to which body has primary competence and responsibility; and in any case whether the CSD, as a consultative body, should be entitled to consider such transactions and as appropriate submit recommendations.[22]

Stimulated by this working party report, the CSD's parent, the Committee on Commodity Problems established its own working party to respond to the issues raised by the CSD's report. The CCP working party completed its work in 1969 and reported to the CCP the same year. In its report, the working party offered a series of recommendations to deal with the problems raised by the CSD working party. In several important respects, the working party offered alternative approaches for resolution by the CCP.[23] The CCP resolved most of the issues raised in the working party report and forwarded its recommendations to the FAO Council.[24] In January 1970, the Council, in accordance with its normal procedures, endorsed the CCP's recommendations and requested the Director General to transmit the text of the substance of the Council's action on this matter to the FAO membership for their acceptance.[25]

Clarifying the Jurisdiction of the
FAO Control System

We have already noted that the effectiveness of the FAO control system depends to a large degree upon the extent to which transactions are subject to CSD procedures. Therefore, the second problem identified by the CSD working party report—the requirements for reporting and consulting with respect to various transactions—goes to the heart of the FAO system.

Rather than attempting to work with the central concepts of the Principles of Surplus Disposal—"surplus," "surplus disposal," "concessional sales"—the FAO undertook to solve its jurisdictional problems via a process of inclusion and exclusion. The working group of the Committee on Commodity Problems listed every transaction that deviated from the commercial paradigm—sales of commodities at prices prevailing in the respective domestic markets, payable in cash, in convertible currency. From these, the FAO, on the basis of the recommendations of the Committee on Commodity Problems, designated the transactions that would fall within CSD jurisdiction. Despite the strong recommendation of the CSD working party that all transactions included within CSD jurisdiction should be subject to similar reporting and consultation requirements, this was not done, and in many cases, full prior reporting and consultation were not required for all categories of the included transactions.[26]

The CCP working party classified all agricultural transactions into the following categories.

1. Gifts or donations of commodities from a government to a government of an importing country, an intergovernmental organization or a private institution for free distribution, directly to the final consumers in the importing country;
2. Gifts or donations of commodities from a government to a government of an importing country, or an intergovernmental organization or a private institution for distribution, by means of sale on the open market of the importing country;
3. Monetary grants by the government of an exporting country to an importing country, for the specific purpose of purchasing a commodity from the exporting country;
4. Monetary grants by a government either to a supplying country (or countries) or to a recipient country for the specific purpose of purchasing a commodity from the exporting country (or countries) for delivery to the specific recipient country;
5. Monetary grants by a government to an intergovernmental organization for the specific purpose of purchasing commodities in the open market for delivery to eligible importing countries (developing countries);
6. Transfers of commodities under the rules and established procedures of the World Food Program;
7. Sales for the currency of the importing country which is not transferable and is not convertible into currency or goods and services for use by the contributing country;
8. Sales for the currency of the importing country which is partially convertible into currency or goods and services for use by the contributing country;
9. Government-sponsored loans of agricultural commodities repayable in kind;
10. Sales on credit in which, as a result of government intervention, or of a centralized marketing scheme, the interest rate, period of repayment (including periods of grace) or other related terms do not conform to the commercial rates, periods or terms prevailing in the world market. In particular with respect to period of repayment, credit transactions are distinguished as follows:
    a) 10 years or more;
    b) Over 3 years and under 10 years;
    c) Up to 3 years
11. Sales in which the funds for the purchase of commodities are obtained

under a loan from the government of the exporting country tied to the purchase of those commodities, distinguished as follows with respect to periods of repayment:

    a)   10 years or more;

    b)   Over 3 years and under 10 years;

    c)   Up to three years

12. Transactions under categories 1 to 4 and 7 to 11, subject to tied usual marketing requirements or to tied offset purchasing requirements;

13. Transactions under categories 1 to 4 and 7 to 11, tied to the purchase of fixed quantities of the same or another commodity from the exporting country;

14. Sales in which, as a result of government intervention or of a centralized marketing scheme; (a) prices are inconsistent with price provisions of an international agreement for the commodity concerned; or (b) prices are lower than prevailing world prices 2/; or (c) sales made in such ways as to disrupt prevailing world prices or the normal patterns of international trade;

15. Subsidized exports and imports, including special transport arrangements;

16. Barter transactions not involving price concessions: (a) government sponsored; (b) not government sponsored;

17. Barter transactions involving price concessions: (a) government sponsored; (b) not government sponsored;

18. Sales for noncovertible currency: (a) involving price concessions; (b) not involving price concessions;

19. Any other categories of government-sponsored transactions which may interfere with normal commercial trade;

20. Transactions which conform to the usual commercial practices in international trade and which do not include those transactions listed above.[27]

Each category was analyzed with a view to determining the appropriate notification and consultation requirements. In all cases of serious disagreement among the working party members, the final decision was left to the Committee on Commodity problems itself. The CCP resolved most of the disputes and in large measure its recommendations were accepted by the FAO Council.

The scheme that finally emerged substantially conformed with the past practices of the CSD. With one partial exception, the FAO Principles are to be applied to the first thirteen categories and not to the remaining seven. The line was drawn to exclude transactions conducted below market terms by virtue of government intervention but not involving the following: credit arrangements of over three-years length, subsidized exports and imports, barter transactions, and sales under nonconvertible currency clearing arrangements. Of those categories generally made subject to FAO jurisdiction, an exception was made for transactions effected through intergovernmental organizations (including the World Food Program) whose commodity transfers are already subject to special consultative rules, or through intergovernmental organizations (including UNICEF and UNRWA) whose operations were deemed to be of such a nature and volume as not to constitute a substantial danger of harmful interference with normal patterns of production and international trade. Emergency transactions and government-to-government transactions of relatively small size and not involving sales in the local markets of the recipient country and therefore not likely to result in harmful interference with normal patterns of production and international trade shall be notified to CSD *ex post facto* as soon as practicable. Finally, transactions otherwise subject to FAO jurisdiction which are conducted through private charitable organizations need not be reported transaction-by-transaction. Instead, the charities shall periodically notify the members of CSD in a reasonably comprehensive form of the relevant data on the current pattern of programs and projects, so that a member nation which considers its commercial trade endangered may request bilateral consultation. Also, there was general agreement that the lists of transactions were not exclusive and that some new types of transactions might be identified in the future. The CSD was authorized to consider such additions or deletions.[28]

The Use of Open Market Transactions (Items 1 and 2). An important aspect of the final formulation is the distinction drawn between gifts and donations for free distribution directly to the final consumers in an importing country and those for distribution by sale on the open market of the importing country. Nonopen market transactions present a significantly smaller danger to normal commercial trade than gifts made directly to targeted consumers. These latter transactions are usually small in size and related to chronic or acute emergency feeding situations where there is little likelihood that the consumers would have purchased the commodities commercially without food aid.

Sales Made at Reduced Prices. Item 14 of the CCP working parties comprehensive list of transactions included sales in which, as a result of government intervention or of a centralized marketing scheme (a) prices are inconsistent with price provisions of an international agreement for the commodity concerned; or (b) prices are lower than prevailing world prices; or (c) sales are made in such ways to disrupt prevailing world prices or the normal patterns of international trade. These were excluded from CSD jurisdiction on the belief that such transactions could be better handled in the context of specific commodity agreements such as the Wheat Trade Convention or the GATT. Excluding Item 14(a)—sales in which prices are inconsistent with price provisions of an international agreement for the commodity concerned—seems logical since the CSD is not and should not serve as a watchdog for the enforcement of commodity agreements which uniformly provide their own machinery for this purpose. Inclusion of Item 14(b)—sales in which prices are lower than prevailing world prices—would bring within CSD jurisdiction the entire range of export subsidy operations, including commercial sales as well as possible food aid transactions. The CSD's clear orientation and limitation to food aid problems would seem to preclude CSD jurisdiction in this area. Item 14(c)—sales which might disrupt prevailing world prices or the normal patterns of international trade—presents a slightly different problem. The FAO General Principles (2 and 3) are directed towards surplus disposal practices which might disrupt world commodity prices or cause harmful interference with normal patterns of international trade. And though the Principles technically are limited to "surplus" engendered transactions, there is now a clear authority for the CSD to expand its functions beyond surplus-engendered transactions. But as with item 14(b), 14(a) transactions include many commercially oriented sales, and the CCP wanted the CSD to concentrate on noncommercial, food aid type operations. Furthermore, inclusion of both items 14(b) and (c) within CSD jurisdiction would require the CSD to make specific judgments as to which transactions did and did not disrupt world prices and normal patterns of commercial trade, and this is precisely the kind of decision the FAO wishes to avoid. The GATT does provide procedures for *ex post facto* consultations and reporting in cases of policies or transactions causing market disruption, as well as procedures for reporting on export subsidies, surplus disposal and liquidation of government stockpiles. Still, some delegates believed that 14(b) and (c) transactions should be subject to some CSD jurisdiction as a matter of principle, while others stressed the practical difficulties of prior consultation on such matters and the problems involved in defining such concepts as "prevailing world market prices." This group, therefore, deemed GATT complaint procedures the better approach.

Credit Sales. Items 10 and 11 of the CCP list includes credit transactions sponsored by governments in which the interest rate, the repayment period, or other related items depart from the terms prevailing in world markets. There was no dispute over including transactions providing credit terms longer than three years (Items 10(a), (b); 11(a), (b)). But Items 10(c) and 11(c) identify transactions with credit terms of less than three years. These would include both commercial and quasicommercial transactions. Some members of the CCP Working Party who believed that three months constituted a normal credit term, proposed that such transactions should be subject to consultation and reporting, particularly where the period of repayment approached three years or where the interest rate was less than that prevailing in world markets. They suggested that consideration be given to methods of defining "commercial" credit terms, bearing in mind differing rates of interest. Other delegates suggested that credit sales with repayment up to three years should be subject to notification rather than prior consultation, as the latter would give rise to serious administrative problems. The working group noted that the GATT already required a notification of export credits involving concessional terms or subsidies and that the GATT Committee on Agriculture was working on the matter. Here again, Argentina pressed its argument that any agricultural credit sale fell within FAO jurisidiction. Finally, the working party excluded 10(c) and 11(c) transactions. This decision was ultimately ratified by the FAO Council.

Export and Import Subsidies. The acceptance by the CSD of jurisdiction over Item 15 transactions—subsidized exports and imports, including special transport arrangements—would entail a wholesale departure from the FAO's conception of the subcommittees role in the food aid-commercial trade arena. Obviously, the range of subsidized import and export transactions extends far beyond both food aid and surplus disposal. The CCP working party had little difficulty in deciding that these transactions were best handled through the GATT. As previously noted, Article XVI of GATT requires member countries maintaining subsidies which directly or indirectly increased exports or reduced imports to notify the organization in writing of the nature and extent of the subsidization. Such notifications must be made annually and a form is prescribed for the purpose. Under these circumstances, it is interesting that some members of the working party were dissatisfied with the GATT procedures and wanted to establish co-ordinate jurisdiction in CSD. More specifically, they wanted the *ex post facto* reporting required by GATT to be more systematic and comprehensive and they deemed annual reporting to be of limited use. As a consequence, some members reserved their right to raise question on Item 15 transactions in the CSD. This dissatisfaction with GATT procedures also is being discussed in the GATT Committee on Agriculture.[29]

Barter Deals (Items 16 and 17). Barter transactions, government-sponsored and private, with and without price concessions (Items 16 and 17) were considered and finally excluded from CSD jurisdiction. The CSD was seriously concerned with United States barter transactions. But now that this country has clearly identified the purpose of its barter operations as commercial rather than food aid, and has cured some of its most objectionable features, these transactions are no longer considered a problem.[30] Other countries' barter operations are closely related to problems of bilateralism, and are seen to distort normal commercial trade by preempting commercial markets to the detriment of other suppliers. As with export-import subsidies, the thrust of the operations are almost exclusively commercial with little or no food aid component. Presumptively, this is why the CCP working party recommended against including them within CSD jurisdictions, and was content to have them handled through the GATT. But here again, some countries lacked confidence in GATT's ability to handle barter problems and preferred that government-to-government barter deals involving clearly identifiable concessional elements be made subject to prior bilateral consultation in the CSD. There was no dispute over excluding private barter transactions.[31] Given the existing orientation of the CSD, the exclusion of barter transactions is eminently proper.

Nonconvertible Currency Clearing Transactions (Item 18). This class of transactions was intended to include sales for nonconvertible currencies arising within clearing and other bilateral payments arrangements. This feature distinguishes them from the kind of local currency sales described in Items 7 and 8. These latter kinds of local currency sales are exclusively food aid transactions and—up to the last few years—were the principal vehicle for United States food aid (and given United States predominance, the principal vehicle for all food aid). Here again, the strong commercial orientation of Item 18 transactions counterindicates CSD jurisdiction and points towards treatment under the GATT or particular commodity agreements. But despite this, once more, certain countries pressed for some CSD jurisdiction, arguing that in some cases the necessity for clearing bilateral accounts through purchase of noncompetitive products of the trading partner in a bilateral arrangement involved a sufficient concessional component to warrant such jurisdiction.[32]

Other Government Sponsored Transactions Interfering with Normal Commercial Trade and Transactions Conforming with Usual Commercial Practices (Items 19 and 20). The purpose of this item was to give the CSD the flexibility to increase its jurisdiction to include additional transactions with significant food aid features which might subsequently be found to interfere with commercial trade. Although excluded from the list of FAO cognizable transactions, the same effect was achieved by the grant of authority to the CCP to modify the list to include new types of transactions. The final item, "Transactions Conforming with Usual Commercial Practices" obviously was included to make the list exhaustive of all agricultural trade, and was never intended to be made part of CSD jurisdiction.[33]

Jurisdiction over Grey Area Transactions. As we have noted, the 1968 CSD working party examining the role of the Subcommittee was very anxious to clarify the jurisdiction of the CSD with respect to transactions lying somewhere between clearly identifiable food aid and commercial export facilitation. The issue was partially resolved by establishing the catalog of transactions cognizable by the CSD and excluding Items 14-20, and 10(c) and 11(c) from the list of transactions ceded to FAO jurisdiction. The included transactions do not extend beyond transactions universally conceded to be surplus disposals or concessional sales. However, the status of intermediate transactions was raised in another aspect of the reformulation process; the proposed modifications of the terms of the CSD's charter.

Modifying the CSD's Charter. The changes in the FAO control system discussed herein require changes in the CSD's formal terms of reference. These had stipulated the following functions for the CSD:[34]

1. to keep under review developments in the disposal of agricultural surpluses, and to assist FAO Member Nations in developing suitable means of surplus disposal;
2. to provide a forum for the discussion of proposals, programs, policies or transactions of Member Governments for the disposal of agricultural surpluses

in the light of the principles recommended by the Seventh Conference Session and in the Report of the CCP Working Party on Surplus Disposal, and to promote the observance of these principles.
3. to report periodically to the CCP, it being understood that copies of its reports and summary records of its proceedings, including any conclusions, should be circulated to FAO Member Nations as soon as possible.

The CCP working party proposed two changes to the existing terms of reference of the CSD. The first change involved the addition of a new paragraph as follows (changes from original wording in italics):

to provide a forum for *consultations and notifications, including usual marketing requirements, regarding the transactions of Member Nations and Associate Members of the Organization of the types identified in the attached catalogue and any other types of transactions as may be subsequently agreed by CCP*, in the light of Guiding Lines and Principles of Surplus Disposal endorsed by the Conference.

This change was adopted by the Committee on Commodity Problems at their forty-fourth session in September-October 1969.[35] This language establishes CSD jurisdiction over the catalog of transactions that are subject to consultation and notification and establishes procedures for modifying the catalog.

In addition, the CCP working party proposed to expand the charter of the CSD to deal with transactions difficult to classify in terms of the adopted catalog. These are the so-called grey area sales. Under the original terms of reference of the CSD, the Subcommittee was "to provide a forum for the discussion of proposals programs, policies, or transactions of Member Governments for the disposal of agricultural surpluses in the light of the principles recommended by the Seventh Conference Session and in the Report of the CCP Working Party on Surplus Disposal and to promote the observance of these principles."[36] Three alternatives were proposed. Under the first proposal, the following language would be added to item (a) of the original terms of reference:

it being understood that these Principles and Guiding Lines should not be interpreted as applying only to surplus disposal in the narrow sense but also to any transaction containing a government-sponsored element of concession or special conditions which might involve a danger of harmful interference with normal patterns of international commercial trade regardless of whether the transaction is specifically related to surplus situations in the commodity or country concerned.[37]

This language was proposed by these working party members who believed that the FAO Principles of Surplus Disposal applied to any transaction which might involve a danger of harmful interference with normal patterns of international commercial trade, and they considered that the Subcommittee should accordingly be empowered to hear complaints on such cases as may be raised by member nations. This formulation would give the CSD broad authority over any government-assisted transaction departing from strict commercial terms, without regard to the surplus status of the commodities involved. In effect, it would bring transactions 10(c), 11(c), and 14-19 within the ambit of the CSD.

The second formulation focused upon food aid. It would add the following to paragraph (2).

it being understood that these Principles and Guiding Lines should not be interpreted as applying only to surplus disposal in the narrow sense but also to other food aid operations regardless of whether these are specifically related to surplus situations in the commodity or country concerned.[38]

This language would give the CSD jurisdiction over all food aid operations whether based upon surplus products or not. It would require the CSD to develop standards for distinguishing food aid from commercially oriented transactions at below market terms.

The third alternative—the one ultimately adopted by the Committee on Commodity Problems—is also the least specific. It would add the following to the paragraph (2).

and more generally to provide a forum for the examination of any difficulty that may arise in the application of the Guiding Lines and Principles of Surplus Disposal endorsed by the Conference, and to promote observance of these Principles, it being understood that these Principles and Guiding Lines should not be interpreted as applying only to surplus disposal in the narrow sense.[39]

By adopting this formulation the FAO has refused to provide a definitive resolution of existing differences of opinion over the status of nonsurplus food aid transactions and quasicommercial sales. It does provide a basis for later resolution of these problems by explicitly negating interpretations of the FAO Principles that would limit their applicability solely to transactions based upon officially designated surpluses.

Unresolved Problems of CSD Operations. The efforts to clarify the CSD jurisdiction were only partially successful. The extent of the CSD's authority over the thirteen categories of transactions was firmly established. Member nations must notify and consult with affected nations with respect to the listed transactions in accordance with the procedures established by the Subcommittee. Also, it is now clear that the FAO Principles are not limited to surplus disposals, narrowly defined. However, many FAO members consider that there exist categories of transactions having clearly identifiable concessional elements or elements that could otherwise adversely affect normal commercial trade that have not been included in the list and that should be subject to consultation and notification.

Those nations concerned over the exclusion of important transactions feared that the noninclusion of these transactions under the procedures recommended could undermine the effectiveness of CSD operations and weaken the concepts of reciprocity and equivalent advantages on which such procedures should be based. The admonition (in the CSD terms of reference) against an overly narrow construction of CSD jurisdiction and the provision for subsequent definition of the catalog of included transactions is a concession to this viewpoint.

Relationship of CSD and GATT. Much of the disagreement over the appropriate reach of the FAO Principles focuses upon the question of whether certain transactions are based on surplus or concessional sales, and therefore covered by the Principles, or whether they primarily involve export aids to essentially commercial clients and thus fall within the jurisdiction of the GATT. In many cases, those who push for wider FAO coverage are motivated by dissatisfaction with GATT as an effective mechanism for protecting their commercial interests in agricultural trade. There was at least some support for expanding CSD jurisdiction to include sales made at reduced prices or in ways that disrupt prices, subsidized exports and imports, barter transactions, and even noncommercial currency clearing transactions. Ordinarily, one would think that all of these were far more suited to treatment by GATT or that they would fall within the scope of particular commodity agreements. Apparently, some countries believed that they were more likely to receive a sympathetic ear for their problems within the CSD. Since GATT encompasses heavy industrial traders as well as agriculturally oriented nations, and given GATT's recognized failures with respect to agricultural trade, it isn't entirely surprising that agricultural producers believe they can do better in an organization within the Food and Agriculture Organization with its obvious agricultural orientation, particularly in a Subcommittee of the Committee on Commodity Problems, which traditionally represents the views of agricultural exporters. It is interesting to note that GATT has begun to take agricultural export subsidy problems more seriously, although as yet nothing concrete has happened in this regard.[40]

Future Expansion of CSD Jurisdiction

To satisfy those countries seeking broader jurisdiction by the FAO over noncommercial transactions, the Committee on Commodity Problems authorized further revision of the CSD charter which could broaden the jurisdiction of the FAO control system. The Committee on Commodity Problems found general agreement that the adopted list of transactions was not exclusive and that some new types of transactions might be identified in the future. The CSD was authorized to examine proposals by member nations for additions to or deletions from the list of transactions and modifications to the catalog of transactions in the Annex to the terms of reference of CSD. If the CSD, after taking account of arrangements in other international organizations, concluded that the type of transaction concerned fell within the scope of the FAO Principles of Surplus Disposal, it could request the CCP to decide whether it should be added to the categories of transactions subject to consultations and/or reporting.

*Procedures for Notification and
Consultation*

It is apparent that since the FAO control system is based upon the concept of negotiation rather than authoritative adjudication, the procedures employed to conduct these negotiations are a crucial component of the control system. The 1968 CSD working party, in its review of the role of the CSD, found existing procedures generally to be satisfactory. But, as has been discussed earlier in this chapter, there has been some dispute over the extent to which the FAO Principles explicitly require prior notification and consultation. The FAO, in its deliberations on the changes with respect to the FAO Principles recommended to it in 1969 by the Committee on Commodity Problems, underscored the importance of establishing effective consultative procedures. The Council considered that the development by the Committee of agreed procedures for consultation and notification under the FAO Principles for Surplus Disposal constituted an important step forward, and that adherence to the procedures recommended by the CCP would make an important contribution to more orderly conditions in international trade for agricultural commodities, which would be in the interest of all member nations. It therefore invited member nations to cooperate fully in implementing the agreed procedures.

The notification and consultation requirements recommended by the FAO Council are included in an Annex to FAO Council Resolution 1/53, entitled "Procedures for Notification and Consultation Under The Principles of Surplus Disposal Recommended by FAO."[41] The first two sections of the annex follow.

1. All reporting and consultative obligations and procedures shall be based on the principle of reciprocity among Member Nations and Associate Members.
2. Before carrying out any transaction in agricultural commodities of a type mentioned in the Catalogue of Transactions, and taking into account the special situations covered in paras. (3), (4) and (5) below the supplying country shall:
   a. undertake bilateral consultations with countries substantially interested by reason of their exports of the commodity concerned to the recipient country;
   b. notify the CSD of the main features of the proposed transaction in order to provide other countries directly interested in exports of the commodity an opportunity for bilateral consultations, it being understood that this would not result in any lengthening of the total period of consultation.

These Procedures have been interpreted by the Committee on Commodity Problems on the basis of a report by the CSD. The Subcommittee considered that the principle of reciprocity requires not only reciprocal observation of consultative procedures in form but also willingness on the part of suppliers to apply those procedures in such a manner as to take fully into account the expressed interests of all affected parties.[42] In general, this means that the extent to which one country is obliged to supply information to another depends upon the kind of information it receives from that country. There is some history in the CSD of disagreement over how much information a food aid donor could be asked to supply. This could be a problem with respect to trade information sought from smaller countries. Often, they do not have the requested figures at hand and are understandably reluctant to invest the time and manpower necessary to obtain them. Other than adopting the concept of reciprocity as the touchstone, the FAO working groups were unable to establish clear standards regarding the amount and kind of statistics countries must supply to satisfy the notification and consultation requirements. More specifically, reciprocity has been interpreted by many CSD members as requiring food aid donors to discuss the size of proposed food aid transactions with third countries before discussing this matter with the recipient. France, and most of the EEC countries disagree. They find it impossible or impractical to avoid discussing the size of a transaction with a potential recipient before discussing it with other nations. Therefore these countries interpret FAO consultation rules to require simultaneous discussion of the program's size with the recipient and third countries. For at one point the EEC took the same position with respect to usual marketing requirements. But as we shall see in Chapter 8, the EEC has changed its mind on this point. Certainly, it would seem that some discussions of the size of the transactions' size must be conducted with the recipient before bringing the matter to the CSD, since it would be extremely awkward for a potential donor to propose a food aid deal without knowing the recipient's desires and needs in this regard. The extent to which the figure is subject to change in response to third country complaints is the real issue.

Paragraph (2) of FAO Council Resolution 1/53 codifies the generally accepted views of CSD members towards consultation and notification, and the CSD Report supplies the necessary specifics. The FAO consultation system is broken into two parts. The first relates to bilateral consultations between the country supplying the agricultural product and "countries substantially interested by reason of their exports of the commodity concerned to the recipient country." An important aspect is the identification of the countries that must be consulted. The CSD Report specifies that this decision shall be made on the basis of recent trade statistics. Countries may also request to be consulted and the supplying country must "consider" such requests. The length of the consultation period is a second important feature. The notifying country is obligated to provide no less than 14 calendar days, from the time of formal notification, for the country consulted to make observations or raise objections. If there is no reply within that period, the notifying country may assume there are no objections to the proposal. Under "extraordinary" circumstances, the period may be shortened. If so, the notifying country shall explain the reasons for departure from the 14-day rule. If more than 14 days are requested by a country being consulted, the notifying country, while not obligated to extend the consultation period, must "consider sympathetically" such requests. The place of consultation is determined by the notifying country and the notification is to be made on a standard form drafted by the CSD.[43] The second branch of the consultation process relates to notification to the CSD. The CSD Report recommends that the notification be received in time to provide advance notice of at least three working days before the agreement is signed. The CSD Report stressed that notification to the CSD does not provide for consultation in the same sense as envisaged for bilateral negotiations. It is expected that countries subscribing to Resolution 1/53 will conduct bilateral consultations with all countries having a known trade interest related to the proposed transaction. Notifying countries are expected to make a thorough effort to determine those countries to be consulted bilaterally. However, if oversights occur, the primary role of the notification to CSD is to give any country so overlooked an opportunity to become aware of the fact at this early stage and to take the steps it deems appropriate. The form of notification is the same as that used in bilateral consultations.

The Relationship between the CSD and
Other International Organizations

Food aid operations of international organizations are given special treatment. The World Food Program and the programs of other UN relief organizations such as UNICEF and UNRWA fall into categories 1 and 2. But upon the recommendation of the CCP working party, FAO Council Resolution 1/53 specifically excludes such transactions. WFP transactions are already subject to special consultative rules and the operations of intergovernmental organizations like UNICEF and UNRWA operations were deemed sufficiently small and nonmarket-oriented to constitute no substantial danger of harmful interference with normal patterns of production and international trade. UNICEF and UNRWA operations present no problems. But the situation with respect to the World Food Program is more complex.

The World Food Program and Commercial Agricultural Trade. From its inception, the potential impact of World Food Program activities on both the agricultural sector of the recipient country and international agricultural trade has been a prime consideration in the adoption and administration of the Program. Developed agricultural exporters feared further deterioration of the already very serious surplus problems in basic food grains. Developing countries were afraid that new food aid programs might be substituted for "hard" foreign aid and that food aid might impede the indigenous development of the recipient's agricultural capacity. The socialist countries saw the plan as a United States scheme for dumping its agricultural surpluses. Therefore, the basic texts establishing the program explicitly required that the program be administered to avoid any possible disruption of agricultural commerce within the recipient or of international trade.

The basic structure of the World Food Plan was established by General Assembly Resolution 1496 (XV).[44] Article 9 of this Resolution required that any program based upon this Resolution "proceed in accordance with the Principles of Surplus Disposal and Guidelines of the FAO." More specifically, such programs were to be conducted "with adequate safeguards and appropriate measures against the dumping of agricultural surpluses on the international markets and against adverse effects upon the economic and financial position of those countries which depend for their foreign exchange earnings primarily on the export of food commodities. . . ." The World Food Program itself was established through Resolution 1714 (XVI)[45] of the United Nations, and FAO Conference Resolution 1/61.[46] Article I(1) of the UN resolution approves an experimental World Food Program subject to the safeguards included in FAO Conference Resolution 1/61 and paragraph 9 of UN General Assembly Resolution 1496 (XV). Article 13 of the FAO Conference Resolution 1/61 requires the governing body of the World Food Program (Intergovernmental Committee) to ensure that

i. in accordance with the FAO Principles of Surplus Disposal and with the consultative procedures established by CCP, and in conformity with United Nations General Assembly Resolution 1496 (XV), particularly paragraph 9, commercial markets and normal and developing trade are neither interfered with nor disrupted,

ii. the agricultural economy in recipient countries is adequately safeguarded with respect both to its domestic markets and the effective development of food production.

The protection of commercial trade and the recipient's agricultural economy required by these basic texts is built into the World Food Program by Articles 20 and 21 of its General Regulations. Article 20 requires that:

Adequate consideration shall also be given to safeguarding commercial markets and the normal and developing trade of exporting countries in accordance with the FAO Principles of Surplus Disposal, as well as safeguarding normal commercial practices in respect of acceptable services.

The procedures to be employed for this purpose are provided in Article 21:

a. At an early stage in the preparation of a project which may be of such significance as to threaten to interfere with or disrupt commercial markets or normal and developing trade, he shall consult with the countries likely to be affected.

b. He shall also inform the chairman of the Consultative Subcommittee on Surplus Disposal of the FAO Committee on Commodity Problems of such preparations.

c. If questions concerning any proposed project are raised before the Consultative Subcommittee, its views should be promptly reported to the Executive Director, who shall take them into account before proceeding with the project.

d. To facilitate the consideration of policies within the field of surplus disposal, he shall make available to the Consultative Subcommittee documents relevant to these subjects prepared by the Program.

The Interrelationships of the WFP and CSD

Despite the unmistakable concern of both the UN and the FAO that the World Food Program be administered to minimize the impact of WFP programs on commercial agricultural trade and the explicit incorporation of the FAO Principles into the WFP's charter, the history of the World Food Program has been marked by a consistent, if muted, friction between the administrators of the WFP and the CSD. The source of the problem is clear enough. The objective of the WFP is to use its resources to maximize humanitarian relief and economic and social benefits from the cash and food resources entrusted to it. Considerations of possible adverse effects upon commercial trade are seen, correctly, as impediments to the attainments of its goals. The CSD, although gradually expanding its horizons, still primarily is the tool of agricultural trading interests. Thus, conflict is inevitable.

Formal relationships between the WFP and the CSD are established by a set of jointly adopted procedures for notification and consultation and a series of interpretative comments by the governing bodies of both institutions. There are two sets of requirements. The first set identifies those transactions requiring various degrees of notification and consultation. These are set forth in the following table:

Types of WFP Aid	*Consultation*
a. Meeting emergency food needs and emergencies inherent in chronic malnutrition (this could include the establishment of food reserves);	a. Prior consultation would not be required, except where concessional sales are involved, or where the establishment of food reserves is contemplated.
b. Assisting in preschool and school feeding;	b. Prior consultation would not be required (subject to review in light of experience).
c. Implementing pilot projects,	

using food as an aid to economic and social development, particularly when related to labor-intensive projects and rural welfare.

c. Prior consultation should be required in all cases.[47]

The second set of requirements established the procedures to be followed for those transactions requiring notification and consultation.

a. On being informed of a proposed project under the World Food Program, the Washington representative of the Program will consult with the representatives of those countries regarded as having a trade interest which might be adversely affected by the World Food Program proposals.
b. In his contact with these third country representatives, the representative of the World Food Program will provide all relevant information.
c. The representatives of countries so consulted will communicate the reaction of their countries to the World Food Program representative as quickly as possible.
d. At the time the World Food Program representative consults third country representatives, he will inform the Chairman of the Subcommittee that bilateral consultations are in progress on a specific project.
e. Following bilateral consultations, the World Food Program representative will provide relevant details of the project to the Chairman of the Subcommittee for circulation to all members.
f. Should the representative of any member country of the Subcommittee wish to do so, he may request bilateral consultation with the representative of the World Food Program.
g. If the World Food Program representative receives no reactions within ten working days of the date of the notice, he will assume that there is no objection on the part of the Subcommittee member countries.
h. Members may of course raise for discussion in the Subcommittee any matters relating to the consultative aspects of World Food Program projects.[48]

These arrangements draw a clear line between direct donations of foods to needy or hungry people, which require no consultation, and programs for economic or social development which are subject to standard CSD notification and consultation procedures.

There seems to be some disagreement between the CSD and the office of the Executive Director of the WFP and perhaps between the WFP secretariat and the Intergovernmental Committee with respect to the impact of WFP projects involving a significant sales element on the demand for commercially supplied agricultural products. The effect of these transactions is not always easy to analyze. Some of these problems will be discussed in the subsequent chapters dealing with specific food aid/commercial trade problems. On the procedural level, the CSD has not been entirely satisfied with the information and analysis provided by the secretariat pursuant to its notification requirements. At one point, the CSD found that the WFP secretariat, in formulating projects where sales are involved, "almost invariably" finds that no displacement of commercial sales would take place or that there would be sufficient control and follow-up in the field to minimize such displacement. Moreover, in cases where there might be displacement of commercial sales by the sale of WFP commodities, the WFP secretariat citing paragraph 6(1)(b) of the FAO Principles, follows the pattern of stating that there exist offsetting economic benefits to the recipient.[49] Without directly challenging the standards applied by the WFP secretariat, the CSD claims that it is not given sufficient information and analysis by the WFP to enable the CSD to judge the matter for itself.[50]

To remedy this situation, the CSD suggested substantive and procedural standards to be applied to WFP programs involving sales of commodities. These were largely accepted by the Intergovernmental Committee. The CSD recommended the following guidelines.

General Principles

i.   Sales of WFP commodities should continue to be regarded as exceptions, such decisions being based on one main question: Is the sale absolutely essential to the project?
ii. In general, sales should be excluded from a proposal if commercial sales would knowingly be displaced. If despite this, the WFP proposes to go ahead with the sale, then the overriding economic benefits to the receiving country should be adequately explained.
iii. If the sale is essential, the WFP would be expected to explain why this is so, and the guidelines in paras. (a) through (c) below should apply:

    a.   Where WFP commodities are to be sold on the open market, the WFP Secretariat should carefully analyze the recipient country's supply pattern for each of the commodities involved and determine whether special safeguards to assure against displacement of commercial marketings are essential. The results of the Secretariat's analysis, together with the data used, should be provided, along with information on special safeguards and on the administrative machinery for implementing the sales.

    b.   Where WFP commodities are to be sold at prices below *prevailing local levels*, the channels through which such commodities would move should be isolated from the usual commercial channels, so far as possible. The WFP would be expected to provide information which would support this type of sale.

    c.   Proceeds from sales should continue to be used only to finance activities under the project, including payment of wages, purchase of local tools, equipment, and local ingredients. Information on the use and control of the proceeds should be provided, along with an indication as to how such sales would lead to purchases of the same types and quantities of food as were initially supplied under the project.

iv. *Livestock feeding projects*

With respect to livestock feeding projects, the determination of whether or not there is likely to be market displacement can best be made if it is known that the WFP feed is distributed under controlled conditions to livestock producers undertaking new livestock enterprises which they would not undertake in the absence of this assistance; or that the WFP feed is utilized in a mixture which would not otherwise be available and which will be distributed under controlled conditions to participating livestock producers. If the producers receive feed at subsidized prices, such prices should be gradually increased so as to reach the market price level by the time of WFP's withdrawal. The CSD believes that lack of attention to these details could result in discouragement of local feed grain production or in displacement of markets at a later date even though such effects may not exist in the initial stage.

White, with some possible exceptions, the livestock feeding projects thus far undertaken probably meet the criteria suggested above, the WFP documents do not clearly indicate that they do. The CSD suggests, therefore, that in the preparation of future livestock feeding project summaries, the WFP Secretariat should specify the arrangements which have been made or are planned to meet these criteria. The CSD is mindful that the criteria may not be fully applicable to an occasional potentially good livestock feeding project.

v. *Price stabilization projects*

With respect to price stabilization projects, the question of possible market displacement is directly associated with the competence with which the project is planned and administered. The CSD, therefore, believes that its assistance to the WFP on price stabilization projects will necessarily be limited until it has received and reviewed reports on projects already undertaken with a view to assessing the extent, if any, of market displacement.[51]

The thrust of the guidelines is towards a more restrictive attitude towards sales. But the Secretariat of WFP has resisted undue restriction of what it deems a useful device for implementing its programs.[52] The controversy is a prime example of the limited nature of the FAO control system. The FAO greatly prefers that the WFP give food rather than sell it through commercial channels. But it lacks the power to forbid the sales. Instead, it requires fuller documentation of these transactions, including explicit justifications in terms of overriding benefits to the recipients.

The ultimate resolution is a compromise. The Intergovernmental Committee (IGC) of the WFP was reluctant to burden the Secretariat with the requirement of undertaking "costly and extensive investigations" to satisfy CSD requests for more information and analyses. But it did admonish the Executive Director to be more restrictive in its use of sales. Apparently, the Executive Director agreed to adopt, as an additional criterion for the selection of projects, the test of whether a project involves sales on the open market.[53] As a result of this interchange, the WFP provided the CSD fuller descriptions of the projects subject to CSD procedures. However, consistent with the IGC's reluctance to impose additional burdens on the WFP Secretariat, these were not accompanied by specific analyses of the impact of the transactions. The CSD has continued to criticize proposed sales, but in each case, it has limited itself to conveying its objections to the WFP Secretariat, or, in the most recent case, to the Intergovernmental Committee itself.

Given the institutional kinship of the CSD and World Food Program, it is not surprising that no formal action was recommended with respect to WFP-CSD relationships. Any adjustments that might be required would in all likelihood be accomplished through direct discussions of the kind described above. The rapid growth in size and ambition of the WFP programs is likely to bring further conflict with the CSD. Even now, the CCP working party which developed the recent modifications to the FAO system expressed some concern with the very much larger feeding programs now under way.[54] Under present arrangements, feeding programs are reported to the CSD but do not require prior consultations. The working party suggested that some modifications of these arrangements might be in order. This concern will certainly increase if the WFP decides to implement its long-standing interest in exploring the possibilities of a program approach to food aid, under which food aid is channeled through the commercial market in support of the balance-of-payments during the whole period of national plan. According to the Report of the Intergovernmental Committee of the World Food Program on Food Aid and Related Issues during the UN second development decade, if additional resources are made available, the WFP should seriously consider initiating programs that use food aid in support of the national plans of developing countries (in other words, the much criticized and feared program approach, where food aid is given through the commercial markets). If this should occur, drastic changes in WFP-CSD relationships would be necessary if the CSD is to play the same role vis-a-vis WFP programs and national programs. One solution might be to give each body formal representation on the other's governing board. Or the WFP might formally be given final authority to weigh the benefits and commercial trade dangers of large-scale WFP programs operating through normal commercial channels.

In all events, the current sniping should cease. The CSD's concern with the potential danger of large-scale market-directed WFP programs is understandable. But the fact is that this is exactly the form that United States Food for Peace programs have taken, even though in most instances the programs could not meet a strict additionality test. In practice, this has been recognized by the CSD which has focused its attention on preventing the use of food aid as an offensive trade weapon, and building in maximum protections to commercial trade through devices like usual marketing requirements, World Food Program market operations would be much less dangerous than national programs since there is no temptation to use food aid to improve the donor's commercial position. Undoubtedly, some of this friction stems from the greater vulnerability of the WFP to criticism when compared to individual countries. Therefore, the FAO Council or Conference should determine the general acceptability of this kind of food aid, recognizing that full additionality won't always be possible. Then, the CSD and WFP should concentrate on developing adequate protective measures such as usual marketing requirements.

Interest of Developing Countries. The CSD working party review of its functioning recognized that the daily work of the Subcommittee tended to focus upon the problems of exporting countries. But as stated by the working party, the FAO Principles do give great weight to the benefits to developing countries obtainable through food aid. This, together with the possibility that some developing exporting countries might themselves become food aid donors, "suggested" to the working party that CSD activities might soon become more useful to developing countries.

The recent actions of the FAO continue to show concern with the problems of developing countries. Many of these actions were the result of FAO Council modifications of CCP proposals (which body continued to be less sensitive to food aid recipient's needs than the FAO Council). The FAO Council reaffirmed that governments of recipient countries were not responsible for prior consultation and reporting. Secondly, the new procedures adopted by the FAO were not to be an obstacle, or cause undue delay in the provision of food aid urgently needed by a developing recipient country. Finally, special consideration was to be given to the interests of developing exporting countries which depend heavily on export earnings from agricultural commodities. The Council resolution also made reference to safeguarding local production and markets of developing countries. This can be considered largely ritualistic since recipient countries can protect their internal markets without help from international controls.[55] But one aspect of recent modifications in the FAO control system may have very serious consequences for developing countries. This is the incorporation of the usual marketing requirements (UMR) into the FAO Principles. The UMR (which will be discussed in the next chapter but one) which has been the principal tool used by the United States to protect commercial markets. It requires food aid recipients of particular agricultural products to purchase a minimum quantity of the same or closely related products on commercial terms. Since the level of the UMR directly affects the utility of food aid to the recipient, developing countries will have a powerful interest in the way the new FAO requirements are administered through the CSD.

National Food Reserves

Although national reserve plans have been considered for many years, the first such program was undertaken by the World Food Program in 1971 to establish wheat reserves in Turkey. The concept of using food aid to establish commodity reserves raises in unusual form all the issues implicit in the consideration of usual marketing requirements. This concept also raises peculiar problems with respect to compliance with the requirements of the FAO Principles.

To stabilize the prices of bread grains, the staple of the Turkish diet, a Turkish governmental agency, the TMO, is empowered to regulate the supply and price of wheat. This is accomplished by the TMO holding stocks of wheat and buying and selling wheat on the local market, fixing guaranteed purchase and sales prices, and undertaking imports and exports, where appropriate, in fulfillment of these functions. In discharging its functions, the TMO annually handles stocks of about 1,200,000 metric tons. Short crops have periodically depleted these stocks, and Turkey wanted to establish a national wheat reserve to guard against shortages of domestic grain production. The minimum size for this reserve has been established at 400,000 tons of wheat—a bit more than a one-month market requirement—and the World Food Program has agreed to furnish this amount as soon as possible. The initial agreement will cover a five-year period and is estimated to cost $35 million, including shipping and insurance. The reserves may be used to meet emergency needs and to stabilize prices in periods of shortage of home-grown wheat. Up to 10% of the reserve may be used by the WFP to make food available in other countries with emergency needs, in which case the WFP will replenish the reserve so used.

The World Food Program and the Turkish government have agreed upon safeguards against disruption of normal commercial trade patterns. Turkey has agreed to permanently maintain wheat stocks at the level provided by the reserve. Whenever wheat is drawn from the reserve, Turkey will replenish the reserve at the close of the current crop year. The replenishment will be made through domestic commercial purchases, commercial imports or food aid. Turkey agreed never to export wheat from the reserve. In addition, it agreed to export no wheat at all during the period when the World Food Program was delivering substantial amounts of wheat for the reserve. Turkey further agreed to consult with any third country which believes that the operation of the reserve has injured its export interests. Turkey also agreed to increase the reserve under certain conditions. If domestic production of bread wheat increases to a level whereby after all domestic requirements are met and a surplus equal or greater than the reserve remains for export, Turkey will increase the size of the reserve by at least 10 percent of the amount contributed by the WFP, until the size is doubled. Although the Turkish government must submit reports to the WFP pertaining to the use of the reserves, it is not subject to any other direct administrative controls.

Because the actual use of the reserves is deferred to uncertain future times, this kind of arrangement presents special problems. The impact of the use of reserves upon commercial trade depends upon the same factors operative with respect to food aid shipments designated for immediate use. If the food is used to meet needs that otherwise would not be met through commercial purchases, no displacement of commercial sales will occur. Or if the food aid assists economic development which ultimately raises the effective demand for commercial food purchases, additionality requirements will be met. But if reserves are used to meet needs that otherwise would be satisfied through commercial purchases, this would result in displacement of commercial sales in violation of the FAO Principles. Since reserves used to overcome shortages of domestic production will be sold through normal channels to meet commercial demands, the only situation in which it is likely that the reserves will not displace commercial sales would be where reserves are used in disaster areas to feed people who could not afford to buy bread.

If displacement of commercial sales occurs, the CSD has taken the position that the reserves must be replenished by commercial purchases in order to preserve the preuse level of commercial imports.[56] Under the Turkish-WFP program, commercial markets are to be protected by requiring replenishment of the reserve after each use by mandatory minimum increases of the reserve if, in any given year, Turkey produces exportable surpluses at least as large as the reserve. The replenishment provisions will work if the purchases for this purpose are made from commercial sources; but the result is uncertain if they are made with food aid. Commercial purchases, whether from domestic or foreign sources, will compensate for any trade displacement caused by the initial use of the reserve. If the reserve is replenished with food aid, there will be a net displacement of commercial sales unless the wheat reserves were used in disaster situations. The provisions for using exportable surplus domestic production to augment the reserve should help commercial sales by withdrawing that amount of wheat from commercial markets. The practical utility of this feature depends upon the prospects for increasing domestic production to the extent necessary to trigger the augmentation requirement.

Reserve plans also present administrative problems which the Turkish plan does not fully take into account. For direct food aid transactions, a single review in accordance with FAO procedures will suffice. But in the case of reserves, the question of market displacement arises every time the reserve is used. That is, every use of the reserve must be tested to determine whether displacement of commercial sales is likely to occur, and, if it is likely, what steps will be taken to replenish the reserves with commercial purchases. The problem is further complicated by the possibility of replenishing the reserves from domestic production, imports, or food aid—all of which will have a different impact upon commercial trade patterns.

Therefore, a fully effective control system requires the establishment of general guidelines in advance and a permanent administrative system to review every use of the reserve. The guidelines would stipulate the kind of replenishment required by each major kind of use anticipated for the reserves. After each use of the reserves, the administrative body would determine the nature of the use and the appropriate action with respect to replenishment. The Turkish system requires Turkey to consult with any exporter believing itself injured by the reserve's operations. It is not clear if this permits a third country to complain against Turkey's failure to comply with its undertakings pursuant to its agreement with the World Food Program, or to any activities of the reserve scheme. If Turkey complies with the agreement, the only situation which could give rise to a legitimate complaint would be where Turkey uses food aid commodities to replenish uses of the reserve which displaced commercial sales. In this situation, countries which normally export wheat to Turkey could complain if Turkish imports are reduced, and this reduction is traceable to use of the reserve.

This is a very clumsy arrangement. The vital consideration is the use of the reserves which required the replenishment. If the reserve was used in a way which would have been appropriate for food aid, wheat replenishment via food aid would be appropriate. Otherwise not. But complaints registered after Turkey has obtained the food aid come much too late. At this point, it is very unlikely that Turkey will refuse the food aid solely because a prior use of the reserve caused displacement of commercial sales. Actually, the injured third country, rather than making a fruitless complaint to Turkey, would be far better off if it could make the complaint to the donor through the FAO system. Under existing procedures, this can be done.

The crucial feature of reserve plans with respect to protection of commercial trade is the method used to determine if replenishment is necessary. These decisions on the necessity for commercial purchases (and in the event commercial purchases are deemed necessary, the source of the required commodities) must affect the country maintaining the reserve and third party exporters to the reserve-holding country much in the way that usual marketing requirements affect these parties. Under the Turkish plan, these decisions are made by Turkey, pursuant to the restrictions imposed by agreement with the World Food Program. Obviously, this task is best discharged by people without direct interest in the outcome. This would indicate that reserve programs undertaken and administered by the World Food Program should be easier to administer than nationally sponsored programs. To establish a credible decision-making group under bilateral reserve programs, it may be necessary to include other exporters in the decisions or to coopt personnel from international institutions. Another possibility would be to subject these decisions to normal FAO consultation procedures. The feasibility of FAO review depends upon the frequency with which the reserves are used as transactions increase; the larger the administrative burden imposed by the review system. So far, this problem has not arisen since the only national reserve plan supported by food aid is under WFP auspices.

In the Turkish scheme, the World Food Program chose to rely upon guidelines imposed in the basic agreement, leaving their implementation entirely to Turkey. Pursuant to the terms of the agreement, Turkey decides when and how replenishment is to be accomplished. It also is responsible for consulting with

potentially affected third countries. This approach is the simplest administratively and creates minimum interference with the recipient's political processeses. It
also provides the least protection to third country exporters. It is impossible to
predict the sources of this approach *a priori*. Therefore, it will be necessary to
observe experience with this plan closely for guidance on the appropriate methods for future reserve schemes.

In 1971, the first year of the reserve plan's operation, a combination of a
bumper crop and the lack of storage capacity has forced the WFP to waive certain restrictions of the arrangement. Turkey was permitted to export up to
2,000,000 m.m.t. of wheat despite the explicit prohibition of exports during the
period when the WFP is shipping wheat to Turkey for the reserve. One hundred
thousand tons is destined for Iran under the emergency aid arrangements operative between Turkey, Iran and Pakistan. Another 50,000 tons will be added to
the reserve and the remainder will be sold commercially. Turkey agreed not to
accept any food aid imports for the reserve in 1972. Under the circumstances,
there seems to be no alternative to the waiver. This does illustrate the necessity
for great administrative flexibility necessary under this kind of scheme, principally due to the inherent national and international variability in wheat
production.

Expanding the Scope of CSD Operations

Under its current charter, the CSD is only concerned with food aid as a threat to
commercial trade. This role brings the Subcommittee into conflict with national
and international institutions such as the World Food Program, UNCTAD, and
the Economic and Social Council of the U.N., which view food aid as an effective tool of international development and relief. Its activities also trench upon
the responsibilities of other organizations concerned with agricultural trade
problems such as GATT, the International Wheat Agreement, the Food Aid Convention, the International Sugar Agreement, and the OECD. Obviously, the ideal
method for handling food aid would be for the same institution to have responsibility both for maximizing the benefits of food aid and for the controlling of all
potential adverse side effects. Possible ways of accomplishing this will be discussed in Chapter 11.

Although the Subcommittee is generally satisfied with its performance in the
past, it is uneasy about the future. According to its analyses, its existing terms of
reference give it a wide mandate to deal with problems of surplus disposal and
instruct it to be flexible and adaptable in its approach to them. The Subcommittee believes its usefulness has resulted from and is directly correlated with its
adaptability in dealing with all aspects of these problems, including nonsurplus-
based food aid. This adaptability is, however, now threatened by differences of
judgment as to precisely what is meant by surplus disposal in the contemporary

situation, which is complicated by new concepts such as planned production for food aid and by changes in the nature, extent and location of surpluses. The Subcommittee's name in itself may be deemed to prejudice these issues and may need to be changed. Such differences of judgment appear to derive directly from current uncertainties at the government level as to (1) the direction in which intergovernmental discussions and consultations on surplus disposals, food aid and related issues should be oriented; (2) the objectives which ought to be pursued in the light of current trends and developments; and (3) the kind of institutional arrangements which would best meet those objectives. Clearly, these issues cannot be decided within the CSD itself, but must be resolved at higher intergovernmental levels.

Conceivably, the CSD's functions could be expanded to include responsibility for formulation of policy with respect to food aid and surplus disposal as it affects international trade. Although there is no sign that a change of this magnitude is imminent, elements in the FAO have shown some interest in expanding the CSD's focus by making it the central point in the food aid giving sphere for assembling, analyzing and distributing information on food aid operations. This suggestion was made in a letter from the Executive Director of FAO to the Chairman of the CSD, dated March 29, 1968. This matter was included in the overall review of its functions undertaken by the CSD in 1968.[57]

The CSD study committee concluded that it could perform this function, but it carefully refrained from taking a position on whether it should. Previously, in the response of the Chairman of the CSD to the 1968 inquiry of the Executive Director of the FAO, the Subcommittee took pains to emphasize the CSD's determination to steer clear of any wider involvement with food aid policy.[58] It did believe, though, that giving this function to any other body would lead to duplication, and that by undertaking the information function, the CSD would have better data with which to perform its current duties.[59] But even the inclusion of an information-gathering function worried some export-minded countries on the Committee on Commodity Problems. The parent CCP endorsed the concept of such a service, but recommended that it be run by the FAO Secretariat rather than the CSD. The reason for this decision is enlightening. The CCP wished to avoid placing any responsibility on the Subcommittee which would detract from its primary function of ensuring the observance of the FAO Principles of Surplus Disposal and of safeguarding normal commercial trade. By this action, the FAO clearly identifies the CSD as a narrowly focused institution, whose mission is to protect commercial trade from injury by food aid. The responsibility for maximizing the potential of food as a development tool is to be placed elsewhere. At the moment, no single body short of the FAO Council and Conference is authorized or able to take responsibility for formulating policies capable of resolving the inherent conflicts between maximizing the utility of food aid to developing recipients and maximum protection to commercial trade interests. But to discharge this function, the Conference and Council require expert staff work which would narrow the issues and present alternatives in a form which could be acted upon by the Council and Conference. Under the current organization of FAO, there is no place within the organization authorized to undertake these tasks.

Food Aid Information Service

Although the responsibility for gathering and disseminating information on food aid activities was not located in the CSD, the operation has important and interesting relationships with CSD functions. Dissemination of the information gathered through the service is through a Food Aid Bulletin, published quarterly from information gathered by the Basic Food Stuffs Service of the FAO. The first issue was published in July 1970. The scope of information to be collected is defined by the catalog of transactions made subject to CSD jurisdiction—types 1-13, excluding 10(c) and 11(c). Moreover, the principal source of information is to be the notification by governments and the World Food Program to the Subcommittee. Although the Principles of Surplus Disposal apply to all agricultural commodities, the service only will cover basic foodstuffs including cereals (wheat, maize, barley, sorghum, oats, rice); livestock and dairy products (meat, butter, milk and milk products); and other basic foodstuffs (oilseeds, oils and fats, sugar, fish and other miscellaneous foods). It was understood that the commodity coverage would be open to extension if the CCP so decided at a later date. In addition to the information available from CSD notifications, in order to help developing countries plan their economies, the Food Aid Bulletin attempts to keep abreast of prospective food aid programs to the extent that this information is available from published or other sources. The FAO Secretariat was directed to explore the possibility of obtaining relevant food aid data from the OECD, the World Bank, the International Wheat Council, and individual governments. Certain countries wished to go even further. It was suggested that the information service should attempt to gather information about the food aid needs of developing countries which would be useful to potential food aid donors.

The final product of the FAO political process is at best odd and at worst rather useless. The transactions covered (items 1-13) make this aspect of the service's coverage identical with that of the CSD. But, we have seen that the CSD's jurisdiction is considerably affected by its initial concern with surpluses, modified to some degree by recent increased interest in food aid. The additional functions of the service with respect to food aid availability are largely afterthoughts, and might well be concessions to recipient-minded interests, who do not share the CCP's overriding concern with trade protection. While it might be useful for the CSD to begin collecting and publishing information on food aid activities as a step towards closer integration of the positive and negative aspects of food aid, it is difficult to see what purposes are served by an information service detached from any operational or policy-making responsibilities for food aid/commercial trade problems. All countries seriously concerned with protecting commercial agricultural exports are represented on the CSD, and therefore have direct access to the information service's prime source of information. Countries seeking food aid require better sources of information than the secondhand stuff gathered by the information service. This is not to imply that greater centralization of and coordination of food aid is not desirable only that the information service is not going to contribute much to this process. As an additional function of the CSD, the service could be a useful starting point for more sophisticated analyses of food aid/commercial trade problems. As an independent operation, detached from any organization directly concerned with these problems, it makes little sense.

The Future of the CSD. Experience justifies the CSD's conclusion that the FAO control system has fulfilled the role established for it in 1954 with respect to the relationships of food aid and commercial trade. It has been flexible and adaptable in dealing with a wide range of problems. And with the exception of tying, it seems to have resolved most of the outstanding food aid/commercial trade conflicts. However, in discharging its function, it is limited by the nature of the FAO Principles, its lack of decision-making powers and the narrow scope of its focus. With the exception of the recently adopted standards relating to UMR, the Principles themselves are general and imprecise. Normative prescriptions of this generality are sometimes used in domestic legal systems. But in domestic systems, legislation of this generality is made effective through the medium of quasiadministrative agencies empowered to flesh out the general prescriptions through rule-making and through authoritative adjudication of disputes falling within the agency's jurisdiction. The CSD, though, has no such powers, and is strictly limited to providing a forum for consultations and negotiations and to making recommendations which are not binding upon the governments concerned. Given the political sensitivity of agricultural problems, under the existing state of the international order, an international organization probably could not achieve any greater centralization of authoritative decision-making power.

Notes

1. *Disposal of Agricultural Surpluses Principles Recommended by FAO* [hereinafter *FAO Principles*] 17.

2. FAO/UN, CCP/CSD/68/44, *Role of Subcommittee CSD in Light of Current and Prospective Developments in Agricultural Surpluses and Food Aid* [hereinafter *Role of Subcommittee*] at 4.

3. Ibid.

4. Resolution No. 11/59, *Operation and Adequacy of FAO Principles of Surplus Disposal and Guiding Lines.*

5. See discussion of United States food aid programs, Ch. 2.

6. FAO/UN, CCP/CSD/68/44, *Role of Sub-Committee (CSP) in Light of Current and Prospective Developments in Agricultural Surpluses and Food Aid* (26 July 1968).

7. UN/FAO, CCP/CSD/68/44, *Report of Subcommittee (CSD) in Light of Current and Prospective Developments in Agricultural Surpluses and Food Aid* (26 July 1968).

8. UN/FAO, CCP/CSD/5B17, *Report on Consultative Machinery and Procedures* 10 (21 Apr. 1968).

9. UN/FAO, CCP/CSD/58/7, *Report on Consultative Machinery and Procedures* 10 (21 Apr. 1968).

10. *FAO Principles* at 20-21.

11. *FAO Principles* at 21-22.

12. FAO/UN, CCP/CSD/68/44. *Role of Subcommittee*, at 20.

13. FAO/UN, *Food Aid Bulletin*, ESC: FAB/71, Oct. 1971, at Tables 2, 13.

14. UN/FAO, CCP/CSD/58/7, *1958 Report on Consultative Machinery and Procedures*, 9-10.

15. *Report of Thirtieth Session of the Committee on Commodity Problems* 16-26 (June 1958).

16. The EEC position of consultations under FAO procedures is stated in FAO/UN, CCP/CSD/71/69, *Food Aid Policy of the EEC* (22 July 1971 and FAO/UN, CCP/CSD/71/152, *Implementation of The Food Aid Policy of the EEC*.

17. CCP Resolution No. 2/44, para. 4, CCP 69/28, *Report of the forty-fourth session of the Committee on Commodity Problems*, para. 136.

18. United States government officials claim that the United States' practice of presale consultations with all potentially affected parties was not the result of political pressures or legal requirements but were initiated by the United States itself, acting in accordance with its enlightened self-interest. It made little sense, they claimed, to antagonize Canada, Australia and the Netherlands, for both are friendly allies and good customers of United States exports. Moreover, 30 less-developed countries (or LOCs as they are called in bureaucratese) depend on varying degrees on agricultural exports and it would be silly to help these countries with one hand and harm them with the other by threatening vital sources of foreign exchange ... Memorandum from Howard Gabbert of the Food for Peace Division of the Agency for International Development, dated Oct. 31, 1969 (available in author's files).

19. Swerling, *Current Issues in Commodity Policy, Essays in International Finance*, at 5 (1962); Maiden, *Some Aspects of Commodity Policy*, 4 *Australian Journal of Economics*, 3, 9 (1960).

20. UN/FAO, CCP/CSD/68/44, *Role of Subcommittee*, supra, *in Light of Current and Prospective Developments in Agricultural Developments and Food Aid* (26 July 1968).

21. Id. at 29.

22. Id. at 30.

23. FAO/UN, CCP 69/13/1, (CCP: FU/CSD 69/16). *Report of The CCP Working Group on CSD Functions* (15 July 1969).

24. UN/FAO, CCP 69/28, (CL 53/4) *Report of the forty-fourth session of The Committee on Commodity Problems*, 23-32 (10 November 1969).

25. UN/FAO, Council Resolution 1/53, *Consultative Obligations of Member Nations Under FAO Principles of Surplus Disposal*.

26. The catalog of transactions subject to some form of CSD control is included in Appendix A.

27. FAO/UN, CCP: 69/13/1 (CCP: FU/CSD 69/16), *Report of the CCP Working Group on CSD Functions* 6-7 (15 July 1969) [hereinafter cited as *CCP Working Group*].

28. FAO Council Resolution 1/53, Annex (Nov. 1969).

29. *CCP Working Party Report* at 11.

30. See Chapter 2.

31. *CCP Working Party Report* at 11.

32. Id. at 11.

33. Id. at 12.

34. The question of usual marketing requirements will be discussed in Chapter 8.

35. CCP Resolution No. 2/44, *Report of the Forty-fourth session of the Committee on Commodity Problems*. CCP 69/28, at 28-29.

36. *FAO Principles* supra note 1, para. 28, at 17.

37. FAO/UN, CCP: 69/13/1 (CCP: FU/CSD 69/16), *Report of the CCP Working Group on CSD Functions*, para. 67 U/CC (15 July 1969).

38. Ibid.

39. CCP Resolution 2/44, op. cit. supra.

40. UN/FAO, CCP/FU/CSP 69/4/1. *Rules and Functions of the GATT in the Field of Export Subsidization and Disposal of Commodity Surpluses* (17 Dec. 1968), UN/FAO/CCP/CSD/68/44. *Role of Sub-Committee (CSD) in Light of Current and Prospective Developments in Agricultural Surpluses and Food Aid* 15 (26 July 1968).

41. FAO Council Resolution 1/53 (Nov. 1969).

42. UN/FAO, CCP/CSD/70/74, *Report on CSD Consultation and Reporting Procedures* (24 September 1970).

43. UN/FAO, CCP/CSD/70/74, *Report on CSD Consultation and Reporting Procedures* 2 (24 September 1970). The form recommended by the CSD for notifications is reproduced in Appendix C.

44. 27 October 1960, adopted unanimously.

45. 19 December 1961, adopted by a vote of 89 to 0, with 9 abstentions.

46. 24 November 1961.

47. UN/FAO, CCP/CSD/65/7, *Consultative Arrangements Between The World Food Program and the Consultative Sub-Committee on Surplus Disposal*, (6 February 1965).

48. Id. at Appendix B.

49. UN/FAO, CCP/CSD/66/23, *Report on WFP Sales Policy and Consultative Procedure*, (8 March 1966).

50. Ibid.

51. The Intergovernmental Committee of the WFP also accepted a CSD request to increase the notice period from six to ten days. Id. at 5.

52. *See* WFP/FGC/15/17, *WFP Sales Policy* – Note by the Executive Director, (2 March 1969).

53. Id. at 29.

54. UN/FAO, CCP: 69/13/1. *Report of the Working Group on CSO Functions*, pp. 21, 34 (15 July 1969).

55. Annex to Council Resolution 1/53, (7), (8). (Nov. 1969).

56. UN/FAO, CCP/CSD/56/65 Revised, *Report of the Working Party on National Reserves* 3 (14 Dec. 1956). This report provides a comprehensive review of the relationships of national reserves with commercial trade protections.

57. UN/FAO, CCP/CSD/68/44, *Role of Sub-Committee* at 25-29.

58. UN/FAO, CCP/CSD/68/26, *Chairman's Reply to Letter from FAO Director-General Regarding Added Function for CSD* (9 May 1968).

59. Id. at 2.

Part III: Techniques of Food Aid Control

To this point, we have presented the range of food aid programs, the basic economic relationships between food aid and commercial trade, and the basic legal strictures pertaining to food aid and the institutions available for enforcing these strictures. The next step is an examination of the specific techniques employed to control the unintended impact of food aid transactions on commercial trade and to prevent countries from using food aid as a bribe or club to induce increases in its own commercial sales. The adverse effects of food aid may result directly from the substitution of food aid for commercial imports or from exports which are facilitated by the acquisition of low-price food aid commodities. The principal tool for protecting the "normal" level of commercial imports by food aid recipients is the establishment of minimum levels of commercial imports for food aid recipients. These are called usual marketing requirements (UMRs). UMRs have been employed by the United States from the outset of its food aid programs, and have just been incorporated into the FAO control system. The International Wheat Agreements have endorsed the use of UMRs since 1967. Food aid assisted exports by recipient countries are controlled through direct prohibitions upon such exports. In situations where exports contribute to the recipient's long-term economic development, this country has employed the device of "offsets" which require food aid recipients to match

excess exports with additional commercial purchases.

Paradoxically, the most serious forms of export aggrandizement through food aid programs are closely related to the devices developed to protect normal commercial trade. These two-edged devices are UMRs and offsets in which some or all of the commercial purchases must be made from the food aid donor. These are called tied UMRs and tied offsets. In theory, the level of tied UMRs is based upon the history of the recipient's commercial purchases from the food aid supplier. "Unrestricted tied sales" require the food aid recipient to maintain a minimum level of commercial purchases from the donor without regard to the prior levels of such purchases. These latter arrangements are universally condoned, but sometimes employed.

The close interrelationships between "defensive" and "offensive" control devices complicates orderly examination of these problems. I have decided to divide the discussion into four chapters. Thus, Chapter 7 will focus upon unrestricted tied sales, Chapter 8 will include both untied and tied UMRs, Chapter 9 will discuss methods for controlling food and assisted exports, and Chapter 10 will describe the means employed by the United States to enforce market protection requirements. The discussion of UMRs in Chapter 8 will be introduced by a minute examination of United States practices and experience, followed by

184

an analysis of the issues raised by the recent FAO adoption of UMRs as part of the FAO principles. Since there has been relatively little international ef-fort to deal with food aid induced export problems, Chapter 9 will deal al-most exclusively with United States practices.

7

Unrestricted Tying — Food Aid or Trade Warfare

Although the international community unequivocably condemns the use of food aid to directly increase the donor's commercial sales, in an era when agricultural trade is in a chronic surplus situation, the pressures to so use food aid can become very strong. Tying can be a very effective method of boosting a food aid donor's agricultural exports. Recipients of food aid can be required to increase their commercial purchases of given agricultural products from the donor as a condition to receipt of the same or other commodities on concessional terms. It would be rational for potential recipients to accept such tying arrangements so long as the concessional-commercial package as a whole yields goods at cheaper prices than would be otherwise available. The burden would be borne by third country exporters whose expected sales would be thereby diverted to the food aid donor.

The FAO has declared so-called "unrestricted tied sales" to be clear violations of the FAO Principles. "Unrestricted tied sales" are those in which food aid is made contingent upon a given level of commercial imports from the donor not limited to the normal imports from the supplying country and without provision for safeguarding the normal commercial trade of other exporting countries.[1] But many countries regularly conduct their commercial export trade as well as their food aid through centralized government and quasi-governmental marketing organizations.[2] Therefore, in situations where an agricultural exporter simultaneously negotiates food aid and commercial sales with the same country, the possibility is always there that the two are to some degree connected. Even if exports are largely the function of the private sector, the government agencies responsible for food aid can (and apparently do) informally pressure food aid recipients to purchase the donor's products. So long as the price is at prevailing market levels food aid recipients may well comply in order to protect future food aid possibilities.

The FAO Principles also require that food aid donors take steps to ensure that food aid does not disrupt normal trade patterns. This may reasonably be interpreted to include the right of the donor to protect its own commercial sales. Thus, commercial purchase requirements based upon a prior history of commercial sales to the food recipient, though certainly controversial, have been defended on the general grounds that a food aid donor is entitled to maintain its prefood-aid level of commercial sales. If commercial purchase requirements include provision for commercial purchases from exporters other than or in addition to the food aid donor, these arrangements would be consistent with protection of normal trade patterns. But where the entire commercial purchase requirement is tied to the donor, the transaction moves onto uncertain grounds.

Arrangements tying food aid to commercial purchases from the donor, unrelated to prior trade patterns, are clearly predatory and constitute specific violations of the FAO Principles, and probably violations of Articles VI and XVI of the GATT.[3] A working group of the Consultative Sub-Committee on Surplus Disposal has put the matter well

It is an approach to food aid and market development which is consciously aggressive in intent and practice. It also has a considerable potential for perverting the basic purpose of food aid, since the tendency would be to use a small amount of aid to obtain the largest possible amount of trade on commercial terms. In effect, this would turn the transaction into a cut-rate commercial sale which would both minimize the benefit to the recipient country and undermine internationally agreed minimum prices where these apply.

The Working Group realizes that pressures are present in many exporting countries to use food aid as a device to promote their commercial sales at the expense of other suppliers. Adoption of this practice by any country would make it extremely difficult for other exporting countries to adhere to a policy of self-restraint in this matter. It is not sufficient to deplore such pressures; it is necessary to contain them if a progressive deterioration of trading and surplus disposal practices is to be avoided.[4]

In fact, it is not always easy to distinguish "unrestricted tying" from so-called "grey area" concessional sales. Grey area transactions are concessional sales in which the terms closely approximate commercial levels. At the margin, they tend to be indistinguishable from good old-fashioned price-cutting. Transactions in which transfers on unmistakeable food aid terms are linked to commercial sales have the same impact upon donors, recipients, and third countries as any other form of price-cutting. To determine the real terms of a transaction with tying features, one must total up the food aid and commercial components and determine the average price per ton of all the commodities involved in the transaction. The extent to which the transaction departs from commercial standards will depend upon the mix of food aid and commercial sales and the degree of concession granted in the food aid position. If the net cost to the recipient is well below market levels, we should identify the transaction as food aid. The closer the terms approximate commercial levels, the nearer it comes to price-cutting. But this is exactly the situation with respect to grey area transactions—the prices and terms lie somewhere between food aid and commercial levels.

Administratively, unrestricted tying may be more dangerous to international trade than straightforward grey area deals. With respect to countries which give food aid and handle exports through a governmental or quasigovernmental entity, it may be very difficult to be sure if food aid and commercial transactions actually are tied together. Recent wheat transactions involving Italy provide some good, recent examples of this problem. Italy had donated 75,000 tons of wheat to the United Arab Republic under the Food Aid Convention. During the same period, Egypt agreed to purchase 450,000 tons of wheat commercially. Italy also was alleged to have offered to donate 10,000 tons of wheat to Lebanon in exchange for a commercial deal for 10,000 to 20,000 tons of wheat. Though the transactions were reportedly transacted together, Italy claims that the food aid was not tied to the commercial sales. Rather, these transactions are attributable to the traditionally close ties among the countries in the Mediterranean region—politically, financially and economically. According to Italy, for some time, it has been a source of wheat supply for the UAR. Moreover, the 450,000 tons commercial purchase was a three-year agreement. However, there was no reason to believe that there was a link between the two transactions. Competing exporters didn't believe this, and feared the consequences if this sort of thing continued. More specifically, they believed that there would be a snow-balling effect. The recipient countries would expect and might demand this kind of arrangement and the commercial market would be carved up roughly in proportion to the size of each exporter's food aid program.

This case is a good example of the difficulties which would face the CSD in implementing the changes in the FAO control system discussed in Part III. It is characteristic of a case which looks different, depending on whether it was viewed from the position of the recipient, the supplying or the competing exporting country. Tied transactions are covered by Item 13 in the new CSD catalogue of transactions. However, the new CSD guidelines provide no basis for identifying various types of tying. If the CSD is to cope with these transactions effectively, it will have to devise objective rules in order to identify transactions featuring unacceptable tying features. Under these circumstances, grey area transactions may be easier to handle. Sales on terms somewhere between food aid and commercial levels are completely visible and may be analyzed and discussed on a firm factual basis. Such discussions have the potential of establishing clearer standards, thus leading to permanent solutions, while in the case of unacknowledged tying, one cannot even begin discussions, since there is no agreement that a problem exists.

Under this analysis, a black-and-white approach to unrestricted tying relies on form rather than substance. While the FAO may be forgiven for seeking some firm footholds in the exceptionally swampy field of international trade morality, the extent to which unrestricted tying represents a sharp departure from accepted conduct norms entirely depends upon the terms of each transaction. Exactly the same ambiguities which surround transactions or near commercial terms apply here. Thus, as consensus develops on the level of concessionality necessary to distinguish food aid from price-cutting, these same standards should apply to unrestricted tying. The legitimacy of the transaction should not depend upon the form of the transaction, but upon how great a concession the recipient receives in his total transaction with the putative donor.

United States Practices

Although the United States does engage in certain forms of tying deemed improper by competing exporters, it has not been guilty of unrestricted tying practices.[5] Furthermore, based in part upon long-term pressure from competing agricultural exporters, the United States has abandoned most economically significant tying practices.[6] In this regard, a United States representative in the CSD asserted that it was not United States practice to make the supply of one commodity conditional on the commercial purchases of another commodity, and that this policy would be continued. This may be due in part to sensitivity to international norms, and perhaps in part to the absence of a substantial governmental role in agricultural trade. Unlike many other agricultural exporters, the United States does not enter into commercial sales agreements with other countries.[7] Practically all such transactions are conducted through private channels. Thus, the opportunity of the government to quietly link food and sales to acceptance of commercial products is limited. Any such connection would have to appear openly in the terms of the food aid agreement, and be subject to loud protest from our trading "partners." But it is interesting to note that where the United States engages in state trading—barter deals are an example—questionable practices have developed.[8]

Guaranteeing the United States a
"Fair Share" of Commercial Markets

If direct export expansion through tying devices has not been attempted, efforts to protect existing markets for the United States commercial exports has played a prominent part in the Food for Peace legislation and attendant administrative practices. The language and history of this legislation clearly requires that the program be administered to ensure that concessional sales constitute a net addition to the recipient's "normal" agricultural imports. This is designed to protect United States commercial exports to these countries and is administered through the use of UMRs tied to the United States. If the concessional sales are in addition to commercial sales by *all* countries, this policy would be consistent with the objectives of the FAO Principles, since the same commercial export opportunities would be available as would have been the case absent the food aid. To the extent food aid displaces commercial sales, but the United States retains its own share of commercial sales through the tied UMR, the entire loss of commercial opportunities would be borne by third country exporters.

To date, the only explicit legislative attempt to use food aid to guarantee United States commercial sales focuses upon the division of future expanded commercial sale opportunities in food aid recipient nations. Section 103(0) of the Food for Peace Act requires the President to "(t)ake steps to assure that the

United States obtains a fair share of any increase in commercial purchases of agricultural commodities by the purchasing country."[9] This provision grew out of a concern with the drop in overall and government-sponsored exports of agricultural commodities suffered by the United States between 1966 and 1967.[10] Its purpose, according to the House Committee Report, is to emphasize the development of commercial markets for American agriculture. That is, when a country has progressed towards a commercial sale basis, Congress wanted to see that the United States farmer and taxpayer would be a beneficiary of the newly developed commercial opportunities. It would be unfair, argues the Committee, for the United States to assist the country's development through concessional sales only to lose the emerging commercial markets to competing exporters. The term "fair share," according to the House Committee, is not to be construed as a constant or declining percentage "but is to be a growing or increasing amount *(sic)*" as the economies of the recipient countries improve.[11]

The Administration opposed this enactment. It believed that the United States had been getting its fair share of the commercial imports from major food aid recipients such as India and Pakistan. And any attempt to require such purchases would be misunderstood and would do more harm than good.[12] The performance of several large Food for Peace recipients with respect to commercial imports of cotton and wheat during the past six years may be judged from Table 7-1.[13]

The trade figures for fiscal 1971 show a similar pattern. Japan imported over 100 million bushels of wheat, a record for United States wheat exports to a single country. Yugoslavia, a former food aid recipient, imported 15 million bushels. Commercial wheat exports to Korea and Taiwan continued to expand, and poor growing conditions led to wheat purchases by Turkey and Spain. Raw cotton exports to Hong Kong, Thailand, Taiwan, Japan, and Korea all increased over fiscal 1970 levels. Yugoslavia also imported 259 million pounds of soybean oil, all on commercial terms.[14]

As could be expected, enactment of 103(0) was criticized by competing exporters. They feared that the new legislation might lead to increased tying. And as interpreted by the House Agriculture Committee, Section 103(0) seems to call for a return to dubious past practices. For it is difficult to see how the United States can be guaranteed any given share of commercial sales without resorting to some kind of preemptive device such as tying food aid sales to given purchases of United States products on commercial terms. Total United States commercial sales probably could be increased without preemptive devices simply by reducing concessional sales and competing for the increased commercial imports likely to result therefrom. An increasing share of commercial imports, though, may be attained only by excluding other exporters.

The administration of Section 103(0) by the United States has not justified the fears of its international critics. In the CSD, the United States has asserted that its concept of "fair share" of an expanding market was intended to be con-

Table 7-1
P.L. 480 and Commercial Exports to Selected Countries

	61-62 P.L. 480	Commercial	62-63		63-64		64-65		65-66		66-67	
India												
wheat	1,991	560	3,436	115	4,451	0	5,902	1	7,226	84	3,927	184
cotton	143	54	282	55	189	85	242	121	11		117	150
Korea												
wheat	337	26	611	46	626	85	507	23	547	7	331	341
cotton	234	15	267	14	229	43	243	49	235	87	173	168
Pakistan												
wheat	675	45	1,389	–	1,626	–	1,767	–	841	132	969	69
cotton	36	0	9	2	10	0	8	1	6	0	0	3
Taiwan												
wheat	325	9	335	2	298	15	316	74	16	124	–	280
cotton	115	113	120	115	69	140	135	62	71	114	176	182
Tunisia												
wheat	358	30	220	34	82	8	164	1	43	25	98	44
cotton	0	0	0	0	1	1	2	7	10	3	2	12
Bolivia												
wheat[a]	83	10	130	4	101	9	95	40	97	4		5
cotton[b]	5	0	5	2	7	0	2	4	4	0	4	6

[a] Exports of wheat are measured in thousands of metric tons.
[b] Exports of cotton are measured in thousands of bales.

sistent with its international obligations, particularly, the FAO Principles of Surplus Disposal. Other relevant considerations would be comparative advantage and pertinent government policies, directly or substantially affecting the situation; including the policies of the recipient country as well as those of other competing countries. This position is consistent with the statutes' legislative history. Although the Senate-House Conference committee did not change the language of the House-sponsored provision, the Conference Report mitigates the aggressive tone of the House Agriculture Committee Report. First, the Conference report recognizes that any arrangements designed to benefit United States commercial exports must be consistent with international agreements[15]—presumptively, the FAO Principles of Surplus Disposal and the Guideline for Concessional Transactions of the International Grains Arrangement of 1967.[16] And, rather than demand the reservation of an increasing share of nascent commercial markets for the United States, the conferees state that Section 103(0) only requires that the United States "benefit equitably from the development of new commercial markets," in those countries now receiving United States food aid and that the United States "achieve a growing commercial market for agricultural products as the respective developing nations expand."[17] Thus, according to the conferees, the objective of Section 103(0) is to expand markets for United States products, but not necessarily as the House would have had it, to expand the United States' share of existing and potential commercial markets for its agricultural exports in food aid recipient countries.

As we have noted, the EEC is concerned with the impact of food aid on commercial trade, and has required that food aid include language designed to protect normal patterns of commercial trade.[18] However, it has not resolved the more specific issues of the use of unrestricted tying, and UMRs—tied and untied. With respect to tying, the position of both the EEC and individual members of the Community is a bit obscure. Several EEC countries have imposed conditions on food aid donations under the Food Aid Convention that may amount to unrestricted tying. But the EEC representative did not dissent when the Committee on Commodity Problems condemned commercial purchase requirements connected to food aid transactions (but not based upon a prior history of commercial purchases from the food aid donor). It appears that this problem is one for the Community and is not within the jurisdiction of the individual community members. However, the EEC has not yet officially resolved this matter. But the EEC was very firm on the use of UMRs. It would not impose them unless they were formally made part of the FAO Principles. The United States was equally insistent. It would not continue to impose them if other nations did not follow suit. These attitudes certainly contributed to the adoption of UMRs by the FAO in early 1971.

An Example of Tying Problems—The
New Zealand—Peru Dairy Transaction

Unavoidably, this study has concentrated on United States practices. Therefore, we should be able to gain better focus on these problems through discussion of a transaction not involving the United States which raises many of the fundamental issues with respect to tying. (It's also refreshing to see the United States dishing it out, rather than taking it.) This involves a sales agreement between New Zealand and Peru for dairy products which became a cause celebre in the CSD because of features which could be interpreted as "unrestricted tying."

New Zealand has been the principal supplier of dairy products to Peru. At the time of the transaction in question, New Zealand was supplying about 75% of Peru's total import needs of skimmed milk powder which totalled from 10,000 to 11,000 tons. Commencing on January 1, 1970, New Zealand agreed to give Peru a credit of U.S. $10 million which could be used to purchase from New Zealand up to 9,000 metric tons of skimmed milk powder and 3,500 metric tons of anhydrous milk fat. The credit was intended to finance the approximate proportion of the designated dairy products which New Zealand has supplied to Peru on commercial terms in recent years. Repayment is to be made within ten years with interest at 5-3/4 percent per annum, with the first of ten semiannual principal payments deferred until December 31, 1975. The milk products were to be purchased through normal commercial channels under arrangements which assured that the prices should be competitive with those prevailing for normal commercial sales. An untied UMR was imposed. In addition to the purchases to be financed under the credit, Peru was obliged to purchase commercially from any source, 2,700 metric tons of dried milk and 1,000 metric tons of milk fat. The total of the amount to be purchased under the New Zealand credit and the amount to be purchased globally outside the credit, approximates Peru's expected total needs for the period of agreement.

Does this transaction constitute tying of the kind unequivocally condemned under the FAO Principles? Certainly, the availability of the credit is tied to purchases from New Zealand. But the agricultural commodities are supplied by the donor in almost every concessional sale. Only in the case of the donations by nonfood producers under the Food Aid Convention will a recipient be able to use the donor's funds to purchase products from other countries. Therefore, a meaningful definition of unrestricted tying must refer to arrangements whereby a recipient is obliged to make commercial purchases from the donor in addition to those received under concessional terms, where those purchases are not related to a history of prior commercial purchases. Indeed, as we shall see in Chapter 8, under typical United States practice, if the United States had a history of supplying 9-10,000 m.t. of skimmed milk powder to Peru, it would have required Peru to maintain the old level of commercial purchases from the United States—9-10,000 metric tons in addition to the commodities supplied as food aid. All New Zealand has done is to transmute its normal commercial sales to Peru into concessional terms; accepting the resulting revenue loss. That is, the normal pattern of trade has been for Peru to purchase the major part of its import requirements of skimmed milk powder and anhydrous milk fat from New Zealand on normal commercial terms. Other things being equal it could have been anticipated that this pattern would persist into the future. However, the Peruvian government desired to replace those purchases with a concessional arrangement and New Zealand was willing to comply. Given this situation, New Zealand was their preferred supplier and an agreement was negotiated. But New Zealand has not wooed the Peruvian government away from purchasing from other sources. Indeed, New Zealand has sought through the measures reported above, to ensure that other countries which have supplied these products to Peru in the past—and indeed, any other dairy exporting countries—will continue to be able to compete for the Peruvian market. Thus, New Zealand has not deprived other exporters of their expected markets. These have been protected by the UMR of 2,700 m.t. for skimmed milk and 1,000 of anhydrous milk fat. The departure from the FAO standards lies in the failure to achieve additionality; a related, but decidedly different matter. To the extent additionality requires that in granting food aid, the prior level of commercial sales to the recipient must be preserved, this transaction violates FAO Principles, since there is no reason to believe Peru's commercial purchases will exceed the 2,700 metric ton commercial purchase requirement, thus reducing expected commercial purchases from 10-11 thousand metric tons to 2,700 metric tons. The difficulties raised by an overly literal interpretation of additionality have been discussed elsewhere and will be reexamined in Chapter 11. But whatever the answers to those questions, the transaction does not involve tying. It doesn't even fall into the "grey area" since the terms of the credit are clearly concessional.

The lesson in this is that food aid/commercial trade relationships are exceptionally complex and there are no simple rules for distinguishing appropriate from inappropriate trade conduct. Financial linkage of concessional and commercial transactions could represent extremely aggressive commercial competition, or practices produce results which do not depart very far from normal dealing. The result in a particular case depends upon the terms of the concessional deal, the normal pattern of trade between the donor and recipient, and the steps taken to assure additionality. At all points, one must focus upon the net effect of the entire transaction rather than the form it takes.

Notes

1. UN/FAO,CCP 69/28, *Report of the forty-fourth Session of the Committee on Commodity Problems* 33-34 (10 November 1969).

2. E.g., Canada, Australia, Argentina, New Zealand.

3. See Chapter 4.

4. UN/FAO, CCP 69/613/3, *Report on Tied Sales* 14 (July 1969).

5. Tied Offsets may be an exception. These are discussed in Chapter 9.

6. *Comptroller General's Report on Review of Precautions Taken to Protect Commercial Dollar Sales of Agricultural Commodities to Foreign Countries* at 15-19 (Aug. 1966).

7. The Commodity Credit Corporation is authorized to sell products it has accumulated by virtue of its price support operations. 63 *Stat*. 1055 (1949); 70 *Stat*. 6 (1958), 7 U.S.C.A. § 1427 (1970).

8. United States barter practices are discussed in Chapter 2.

9. 82 *Stat*. 450 (1966), 7 U.S.C.A. § 1703 (0) (1970).

10. *H.R. Rep.* No. 1297, 90th Cong., 2d sess., 41 (1968).

11. Id. at 35.

12. *Hearings on World War on Hunger before the House Committee on Agriculture*, ser. W. 89th Cong., 2d sess., 204-07, 279-81 (1966).

13. *Hearings on the Extension of P.L. 480 Before the Senate Committee on Agriculture and Forestry*, 90th Cong., 2d sess., 159-60 (1968) (Hereinafter cited as *1968 Senate Hearings*).

14. USDA/FAS, *Foreign Agriculture*, Aug. 9, 1971, 5-7.

15. *H. Conf. Rep.* 1642, 90th Cong., 2d sess., 4 (1968).

16. *FAO Resolution No. 14 (53) Disposal of Agricultural Surpluses, Principles* Recommended by FAO, 10-11 (1963) Wheat Trade Convention, International Wheat Agreement, 1971, Article 9.

17. *H. Conf. Rep.* 1642, supra, at 45.

18. See Chapter 4.

8 Usual Marketing Requirements

If additionality—food aid must supplement, not displace commercial sales—is the central concept of the international community's efforts to control the impact of food aid upon commercial agricultural trade, the "usual marketing requirement" (UMR), is the principal tool for achieving additionality. In general terms, a usual marketing requirement obligates the recipient of food aid commodities to purchase additional amounts of these same commodities commercially. Ideally, the UMR should be set at a level equal to the commercial purchases that could be expected without food aid. The United States first formulated and developed the UMR in order to satisfy both the portions of its own P.L. 480 legislation requiring protection of the United States commercial agricultural exports, and the additionality requirements of the FAO Principles. When evidence began to accumulate that other major agricultural exporters with surplus problems were using their growing food aid operations to assist their commercial sales, the United States insisted that UMRs be required in all transactions. One way of accomplishing this would be to incorporate UMRs into the FAO Principles themselves. After two years of very difficult negotiations this was accomplished in January 1971.

One of the prime reasons for the difficulties encountered in incorporating UMRs into the FAO Principles is that the establishment and implementation of UMRs raise important and complex problems, going to the heart of food aid. If set too high, they can neutralize much of the economic benefits food aid is supposed to provide developing countries. If too low, food aid could cause serious disruption in the superdelicate structure of international agricultural trade. Moreover, if the commercial purchases required must be made from the food aid donor—tied UMRs—these can serve as an effective device for improving the donor's commercial trade position at the expense of competing exporters. This chapter will first analyze the basic nature and economic impact of UMRs and compare them with other means for protecting commercial sales. Then, it will discuss United States practice with respect to UMRs and the criticisms of these practices by other countries. The chapter will conclude with a presentation and analysis of the UMR requirements now mandated by the FAO Principles.

Nature and Economic Impact of UMRs

There are three basic variations of usual marketing requirements, with differential impact upon the food aid donor, the food aid recipient, and third country

195

exporters. This section will commence with a discussion of the common features of all three forms and then analyze the precise impact of each of the varieties upon the parties likely to be affected by them.

A usual marketing requirement may be defined as a condition of a food aid transaction which requires the food aid recipient to supplement the commodities it receives through food aid with a certain amount of additional purchases of these same commodities on commercial terms. According to the particular form of UMR employed, these purchases may be made from any exporter (including the food aid supplier), solely from the food aid supplier, or from any exporter except the food aid supplier. Hybrids are also possible whereby the food aid recipient must purchase some fraction of the total UMR from the supplier or from nonsuppliers.

Since the UMR requirement of the FAO Principles is patterned so closely upon United States practices in this regard, the description of the process by which the United States, at least in theory, sets the level of the UMR may be deemed the paradigm for this particular control tool. According to a United States Deputy Assistant Secretary of State for Economic Affairs, a usual marketing requirement:

is included in P.L. 480 agreements whenever there is a strong presumption that commercial sales would take place in the absence of P.L. 480 sales. The exact quantity that would have been bought commercially in these circumstances is, of course, impossible to predict, but several guides have been found useful in establishing the minimum requirement. The most frequently used criterion is the average of commercial imports during the most recent period for which complete statistics are available. The base period generally selected is five years, but this period may be shortened to reflect recent trends more accurately. If there is reason to assume that, because of special circumstances, no base period would adequately reflect the commercial imports that could be expected during the coming year, the usual marketing requirement may have to be adjusted accordingly.

Whenever a new agreement is negotiated, the usual marketing requirements are carefully reviewed. All new developments since the previous agreement, including changes in demand for imports and changes in foreign exchange reserves, are taken into consideration. Other things being equal, if a country's external financial situation has improved appreciably, the country would be expected to purchase a larger portion of its requirements commercially. Conversely, if a country's foreign exchange earnings had been substantially reduced, the usual marketing requirements may have to be reduced.

The interest of developing countries in multiyear programs, stimulated by the desire for more effective planning, raises the question of how to avoid "freezing" the commercial quota for several years. In some cases, this problem is being met by building growth factors into usual marketing requirements established for three or four years hence, on the basis of trends in commercial imports and consumption. In addition, provision is made for an annual review which provides an opportunity to reassess the situation.[1]

The negotiation of UMRs is complicated by the difficulty of obtaining accurate trade data. Countries greatly vary in their sophistication in keeping records of imports and exports. And although a number of international organizations attempt to maintain accurate and timely records of international transactions pertaining to their interest area, they too are ultimately dependent upon the individual countries for their raw data. In negotiating UMRs, recipient countries naturally try to rely upon those figures which will yield the lowest possible UMR. Wheat has been a troublesome commodity in this regard. Recipient countries often attempt to use the statistics maintained by the International Wheat Council (the administrative organ of the International Wheat Agreements). But the United States has insisted that the Wheat Council's figures, which are based upon the information given to it by the member nations of the Wheat Agreement, understate actual imports. For this reason, the United States insists upon examining the raw records kept by each importing country, which are usually higher than the Wheat Council's figures.

Generally, global usual marketing requirements are of some benefit to certain United States interests, more helpful to third country exporters, and are potentially harmful to the recipient of food aid.[2] If a country is forced to make some commercial purchases of the food aid commodity, the United States and other exporters get that much more chance for commercial sales. The real benefit attributable to the marketing requirement depends upon the degree to which the import level imposed compares with that which would have prevailed had the recipient been permitted free choice in the matter. Obviously, if the same level would have been reached, the marketing requirement is economically sterile. Psychologically, it might serve to reassure third country exporters fearful of losing all opportunity for commercial sales to that country. If the mandatory commercial import level exceeds that desired by the recipients, the United States and third country exporters may be benefiting at one recipient's expense.

Short-Run Economic Impact of Imposing Usual Marketing Requirements Compared to its Major Alternatives. Positive commercial purchase requirements of the type employed by the United States constitute but one of several possible methods of preserving commercial markets in food aid recipient countries. Another approach would be to limit concessional sales to each country to some figure below its estimated total import requirements. Under a third variety, commercial purchases could be made a fixed percentage of concessional sales (or vice-versa). Each of these alternatives will affect the recipient differently, both in terms of total commercial and concessional sales, overall benefits, and the division of its resources between food and nonfood items. In several respects, either the food and donor or the recipient or both might profit through use of one of these alternative control methods.

Effect of Usual Marketing Requirements

The current system of fixed levels of mandatory commercial purchase requirements imposed as a precondition to any concessional sales tends to induce the recipient to increase purchases of the concessional commodity at the expense of other goods. Within a narrow range, it also may permit an actual increase in total commercial purchases, and under most assumptions will result in the largest total food consumption. The situation is best explained through use of an indifferent curve analysis (see Figure 8-1).

The horizontal (x) axis will register imports of a product possibly available under food aid. The vertical axis (y) will measure imports of all other items. Located on each numbered indifference curve are combinations of food and other imported items yielding the same level of satisfaction. At each point on the curve, the slope of a tangent represents the rate at which food must be substituted for all other products to maintain a given level of satisfaction. Starting with either axis, and traveling upwards or to the right, the indifference curves represent higher welfare levels. This is self-evident since moving upwards or to the right always increases the supply of one or both products without reducing the other. The straight lines, called budget lines, represent the total available foreign exchange. The slope of the line is determined by the relative prices of food and by the nonfood items and every point along the line represents the various combinations of food and nonfood that may be purchased within available foreign exchange at current prices. Satisfactions are maximized by purchasing that amount of food where the budget line is tangent to the highest indifference curve. This means that any change in the combination of food and other items will result in a lower level of satisfaction.

In the absence of food aid, the budget line is ab, which is tangent to indifference curve Wo, at K. This means that satisfaction is maximized by purchasing X_c^o amount of food and Y_c^o amount of other products. If unlimited amounts of food aid were available, the budget line would be ac. This is tangent to indifference curve W_2 at point c and results in food purchases of X_f' and purchases of other commodities of Y_f'. Under these conditions, both food and nonfood purchases are increased.

The impact of the current practice requiring a given level of commercial purchases as a prerequisite to any concessional sales varies as the purchase requirements are altered. Let us start from the situation in which no food aid is available. Next, food aid becomes available, but commercial purchase requirements are set at the level of commercial sales prevailing immediately before the onset of food aid. Once commercial requirements are met, the recipient may purchase an unlimited amount of food at the lower concessional prices. Therefore, he will substitute food for other commodities, increasing his food consumption until he reaches point M on curve I_z, which is tangent to his new budget line aLt. This budget line follows the original path for commercial purchases until it hits point

199

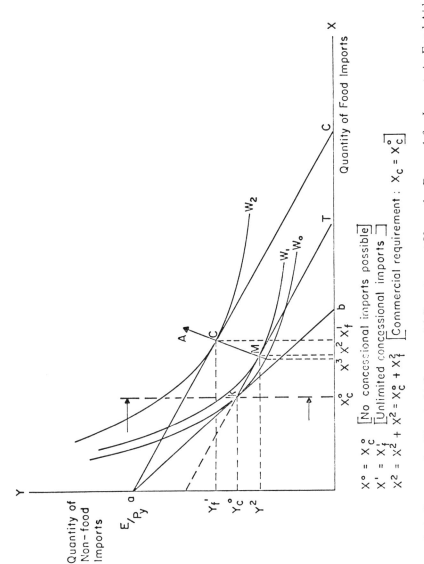

Figure 8-1. Impact of a Threshold Commercial Requirement Upon the Demand for Imports in Food Aid Receipient Country.

L, the old equilibrium point where it turns upward and continues in a path with the slope representing the concessional sale price of food. If commercial purchase requirements are then reduced below the prefood aid levels, the recipient will first save money by substituting concessional purchases for commercial purchases up to the minimum required commercial purchase level. Then he will use these savings to purchase more food and other products. That is, for every substitution of concessional for commercial sales, the recipient saves the difference between the commercial and concessional prices of each unit. The extra income is then spent on food and nonfood. But in addition to the extra income, the price of food has been reduced for additional purchases (assuming unlimited food aid availability). As commercial purchase requirements are reduced to zero, the various equilibrium points will follow path P_C until commercial requirements are reduced to zero, which is the equilibrium point for the recipient having unlimited food aid availability. Technically, this is called an income expansion path at concessional food prices. Unlike the first move after food aid first became available (where the recipient increased food but reduced purchases of other commodities), after the introduction of food aid, as commercial purchase requirements are reduced, purchases of both food and nonfood will increase.

Starting from the prefood aid equilibrium position, if commercial requirements are increased above current levels, we get some interesting results. As previously stated, after food aid becomes available, if commercial purchases are set at existing levels, the purchaser will buy more food and less other products, moving to point M. As commercial purchase requirements are increased, the recipient will be forced to give up concessional purchases to meet commercial purchase requirements. This will have the effect of decreasing total income by the difference between the commercial and concessional prices. But since food has become a cheaper good, the quantity purchased may remain greater than in pre-Food for Peace days. The path followed will not only show the effect of increased income, but will reflect the fact that food has become cheaper than other products since it may be purchased at concessional prices. As commercial purchase requirements increase, the equilibrium points follow the same income expansion line C produced by decreases in commercial requirements, but in the opposite direction. This process will continue until the equilibrium point reaches the same indifference curve that the recipient could reach without food aid. However, now more food and less other products will be purchased. If commercial purchase requirements are increased further, this would drive the recipient to an indifference level below that achievable without food aid (W_O). At this point, it will withdraw from the food aid program and jump back to the original pre-food aid position. This jump creates a discontinuous function between points X_3 and X_C°.

Thus, the current practices with respect to commercial purchases have the following characteristics. When the program is first instituted with commercial purchase requirements set at existing commercial import levels, the recipient will buy more food at concessional prices and give up other products. Both total and commercial food purchases may be increased to some extent by increasing mandatory purchase requirements above prevailing levels. But the possibilities here are limited and a point is soon reached where increased purchase requirements will drive the recipient out of the program. Total food sales may also be increased by reducing required commercial purchase requirements. As commercial purchase requirements go to zero, concessional sales replace commercial sales and both food and nonfood purchases increase over prefood aid levels. When requirements reach zero, all food purchases are on concessional terms, but total food sales are at their highest point. Under most preference functions, at this point, purchases of nonfood products also will be greater than in the prefood aid era.

Besides the direct economic impact, current commercial import requirements burden the food aid recipient with the risks of the donor overestimating total food and fiber needs. An overestimation of total import needs by the donor would face the recipient with some unpleasant alternatives. Under current arrangements, the commercial import quota must be met fully, no matter how much or little of the available concessional purchases are actually made. Under these conditions, if the recipient takes as much food aid as had been anticipated, fulfillment of its mandatory commercial purchases will cause it to import more than an optimum amount of food. If it cuts back concessional purchases, it will be substituting commercial purchases for concessional sales, thus spending more on food imports than it or the donor might desire. Under most demand conditions, the recipient will optimize by reducing some concessional purchases. Since the price of food has been reduced, total food purchases probably will be greater than the levels deemed best by both donor and recipient.

Controlling Commercial Purchases via
Manipulation of the Food Aid Level

Commercial imports also may be protected by restricting the availability of concessional products rather than fixing a minimum level of commercial purchases. In effect, this is the system employed where no commercial purchase requirements are imposed. If the maximum amount of concessional sales made available to a given recipient is set below the total anticipated needs for the commodity concerned, some commercial sales will be assured if the demand functions have been correctly estimated. This procedure, though, will have somewhat different effects on commercial purchases and total purchases than the imposition of minimum commercial purchase requirements would have. This situation is described by Figure 8-2. Starting at the equilibrium point for food purchases at commercial prices, K, Food for Peace is introduced unit by unit. If food aid at lower prices is available, the recipient will certainly buy as much food at the lower

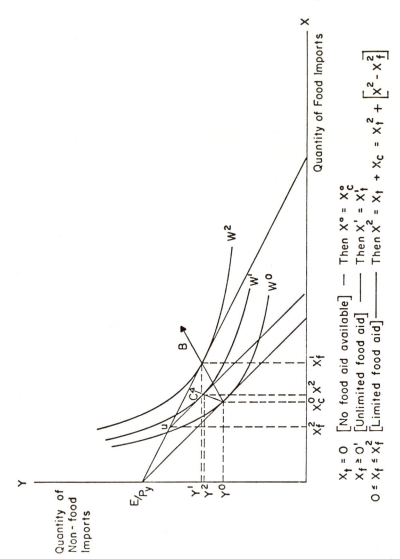

Figure 8–2. Impact of a Food Aid Restriction Upon the Demand for Imports in a Food Aid Recipient Country.

prices than he did at the higher prices. Therefore, he will at least substitute the concessionally priced commodity for one unit of commercial product. But, by so doing, he increases total available income by the difference between the food aid price and the commercial price. He is then able to spend this additional income on both food and other products in accordance with his general preferences. We must note, though, that since only one unit of concessionally priced commodity is available, and he has already used this to substitute for a commercial purchase, additional food must be bought at commercial, not concessional prices. As more and more food aid becomes available, the effect on the recipient will be equivalent to that of receiving additional income equal to the difference between the commercial and concessional prices for the amount of commodity that can be bought on concessional rather than commercial terms. Thus, for a time, the equilibrium points for each level of food aid will follow an income expansion line with food prices at the commercial level. This is indicated by line B on figure 8-2. Point u is reached when enough food aid has been made available so that no commercial purchases need be made. Up to this point, additional food aid has increased both total food and total nonfood purchases. But beyond this, if more food aid is provided, no more savings are available by substituting food aid for commercial purchases. Rather, additional food purchases can be made at concessional rather than commercial prices. Since the effective price for more food is lower than previously, it will now pay to substitute food for other products. This reaction is pictured by a downward turn in the expansion path, forming a kink at u. The purchaser will continue moving along this new, downward sloping path until c is reached, when no more food is desired even at concessional prices. This is the same point as that reached when unlimited food aid is available and when commercial purchase requirements are reduced to zero.

Under these arrangements, u is a critical point. Up to then, increased food aid resulted in increases in both food and nonfood purchases. Beyond this point, further food aid only will result in increased food purchases at the expense of other goods. Thus, if the donor does not wish to decrease importation of other products (and if these other products include capital goods necessary for economic development, the United States at least, probably would not wish them reduced) it must limit food aid to a level below that necessary to reach u. Of course, if increased food sales and greater consumption are the objectives, the donor might take a different attitude.

Controlling food aid levels rather than imposing fixed minimum commercial requirements removes the risk of miscalculation from the recipient. If total import needs are overestimated, too much food aid will be available. This may induce the recipient to move beyond the kink, and begin substituting concessional food for development imports. If food needs have been underestimated, insufficient food aid will be available and commercial food purchases will be larger than anticipated or desired. Here, though, no adverse substitution effects will occur whereby food is bought at the expenses of development imports.

Comparing both methods of control, it would appear that controlling food aid is at once more efficient and more dangerous than imposing fixed minimum commercial purchase levels. According to the well-known welfare principle, the efficiency of economic assistance is maximized where the assistance induces least substitution. Thus forms of assistance which change the relative prices of products are less efficient than those providing increased income at existing price ratios. For example, direct welfare payments are more efficient in this sense than subsidizing the price of particular commodities. This may be particularly relevant in our situation, where there exists a strong interest in maximizing resources devoted to developmental rather than sumptuary ends.

Food aid transactions imposing fixed commercial purchase requirements have the maximum product substitution effect. By making food aid available only after minimum commercial purchases are made, the price of additional agricultural commodities is lowered relative to other products. This has the effect of increasing the consumption of food aid products, relative to other alternatives. By contrast, and short of the kink, fixing maximum levels of food aid does not change the relative prices of food aid and other products. The availability of food aid has the effect of increasing total disposable income which is spent in accordance with prefood aid price relationships. This arrangement induces no product substitution and is therefore the most efficient in the sense we are using the term. More specifically, it does not impel the food aid recipient to give up developmental imports for cheap food.

But, given the uncertainties inherent in this area, and the exigencies of international politics, commercial purchase requirements may be a safer course than exclusive reliance on food aid level control. Clearly, demand functions for underdeveloped countries for imported agricultural commodities are extremely difficult to construct. Not only are consumer wants difficult to divine, but seasonal variations in domestic production will sharply alter the need for imported food and fiber. Under these circumstances, if food aid needs are overestimated, the recipient well may be driven past the kink and onto the area of expansion line where concessional prices prevail and food is thereby substituted for other products. Indeed, a rather small overestimation can have very marked impact if it drives the recipient past the kink. By contrast, the expansion curve under the commercial requirement system is monotonic—moves in one direction—and miscalculations will never cause radical change.

Furthermore, the existing system might be psychologically more appealing to third country exporters and export-minded segments of the donor country. Under this system, all parties immediately know and can rely upon a given level of commercial export opportunities to the recipient country. The other approach may give them equal if not greater protection, but they have no way of knowing this until the financial year ends, unless they wish to duplicate the onerous and speculative chore of estimating the recipient's total demands. Thus, there is much political advantage in having a specific visible import figure as proof that commercial export interests have been duly protected, even if the level is lower than might be the case under the alternate system. So, in choosing between the two systems, we must match economic efficiency against uncertainty and political benefit.

Fixed Commercial-Concessional Ratios

But perhaps this hard choice may be avoided through employment of yet a third plan. This would be to fix commercial purchases as a percentage of concessional ones. That is, for x amount of concessional purchases, the recipient need purchase y amount commercially. The ratio might be set so that if total imports reach the estimated level either total concessional or commercial purchases will reach predetermined optimum figures. Obviously, both figures may not be optimized simultaneously.

Fundamentally, the impact on the recipient will be identical to a simple reduction in the price of the food aid commodity. At all times, the price will be a weighted average of the commercial and food aid price, in accordance with the stipulated ratio. $P = \dfrac{P_f + K\rho c}{1 + K}$, where P is the price, P_f is the concessional price, Pc is the commercial price, and K represents the amount of commercial purchases needed to match each concessional one. Commencing with all commercial transactions, as the proportion of food aid increases, the effective price for the product is reduced. As the proportion of food aid is increased, the recipient again reacts in two ways. First, since he can buy the same amount of commodities with less money (the difference between the commercial and concessional prices, multiplied by the quantity of concessional purchases), his income has been increased. The extra income is then spent on food and other items. Additional food may be purchased on the same terms as the original amount; for every unit of food aid, a given amount of commercial purchases must be made. This differs from both the commercial requirement or food aid limitation cases where additional food is purchased at concessional (commercial requirement case) or commercial (food aid limitation case) prices. Thus, both more food and more other products will be purchased, with impetus towards increasing the proportion of food since it has become relatively cheaper. This alternative is illustrated in Figure 8-3.

The path followed by the equilibrium points as the proportion of commercial purchases decreases lies midway between that of the other two cases. Starting from all commercial purchases, food and nonfood purchases both increase along path C. Food purchases rise less slowly than with commercial purchase requirements, but more rapidly than with food aid limitations before the kink. Concurrently, nonfood expenditures rise more rapidly than under commercial requirements but more slowly than in the prekink food aid limitation case when the proportion of commercial purchases reaches zero. Purchases will be at point   , the all food aid equilibrium point.

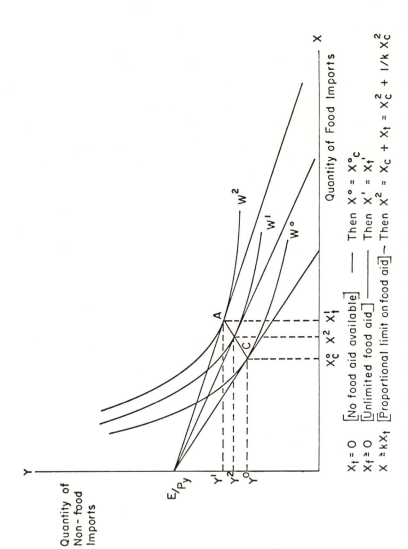

Figure 8–3. Impact of a Proportional Food Aid Restriction Upon the Demand for Imports in a Food Aid Recipient Country.

This third alternative has several advantages over either of the other two approaches. Compared to fixed commercial purchase requirements, it does not induce an immediate shift to greater food purchases at the expense of other goods. Compared to limiting food aid, it doesn't run the risk of sharp changes in food-buying behavior if the demand curve is misestimated and the kink is passed. Moreover, if it does not guarantee a fixed amount of commercial sales, it does ensure that so long as any imports are made, some commercial sales will be assured. Moreover, the risk of overestimating import needs is minimized. If imports are lower than expected, the commercial requirements will be reduced along with the concessional purchases.

The principal disadvantage of a proportional system is that it will be extremely difficult for the recipient to maintain the proportions during any yearly period. Of course, expected needs may be estimated in advance and arrangements for given levels of commercial purchases made accordingly. But, if estimates are miscalculated, given the lead time necessary for food imports, it will be very difficult to make the necessary adjustments in commercial purchases before the year's out. Of course, a system could be devised where necessary adjustments were made in connection with the following years food aid program. Actually, such adjustments are quite common under the existing system.

The Impact of UMRs on the Donor and
Third Country Exporters

The food aid recipient only is interested in the level of the UMR. But third country exporters are interested in both the level—the higher the UMR, the better the opportunity for commercial sales—and the extent to which the sales are tied to the food aid donor.

Usual marketing requirements may appear in any one of three alternate forms. A fully tied marketing requirement obligates the recipient to purchase specific minimum quantities of particular commodities from the food aid donor. A global requirement obligates the country to purchase minimum quantities from the food aid donor or any other country.[3] A third alternate combines these two; an overall global purchase requirement is imposed, of which a stipulated portion is to be purchased from the donor.[4] A fourth possibility is that the commercial purchases may be made from anyone except the donor. All these alternatives are subject to the FAO prohibition on unrestricted tied sales. That is, to the extent the commercial purchases are tied to the donor, the level of the tied purchases must correspond to a history of supportable expectation of an equivalent level of commercial sales, without the food aid.

The Benefit to Third Countries of Mandatory Commercial Import Levels. The greatest benefits from worldwide marketing requirements flow to third country exporters. Under this system, third country exporters have been guaranteed the opportunity to compete for a stipulated level of commercial sales to the country involved. Of course, if food aid levels were calculated correctly, they would have this opportunity without imposing mandatory quotas. But stipulated requirements do afford the psychological benefit of an assured minimum market. The donor also has the opportunity to sell commercially within global marketing requirements. But, through its control over the level of its food aid program, the donor can guarantee itself the desired amount of concessional sales and also control the size of the potential commercial markets without imposing commercial purchase requirements. Marketing quotas just guard against miscalculations, and worldwide quotas merely give the donor a chance, not the certainty of sales. Besides, the ratio of concessional versus commercial sales effects only the donating government, since under most food aid programs, private parties receive the same compensation for concessional sales as commercial ones. Perhaps the chief benefit of marketing requirements to the food aid donor is political. At minimum cost, it is able to satisfy both its legislators concerned with balance-of-payments and its exporter friends whose commercial markets it is actively interested in preserving.

Marketing requirements tied to the donor without an accompanying global requirement, benefit both the recipient and the United States at the expense of third country exporters. The gain to the United States is obvious—it maximizes concessional sales and guarantees itself commercial markets. The mix of concessional and commercial sales may be set at precisely the level providing the ideal mix of concessional sales while preserving an assured market for commercial sales. Moreover, it has the chance of increasing its normal share of the commercial market through tying arrangements. To obtain concessional sales, the recipient must make commercial purchases. Even if the United States purchase requirements are set above the United States' normal expected share of the market, if the commercial purchase requirement is set below the recipient's anticipated level of commercial imports, the recipient should have no serious objections to purchasing commercially from the United States rather than elsewhere.

Donor-tied purchase requirements included within a global marketing requirement affect the recipient no differently than straight global requirements, but they do have impact on third country exporters. To the recipient, the only important figure is the global requirement. Although a recipient might have sound political reasons for allocating its commercial purchases to particular countries, requiring recipients to purchase a certain amount of its commercial imports from the food aid donor rather than other exporters, does not cause it economic harm. Moreover, the food aid donor does as well under a system combining global purchase requirements with donor-only purchase requirements, as it does with donor purchase requirements alone. In both cases, the donor gets an assured minimum amount of commercial sales. Third country exporters are in an intermediate position. They are better off under a combined global-donor requirement than with a straight donor requirement, but they are worse off than with a pure global requirement. It is not entirely clear how this arrangement stacks up against not imposing any commercial import requirements at all. In the latter case, third country exporters would get a chance to sell to the entire market remaining after concessional sales are concluded, instead of just that portion left after satisfying the donor's requirements. On the other hand, these exporters would have no way of knowing the level at which the donor would fix concessional sales and therefore they could not be sure of the size of the potential market left for commercial sales. Probably third country exporters would prefer having the assured potential market guaranteed via global requirements, even with a corner of the market reserved for the donor. To the extent food aid sales replace commercial sales, all potential exporters are harmed in proportion to the share of the market usually enjoyed by these exporters. Commercial purchase requirements tied to the donor are designed to minimize these losses to the donor at the expense of other exporting nations. But if there is displacement of commercial sales, it seems difficult to justify the donor shifting the entire displacement burden to other countries, particularly to the extent that the donor benefits from concessional sales themselves. Also, reservation of a portion of the food aid recipients' commercial imports for the donor smacks of bilateralism inconsistent with our constant support of free, multilateral trade. All in all then, if global commercial purchase requirements are employed, all countries, including the donor, should get an equal crack at these markets, rather than reserving a portion solely for the donor.

Tied UMRs

Mandatory commercial purchase requirements imposed upon food aid recipients should assist all countries anxious to preserve markets for normal export of the relevant agricultural products. While the level of the required purchase certainly is a matter of great concern to such exporters, the source from which the purchases are to be made is of equal, if not greater, interest. We have seen that source restrictions may take one of three forms—worldwide (global); donor-only; and a combination of worldwide and donor-only.

Understandably, United States-only quotas have drawn the sharpest criticism from third countries. Equally understandably, failure to tie commercial sales to the United States has drawn fire from the General Accounting Office and Congress. The picture has been complicated by the Guidelines to Concessional Sales included in the International Wheat Agreement, 1971, which for the first time, internationally recognize and impose limitations on the form of usual marketing requirements for wheat. And, the inclusion of mandatory UMRs in the FAO Control System, of course, is of prime importance here.

According to the United States Representative to the CSD, tied UMRs are the most practical way of complying with Section 103(n) of the Food for Peace Act. This section requires the President to take maximum precautions to assure that sales for dollars on credit terms under this Act shall not displace any sales of United States agricultural commodities which would otherwise be made for cash dollars. The United States-only UMR, when employed, it is claimed, is related directly to the record of commercial imports into a particular country. Its purpose is to protect legitimate interests of the United States, and not to invade other suppliers' established markets. Again, according to a U.S. spokesman, tied UMRs are employed wherever circumstances indicate that such a provision was needed to protect the United States. Such protection may be needed, for example, where the United States would not otherwise have a fair opportunity to compete in the commercial market of the P.L. 480 recipient country because of export subsidies, bilateral payments and barter arrangements, and similar special arrangements favoring other suppliers. Since decisions are made on a case-by-case basis, depending on all the circumstances surrounding a specific proposal, it follows that there is no list of commodities for which usual marketing requirements must include a United States-UMR component.[5]

Tied-UMRs have been repeatedly criticized in the Committee on Surplus Disposal. The CSD's Fourteenth Report to the Committee on Commodity Problems believed that tied sales "could result in harmful interference with normal patterns and evolution of international trade." The CSD took similar positions in 1964, 1966, and 1968. The concern in 1968 was with the newly enacted Section 103(0) of P.L. 480 which CSD members feared would be used as an offensive measure to enlarge United States commercial trade.[6] The most recent CSD examination of the tying problem is discussed in a Report on Tied Sales made in July 1969 which reviews United States tying practices.[7] The CSD itself took no position on the legitimacy of tied sales under the FAO Principles. However, some members continued to condemn these practices as violations of the Principles, while the United States defended its practices as entirely legitimate and consistent with the additionality requirement. The United States and almost all other exporting members of the CSD have reached impasse on this subject. The exporters are convinced that tied UMRs violate the FAO Principles, but the United States insists on their continuance. The inability of the CSD to resolve this issue represents one of the few outright failures of the FAO Control System.

Since the FAO Principles, until 1971, do not refer to UMRs as such, there is no direct textual basis for an attack upon tied UMRs. Rather, the allegation is that tied UMRs violate the spirit of the Principles because of the danger that such practices result in commercial gains by the donor country at the expense of other exporters. The argument against tied UMRs is straightforward enough. According to the critics, a tied UMR provides the donor with a guaranteed market which sometimes amounts to the entire UMR; that is, competition from other exporting countries is automatically excluded within the tied portion. For the untied portion of the UMR, as well as for any commercial sales beyond the UMR level, the donor retains the opportunity to compete with other suppliers. Furthermore, the commercial market presence afforded to the donor by the existence of the tied UMR gives it a competitive advantage over other suppliers. The consequence can be to limit severely the market opportunities of other countries, including those heavily dependent for their economic growth on the export of agricultural products competing with the donor's products.

Tied UMRs, it is argued, are particularly dangerous during a period of mounting pressures in a growing number of countries to make disposals of agricultural surpluses on near commercial terms. Also if such tied UMRs were also adopted by other countries, this could result in dividing up a large part of the recipient country's market by donor countries, to the disadvantage of exporting countries which do not seek or are unable to follow this course. Some CSD members projected that the ultimate result of these developments might be to blur and in time obliterate the distinction which has thus far been maintained between food aid and commercial trade, with adverse effects on both. The resulting market security, it is argued, runs counter to competitive principles causing potential international markets to be arbitrarily divided among exporters, with no opportunity for the play of competitive forces which will tend to reward the most efficient producers and skillful traders. To the extent concessional sales are used as a means of expanding commercial opportunities, competition among exporters may become competition among national treasuries, with little relevance to efficiency of production or the needs of the recipients.

In defense of its tying practices, the United States makes two kinds of arguments. First, P.L. 480 legislation requires tying, and then, tying is justified because of unfair trading practices of other countries which hamper United States commercial exports. As an additional point, which isn't really an argument for tied-UMRs, the United States claims that its practices have not damaged other exporters.

Implicit in the United States position is the proposition that it is entitled to take any steps necessary to protect its prefood aid level of commercial sales and to assure its own share of potential expansion of commercial trade opportunities. It is difficult to reconcile this attitude with the spirit of the FAO Principles or general notions of international trade morality. Assuming that the tied portions of UMRs are computed by simple extrapolation of prefood aid levels of commercial sales, tying ensures that the donor actually will achieve no less than its projected sales and in addition permits it to compete on equal terms with other exporters for the untied portion of the UMR, plus any commercial sales above the UMR. Moreover, it may well be that the combination of the concessional sales plus the tied UMR will permit the donor to establish itself commercially in the recipient country and thereby gain a competitive advantage over other exporters for the remaining untied portion of the market.

As indicated in Chapter 3, it is difficult to evaluate the capacity of untied food aid to preempt commercial markets.[8] If the recipient has a relatively small market, food aid sales may give the donor some advantage in that it won't pay other exporters to set up the necessary parallel marketing facilities. The legitimacy of a food aid donor's claim to some portion of a recipient's commercial imports depends upon the extent to which food aid transactions achieve additionality. If there is absolute additionality, the prefood aid commercial market is unchanged. Under these circumstances, there is no reason why the food aid donor should be able to use his food aid program to secure markets that otherwise it would have to compete for. It would be even worse if the food aid donor actually profited from the concessional sale. In these circumstances, it would gain both from the food aid transaction *per se*, and the market security achieved through the tied UMR. As we have demonstrated in Chapter 3, under current United States domestic agricultural policies, food aid costs the Treasury about half of its dollar value to the recipient. Therefore, depending upon the specific terms of each transaction, the United States could actually profit from concessional sales.[9] The United States is now converting its entire program to a dollar repayable basis. Moreover, a cash dollar down payment is often imposed, and even local currencies may be used to substitute for dollar expenditures in the recipient country. Also, to some extent, food aid may substitute for conventional foreign aid, again saving public expenditures. Beyond direct financial gains, food aid assists the United States, as leader of the western bloc, to achieve the political stability and economic growth in the volatile third world which many believe essential to the United States' long-term interests.

The problem becomes more complex if food aid does not achieve full additionality. This means that food aid has displaced a certain quantity of otherwise anticipated commercial sales. The question is, who shall bear the loss? Through tied UMRs designed to preserve the donor's anticipated prefood aid level of commercial sales, the donor shifts the expected commercial trade losses to other countries. Although no conceptual framework provides an authoritative unequivocal answer for apportioning the loss, some sort of sharing among the donor and third country exporters seems appropriate. An untied (global) UMR or no UMR at all would induce such sharing. All countries would scramble on an even footing for the supplemental commercial imports imposed upon the food aid recipient through an untied UMR, or voluntarily purchased by the recipient if there was no UMR at all.

The United States' argument that tied UMRs are necessary to protect the United States against the unfair trade practices of other countries in the commercial markets of the food aid recipients, amounts to the assertion of the right of an aggrieved country to use self-help to protect itself when and where it can. Indeed, it is the same type of argument President Nixon used to justify his unilateral abandonment of the international gold standard, and the imposition of a "temporary" import surcharge. In theory, violations of international standards of trade practice should be resolved through the machinery established for this purpose—in this case, the GATT. Moreover, acceptance of the FAO Principles by the United States should imply a general commitment not to use food aid as a trade war weapon—offensive or defensive. Admittedly, GATT has not been terribly effective with respect to agricultural trade and, at times, countries do engage in sharp trading practices.

This issue cannot be resolved within the context of this inquiry. If consideration were limited to international standards pertinent to food aid, tied UMRs should be prohibited. If full additionality is obtained and food aid does not shrink commercial markets, UMRs distort trade patterns by providing secure markets where normal commercial trade rules affords no such protection. If commercial markets are reduced, tied UMRs permit a food aid donor to unilaterally impose the loss of commercial sales caused by food aid upon the nonfood aid donating countries. This may be even more inequitable if a surplus-holding food aid donor is using relatively inexpensive food aid as a partial substitute for conventional foreign aid, while the injured third countries are meeting all their foreign aid burdens with full-priced conventional aid. Under these circumstances, the food aid donor is transferring its foreign aid responsibilities to other countries which are already shouldering their proper share of the burden.

But given the imperfect state of our international order, even in economic matters, this issue can't be solved solely by the FAO Principles, or any clearly established set of conduct norms. There simply are no very effective remedies for many of the alleged injuries suffered by nations caused by questionable trade practices of competing exporters. Under these conditions, limited self-help is expectable and probably justifiable. The validity of such measures only may be judged by examining both the kind of injury suffered, the form of the self-help measures, and the impact of these measures on the international community. Further evaluation of United States practices in this regard will be made in the next section which is devoted to a detailed examination of United States UMR practices.

United States UMR Practices

The pivotal concept underlying the purchase-oriented controls employed by the United States is the level of the potential food aid recipient's commercial purchases without the availability of the relevant agricultural products at less than market terms.[10] This is computed by determining the commercial import level price up to the advent of food aid and adjusting it in light of such factors as consumption trends and the recipient's current financial status.[11] Obviously, this formulation allows for considerable administrative discretion. Once the "normal" level is found, it forms the basis of the usual marketing requirement. Technically, these purchase requirements are legally based on a clause in the underlying sales agreement in which the recipient promises that the food aid it receives will not disrupt commercial markets for the products involved.[12]

The United States employs three basic forms of UMRs. For all wheat transactions and certain other transactions, the UMR permits commercial purchases from any country "friendly" to the United States (global UMR). In certain cases, other formulations of the concept of "friendly" countries have been used in order to salve the sensibilities of countries which do not wish to openly classify certain Communist or other nations as "unfriendly." For most other transactions, an overall level of mandatory commercial purchases is set, with a specified *minimum* portion of the total UMR to be purchased from the United States (tied UMRs). Finally, in a few cases, the entire UMR may be tied to the United States, with no untied portion on a global basis. The determinants of the type of requirement to be imposed in each case are extremely complex. Moreover, important changes have been made in response to pressure from third country exporters and as one effect of the recent trend towards closer union of concessional sales with economic development efforts.

Though no single formula will predict when and in what form commercial import requirements will be imposed in concessional sales to all countries, for all products, fairly reliable generalizations may be made on a product-by-product basis. Largely speaking, the form of commercial import requirements vary with the United States surplus holdings of the product involved, its relative position as an exporter of the product, the identity and commercial interest of competing exporters, the import history of the recipient country, the status of United States political interest in a particular country, and the patterns established for other food aid recipients in the region—particularly political or economic rivals of the recipient (for India, treatment of Pakistan is important, and vice-versa). Although these standards are highly complex and are sensitive to shifts in domestic, foreign, or international economic and political parameters, generally, the kind of UMRs employed in each country or area tend to remain constant.

Analysis of United States Practice by the
Subcommittee on Surplus Disposal

The next section of this study will attempt to formulate the principles employed by the United States in establishing usual marketing requirements. The work is based upon an examination of all P.L. 480 agreements through mid 1968, and selected agreements through mid 1971.

In 1969, the Subcommittee on Surplus Disposal, as part of its most recent examination of tying, attempted to determine the direction of United States tying practices through an examination of all P.L. 480 agreements which had been signed during the five-year period beginning with 1963.[13] Their findings are consistent with mine. Before presenting my results, it would be helpful to summarize the CSD's work. The CSD working party found that slightly more than 10 percent by value of the usual marketing requirements established for commodities programmed under P.L. 480 were "tied," or about 25 percent when wheat and wheat flour are excluded. The commodity tabulations indicate a persistent use of tied UMR provisions but no clear cut trends over the 1963-67 period. For the individual commodities, a few tendencies up or down are apparent, but these seem to reflect short-term shifts in the identity of food aid recipients rather than changes of policy. However, over the period covered, UMRs for vegetable oils, cotton, tallow and tobacco were frequently and consistently tied to the United States. Broken down by commodity, their results were summarized as follows:

i.   *Wheat and Wheat Flour.* Tied usual marketing requirements have not been imposed since 1959.
ii. *Rice.* No trends were observed in either the volume of tied UMRs or the proportion of usual marketing requirements which were "tied." The relatively low level of usual marketing requirements and the relatively high percentage tied in 1967 are due to the fact that the bulk of available rice was programmed for Viet Nam and Indonesia, which had no usual marketing requirements, while the remaining sales were confined to one or two African countries which are largely United States markets.
iii. *Feedgrains.* The amounts and proportions of tied UMRs dropped to almost nothing in 1966 and 1967. This reflects a shift in feedgrain programming to developing countries having only a limited history of commercial imports from the United States.
iv. *Vegetable oils.* The proportion tied was about one-fourth throughout the period.
v.   *Cotton.* Tying applied to one-fourth to one-third of the usual marketing requirements during the last four years of the period.
vi. *Inedible tallow.* Except in 1965, when the amount programmed was very small, the United States reserved to itself from one-half to three-fourths of the usual marketing requirements.
vii. *Tobacco.* The proportion of tied UMRs varied from one-fourth to one-half of the usual marketing requirements.
viii. *Dairy products, pulses, poultry and meat.* For all three of these groups, the magnitudes are too small to permit generalizations. The usual marketing requirements were usually either small or nonexistent and in most instances, there were no tied UMRs.[14]

These conclusions were based upon Table 8-1.

Except for 1966, the number of recipient countries which had signed agreements containing tied UMR provisions averaged about a dozen. In 1966, 18 countries had signed agreements involving tied UMRs. Out of the 136 instances of tied UMR provisions which were cited in agreements signed during the five-year period, over two-thirds involved vegetable oils, cotton and tobacco (see Table 8-2 below).

Table 8-1[a]

Usual Marketing Requirements and Tied UMRs for Selected Commodities Programmed under Public Law 480 Agreements Signed 1963-1967

Commodity	1963	1964	1965	1966	1967
			(in 1,000 M.T.)		
Wheat/wheat flour					
(i) Total UMR	1,499	2,873	857	3,743	3,367
(ii) Tied UMRs	0	0	0	0	0
(iii) "Tied" as % of UMR	0	0	0	0	0
Rice					
(i)	67	623	283	76	68
(ii)	33	20	0	30	64
(iii)	49%	3%	0	39%	95%
Feedgrains					
(i)	262	657	671	319	269
(ii)	241	312	467	15	0
(iii)	92%	48%	70%	5%	0
Vegetable oils					
(i)	40.0	208.4	72.4	133.6	96.8
(ii)	8.0	48.8	19.4	35.2	25.4
(iii)	20%	23%	27%	26%	26%
			(in 1,000 bales)		
Cotton					
(i)	56.0	1,011.7	352.9	836.9	1,175.4
(ii)	52.6	361.6	88.2	197.0	372.8
(iii)	94%	36%	25%	24%	32%
			(in 1,000 M.T.)		
Inedible tallow					
(i)	17.4	87.5	5.0	48.5	69.0
(ii)	12.0	41.6	0	25.5	51.8
(iii)	69%	48%	0	53%	75%
Tobacco					
(i)	11.8	4.8	4.2	13.6	7.4
(ii)	3.5	2.7	1.1	3.6	3.4
(iii)	29%	56%	26%	27%	46%

Not adjusted for multiyear agreements.

[a]UNIFAO, CCP/CSO/69/51, *Report on "Tied Sales"* 7 (July 1969).

Table 8-2
**Incidence of Tied UMR Provisions in Public Law 480 Agreements Signed
1963-1967, by Selected Commodities**[a]

Year	1963	1964	1965	1966	1967	(1968)[b]	Total
Total No. of Tied UMRs[c] of which:	13	32	21	27	32	(11)	136
Vegetable oils	2	9	6	6	10	(0)	33
Tobacco	4	8	7	7	4	(2)	32
Cotton	2	4	3	6	7	(5)	27
Feedgrains	4	3	3	4	2	(1)	17
Tallow	0	3	1	2	6	(3)	15
Rice	1	3	1	1	2	(0)	8
Poultry & meat	0	1	0	1	0	(0)	2
Dairy products	0	1	0	0	1	(0)	2

[a]UNIFAO, CCPICSO/69/51, *Report on Tied Sales* 8 (17 July 1969).

[b]The subsequent column consists only of tied UMR provisions cited for years subsequent to 1967 in agreements signed by the end of 1967. Therefore, the figures are residual and are not comparable to the preceding years.

[c]Adjusted for multiyear agreements.

The Working Party also attempted to analyze the data by country in order to study the relationship between the use of tied UMRs and the pattern of commercial imports. Various deficiencies in the data limited the Working Party's capacity to draw many firm conclusions. These were:

i. The usual marketing requirements, both in total amount and in the portion reserved for the United States, tended to increase over the 1963-1966 period. They generally appeared to be in line with the historical record, although in some cases insufficient allowance may have been made for rising trends in commercial imports.
ii. There were significant commercial imports additional to those covered by the UMRs, although there was no constant relationship. Levels of commercial imports, in total as well as from the U.S., showed no general trends or consistent patterns; such levels obviously are influenced by factors other than UMRs specified in the P.L. 480 agreements.
iii. In the small number of cases where available data permitted analysis, the tied UMRs enabled the United States to maintain its trade and did not appear to have the effect of displacing other suppliers. In some cases, the U.S. was apparently the historically predominant supplier; where the U.S. is fully competitive, the need for tying the UMRs may be questioned. Also in some instances, the existence of a tied UMR may have prevented a shift of com-

mercial imports from U.S. to non-U.S. sources that might otherwise have occurred for purely commercial reasons.[15]

Author's Analysis of P.L. 480 Agreements

The author's analysis of United States UMR practices confirms many of the Working Party's conclusions. However, this analysis explores aspects not included in the CSD analysis. Discrepancies with the CSD's results will be noted and, where possible, rationalized.

Wheat and Flour. Central to any discussion of concessional sales is the treatment of wheat and flour. First, these products historically have dominated United States (and worldwide) food aid transactions. From the onset of P.L. 480, they have totalled $9.63 billion or 49% of the $19.58 billion of United States food aid.[16] Second, wheat has been a chronic international surplus problem of fluctuating intensity for many years.[17] Then, wheat has been the most important commercial export crop for the United States[18] and, relative to their economy, an even more important export for Canada, Australia, and Argentina—countries of obvious importance to United States foreign policy.[19] Finally, largely via concessional sales, the United States has vastly increased its share of world wheat exports, preempting to some extent markets formerly enjoyed by Canada and Australia.[20] These losses, however, were compensated by gains in other markets.[21]

The history of usual marketing requirements practices for wheat have passed through several phases. These were: no requirements; purchases tied to the United States; a combination of worldwide and tied United States requirements; and finally, the current practice of imposing only worldwide requirements in all wheat sales. The very first agreements covering concessional wheat sales contained no specific marketing requirements.[22] The next set of agreements required a given level of commercial purchases of wheat from the United States.[23] Then a new pattern developed. Sales to South Asia carried usual marketing requirements which could be met by purchases anywhere in the non-Communist world (global requirements).[24] For other portions of the world, the pattern was global requirements combined with a portion to be purchased in the United States.[25] Finally, commencing sometime in 1959, all requirements for purchase in the United States were dropped, and global marketing quotas were and are imposed in almost every agreement.[26]

The current policy coincided with the 1958 amendment to the P.L. 480 Act requiring that the program be administered to protect the normal patterns of trade of friendly nations, as well as the usual marketings of the United States.[27] However, the United States claims that the reason it stopped using tied UMRs for wheat sales is that United States commercial sales are sufficiently protected by the International Wheat Agreement. This is a bit hard to believe. Overall, the Wheat Agreement has not been very successful in maintaining wheat prices.[28] Possibly, the long-term association formed by the succession of wheat agreements has had the effect of curbing questionable trade practices in that commodity. However, it is more likely that wheat sales are untied in response to strong pressure from Canada and Australia. The reference to the Wheat Agreement may be the Administration's excuse to Congress for abandoning tying.

The General Accounting Office also believes that the move away from tied UMRs is politically motivated. It found nothing in the language of the 1958 P.L. 480 amendment to force the elimination of United States quotas.[29] Rather, the same increased sensitivity towards P.L. 480's impact on world trade which induced the Administration to amend the Act also militated in favor of the shift towards elimination of the United States purchase requirement and substitution of global purchase requirements. Both changes are necessary, to effectively meet the concerns of other wheat exporters. Just eliminating the United States purchase restriction would not in itself guarantee commercial markets for third countries. Usual global marketing requirements, though, will assure that concessional sales do not fill the recipient's entire requirements for wheat and that some market will remain for commercial sales.

There is some evidence that the balance-of-payments crises affecting the United States in 1972 may well induce the United States to revert to its previous practice of tied UMRs for wheat sales. We have discussed the equivocal status of tied UMRs under the FAO Principles. Moreover, Article 9 of International Wheat Agreement provides guidelines for concessional transactions which is an added deterrent to tied wheat UMRs. Article 9(2) requires members to take measures "to ensure that concessional transactions are additional to commercial sales which could reasonably be anticipated in the absence of such transactions." These "measures" are to be consistent with the FAO Principles and "*may* provide that a specified level of commercial wheat, agreed with the recipient country, is maintained on a *global basis* by that country." Although the term "global basis" may be somewhat ambiguous, under its most reasonable reading, it should preclude tied UMRs for wheat. Of course, the United States could (and probably will) seize upon the word "may." But the argument is weak. Read in context, "may" refers to the option of whether or not to impose UMRs. Once they are imposed, it would seem clear that they must be on a global basis.

Probably the issue will be resolved politically, not legally. If the United States reties wheat UMRs, exporters heavily reliant on wheat exports will retaliate. The first victim might be the already beleagured International Wheat Agreement. If this fails, Canada and the EEC have large wheat stocks which can be sold below commercial levels. Also wheat exporters could begin to tie their contributions under the Food Aid Convention. All in all, the United States is in a relatively weak position on wheat because wheat exports aren't as important to it as they are to other countries.

Exceptions to Global Marketing
Requirements

There are some exceptions to the general pattern of global marketing requirements for wheat sales. But almost all deviations may be explained by special
circumstances. Countries with histories as wheat exporters have not been required to make commercial purchases. Syria and Turkey are examples.[30] This
policy is consistent with the concept of basing marketing requirements on historical import levels—wheat exports have no history of imports. But to the extent
the commercial purchase requirements are designed to ensure that concessional
sales to not substitute for *potential* cash sales, this practice is questionable.
Countries permanently shifting from export to import positions might well be
potential cash customers, absent food aid. Along similar lines of reasoning, marketing requirements have not been imposed upon rice-eating countries such as
Taiwan and Korea, receiving this first substantial wheat imports through concessional sales.[31] Subsequent sales however, do impose commercial purchase requirements—presumptively as tastes for wheat products developed, and the pace
of economic development quickened.[32]

Wheat sales to certain Communist and bloc-leaning nations get special treatment. No commercial requirements have been imposed in food aid transactions
with Yugoslavia.[33] In fact, the United States has been supplying almost all of
Yugoslavia's wheat imports, first through Title P.L. 480 sales and then commercially.[34] The food transactions were part of the general commitment of the
United States to support Yugoslavia's independence. Poland also was excused
from mandatory commercial wheat purchases, but she has been obliged to purchase 200,000 metric tons of feed grains annually from the United States, even
though feedgrains were not included in that or other P.L. 480 agreements with
Poland.[35] This transmutation of wheat sales into required feedgrain purchases is
unique. Conceivably, it resulted from the United States' desire to derive maximum benefit from the transaction without upsetting the established pattern of
not tying wheat sales to the United States. Since Poland normally gets its wheat
from Russia and does not purchase any wheat from the United States, imposition of untied commercial wheat purchases would be of little benefit to this
country.[36] Tied wheat purchases though, would run counter to the strongly
established pattern against such practices and would surely upset Canada,
France, and Mexico, which are large, commercial exporters to Poland.[37] But as
we shall note subsequently, feedgrain purchases have been occasionally tied to
the United States, and since no other non-Communist nation exports feedgrains
to Poland, requiring feedgrain rather than wheat purchases from the United
States would give the United States the opportunity to achieve its objectives
with minimum injury to friendly exporters or established patterns of conduct.[38]
In calendar 1964, Poland imported almost 211,000 tons of feedgrains from the
United States, just filling its quota.[39] But, in fiscal 1966, when no purchase re-

quirements were imposed, Poland imported only 158,000 metric tons, tending to show that the quota had been effective in increasing United States commercial exports to Poland.[40]

Rice. Rice has always been the most volatile item in world grain trade. After a period of world shortage, largely caused by the war-induced decline of rice production in Viet Nam, commencing in 1968, rice surpluses have built up rapidly and there is no sign of an early change in this situation.[41] As with wheat, the United States is the world's largest rice exporter. In 1970, the United States exported 1.69 million metric tons out of total world rice exports of approximately 6.5 million tons, or 26% of the market. Since Thailand is an important ally and Burma a touchy neutral, the United States might be expected to take precautions to ensure that concessional rice sales do not cut into traditional markets of these nations.[42]

Up to now, and with one important exception, the underlying trade picture and the pattern of Food for Peace transactions and conditions for rice closely resemble those pertaining to wheat, albeit in reduced dimension. Rice sales rank fourth in P.L. 480 transactions,[43] but they form a large portion of total United States rice exports. In fiscal 1969, rice exports totalled $315.5 million of which $168.2 or 53% was shipped under Food Aid.[44] The pattern of usual marketing requirements for rice transactions reflects both the trade position of the United States and our concern with Thailand, the second largest producer.

The prototype agreement for rice sales, like those for wheat, requires commercial purchases of rice on a free-world basis.[45] But with rice there are more exceptions. A few agreements impose no commercial purchase requirements. The only significant transactions in this category were with the Dominican Republic,[46] Indonesia,[47] and Vietnam.[48] Unusual circumstances have surrounded all these transactions. The treatment of the Dominican Republic stems from the instability in that country following Trujillo's overthrow in 1961.[49] The Indonesian arrangements are attributable to the desire to reestablish financial and economic sanity in Indonesia following the coup that ousted Sukarno. And obviously, all bets are off in Vietnam. Moreover, this tragic country was a net exporter of rice in better days and therefore had no historical import level. A few rice agreements tie a substantial portion of total mandatory commercial rice imports to the United States. These aberrations, though, are for very small amounts and apply to European or Latin American countries, not within the normal trading areas of Thailand or Burma.[50]

Feed Grains. The pattern of commercial purchase requirements with respect to feedgrains differs somewhat from wheat and rice and seems dictated by the predominant position of the United States in the export market of these products and the relative absence of friendly nations likely to be adversely affected by Food for Peace transactions in these commodities. In fiscal 1970, the United

States accounted for 46% of total feedgrain exports. The remainder is divided among a number of countries, including Argentina, France, Australia, Brazil, Canada, Mexico, and South Africa, none of which has more than 10% of the market. But these exports do represent significant portions of the total export earnings of Argentina and Thailand.[51] As with wheat and rice, some type of commercial purchase requirements are usually imposed. But more exceptions exist, particularly outside of the normal market areas of Thailand and Argentina.[52] Most purchase requirements are on a free-world basis.[53] But occasionally, substantial United States purchase requirements may be found combined with global requirements, again usually outside the normal market areas of Argentina or Thailand.[54]

Edible Oils. The United States accounts for 90% of the world exports of soybeans and soybean oils. This gives it some latitude to conduct Food for Peace transactions in this commodity substantially without fear of harming the trade of friendly nations.[55] However, the United States export position is somewhat less commanding with respect to soybean oil, with 68% of the market. The other leading soybean oil exporters are the Netherlands with about 11%, and Denmark and Germany with about 7%.[56] Since it is the policy of the United States to tie UMRs where there is a history of United States commercial sales, we should expect considerable tying here. And this is the case. Edible oils have constituted about 5% of Food for Peace sales.[57] But Food for Peace sales have represented 61% of total United States exports of this commodity.[58] Generally, United States policy has been both to stimulate increased consumption of these products and to appear to take a hard pro-United States line in conducting food aid transactions therein.[59] Consequently, almost without exception, every agreement includes a commercial purchase requirement.[60] And in the large majority of cases these purchases are fully or partially tied to the United States.[61] The Netherlands, Denmark and Germany have complained of these practices in the CSD, but since the demand for soybean oils has been strong, the United States has escaped the intense criticism generated by tied UMRs in wheat sales. Complications do arise when vegetable oils are sold to olive oil exporting countries such as Tunisia and Turkey. These problems are handled through export limitations which will be analyzed in detail in the next chapter.[62]

Cotton. Cotton is a major food aid commodity with transactions totaling $2.22 billion through December 1970.[63] The requirements for commercial purchases of cotton reflect the surplus status of this crop in the United States, the fluctuating political attitude towards Egypt, and the intimate relationship of raw cotton sales with cotton textiles. For some time, cotton has presented very troublesome domestic oversupply problems for the United States.[64] Internationally, the United States is the world's leading cotton exporter, followed at some distance by Brazil, the UAR, and the Sudan and Pakistan.[65] Moreover, cotton represents a very important source of export earnings for large developing countries such as Egypt, Sudan, Mexico, Brazil, Turkey, Syria and Pakistan.[66] Under these circumstances, the United States has aggressively sold short-staple cotton under Food for Peace. But until very recently, in order to protect the export markets of Egypt, Sudan, and Peru in these products, and despite severe Congressional pressure, the United States has refrained from including long-staple cotton in its food aid programs.

The 1966 revision of the Food for Peace Act applied new pressure to increase concessional cotton sales. Section 103(i) of the Act directs the President to promote progress toward assurance of an adequate food supply by encouraging countries with which agreements are made to give greater emphasis to the production of food crops rather than to the production of such nonfood crops as are in world surplus.[67] Section 109(a)(1) makes a potential recipient country's performance on this count a factor to be considered prior to making concessional sales.[68] Chronically, surplus cotton is the chief target of both provisions, with tobacco of secondary interest. Armed with this language, Representative Poage of Texas, a large cotton producing state, then Vice-Chairman and now Chairman of the House Agricultural Committee, exerted great public and private efforts to force the Administration to induce India and Pakistan to divert their native cotton acreage to food products and obtain all their cotton from the United States under Food for Peace.[69]

In view of the size of United States cotton holdings, this arrangement seems attractive.[70] Nevertheless, it may not make economic sense with respect to a particular country at a particular time. From the viewpoint of the recipient country, the wisdom of this type of transaction depends upon the price of United States cotton, including transportation, and reliability of the supply from the United States at a given price, and the alternative uses for land now devoted to cotton production. It is understandable, moreover, that a country with a relatively primitive and unresponsive economic system would not be anxious to make short-run changes in their agricultural patterns if cotton growing figures in their long-run economic plans.[71]

Based upon Food for Peace statistics, Section 103(i) has not measurably increased cotton sales under P.L. 480. During the period from 1954-1966, P.L. 480 cotton sales averaged $149.1 million per year. During the four-year period since the enactment of 103(i) P.L. 480, cotton sales averaged 131.0 million.

Concessional cotton sales agreements generally have required mandatory commercial purchases, including substantial tying to the United States.[72] But since cotton is but an intermediate product, the critical problem is control of possible increased cotton textile exports attributable to raw cotton sales.[73] Most current cotton recipients are traditional textile exporters. Therefore, any concessional cotton sales either will displace commercial raw cotton imports or will increase the availability of exportable textiles. Assuming that minimum commercial purchase requirements ensure that P.L. 480 cotton does not displace "normal" cotton imports, concessional cotton sales must lead to increased textile exports. Moreover, the sentiment favoring promotion of increased internal food consumption as the basic objective of concession sales to developing countries understandably does not apply with equal force to increased domestic consumption of textiles. Therefore, absolute prohibition of such exports would be self-defeating. The existing pattern of regulation whereby additional textile exports are permitted, if matched by commercial purchases of an equivalent amount of cotton from the United States, seems a logical response to these factors.[74] The specific techniques applied by the United States to counter food aid induced textile exports are analyzed in Chapter 9.

Tobacco. Tobacco seems an unlikely candidate for a humanitarian or developmentally oriented food and fiber aid program. Nevertheless, tobacco sales under Food for Peace have totaled $566 million since 1954.[75] In 1966, a determined effort was made on the floor of Congress to bar the noxious weed from the program.[76] The effort only succeeded in barring tobacco donations, rather than sales—a distinction understandable solely in political terms.[77] Whether due to Senator Williams' efforts or not, tobacco transactions under P.L. 480 have sharply declined in the past three years.[78] But underdeveloped nations do spend foreign exchange to import tobacco.[79] And this country at various periods has accumulated sizeable surpluses of this product.[80] Therefore, inclusion of tobacco within the concessional sales programs might be justified on the basis of foreign exchange savings to recipient underdeveloped countries with overdeveloped nicotine habits.

But the usual marketing requirement patterns for tobacco seem inconsistent with a development rationale. As with cotton, minimum commercial purchase requirements are almost always imposed, including a substantial United States purchase requirement.[81] Similar to its position with soybean oils and feedgrains, the United States is the dominant exporter of all types of tobacco.[82] Moreover, United States tobacco possesses unique qualities which practically puts it in a class by itself.[83] Therefore, United States marketing requirements are unlikely to harm other exporters. But if market expansion vis-a-vis other exporters is not the goal of mandatory purchase requirements, then their purpose must be to prevent the displacement of commercial sales. However, it is only through such displacement that the recipient can conserve foreign exchange in order to facilitate economic development. And if the tobacco program does not aid economic development, the only purpose it can serve is to dispose of U.S. tobacco surpluses through increased tobacco consumption by the recipient—a very questionable objective.

Of course, the tobacco marketing requirements may be set low enough to permit some displacement. The GAO claims this to be the case.[84] Assuming some displacement, we end up with an equivocal situation. Concessional tobacco sales save some foreign exchange and promote some additional use. Since third country exporters are not affected, the program can be justified if substantial amounts of foreign exchange are freed and used for development purposes. Perhaps, the moral implications are best left to the judgment of the importing nations.

Donations. Donations under Title II of the P.L. 480 legislation are not subject to the market protection requirements imposed by United States legislation on concessional sales. However, donations can have just as much impact upon the commercial sales of the donor and third country exporters as any other form of food aid. This is recognized by the inclusion of government-to-government donations in the catalogue of transactions subject to the CSD notification and consultation procedures. The danger of donations to international trade is also implicitly recognized by Article 9 of the International Wheat Agreement, 1971, which imposes guidelines for concessional transactions. The principle motivation for Article 9 was to cover food aid transactions agreed to under the accompanying Food Aid Convention and the preferred forms of food aid under the Convention are sales for local currency and gifts.[85]

But despite the potential disruptive effect of large donations which are made through normal market channels, the United States has not been imposing UMRs on Title II donations. This includes donations made to satisfy United States obligations under the Food Aid Convention. The dangers to commercial trade are reduced by the fact that in many cases, countries receiving substantial Title II donations also are receiving food aid under Title I which include UMRs. In fiscal 1970, the countries which received substantial donations of food aid and did not also have Title I programs were Nigeria, Western Africa, Jordan, Poland, Algeria, Tanzania, Jamaica, and Peru. Nigeria was recovering from its ghastly civil war, Jordan has special status as a United States client state, Poland as a communist country is always a special case. We have no formal diplomatic relations with Algeria, and Tanzania and Western Africa are not normal markets for western food exports. The aid to Peru was made as part of a consortium responding to its earthquake disaster, and the United States was not the principal donor. However, the United States has agreed that in the future it would give particular attention to those cases where Food Aid Convention programs were substantial and where no UMR was established in connection with Title I Programs.

UMR Practice of Other Nations. The UMR practices of nations other than the United States has been very mixed. Undoubtedly, the increasing participation of new nations in food aid and the incorporations of UMRs into the FAO Principles will produce clearer patterns in the future. Up till now, the programs of most other countries have been too small and scattered to permit development of sophisticated UMR practices. In most cases, they have given food aid to countries which also receive food aid from the United States, and the smaller donors have relied upon the United States to set the UMR. Indeed, one of the principle unresolved problems with FAO's implementation of its new UMR requirement is the establishment of rules to determine how UMRs are set where a recipient is receiving food aid from more than one country. This will be discussed more fully in the next session of the UMR under the FAO Principles.

Usual Marketing Requirements under the FAO Principles

After a particularly difficult struggle, the FAO Council in November 1970, amended the Principles to require the imposition of usual marketing requirements in all transactions which are designated by the catalogue of transactions as subject to notification and consultation under the FAO Principles. These recommendations, like those contained in Council Resolution 1/53 relating to consultation and notification, required specific acceptance by the individual FAO members.[86] Although adoption of the concept of usual marketing requirements is a highly significant step in the process of achieving effective control over the food and commercial trade interaction, important matters relating to the nature and implementation of the UMR requirements were left unresolved. The most important of these were the legitimacy of tied-UMRs and the method of establishing UMRs when there are more than one food aid donor to a particular recipient.

Background of the Decision to include UMRs in the FAO Principles. We have often cited the fundamental changes in the food aid situation caused by the entry of new nations as regular food aid donors. We have also pointed out that these countries rarely, if ever, included usual marketing requirement provisions in their agreements, and in some cases, it seemed that food aid was being used as bait for increased commercial sales. For all the criticism of its tied-UMR practices, the United States did provide for a minimum level of commercial purchases on a global basis in almost every transaction in which there was some history of likelihood of commercial purchases. By contrast, the EEC, probably the second most important force in food aid matters, refused to adopt UMRs unless they were made universal through inclusion in the FAO Principles. Under these circumstances, it is not surprising that the United States would not be content to be the only country which consistently imposed market protection requirements in their food aid transactions. The most straightforward method to accomplish this would be to amend the FAO Principles to make the imposition of usual marketing requirements mandatory in all food aid transactions. This step had been anticipated by Article 9 of the Wheat Agreement, 1971, which recommended and authorized, but did not mandate use of global UMRs to protect normal trade patterns.[87] Therefore, commencing in 1968, the United

States exerted constantly increasing pressure to make UMRs mandatory through the FAO control system. When the UMR proposal encountered strong resistence, the United States countered by threatening to stop imposing global UMRs in its own agreements. In November 1970, after two years of difficult negotiations, the FAO Council approved amendments to the FAO Principles that make the imposition of UMRs mandatory for all transactions subject to the FAO notification and consultation procedures. This section of the study will discuss some of the most important features of the new requirements and also analyze in further detail those issues which caused the most difficulties, including the issues which were left undecided because of a lack of consensus. The next section shall set forth the new requirements and the following section shall discuss its controversial features.

Basic Features of the FAO Usual Marketing Requirements Provisions. The new UMR requirements were adopted by the FAO Council in Resolution 2/55. Technically, these requirements were made an integral part of FAO Council Resolution 1/55 which also included the catalogue of transactions subject to notification and consultation and the expansion of the CSD's terms of reference.[88] The operative portion of the Resolution 2/55 appears in the Annex to the Resolution and is reproduced in Appendix B.

The UMR provisions of the FAO Principles may be divided into two broad categories. The first establishes the UMR as the basic method to achieve additionality. The second category provides the substantive and procedural guidelines for establishing UMRs in each food aid transaction. The UMR is defined as the specific agreement by the recipient country to maintain at least a specified level of commercial imports in addition to any imports of the same commodities under the concessional transaction. Under the new rules, such a provision must be included in any transaction undertaken by governments which is included in the list of categories which FAO Council Resolution 1/53 makes subject to prior consultation among interested and affected third countries. The level of the UMR is to be based upon the prior history of commercial imports into the recipient country as modified by the economic, financial and developmental needs of the recipient and by factors indicating that the historical level may not accurately reflect the current situation.

The final form of the UMR requirements reflected the usual tug of war between exporting countries worried about their commercial sales and potential recipients anxious to maximize the inflow of food aid under the simplest possible procedures and subject to minimum restrictions.[89] The divergent ends are clearly evident in paragraphs 4, 5, 6(b)(ii), 6(b)(iv), 6(b)(vi) and 9 of FAO Council Resolution 2/55. Paragraph 6 is the cornerstone of the UMR system. It stipulates the method for computing UMRs and the procedures to be followed in clearing the UMR initially chosen by the donor with other potential exporters. (The role of the recipient in this process was one of the stickier issues in the

FAO deliberations on the new system. This matter is discussed below.) Similar to the United States practice, the computation commences with the history of the recipient's commercial imports during the prior five-year period. This figure may be modified by such factors as an increase in the recipient's production of the food aid commodity which exceeds increases in the recipient's consumption of the commodity, a substantial change in the balance-of-payments position or general economic condition of the recipient, significant trends in recent commercial imports indicating potential changes in future import levels, and the level of prior UMRs. The first factor cited would cover situations like those in India and Pakistan where the adoption of higher yield wheat strains (the Green Revolution) moves the recipient closer to self-sufficiency in the production of the food aid commodity.

The procedures for consultation with potentially affected third countries closely tracks those applicable to other aspects of food aid transactions requiring prior consultation under Council Resolution 1/53. After arriving at a figure for the UMR, the donor must consult bilaterally with those nations whose exports are likely to be affected by the transactions. If the UMR differs from the historical import level, as stipulated by the donor in the notification, an explanation must be provided. The proposed UMR, as determined by the supplier, including modifications resulting from the bilateral consultations, will be included in the notification of the principal terms of the transaction to the Subcommittee on Surplus Disposal normally required under the FAO control system.

Closely Related Commodities. Paragraphs 4(2) and 6(1)(b) of the FAO Principles extend the market displacement protections of the Principles to commodities closely related to, as well as identical with, the food aid commodity. Because of this, some countries very much wanted to impose UMRs for the importation of such commodities. After extended debate and negotiation, a compromise was reached which attempted to protect closely related commodities from adverse food aid impact without actually requiring an additional UMR for such products. The original set of recommendations of the CCP Working Party on the UMR authorized the establishment of UMRs for related commodities via appropriate language in paragraphs (1), (2) and 6(a) of the proposed UMR Resolution.[90] But in the final version recommended by the Committee on Commodity Problems and adopted by the FAO Council, all references to related commodities were deleted from paragraphs (1), (2) and (6) and a new paragraph on related commodities (3), was substituted.[91]

In effect, the new paragraph treats the impact of the proposed transaction on the exports of closely related commodities like any other important feature of a food aid transaction other than the UMR. That is, the supplying country is required to consider whether commercial trade in closely related commodities is likely to be harmfully affected and, if so, it must undertake consultations in accordance with the normal procedures applicable to transactions made subject to prior notification and consultation by the catalogue of transactions.[92] Moreover, a third party may request consultations with a supplying country with respect to related commodities on its own initiative. The deletion of the references to "related commodities" from paragraphs (1), (2) and (6)(a) was strongly opposed in the Committee on Commodity Problems by the Sudan, Canada, and the EEC. One country suggested language that would require that the impact on related commodities be taken into account in setting the UMR on the donated commodity. In the end, only the Sudan recorded a reservation on this point to the FAO Council resolution.

Theoretically, the impact upon related commodities of food aid transactions deserve as much consideration as the effect on identical commodities. Export earnings are fungible. Furthermore, it would appear that the treatment of related commodities under paragraph (3) gives very little protection to countries which, because of food aid, lose commercial sales of related commodities to the recipient. At the same time, the establishment of UMRs for both the donated commodity and related commodities would be an unacceptably restrictive and administratively difficult undertaking. Conceivably, a country that might be injured with respect to related commodities might convince the donor to reduce the size of the food aid transaction or even impose a UMR on related commodities. Although the UMR system makes no explicit provision for such UMRs, neither are they precluded. But both possibilities seem remote. While the terms of proposed food aid transactions may be modified in response to third country protests, the level of food aid is rarely, if ever changed. And it would take very special circumstances to induce a donor to jump into the quagmire of separate UMRs for the food aid commodity and related commodities. The inherent difficulty of predicting the impact of a food aid transaction upon theoretical future commercial sales of the identical product makes it very difficult to determine and negotiate UMRs on the basic commodity which are acceptable to donors, recipients, and third countries. Duplicating the process with respect to related commodities vastly compounds these problems. The undertaking becomes increasingly difficult as the economic relationship between basic and related commodities becomes more remote. Therefore, given the overwhelming technical and political difficulties in setting UMRs for related commodities, the FAO did the right thing in copping out on this issue.

Changes in the UMR Levels. Both the recipient and exporting countries were concerned with the problem of changing previously established UMR levels. The recipients wanted maximum protection against increases in previously established UMRs and the most opportunity to reduce UMRs in the event of economic reverses. The United States, though, opposed any steps which would ease the process of changing UMRs. During the lengthy period when the United States unilaterally imposed UMRs, it had followed a firm policy of strongly resisting changes in UMR levels. This issue is addressed in paragraphs 5, 6(iv) and 9 of the FAO Resolution 2/55. Paragraph 6(iv) establishes the UMR negotiated for the nearest previous period as one of the basic criteria for determining new UMRs. Paragraph (5) requires that if prior UMR levels are to be changed, these changes must take account of the recipient's economic and balance-of-payments position and that the changed UMR should not be an undue burden on the recipient. Paragraph (9) authorizes the renegotiation of UMRs during the life of a particular UMR in the event of substantial unforeseen deterioration in the balance-of-payments and general economic situation of the recipient. The total effect of these provisions is to make the prior UMR a partial ceiling for future UMRs and to authorize downward renegotiation of established UMRs in emergency situations. This gives somewhat more flexibility than desired by the United States, but this is the price exacted by the recipients for their acceptance of the UMR concept.

Establishing UMRs among Multiple
Donors

Although the language might be a bit clearer, Paragraph (8) ensures that where a country receives food aid from more than one source during the same given period, it would be subject to only one UMR during that period. Subjecting a recipient to multiple UMRs would create obvious and unnecessary difficulties. But the FAO failed to agree upon the method of establishing the single UMR in these circumstances.

Although the CCP Working Party offered four alternatives to the Committee on Commodity Problems, these boiled down to three different approaches. The UMR may be set by the first supplier subject to consultation with other potential suppliers through the normal FAO procedures; by the major supplier; or by the first supplier in consultation with the major supplier. The first approach would make the first UMR established the UMR for all other transactions, provided that this figure has been accepted or not objected to by other countries after the UMR had been subjected to the notification and consultation procedures stipulated by subparagraphs 6(c) and 6(d) of the FAO Council Resolution 2/55. This is probably the simplest approach. It would clearly identify the country responsible for establishing the UMR and would provide an explicit procedure for other countries to register their objections, viz. the normal notification and consultation procedures used with respect to all food aid transactions subject to the FAO control system. The obvious disadvantage is that the first supplying country might not be the principal donor and therefore would not be in the best position to establish the best UMR. Also, the country initiating the process would have to make its initial UMR decision in ignorance of the food aid plans of other potential donors. This might well lengthen and complicate the process for arriving at the final UMR.

The second alternative would give the major supplying country the responsibility for establishing the UMR for all supplying countries. Doubt as to which was the major supplying country should be resolved through consultations among prospective supplying countries. This system introduces more ambiguities than the first system and requires more initiative by potential food aid donors. Unlike the first alternative, whereby the UMR proposed by the first supplier automatically applies to all other food aid transactions within the stipulated period unless other countries take positive action to try to change it, the joint UMR depends upon the supplying countries reaching agreement on who is to establish the UMR. It is conceivable that food aid will be held up while the potential suppliers try to reach a decision on this issue. It was the clear advantage of locating responsibility for setting the UMR with the country best able to discharge this function. Also, it tends to induce all suppliers to consult in advance of specific transactions being sent through the FAO machinery, thereby providing more time for negotiation and compromise than is possible under the rather strict time limits applicable to proposals notified in accordance with FAO procedures.

The third alternative would combine the first two. The first supplier would identify the major supplier who would then formulate the UMR in accordance with the notification and consultation procedures prescribed for establishing UMRs.[93] Under this approach, the task of conducting a food aid proposal through the FAO procedures would be bifurcated. The first supplier would identify the major supplier and then follow normal consultation procedures with respect to all aspects of the food aid transactions concerned except the UMR. The UMR would be formulated and taken through the consultation machinery by the country designated as the major supplier.

This hybrid attempts to cure some of the defects of the first two alternatives. Unlike alternative one, the responsibility for determining UMR would be placed upon the major supplier. But instead of relying upon unspecified potential food aid suppliers to identify the major supplier, this task would be imposed upon the first supplier. This formulation does seem to overcome the principal defects of the first two proposals. The responsibility for determining the UMR is placed on the country best able to do so, the question of who is responsible for initiating the UMR determining process is answered, and the UMR determination and consultation process is not unduly complicated or prolonged.

In one sense all formulations which are based upon donor-established UMRs may be faulty. To the extent the donors are also the principal commercial exporters of the food aid commodity, these are the appropriate group to initially set UMR's. But countries seriously affected by food aid may not be donors at all. Certainly developing exporters such as Argentina and Thailand won't be. Under the schemes considered by the FAO, the only opportunity for non-donating affected countries to influence the UMR would be through consultations after a UMR has been proposed by the donor or donors. This puts such countries at a distinct disadvantage. Since UMR's are designed to protect both donating and non-donating third countries equally, there is no reason why all affected countries shouldn't be on equal footing in the UMR setting process. Indeed, if global UMR's were universally employed (no tying to the donor) there is no reason why the donor should have any greater role in establishing UMRs than any other potentially affected third country exporter.

Failure of the FAO to Resolve the Multiple Donor Problems

Despite the obvious need to resolve the question of who sets the UMR and how, and the apparent soundness of the third alternative, the Committee on Commodity Problems was unable to settle this matter. The Report of the Committee on Commodity Problems to the FAO Council did not recognize this failure, but instead papered over this dispute by recommending as paragraph (7) the following:

In determining a UMR for a given period, a supplying country would ensure at the state of bilateral consultations that all the interests concerned were taken fully into account, and use its best endeavors to arrive at a UMR that would be generally acceptable to all the parties concerned.[94]

Although the FAO Council adopted this provision without comment, it is obvious that paragraph 7 adds nothing not already included in paragraph (6) which specifies the procedures to be followed in establishing UMRs. Most countries favor procedures which would ensure that the major donor sets the UMR, on the grounds that the major donor has the most leverage and is therefore the logical country to negotiate the UMR. Those opposing the major-supplier concept fear that the major donor would use its leverage to give preference to its own commercial exports.

Probably, the fact that the United States is likely to be the major donor in most situations underlay much of the opposition to the major-donor concept. Because of this, any formulation which designates the major donor to play the key role in setting UMRs for all suppliers to a particular country means that the United States will perform this function and other food aid donors did not want to cede this much power to the United States. Formulations which might give the UMR setting function to countries other than the major donor were rejected as unrealistic and ineffective. The United States claims that it does not insist upon the major-donor concept. According to the United States, the negotiation of UMRs is a difficult and often unpleasant burden which it would gladly share with other countries. Certainly negotiating UMRs is a chore, but given the United States current trade difficulties, it is likely to be very reluctant to give up any right which might be useful for protecting or expanding its commercial exports.

Another reason for the failure to resolve the problem of setting UMR in multiple donor situations may be the impact of any solution on the problem of tied UMR. Under any system where one country has the responsibility for setting UMRs for all suppliers, the use of tied-UMRs would become very awkward. It is difficult to imagine a country establishing tied-UMRs for its exports without doing the same for other countries. But negotiating UMRs with tying arrangements for each potential additional supplier would be extremely difficult. Equally important, consistent application of UMRs with a string of tied purchase requirements would characterize food aid activities as crude devices to assist commercial exports. It would also lend strong support to those criticizing tying arrangements on the grounds that they lead to a division of commercial markets among food aid donors in accordance with the strength of the national treasuries, rather upon the classic lines of comparative advantage. Since current balance-of-trade problems makes it very unlikely that the United States will materially reduce its tying practices in the foreseeable future (it is more likely to increase them), the multiple donor problem may remain unresolved for some time. However, if food activities of non-United States national donors continues to increase, a point may be reached, wherein a solution can no longer be delayed. It will be very interesting to see what develops in this regard.

The Timing of UMR Negotiations with
Recipients

An innocent looking provision pertaining to the negotiations of UMRs with the food aid recipient nearly derailed the efforts of the FAO to resolve the UMR issue. However, the fifty-fifth session of the FAO Conference managed to find a temporary solution, and in late 1971 the issue was finally resolved. Actually, it was not the provision, *per se*, which caused the difficulty, but its implications with respect to the long-standing controversy over the method of negotiating food aid agreements negotiations with respect to the consultations required by the FAO control system. Subparagraph 6(e) of the CCP Working Party draft stipulated that the final step in establishing the UMR will be the negotiations between the supplying country and the recipient country. France, supported by other countries, proposed that this provision be redrafted to provide that the final step in establishing the UMR will be the negotiation between the supplying country and the recipient country. To considerable extent, France's insistence on this point is based upon its concern that if 6(e) as drafted were adopted with respect to UMRs, it would imply that negotiations on other aspects of the transaction also must be postponed until the completion of the third party consultation process, a result France has consistently opposed as inconsistent with its interpretation of the FAO system.

France's position was deceptively simple. It argued that the first formulation implies that no negotiations with the recipient will occur until after the steps specified in subparagraphs 6(a)-6(d) have been completed. To delay discussions with the recipient over the UMR so long would be, according to France, irrational, ineffective, and contrary to the FAO control system as France understands it. The level of the UMR is crucial to the recipient and if discussions on this vital subject are to be delayed until the conclusion of all the steps specified in paragraph (6), conclusion of the food aid transaction will be unnecessarily delayed. Moreover, delaying negotiations with the recipient until consultations with third countries have been completed might well deprive the recipient of its ability to negotiate a UMR to fit its needs. Of course, should the recipient succeed in convincing the donor to change the UMR, the new figure presumptively would have to be resubmitted to the consultation process. To meet these needs, France argued, negotiations on the UMR must commence much earlier in the process, say between 6(b) and 6(c) and 6(c), that is, after the donor first calculates an appropriate UMR and before commencing bilateral consultations with potentially affected exporters. Under these conditions, subparagraph 6(e) must be redrafted to recognize that negotiations with the recipient on the UMR have commenced before, not after, clearing the UMR through the consultative process.

But as persuasive and reasonable as this position appears, the United States unequivocably rejected it. As discussed in Chapter 6 the timing of consultations under the FAO system has been a continuing sore point between the United States and other exporters. The latter have insisted that third party consultations on food aid transactions must commence before agreement has been reached with the recipient on the basic features of the agreement. Otherwise, they claim, the entire consultation system would be meaningless.[95] The same reasoning should apply even more strongly to UMRs, which are to be the principle means for protecting third country commercial exports. Therefore, the United States was unalterably opposed to any formulation, such as the one proposed by France, that would imply that any discussions with the recipient likely to settle important features of the transaction could commence before consultations are completed with third countries.

The very nature of the consultation-based FAO control system makes it very difficult to choose between the United States and French positions. Undoubtedly, the French are right in stressing the artificiality and clumsiness of a negotiation pattern whereby the donor and recipient cannot negotiate one of the most important and troublesome aspects of the transaction until after this issue is fully vetted among concerned third parties. But the right to be consulted and possibly protest that some aspect of a proposed food aid deal violates the FAO Principles comprise the only internationally recognized rights third countries have with respect to food aid. Therefore, it is understandable that they would resist any steps which would make it more difficult to modify the terms of a proposed transaction before they get their chance to request changes. And prior serious negotiations between the recipient and the donor on the UMR before initiating the required FAO notification and consultation procedures might well make it more difficult to induce a recipient to accept a postconsultation upward revision of the UMR. The United States view finally prevailed and the language proposed by the Working Party was adopted.

The Committee on Commodity Problems and subsequently the FAO Conference, retained the original wording of subparagraph 6(e) making negotiations with the recipient the last step in the UMR setting process, France adopted the UMR proposals, but reserved its position on the timing issue. Subsequently, France removed its reservation and, along with the other EEC members agreed to submit proposed UMRs to third countries prior to discussions with the food aid recipient. In doing so, however, the EEC reemphasized and formalized its determination to negotiate all other apsects of food aid transactions with the recipients *prior* to consultations with third countries.[96] Perhaps, the EEC sees this as a compromise offer to the United States and other countries insisting upon consultation before negotiations on all aspects of food aid. Consultations on UMRs will precede negotiations with the recipient; consultations on all other matters will follow negotiations with the recipient.

Tied UMRs

Although the system for imposing UMRs adopted by the FAO under Council Resolution 2/55 carefully avoids taking any definitive position on the nettlesome problem of tied UMRs, the text of the legislative resolution does touch upon this important subject. In Paragraph (1), the Committee on Commodity Problems reaffirms "the need to establish safeguards to insure that food aid recipients maintain at least the usual *global* (emphasis added) commercial imports of the commodity concerned." "Global imports" means imports from all countries, while tied-UMRs are designed to protect only the commercial imports of the donating country. Thus, the policy expressed in paragraph (1) seems inconsistent with the use of the tied-UMRs widely employed by the United States and to lesser extent by other food aid donors. But the UMR system adopted by the FAO does not preclude such practices. According to paragraph (2), for the purposes of the FAO system, UMRs are defined as the specific agreement by the recipient country to maintain at least a specified level of commercial imports in addition to any imports of the same commodities under the concessional transaction.

This formulation does not preclude use of tied-UMRs. Unlike paragraph 1, paragraph 2 does not make reference to "global commercial imports." Thus, arrangements requiring that a portion of the UMR be purchased from the food aid donor would not be inconsistent with paragraph 2's definition of UMRs nor would they be inconsistent with any other part of Resolution 2/55. Possibly, the reference to global commercial imports in paragraph 1 and the absence of such reference in the operative portions of the resolution was a symbolic gesture towards the critics of tied UMRs. Under existing conditions, this is the most that could be done in this regard, since the United States would not accept any system which attempted to outlaw the use of tied-UMRs. Even if the United States might accept some modifications of its tying practices, it would have been impossible to work this out in time to permit FAO Council approval during 1970.

Practice under the New FAO System

The elapsed time since the adoption of the UMR rules in November 1970 has been too short to provide evidence for evaluating the effectiveness of the new system. But it does appear that the failure of the FAO to agree upon a method for setting UMRs in multiple-donor situations has not deterred some member countries from applying the major-donor concept. Those countries which supported the major-donor concept have acted as if this approach had been adopted by the FAO. That is, they conformed their UMRs to that established by the major donor. This practice conforms with Paragraph (7) of the FAO Resolution 2/55, which is vague enough to authorize practically any solution to the multiple-donor problem. One country defended its use of the major-donor concept on the grounds that it was the only specific concept proposed so far and those countries opposing it had not offered any workable alternative. And though this country was not wedded to the major-donor concept, it saw merit in it and was planning to use it until a better one was found. This seems to be a very realistic and sensible attitude and until the FAO resolves the matter, the major-donor concept may well prevail by default.

Efficacy of Usual Marketing Requirements in Protecting Normal Patterns of Trade

The impact of the recent FAO actions with respect to usual marketing requirements is to universalize United States practices in this regard. UMRs are to be computed and modified in accordance with United States methods. No specific decision was taken on either tied-UMRs or the methods for determining UMRs when there is more than one donor. As we have seen, these issues may be closely related. If the principal donor is to set the UMR, it might be very awkward for it to tie a portion of the UMR to itself without doing the same for the other donors. But the spectacle of a UMR divided among all donors through tying, with little or no unrestricted UMR left for nondonating third country exporters would not have been well received—to say the least. Indeed, it may look so bad that the entire question of tied-UMRs would have to be considered.

Beyond this, we are left with this broader question of the efficacy of the UMR as a device to protect commercial trade patterns compared to other possible approaches. Under the conditions that prevailed when the United States was the sole significant food aid supplier, I believe a good case could be made against use of UMRs because of their adverse impact upon food aid recipients. However, when there are a number of donors, certain types of UMRs might be, on balance, the preferable market protection device, even though the recipient may be injured thereby. The final section of this chapter will wrestle with this problem.

The Impact of UMRs

Earlier in this chapter, it has been demonstrated that to the extent usual marketing requirements are effective, they undercut the economic value of food aid to the recipient country. Usual marketing requirements of particular products are effective only if they induce the recipient to buy more of a product than it would purchase if left to its own devices. But if we assume that each country is the best judge of its own needs, such strictures must lead to a suboptimum distribution of the country's resources, since it will be induced to purchase more food products than is consistent with optimum utilization of its external resources. And, as we constantly admonish foreign aid recipients, resources are scarce and misallocation is a cardinal sin. Thus, one effect of effective mandatory purchase requirements is to rescind some portion of the advantage the recipient has gained from the less-than-market price of food aid commodities.

The impact of usual marketing requirements on the donor and third countries is more difficult to determine. If these requirements induce purchases from third countries which have lost commercial sales because of food aid transactions, this could be seen as some compensation for the damage previously imposed on those countries. However, the redress is made by the underdeveloped recipient rather than the food aid donor. That is, if with respect to wheat food aid to India, minimum commercial purchase requirements are met through increased commercial wheat purchased from Canada, the United States is forcing India to compensate Canada for some of the markets preempted by American P.L. 480 exports. If food aid is a net burden to the United States, this arrangement might be deemed a morally defensible, if somewhat clumsy, method of minimizing undue adverse effects of concessional sales on third parties. But, if as alleged, Food for Peace transactions actually constitute a net benefit to the United States, perhaps more than to the recipient, it is difficult to justify the United States throwing the burden of compensating innocent third country exporters onto the recipients.[97]

Tying mandatory commercial purchases to the donor is even more difficult to justify. Of course, to the extent the donor has lost commercial sales through food aid transactions, it may lay some claim to an appropriate share of those commercial sales made available through usual marketing requirements. This may not really be necessary. As demonstrated in Chapter 3, Australia and Canada's losses in the developing countries have been balanced by increased sales to Socialist countries. But any attempt to increase the donor's normal share of the commercial market through tied mandatory purchases is wholly unjustifiable. Based on our analysis of actual practices, though it would seem that the United States, at least, has not employed tied compulsory purchases arrangements in situations likely to harm friendly third country exporters.

Actually, a strong case may be made for what might be termed reverse tying. That is, the food aid recipient should be obliged to make a given level of commercial purchases from countries other than the food aid donor. This would seem appropriate with respect to situations in which food aid transactions have permitted the donor to make large inroads into the traditional markets of other exporters. Wheat sales in India might be a good example. Here, the United States, with no pre-1954 history of commercial sales to that region has displaced the traditional suppliers—Australia and Canada.[98]

Given the political and economic realities, untied global marketing requirements is the most third country exporters can hope for. The United States Congress has emphasized heavily its determination that Food for Peace be administered to maximize United States commercial sales.[99] And with the current determination to improve the United States trade balance at any cost, the most the Administration would accept are untied global purchase requirements with the United States an eligible source.[100] Moreover, Congress fears that underdeveloped countries have come to view the United States as the residual supplier of food who will always come to their rescue with gifts or concessional sales. Based on this attitude, Congress reasoned, food aid recipients would tend to concentrate their commercial purchases in countries other than the United States. Obviously, this would be highly unfair and ungrateful conduct on their part.[101] As previously noted, it was to counter this supposed tendency and to assure the United States its fair share of commercial purchases that Section 103(o) was added to the P.L. 480 legislation in 1968.[102]

Other nations are likely to take similar attitudes. Until forced by relentless United States pressure to agree to the incorporation of UMRs into the FAO Principles, EEC countries seem to have been making blatant use of food aid to increase their commercial exports. But acceptance of UMRs will not reduce the pressure to find ways of disposing of the agricultural surpluses being induced by the Common Agricultural Policy and since the FAO Principles do not yet preclude tied-UMRs, considerable opportunity for aggressive use of food aid remain.

If exporters likely to be harmed by food aid are themselves developing countries, the detriment caused by usual marketing requirements to developing recipients would be fully justified. And most food aid donors are sensitive to the complaints of such exporters. In 1960, the United States rushed through a four-year sales agreement with India that included $116.0 million worth of rice.[103] No consultations were held with the rice-exporting countries of Thailand, Vietnam and Burma. The Prime Minister of Thailand went on a hunger strike, the State Department was flooded with protest notes, Thailand threatened to withdraw from SEATO and it took several years of delicate diplomacy to repair the damage.[104] Since then, the rice export position of these countries has deteriorated even further. Therefore, the United States, Japan, and any other country interested in maintaining good relations with Thailand and Burma are likely to impose stringent commercial purchase requirements on any food aid transactions involving rice transfers to countries which might be customers for Thai or Burmese rice.

Alternatives to UMRs. Earlier, it has been suggested that commercial imports of food aid commodities also can be guaranteed through less restrictive means. That is, through consultations with the recipient and its own analyses, the donor can set the level of food aid below the recipient's anticipated import needs. From the recipient's viewpoint, this approach has the clear advantage of assuring that no unwanted food purchases need be made. Thus, if domestic production is greater, or the foreign exchange reserves lower, than anticipated, the food aid recipient would not be bound to make unwanted commercial imports. In all probability, though, these same results can be achieved by setting the mandatory purchase requirements well below anticipated needs. Thus, in fiscal years 1965 and 1966, India was required to make commercial purchases of 200,000 metric tons of wheat.[105] Actual commercial purchases totalled 248,000 and 247,000 metric tons, respectively.[106] To the extent this pattern prevails throughout the world, the mandatory purchase requirements probably do not result in unwanted purchases. Furthermore, it seems that these requirements may be postponed. That is, if unforeseen circumstances make it inconvenient for a food aid recipient to meet its commercial purchase requirements in any given year, it can make up the deficit in subsequent years.[107]

UMRs with Multiple Donors. Whatever the case for UMRs imposed by a single donor, in the multiple-donor situation, UMRs may be the best approach. Elimination of UMRs entirely, use of proportional purchase systems, or quotas limited to third countries may make economic and administrative sense.[108] But to be effective, these control methods require full command of the situation by the food aid donor. That is, the donor must be able to closely calculate the recipient's total import needs and also must have the power to control the total amount of food aid each recipient will receive. If commercial trade is to be protected through control of the food aid level, with multiple donors, the various food aid donors must closely coordinate their food aid activities or there will be no assurance that an adequate amount of food will be purchased commercially. Under these circumstances, it might be argued that the UMR system is superior. If donors do not or cannot coordinate their food aid activities, it is possible that the total food aid receipts will be high enough to preclude the need for any commercial purchases. By requiring a UMR in all food aid transactions, all interested parties will be assured that there will be at least some commercial purchases. But, as we have seen, even with UMRs, the results in the multiple-donor situation will be suboptimum unless UMRs are set multilaterally. And, so far, the FAO has been unable to agree upon a method for multilateral setting of UMRs.

If UMRs are set multilaterally, it seems easier to agree upon a joint UMR than upon a joint food aid level. Given the highly competitive and difficult nature of international agricultural trade and the close connection between agricultural export and domestic agricultural policies, countries might be reluctant to commit themselves to food aid levels in advance. Smaller countries might not have the administrative control or interest to do so. These problems would not arise with respect to a joint UMR. Assuming agreement could be reached on the basic trade statistics, potential donating countries should be able to agree upon a joint UMR. One difficulty that would arise under either approach would be the identification of potential donors in advance. This could be solved by setting the UMR in the CSD. This has the additional advantage of ensuring that the views of nondonating third country exporters could be expressed at times when adjustments are still feasible. Under the existing consultation system, countries are consulted only when a transaction is imminent, thereby drastically limiting the opportunity for extensive discussions.

The present situation is that neither UMRs nor food aid levels are set through consultation with all other potential donors and rival exporters. Therefore, each recipient's food aid level will be determined by its success with all potential donors. In most cases, the UMR will be set by the principal donor, despite the refusal of the FAO to formally adopt this system. Under these circumstances, the UMR is the better approach. The current FAO rules require that UMRs are subject to the normal notification and consultation requirements generally applicable to transactions in categories 1-13. Thus, other nations will have the opportunity to comment upon the UMR and if any of them are planning food aid to the same recipient, they can then raise the issue of setting an appropriate UMR on the basis of larger food aid shipments. Discussion of UMRs during bilateral consultations are less satisfactory, since these only are held with countries likely to be harmed by food aid shipments, not with other potential food aid donors. Therefore, this system will be reasonably adequate only to the extent potential food aid donors and potential victims of food aid coincide. This clearly isn't the case with respect to developing exporters which cannot afford food aid programs.

Notes

1. UN/FAO, CCP/CSD, 65/8, P.L. 480 *Consultation Procedures* 2-3 (16 February 1965).

2. But see Chapter 3, where it is implied that for the food aid donor, the benefits and liabilities of exchanges between commercial sales and food aid are unevenly distributed through the polity.

3. See, e.g., Agricultural Commodity Agreement with Somali Republic, March 15, 1968, TIAS 6465, Pt. II, Item III, 19 UST 4698, 4709 (1969). The standard language refers to imports from the exporting countries and other "friendly countries . . . " Id. at Pt. I, Art. III-A-1.

4. E.g., Agricultural Commodity Agreement with Tunisia, March 17, 1967, TIAS 6323, Pt. II, Item III, 18 UST 1777, 1783 (1968). In this case, Tunisia was required to purchase 46,000 metric tons of edible vegetable oils, of which 12,000 metric tons were to come from the United States.

5. UN/FAO, CCP/CSD/69/51, *Report on "Tied Sales,"* Annex (17 July 1969).

6. See Chapter 7.

7. Op. cit., supra.

8. Ch. 3.

9. See Chapter 3.

10. *GAO Report, General Accounting Office, Report to Congress and Department of Agriculture*, Review Precautions Taken to Protect Commercial Dollar Sales of Agricultural Commodities under P.L. 480 (Aug. 1966) at 2-3 [hereinafter *GAO Report*].

11. Id. at 5.

12. See, e.g., Agreement with Afghanistan July 19, 1967, TIAS 6322, P & I, Art. III-A, 18 UST 1766 (1968). Actually, the general prohibition against displacement of usual marketings is included in sales agreements even though no minimum commercial purchases are required. According to the State Department, this practice is followed in order to provide a legal basis for imposing marketing requirements should conditions change from those prevailing when the agreement was concluded. *GAO Report* supra, note 10, at 12-13. Up to the spring of 1967, usual marketing requirements and specific export limitations were included in an exchange of notes accompanying the agreements. E.g., Agricultural Commodities Agreement with Ceylon, March 12, 1966, TIAS 5971, 17 UST 190, 195-97 (1967). Now they appear in Part II, item III of the Agreement itself. E.g., Agricultural Commodities Agreement with India, June 24, 1967, TIAS 6338, 18 UST 2351, 2353 (1969).

13. UN/FAO, *Report on "Tied Sales,"* supra, at 5-10.

14. Id. at 6-7.

15. Id. at 9.

16. 1970 P.L. 480 Report, table 8.

17. During the fiscal year period 1961 through 1964, United States closing stocks of wheat averaged 33.42 million metric tons, while the total closing stocks of the five largest wheat producers during this period (Argentina, Australia, Canada, the EEC, and the United States) averaged 35.60 million metric tons. However, by fiscal 1967, the United States stocks of wheat had declined to the nonsurplus level of 11.57 million tons and the five nation total had declined

to 35.15 million metric tons. In fiscal 1969, United States stocks climbed to 22.29 million and those of the five largest wheat producers to 63.16 million. *International Wheat Council, 1970 World Wheat Statistics* 46-47 (1970).

18. In fiscal years 1955 through 1969, the United States was the world's leading wheat exporter. In fiscal 1969, the United States exported 14.69 million metric tons of a total 44.45 million tons. Id. at 22-23.

19. During fiscal years 1960 through 1964, world exports of wheat were divided among the five major exporters as follows: United States–41%, Canada–22.4%, Australia–11.9%, France–4.8%, Argentina–4.4%. *International Wheat Council, Trends and Problems in World Grain Economy*, 1950-1970, Secretariat Paper No. 6, Table IV (1966) [hereinafter cited as *Trends and Problems*.] In 1967, wheat represented the following percentage of total exports: Canada–7%, Australia–6%, Argentina–1%, France–.8%, United States–3.9%, *United Nations, 1967 World Trade Annual (1968)* [hereinafter cited as 1967 Trade Annual].

20. From the fiscal period 1950 through 1954 to the fiscal period 1960 through 1964, United States increased its share of total wheat exports from 36% to 40%. However, during the same period, it expanded its share of exports to the underdeveloped world from 36% to 68%, while Canada had its share reduced from 23% to 6%, Australia from 17% to 9%, and Argentina from 14% to 5%. Of the 68% exported to the underdeveloped world, 45% was exported under P.L. 480 programs. *Trends and Problems*, supra, note 19, table IV.

21. See Chapter 3, Table 3-3.

22. E.g., Surplus Commodity Agreement with Peru, Feb. 7, 1966, TIAS 3190, 6 UST 563 (1956). In article IV-2 of the agreement, the two governments agreed that they would take reasonable precautions to assure that the sale "will not unduly disrupt world prices of agricultural commodities, displace usual marketings of the United States in these commodities, or materially impair trade relations among the countries of the free world."

23. Id. at 365-66. Surplus Agricultural Commodities Agreement with Italy, May 23, 1955, TIAS 3249, 6 UST 1109, 1122 (1956); Surplus Agricultural Commodities Agreement with Israel, Sept. 11, 1956, TIAS 3635, 7 UST 2469, 2474 (1957).

24. Agricultural Commodity Agreement with Pakistan, Nov. 15, 1957, TIAS 3961, 8 UST 2427, 2438 (1958); Agreement with India, Nov. 13, 20, 23, 1959, TIAS 4354, 10 UST 1882, 1889 (1960). Apparently, the use of free world purchase requirements for wheat grew out of the work of the Consultative Subcommittee on Surplus Disposal and bilateral negotiations with interested exporters. Maiden, *Some Aspects of Commodity Policy*, 4 *Australian Journal of Economics* 3, 9 (1960).

25. Surplus Agricultural Commodities Agreement with Israel, Nov. 7, 1957, TIAS 3945, 8 UST 2205, 2210 (1958); Agreement with Peru, April 9, 1958, TIAS 4045, 9 UST 693, 698-99 (1959).

26. Surplus Commodities Agreement with Colombia, Oct. 6, 1959, TIAS 4337, 10 UST 1799, 1804 (1960); Agreement with Tunisia, March 17, 1967, TIAS 6323, Pt. II, Item III; Agreement with India, Feb. 20, 1967, TIAS 6221, Pt. II, Item III; Agreement with Bolivia, April 22, 1966, TIAS 6013, 17 UST 645, 656 (1967).

27. *72 Stat*. 1790 (1958); *GAO Report*, supra, note 10 at 15.

28. FAO/UN, *FAO Commodity Review and Outlook 1969-70* 156-57 (1970).

29. *GAO Report*, supra, at 17-18.

30. *Trends and Problems*, supra, note 19 at 4; Agricultural Commodities Agreement with Syria, Nov. 9, 1961, TIAS 4944, 13 UST 97, 98 (1962); Agreement with Turkey, Feb. 21, 1963, TIAS 5303; 14 UST 236 (1964), TIAS 5760, 16 UST 66 (1966).

31. Agricultural Commodities Agreement with Korea, March 2, 1962, TIAS 4969, 13 UST 254 (1962); Korea, March 18, 1964, TIAS 5547, 15 UST 250 (1965); Taiwan, Nov. 19, 1962, TIAS 5219, 13 UST 2528, 2530 (1963).

32. Agricultural Commodities Agreement with Taiwan, Dec. 31, 1964, TIAS 5717, 15 UST 2272, 2286 (1965); Agreement with Korea, Feb. 26, 1969, TIAS 6661, 20 UST 522 (1970).

33. Agricultural Commodities Agreement with Yugoslavia of April 28, 1964, TIAS 5568, 15 UST 388, 389 (1964).

34. See *USDA/FAS, The World Grain Trade* 1963-64/1964-65 at 2 (1966) [hereinafter cited as World Grain Trade] ; *USDA/FAS, World Agricultural Production and Trade, Statistical Report*, April 1971 at 9; *Annual Reports on P.L. 480*.

35. Agricultural Commodities Agreement with Poland of Feb. 1, 1963, TIAS 5359, 14 UST 803, 811 (1964); Agreement of Feb. 3, 1964, TIAS 5516, 15 UST 40, 52 (1964).

36. In fiscal 1966, United States wheat exports to Poland, including Food for Peace, were 55,800 metric tons, representing only 3% of her total imports of 1.6 million metric tons. *World Grain Trade*, supra, note 34 at 2.

37. Ibid.

38. Id. at 24-30, 32-58.

39. *United Nations, 1964 Trade Annual*, at I-202-63.

40. *USDA/FAS, World Agricultural Production and Trade, Statistical Report*, 21 (1966).

41. See *FAO Commodity Review 1969-70*, at 25-29, USDA/FAS, *Foreign Agriculture*, June 28, 1971.

42. In the past when the world demand for rice was low, United States Food for Peace operations threatened to seriously impair United States-Thai relations. University of Arizona Agricultural Experiment Station, *Policy for United States Agricultural Export Surplus Disposal* (Technical Bulletin 150), 77-78, 81 (1962).

43. In the period from July 1, 1964 to December 31, 1970, food aid trans-

actions of rice totaled $1.39 billion out of the total $19.58 billion. 1970 *Annual Report on P.L. 480*, Table 8.

44. 1970 *Annual Report on P.L. 480*, Table 3.

45. See, e.g., Agricultural Commodities Agreement with the Philippines, April 23, 1965, TIAS 5785, 16 UST 632, 637 (1966); Agreement with India Sept. 30, 1964, TIAS 5669, 15 UST 1941, 1946-47 (1965).

46. Agreements with the Dominican Republic; Nov. 30, 1962, TIAS 5261, 13 UST 3863 (1963); Sept. 14, 1962, TIAS 5453 (1531); March 18, 1965, TIAS 5758, 16 UST 168, 169 (1966).

47. Agricultural Commodity Agreement with Indonesia, Sept. 15, 1967, TIAS 6346, Pt. II, Item III, 18 UST 2393, 2404 (1969).

48. Agricultural Commodities Agreement with Vietnam March 21, 1966, TIAS 5968, 17 UST 129 (1967).

49. Prior to 1961, the Dominican Republic neither imported nor exported significant quantities of rice. *USDA, Agricultural Statistics* 1964. But in fiscal years 1963-65, she imported a total of 14.6 million dollars worth of rice under Title IV. 1966 *Annual Report on P.L. 480*. Table 12 (1967). However in fiscal 1967, imports were down to pre-1961 levels. *USDA/FAS World Production and Trade, Statistical Report* 13 (1967).

50. Agreement with Liberia, April 12, 1962, TIAS 4996, 13 UST 391, 395 (1962); Agreement with Poland, April 19, 1962, TIAS 4988, 14 UST 401, 402 (1962); Agreement with Poland, TIAS 5539, 15 UST 187, 198 (1964).

51. In 1965, feedgrains accounted for about 15% of Argentina's export earnings and 7% of Thailand's. Id. at 37; *Statesman's Yearbook* 1967-68, at 818, 1490 (1967).

52. E.g., Agreement with Brazil, March 15, 1962, TIAS 5061, 13 UST 1167, 1178 (1962); Israel, May 3, 1962, TIAS 5004, 13 UST 432, 433 (1962); Tunisia, April 7, 1964, TIAS 5556, 15 UST 300, 301 (1964), India, Dec. 31, 1964, TIAS 5729, 15 UST 2392 (1964).

53. See, e.g., Agricultural Commodities Agreement with Israel, June 6, 1966, TIAS 6039, 17 UST 817, 823 (1967); Agreement with the Ryukyu Islands, Dec. 23, 1965, TIAS 5927, 16 UST 1932, 1938 (1966).

54. Agreement with Iceland, March 16, 1962, TIAS 4981, 13 UST 312 (1962); Liberia, April 12, 1962, TIAS 4996, 13 UST 391, 395 (1962); Greece, Oct. 22, 1962, TIAS 5238, 13 UST 2660, 2665 (1963). In some early agreements, a minimum level of government holdings of corn was stipulated, in addition to purchase requirements. Agreements with Mexico, Oct. 23, 1957, TIAS 3935, 8 UST 1895 (1958).

55. *UN/FAO, Monthly Bulletin of Agricultural Economics and Statistics*, Vol. 20, #4 at 25 (April 1971). Cottonseed oil is usually included as an alternate to soybean oil in all sales agreements. E.g., Agreement with Afghanistan, May 22, 1965, 16 UST 1078, 1079 (1966), and is often coupled with soybean oil in official statistics on the program; see, e.g., 1967 *Annual P.L. 480 Report*, at

table 8. But in fact, no cottonseed oil ever has been sold under the program. The United States, the world's largest exporter of cottonseed oil has been sharply cutting production of this product as a result of its efforts to limit production of upland (short-staple) cotton. USDA/AAS *World Production and Trade, Statistical Report* April 1971 at 81. This treatment results from administration anxiety to please ever sensitive Agricultural Committee members hailing from cotton-producing areas.

56. *UN/FAO, Monthly Bulletin of Agricultural Economics and Statistics*, Vol. 70, No. 4 at 25 (April 1971).

57. 1971 *Annual Report on P.L. 480*, Table 8. Barter deals have been excluded.

58. 1970 *Annual Report on P.L. 480*, Table 5.

59. The FAO attributes an increase of per capita supply of edible oils to United States P.L. 480 programs. *FAO Commodity Review* 1967, at 76 (1967). From 1953 to 1967, United States soybean exports have increased from 161 million bushels to 262 million bushels and in fiscal 1971, reached a record 416 million bushels.

60. From 1961-65. The only exception was a $6.3 million sale to Yugoslavia. Agreement of Nov. 28, 1962, TIAS 5223, 13 UST 2578, 2579 (1963). But subsequent agreements with Yugoslavia did contain mandatory commercial purchase requirements. Agreement of April 27, 1964, TIAS 5567, 15 UST 381, 385 (1964).

61. Agricultural Commodities Agreement with Israel of August 4, 1967, TIAS 6314; Agreement with Tunisia, Feb. 17, 1965, TIAS 5767, 15 UST 102 (1966). *But see* Agreement with India, Feb. 20, 1967, TIAS 6221, 18 UST 217, 222-24 (1968) in which edible oils are provided without purchase requirements.

62. *See* Chapter 9.

63. 1970 *Annual Report on P.L. 480*, Table 8.

64. *Statistical Abstract of the United States, 1970, Tables 931, 934 (1971)*. Recently, the cotton problem, has been reduced through new United States supply control policies. *FAO Commodity Review 1969-70* at 95-101 (1970).

65. *FAO Commodity Review 1969-70* at 95-101 (1970), UN/FAO, *Monthly Bulletin*, Vol. 20, #3, at 24 (March 1971).

66. Ibid.

67. 80 *Stat*. 1528 (1966), 7 U.S.C.A. 1703 (i) (1970).

68. 80 *Stat*. 1533 (1966), 7 U.S.C.A. 1709 (a)(1) (1970).

69. *Hearings on World War on Hunger before the House Committee on Agriculture*, ser. W. 89th Cong., 2d sess., 204-207, 279-81 (1966) [hereinafter cited as *1966 House Hearings*].

70. United States cotton stocks stood at 3,665 thousand tons in 1966. *FAO Commodity Review*–1967, 136 (1967); but dropped to 1,414 thousand tons at the beginning of 1969. *FAO Commodity Review and Outlook*, 1969-70, at 95-101 (1970).

71. *1966 House Hearings*, at 192.

72. Agreement with Tunisia, Feb. 17, 1965, TIAS 5767, 16 UST 97, 102, (1966); Ethiopia, Aug. 17, 1965, TIAS 5854, 16 UST 119, 1124 (1966); Agreement with India, Sept. 12, 1967, TIAS 6342.

73. See Chapter 9.

74. Id.

75. *1970 Annual Report on P.L. 480*, table 8. In the year ending June 30, 1970, exports of unmanufactured tobacco under P.L. 480 accounted for 22% of all tobacco exports. *1970 Annual Report* at Table 3.

76. The restrictions on tobacco promoted lively debate between Senator Williams, the sponsor of tobacco and alcohol restrictions, and Senators from tobacco-growing states. 112 *Cong. Rec.* 20573-80 (1966). Through December 31, 1965, $315.7 million worth of tobacco (export value excluding shipping costs) had been included in Title I agreements, and $20.8 millions worth had been sold under Title IV. Id. at 147. The final enactment represented a compromise, 112 *Cong. Rec.* 20578, 20580, between Senator Williams' amendment, which would have banned both products from all aspects of this program, 112 *Cong. Rec.* 20573, and the Senate Committee version, which would have applied no restrictions. Calendar 1943, Title IV, Sec. 402, 112 *Cong. Rec.* 1998 (1966).

77. Sec. 402, 80 *Stat.* 1536, 7 U.S.C.A. 1732 (1970).

78. The value of P.L. 480 for fiscal years 1968, 1969, and 1970 were 31.4 million, 37.2 million, 18.4 million, respectively.

79. In 1969, Uruguay imported 104.6 thousand tons, the UAR, 14.2 thousand tons, and Thailand, 12.2 thousand tons. UN/FAO, *Monthly Bulletin of Agricultural Economics and Statistics*, Vol. 20, No. 3, at 23 (March 1971).

80. In 1966, stocks reached 2.0 million tons. *FAO Commodity Review 1967* at 131 (1967). But at the beginning of 1969, the stocks had fallen to 1.2 million tons. *FAO Commodity Review and Outlook, 1969-70* at 93-95 (1970).

81. Agricultural Commodities Agreement with Israel, June 6, 1966, TIAS 6039, 17 UST 817, 818, 823 (1967); Agreement with Chile, July 27, 1966, TIAS 5828, 16 UST 1725, 1926, 1737 (1966); Agreement with Ryukyu Islands, Dec. 23, 1965, TIAS 5927, 16 UST 1932, 1933, 1938 (1966).

82. In 1969, the United States exported 172.2 thousand tons of the world total of 635 thousand tons. The closest competitors were Greece—71.0 thousand tons; Turkey—70.5 thousand tons, Bulgaria—59.0 thousand tons; India—54.7 thousand tons and Brazil—48.1 thousand tons. FAO/UN, *Monthly Bulletin of Agricultural Economics and Statistics*, Vol. 20, No. 3 at 23 (March 1971).

83. *FAO Commodity Review* 1967, at 130-34 (1967).

84. *GAO Report*, supra, note 10 at 8-10.

85. Food Aid Convention, 1971, Art. II(5).

86. As of June 30, 1971, 20 nations had signified their acceptance of Council Resolution 2/55, including the United States, Australia, West Germany, the United Kingdom, and the EEC. France accepted on Jan. 10, 1972.

87. See Chapter 4.

88. See Chapter 6.

89. FAO Principle 5 states: "In weighing the advantages to countries benefiting from special disposal measures against the possible harm done to other countries, account must be taken of the relationship of possible sacrifices to the economic capacity of the countries concerned, and in particular of the effects of such sacrifices on their rates of development." *Disposal of Agricultural Surpluses, Principles Recommended by FAO* 5 (1963).

90. *See* UN/FAO, CCP 69/28, *Report of the forty-fourth Session of the Committee on Commodity Problems*, paras. 134(c)(7); 134(c)(8), and 134(c)(10)(a) (10 Nov. 1969).

91. See Appendix B.

92. See Appendix B.

93. Actually, this was the fourth alternative proposed by the CCP Working Party. However, alternative three is substantively identical to alternative two and does not require separate discussion. FAO/UN, CCP/UMR 70/3. *Working Party on Usual Marketing Requirements*, 3-4 (9 June 1970).

94. UN/FAO, CCP 70/23, *Report of the Fifth-fifth Session of The Committee on Commodity Problems* 37-41 (30 Oct. 1970).

95. See Chapter 6.

96. See discussion of the consultation process under the FAO Principles in Ch. 6.

97. E. Heady and J. Timmons, *Objectives, Achievements and Hazards of the U.S. Food Aid and Agricultural Development Programs in Relation to Domestic Policy* in *Alternatives for Balancing World Food Production Needs*, Ch. 13 (1967); Wightman, *Food Aid and Economic Development, International Conciliation*, No. 567, at 34-37; H.R.Rep. No. 1297, 90th Cong., 2d sess., 1-17 (1968).

98. In fiscal 1952, the United States exported 28,276,000 bushels of wheat and flour to India, representing 51% of her wheat imports. Canada exported 16,663,000 bushels or 31% and Australia 10,014,000 bushels or 18%. *USDA Agricultural Statistics 1953*, at 10 (1953). In fiscal 1966, the United States supplied 94% of India's wheat imports, Canada 4% and Australia 2%. By fiscal 1969, Australia's share dropped below 1%, the United States share dropped to 71% and Canada's share rose to 22%. Most of Canada's increase, though, was in the form of food aid. *International Wheat Council*, 1970 *World Wheat Statistics*, Table 8a, 8e (1970).

99. Section 103(f) of the Food for Peace Act requires the President to give special consideration to the development and expansion of foreign markets for agricultural commodities. 80 *Stat.* 1527 (1966), 7 *USCA* § 1703 (1970); Section 103(n) requires the President to take minimum precautions to assure that sales for dollars do not displace cash sales. 80 *Stat.* 1528 (1966), 7 *USCA* § 1703 (n) (1970).

100. *H.R. Rep.* No. 1558, 89th Cong., 2d sess., 44 (1966); *H.R. Rep.* No. 1297, 90th Cong., 2d sess. 39-41 (1968).

101. *Hearings before the House Committee on Agriculture on Extension of P.L. 480*, 90th Cong., 2d sess., Serial LL at 157-58 (1968).

102. See Chapter 3.

103. Agreement with India, May 4, 1960, TIAS 4499, 11 UST 1544 (1961).

104. Memorandum from Howard Gabbet, Agency of International Development, dated Oct. 31, 1969. (Memorandum is in author's files.)

105. Agreement with India, Sept. 30, 1964, TIAS 5669, 15 UST 1941, 1947 (1964); Agreement with India, July 26, 1965, TIAS 584, 16 UST 1064-65 (1966).

106. *International Wheat Council, World Wheat Statistics*—1966, Table 34, at 78 (1967).

107. Agreement with India, Sept. 30, 1964, TIAS 5669, 15 UST 1941, 1947 (1964).

108. See Chapter 3.

Controlling Food Aid Induced Exports

We have seen how food aid may affect agricultural trade by reducing the normal commercial purchases of recipient countries. In addition, food aid may permit recipients to alter the pattern of their exports to the detriment of both the food aid donor and third countries. Thus, if food aid purchases of a particular commodity permit a nation to make unwanted exports of the same or physically or economically related products, the interests of other nations interested in similar exports may be adversely affected. Food aid induced exports which tend to upset established commercial interests are subject to the FAO Principles of Surplus Disposal and the Guidelines Relating to Concessional Transactions of the International Wheat Agreement. United States legislation proceeds along very similar lines. But precise interpretation, application, and enforcement of the general guidelines provided by the relevant international agreements and domestic legislation can be very difficult.

Although direct reexports of the same, unaltered food aid commodities are relatively simple to control, proper handling of exports of similar products or products manufactured from the original commodities is harrowing business. As wheat is made into flour, then into gluten, and finally into chemical by-products of gluten, the identity of the original agricultural import becomes increasingly indistinct. Similar problems arise when a wheat-eating country wishes to export rice or when a country which commonly eats one grade of rice wishes to earn foreign exchange by exporting a higher priced variety. Textile exports allegedly attributable to concessional cotton purchases are particularly troublesome. But with respect to the United States, at least, as its food aid program has progressed and grown in maturity and sophistication, these very difficult and sensitive problems have been handled with increased subtlety. This chapter will develop and analyze in some detail the concepts and techniques available to prevent the export ripples initiated by food aid from unduly damaging recognized vested commercial interests.

Although in most cases one can be fairly certain that particular exports are attributable, wholly or partially, to the import of agricultural products under food aid, this conclusion must be based solely on statistical inference. Increases of certain exports usually are caused by a host of factors, food aid being just one. In some cases, the food aid induced exports may be defended as the onset of an economically sound transaction which gives promise of continuation without the benefit of further concessional purchases. Exports of domestic olive oil by countries receiving food aid financed soya beans or soya bean oil is a good example. Therefore, controlling food aid induced exports requires far subtler techniques than those necessary to assure minimum commercial imports by the food aid recipient. Generally, these devices must preclude exports which are harmful to third countries and which make little or no economic sense without food aid, while they must permit normal export patterns and growth and encourage food aid recipients to develop additional export possibilities without assistance. Generally, the administrators of United States food aid programs have responded with a wide array of highly imaginative, ingenious and generally successful control mechanisms. But as with usual marketing requirements, the United States has employed certain tying devices which have been strongly condemned by other exporters.

Basic Legal Structure

Food aid induced exports are generally covered by Article 3 of the FAO Principles and more specifically covered by Article 7. Article 3 requires that food aid transactions must not harmfully interfere with normal patterns of production and trade. Situations in which food aid facilitates the export of commodities by the recipient to markets otherwise served by other countries certainly might fall within this prescription. More specifically, Article 7 requires the beneficiary of food aid to ensure that the food aid commodities themselves are not resold or transshipped to other countries, and that it should take care "to prevent exports of supplies of the same or related commodities which might be freed for sale abroad as a result of the country's imports on special terms." Although the text of the Principles seems to impose the burden of avoiding harmful food aid induced exports upon the recipient, it is broadly accepted that it is the donor's responsibility to include appropriate language in food aid agreements to accomplish this end. Despite its unquestioned authority in this area for a long time, the FAO has been relatively inactive in this regard, apparently satisfied with the way the prime food aid donor, the United States, was handling these matters. But more recently, the FAO has become concerned with certain United States practices, and those of some of the newer entrants into the food aid arena.

Once again, United States practices constitute the only substantial source for analyzing the nature of the food aid induced export problem and the available devices for its solution. Because the FAO has not concerned itself much with export problems, United States practice is even more central. Therefore, our discussion of this matter will center around United States activities. Ocasionally, other country's practices are relevant. Those cases will be discussed in the context of analogous United States practices.

Legal and Administrative Bases for
United States Practices

The legislative basis for United States action with respect to food aid induced exports closely parallels the FAO Principles. Section 103 (g) of the Food for Peace Act obliges the President to obtain commitments from purchasing countries that will prevent the resale or transshipments of commodities received under Food for Peace to third countries or the use of such commodities for other than domestic purposes.[1] This provision would seem to protect third country exporters as well as the United States. Generally, it has been administered that way, but occasionally, one can detect subtle and sometimes not so subtle efforts to turn these restrictions to the advantage of the United States. Actually, read literally, the restrictions in the Food for Peace Act only apply to the agricultural commodities themselves and not to similar or derivative products.[2] However, the Executive Branch has been forced to interpret the statute more broadly. Obviously, it would defeat the clear intent of the law if, for example, a country could import wheat and export flour. Generally, simultaneous imports of rice and exports of wheat also would be bad, though, here counterarguments are possible.

Although the United States recognizes that food aid is intended for domestic consumption and not to enable the recipient country to increase its exports of the same or of a like commodity in raw or processed form, it may be economically desirable for a recipient country to develop exports based upon imports of the kind of commodities being supplied under food aid. Examples are (1) cotton textile exports based on raw cotton imports; (2) exports of higher priced olive oil freed for export by the importation of soybean oil for domestic consumption; and (3) the conversion of domestic wheat production for internal consumption into exportable rice by meeting internal wheat requirements through imports. United States policy is to ensure that such exports are based on real economic advantages and are not the direct and sole result of concessionally priced imports. In these cases, it is United States practice to require that additional exports of this kind be fully offset by additional commercial imports.

Interpretation, application and enforcement of export restrictions causes great difficulties, often leading to squabbles within the United States executive branch between the Department of Agriculture, the Agency for International Development (AID), and the Department of State. As a rule, AID, which is interested in maximizing the developing countries' foreign exchange earnings, takes the most liberal view. The Department of Agriculture may be counted upon to oppose such exports. And State wobbles, depending upon which other exporting country might be affected. By now, though, a sort of case law has been developed which narrows the issues to manageable dimensions.[3]

Basic Control Devices. Certain transactions present particularly difficult problems. These include exports of products economically or physically related to the food aid product such as (1) rice exports by countries importing P.L. 480 wheat; (2) olive oil exports by countries receiving soya beans (or soya bean oil); and (3) textile exports allegedly derived from concessionally priced cotton. Generally speaking, the more developed the food aid recipient, the more difficult it is to segregate and control the economic impact of particular food aid transactions and the more sophisticated the control mechanisms that must be employed.

Every concessional sales agreement contains a catchall clause requiring the importing government to take all possible measures to prevent the resale or transshipment to other countries or the use for other than domestic purposes both of the agricultural commodities themselves and any commodity of either domestic or foreign origin which is the same as or like the commodities purchased.[4] Beyond this, many agreements prohibit or limit particular exports. Occasionally, agreements specify remedial action in case the export provisions are violated.[5]

Tied Offsets. In situations where a food aid recipient might export products economically related to the food aid commodities, the United States has relied upon the device of requiring the recipient commercial to offset some or all of these exports by increased commercial purchases. To the extent these purchases may be made on a global basis, the commercial offset device is an effective method for reconciling the economic development of the recipient with the legitimate export interests of third countries. But the United States has chosen to tie almost all offset purchase requirements to the United States. This practice has come under increasing criticism in the CSD. Such practices are not required by United States legislation and are totally unjustifiable on any basis.

Detailed Analysis of United States
Export Control Practices

Since offset arrangements can be quite complex, analysis of the effectiveness and legitimacy of United States export control practices will be simplified by first examining the specifics of United States practices with respect to the major varieties of export control problems.

Reexportation of the Food Aid Commodity

With very few exceptions, export of the same commodity received as food aid is strictly forbidden during the trade year in which the commodities are to be received.[6] This requirement is consistent with the notion that all food aid trans-actions must result in a *pro tanto* increase in the consumption of the food aid product—if all food aid commodities are consumed by the recipient, increased exports of the same commodity are precluded. Conceivably, though, such exports might be justified if Food for Peace were viewed, in part, as a convenient way of making foreign exchange available to certain countries other than through the normal foreign aid channels—that always painful and cumbersome process of obtaining appropriations and following the expenditure of the funds through every convolution of the economic and financial process. Let us assume that the United States has established a particular foreign aid level for a certain country. But instead of financing goods or services directly, the United States gives it surplus agricultural products, which are to be sold commercially for what they will bring. The net proceeds of the transactions to the food aid recipient may be viewed as foreign aid. Assuming such transactions were permitted solely with surplus commodities, the effect would be to distribute the cost of the benefits received by the recipient among all potential commercial exporters of the products, including the United States. Indeed, such distribution of the for-eign aid burden is one of the most repeated objectives of recent United States governments. Of course, the United States has never seriously considered this kind of dodge. And despite any actual merits of this kind of scheme, it looks so strange that it is unlikely that it ever would be used.

In certain circumstances, exports of food aid commodities have been permit-ted. Almost always, these are situations in which countries recently have moved from food exporter to food importer status. Thus Turkey, Syria, and Cyprus were permitted to maintain some wheat exports while they received P.L. 480 wheat.[7] Or, exports have been permitted to certain traditional customers. Argentina was permitted to export edible oils to a few selected countries.[8] And Jordan was authorized to export wheat to Saudi Arabia while receiving con-cessional wheat.[9]

In some instances, distinctions have been drawn between varieties of the same commodity. Wheat comes in three varieties: hard red for bread; soft mainly for cakes and pastries, and sometimes, for bread in countries such as France that do not produce hard red; and durum for spaghetti and other pasta. Thus, exports of soft wheat by Turkey were prohibited but exports of durum wheat were permit-ted.[10] And Tunisia, a traditional exporter of durum wheat, has been permitted to export this product while bread wheats (hard red) were being imported under P.L. 480.[11] But in Morocco, which at one time exported wheat, durum wheat exports were specifically banned.[12] Pakistan was permitted to export superior grades of rice while receiving concessional sales of lower grade rices.[13] Also, the United Arab Republic, a recipient of concessional wheat and feed grains, was allowed to export seed varieties of these products while it was subject to general prohibitions of wheat exports.[14] Finally, India has been permitted to export short-staple cotton while receiving both long-staple and upland cotton from the

United States.[15] True to the pattern, India is a traditional cotton exporter. It also is a country with severe foreign exchange problems whose fate must be of great moment to the United States.[16] In fact, India generally has received special treatment in all aspects of United States food aid operations.

In some cases, limited exports of identical commodities were permitted for no clear reason. For example, the UAR was permitted to export rice provided these exports were matched by commercial purchases from free world sources.[17] Conceivably, the exports were destined for Russia as part of a barter deal. Similarly, Taiwan was permitted to export tobacco while receiving tobacco from the United States under food aid.[18] Since in recent years, Taiwan continually has increased its exports of tobacco, this exemption seems to have been designed to facilitate development of a potentially valuable export industry for a successfully developing graduate of massive foreign aid.[19]

Usually in these cases, the recipient must pledge to match its exports of food aid commodities with an equivalent amount of commercial purchases from free world sources.[20] It might seem that the requirement that all exports be matched by commercial imports negates any benefits the food aid recipient might have derived from the exports. However, this arrangement does afford food aid recipients certain advantages. For one, the recipient may be unable or unwilling to control its exports to the extent necessary to preclude all exports of the food aid commodity. Also it may wish to preserve traditional markets until such time when it can again become a net exporter of the product involved. Neither of these ends could be reached if exports are banned absolutely. Moreover, to the extent these compensating commercial purchases are tied to the United States in greater proportion than its normal share of such imports, the United States, at least, is a clear gainer.

Food Aid Induced Rice Exports by Pakistan. The fundamental features of food aid reduced exports of the same commodity is well illustrated by the controversy over a recent food aid rice transaction between Japan and Pakistan. Pakistan occasionally purchases rice from Thailand when its domestic production falls short. Pakistan also has been receiving rice as food aid from the United States, and in 1970, from Japan. But Pakistan also annually exports 100,000-200,000 tons of rice. Recently, Pakistan agreed to sell about 10,000 tons of parboiled rice to Ceylon, which in recent years has been consistently unable to meet its domestic needs. Thailand which traditionally exports rice to Ceylon commercially, claimed that Japan's concessional rice sales undercut her commercial markets in Ceylon and thereby violated the FAO Principles. This situation is particularly difficult because of the general squeeze on rice exports and the fact that Pakistan is chronically short of foreign exchange and its rice production and consumption tends to be unstable. Thus, whenever possible, Pakistan wants to increase its export earnings by rice sales, if the rice is not required for home consumption. Japan has serious rice surpluses. Also, it is committed to provide

225,000 metric tons of food aid under the Food Aid Convention, which obligation can be met with rice rather than wheat. Thus Japan is under pressure to supply food aid in rice in the context of a very tight world rice market. Thailand, which depends upon rice as its principal commercial export, understandably will be very sensitive to any transaction which threatens its markets. It is interesting to note that the United States has not given Pakistan any rice food aid in the past five years, roughly coinciding with the period in which Thailand became a key country in our southeast Asia adventures.

The Ban on Similar Products or Commodities

In order to further minimize possible adverse effects of Food for Peace sales on third countries, the ban on the export of the same product has been extended to include "similar" commodities and commodities serving the same general purposes.[21] Generally, if wheat is being provided, exports of all food grains are prohibited. This pattern may be observed in recent agreements with Afghanistan, Tunisia and Somali.[22] But often, just wheat exports were banned. Iceland and the Congo provide recent examples of this variation.[23] If feed grains are provided, usually neither rye, corn, grain sorghums, barley nor oats may be exported.[24] Variations in form stem from the particular ability of the recipient to export certain products. Thus, if a nation has no capacity to export oats or barley, a wheat sale agreement may not bother to specifically prohibit such transactions.

Since rice and wheat are to some extent interchangeable as basic diet staples, sales of one product generally demand restrictions on the export of the other. Thus, wheat sales to Pakistan, Taiwan, and Korea have been accompanied by limitations on rice exports by these countries.[25] For Pakistan, the prohibition did not apply to high-quality rice exports.[26] With respect to Taiwan and Korea, some rice exports are permitted subject to a complex set of limitations.[27] These will be discussed subsequently.[28] The restrictions also run the other way. Thus, rice sales to Ceylon were accompanied by bans on wheat exports.[29]

Products made from edible oils also cause problems. This is well illustrated by recent food aid transactions with Israel. In a recent sale to Israel of 22,000 metric tons of edible vegetable oils, Israel is permitted to export up to 25,000 metric tons of edible vegetable oils, provided that she buys an equivalent amount of oil from the United States commercially. Israel has been permitted to export margarine and/or shortening provided that it purchases commercially from the United States an amount of edible vegetable oil or edible oil bearing seeds equivalent to the edible oil content of the margarine and/or shortening exported. Finally, Israel was permitted to export soybean oil meal, sunflower seeds and peanuts (not for crushing), edible olives, olive oil, desiccated coconut meat and industrial oil and oil seeds without offsetting purchase requirements.[30] In view of the dominant position of the United States in world edible oil exports, this country probably would not increase its market share through this maneuver. But other soybean product exporters, particularly the Netherlands, are very sensitive about food aid related oil product exports.

Perhaps the most controversial cross-product controls apply to the export of olive oil by recipients of soybean oil on concessional terms. Currently, this problem is most acute with respect to Tunisia and Turkey, traditional olive oil producers and exporters.[31] Although soya and olive oils are used for the same purposes, the use by the relatively poor olive oil producing countries of increased quantities of the far cheaper soybean for domestic consumption in lieu of olive oil would have a twofold impact. It would permit domestic cost savings and facilitate increased foreign exchange earnings through greater olive oil exports.[32] But if a food aid recipient is granted unrestricted permission to substitute low-price food aid soybean oil for olive oils in domestic consumption, this may free enough olive oil for export to constitute a threat to rival exporters not now eligible for concessional food sales (such as Spain).[33] Such transactions may be argued to be consistent with the concept of Food for Peace sales as a developmental tool. That is, if the substitution of soybean for olive oil seems a sensible long-run arrangement, making soybean oil available on concessional terms bolsters a natural export. This seems somewhat comparable to using food aid to India in order to meet its expanding food needs and to avoid having food either imported or domestically produced at the cost of other more productive uses of the requisite resources.[34]

Derivative Products

Exports of products physically or economically dependent upon food aid imports are another problem area. A working group of the CSD investigating the relationship between concessional sales of food grains to Israel and increases in Israeli egg exports took the view that "for practical purposes" the Principles have been interpreted to include this kind of transaction within the concept of "related commodities." The relevant standard provisions in United States sales agreements with respect to exports also are somewhat ambiguous. They explicitly prohibit the export of commodities which are the same or like the commodities purchased under the sales agreement, but they do not squarely face the derivative product problem.[35] But since the export of products directly made from imported commodities—particularly those involving minimum processing— might well interfere with normal patterns of production and trade, prohibition of some derived products does seem called for. Thus, if reexports of wheat are forbidden, the same should apply to wheat flour, whose value is almost solely dependent on the wheat content.

In this regard, poultry, egg, or cattle exports by countries receiving P.L. 480 feed grains should be restricted. Largely, these issues have been concentrated in better developed countries such as Poland, Greece, and Israel; really poor nations do not have exportable likestock or livestock products.[36] Usually, potential harmful effect on trade is controlled through direct restrictions on increased exports of the derived products.[37] In one case, the danger that P.L. 480 dried milk might be fed to exportable animals was met by restricting the milk's use to human consumption.[38] The treatment of gluten and similar by-products of flour milling present real headaches. Although they are a product of the original wheat, they differ substantially in form, value, and use from the original products. Moreover, the impact of exports of these products on third country wheat exporters seems remote. At the moment, no consistent pattern has developed regarding the treatment of wheat by-products.

Cotton sales present particularly difficult problems. Cotton textiles constitute a natural export of developing countries and are also widely manufactured and exported by developed nations, including the United States.[39] One result of the struggle of the textile industries in the developed countries to protect their markets from lower priced imports from the developing countries has been the institution of a worldwide network of bilateral agreements under the umbrella of the GATT Long-term Arrangement Regarding Trade in Cotton Textiles. These arrangements are designed to allocate fairly shares of the domestic market of developed countries to textile producers in the developing world.[40]

Export Quotas

The original and perhaps still most common method of regulating unwanted food aid induced exports is a flat prohibition of the export of the products concerned within a stipulated period.[41] But generally, more sophisticated methods of control have been devised, particularly for the more developed food aid recipients for whom outright prohibitions on certain exports would be extremely damaging to their economies.[42] The end product is often quite wondrous. Indeed, some of the devices and arrangements worked out for semideveloped countries like Greece may well be said to approach the acme of sophistication for government-to-government financial and economic dealings.

The most common deviation from the flat prohibition is the export quota. In its simplest form, the food aid recipient is permitted to export up to a given level of specified products deemed related to the commodities received. Thus, Morocco, while receiving edible oils, was permitted to export up to 750 metric tons of the same products to "friendly countries."[43] Similarly, Tunisia, also receiving edible oils, was permitted to export up to 40,000 metric tons of olive oil during fiscal 1967.[44] Poland was given a quota of 7,000 metric tons of lard as permissible exports while receiving edible oils. In addition, Poland promised "to try" to limit total exports to 6,000 metric tons and exports to "Eastern European Countries" to 4,000-5,000 metric tons—the level of existing commitments.[45] Special limitations of exports to particular markets also were attempted with respect to rice exports from Taiwan and Korea. Here, Taiwan was limited to 150,000 metric tons of exports to countries which became markets after January 1, 1955,[46] and Korea was forbidden to export more than 60,000 metric tons to Japan and the Ryukyus.[47]

An old agreement with Turkey demonstrates the degree of complexity that can be reached in the attempt to provide an important developing country with some elbow room in its export efforts without undercutting basic policies. Turkey was receiving concessional feed grains. It was permitted to export barley and oats provided that it promised to use all P.L. 480 corn for human consumption or for the manufacture of glucose and that it refrained from using any corn, including corn of domestic origin, for feed.[48] This Rube Goldbergian arrangement was designed to ensure that the P.L. 480 corn did not displace home grown barley and oats as a feed grain, thereby permitting the export of these products. The ban on the use of domestic corn for feed purposes was necessary in order to preclude P.L. 480 corn from being used for human consumption and for glucose manufacture in lieu of domestically grown corn, which in turn could be used instead of barley and oats for feed purposes, thereby again making these latter products available for export. However, banning domestically grown corn as a feed grain only would be feasible if corn were not ordinarily used for feed purposes in Turkey. Otherwise, such a restriction would disrupt the recipient's normal economic functioning.

Matching and Offsetting Commercial Purchases

Sometimes, exports of the same or related products are permitted provided that the food aid recipient-exporter makes certain additional commercial purchases. These are the arrangements which have drawn fire from the CSD. They provide that either all exports of particular commodities or all exports above a certain minimum must be accompanied on a quantity basis by commercial purchases of the same product (matching) or sometimes, related products (offsetting). Usually exports, even if matched or offset, are limited to a specified maximum. But in the case of at least one commodity, unlimited exports are permitted. In some instances, these purchases may be made on a global basis, and in others, purchases are tied to the United States. Moreover, in some cases, the matching requirements apply to all exports and in others to exports within the quota but above a given minimum.

Conversion to Commercial Terms

The last string to the export control bow is conversion of concessional sales to commercial terms. If export quotas are exceeded or offset purchases not made, the recipient must pay the United States the commercial price for an amount of commodities equal in value to the excess exports. A 1966 commodities sales agreement with Greece including wheat and food grains provides the fullest development of this technique.[49] Paragraph 4 of the Agreement states:

In the event Greece exports any feed grains or more than 350,000 metric tons of wheat and/or wheat flour of either indigenous or imported origin during United States Fiscal Year 1966, the Government of Greece will upon demand of the Government of the United States of America, make payment in United States dollars of an amount equal to the United States dollar value of the quantity or quantities of any such commodities exported by Greece with interest at 6 per cent per annum (in lieu of the rate specified in Article II of the agreement) which shall be computed from the respective dates of individual disbursements by the Government of the United States of America, beginning with the first disbursement and continuing as necessary with the oldest disbursements, which equal the total principal payment demanded by the Government of the United States of America. The amount of this payment of principal will be determined by the Government of the United States of America by multiplying the quantity of exports by Greece of feed grains or wheat and/or wheat flour in excess of 250,000 metric tons by the average unit cost of the feed grains and wheat and/or flour financed by the Government of the United States of America, it being understood that such average unit cost for wheat will be applied to the total amount due the Government of the United States under this agreement in the case of quantities of wheat and/or wheat flour exported by Greece up to the quantity of wheat and/or wheat flour financed by the Government of the United States of America under the agreement and thereafter the average unit price of feed grains will be applied to the total amount due and in the case of any quantities of feed grains exported by Greece the average unit price of feed grains will be applied to the total amount due. Related ocean freight costs may be included in such determination as deemed appropriate by the Government of the United States of America. The foregoing shall not be applicable to quantities of commodities exported by Greece which are in excess of the combined quantity of feed grains and wheat and/or wheat flour specified in Article I of the agreement or the aggregate of the quantity specified in credit purchase authorizations issued pursuant to this agreement, whichever is lesser.[50]

Often, reimbursement is stipulated as an alternative to matching or offset purchases from the United States. Thus, in a sale to Korea of wheat and cotton, the recipient was required to make compensating purchases of raw cotton for all textile exports above 51,000 bales and offset purchases of wheat or barley for any rice exports.[51] Failing this, Korea could meet its obligations by paying the commercial value of the cotton or wheat financed by the United States on concessional terms.[52] In other instances, though, reimbursement is the only permissible adjustment. For example, in a cotton sale to the Congo, the recipient was not required to meet any usual marketing requirements.[53] But should it export upland cotton, it must reimburse the United States in dollars, an amount equal to the quantity of such exports at the per bale commercial value of the concessional cotton received under the agreement, up to the total quantity of concessional cotton received.[54] Simultaneously, this payment eliminates the obligation to pay for an equivalent quantity of P.L. 480 cotton at the concessional terms.

The effect of these reimbursement requirements is to convert a portion of the original concessional sale to a commercial basis. For some reason, use of this technique seems to have become more common in the last few years. It has not been used, though, to enforce usual marketing requirements. That is, reimbursement for concessional sales has not been required when a food aid recipient fails to make the required amount of commercial purchases. Such a practice, though, would be both effective and justifiable. If a country fails to reach the stipulated level of commercial sales, it is fair to conclude that its needs have been overestimated. Therefore, a reduction in the proportion of food aid compared to total imports seems warranted. Conversion of some proportion of concessional sales to commercial terms would have just that effect.

Export Controls of Particular
Commodities

Full comprehension of the potential disruptive effect of food aid on export patterns and the available means for dealing with these problems should be assisted by detailed examination of the control patterns established for major food aid commodities.

Textile Exports. Concessional sales of cotton seem to generate the most frequent application of matching requirements. Here, standard practice is to permit unlimited exports of cotton textiles provided that textile exports above a specified level are to be matched, pound for pound, with commercial imports of raw cotton. A recent agreement with Taiwan is typical.[55] During each of the calendar years 1965 and 1966, Taiwan must import an additional amount of raw cotton equivalent by weight to the cotton textiles exported during each of the calendar years exceeding the level of cotton textiles exported during calendar year 1964.[56] Three-fourths of the cotton imports must be from the United States.[57] Similarly, the 1967 Agreement with India provides for raw cotton imports equivalent to the weight of textile exports exceeding the average level of such exports in fiscal years 1963, 1964 and 1965. Here, all the commercial cotton purchases must be from the United States.[58] In the past, most purchases could be made on a free world basis.[59] More recently, such purchases have been tied in whole or in part to the United States.[60] Possibly, this shift has resulted from a hardening attitude towards Egypt, the chief rival of the United States in the cotton export market.[61]

Edible Oil Exports. For certain recipients, concessional sales of edible oils embody restrictions similar to those prevailing in cotton transactions. These include countries receiving soybean oils which also export olive, copra, peanut oil, or other edible oils and margarine. Traditional olive oil exporters such as Greece, Turkey, and Tunisia are permitted a stipulated level of such exports without purchase obligations. Beyond this though, they must offset exports with commercial imports of soybean oil or soybeans from the United States.[62] The treatment of peanut oil exported by India while it receives concessional edible oils has changed with that country's financial fortunes (or better, misfortunes). Originally, all peanut oil exports had to be matched by additional vegetable oil imports.[63] But the following year, India was permitted unlimited exports of edible oils, including peanut oil, so long as its *total* (emphasis added) commercial imports from the United States exceeded the value of such edible oil exports.[64] Clearly, this "limitation" is but a sham designed to give India the maximum opportunity to earn foreign exchange while maintaining the appearance that prior export controls were being maintained. Given India's importance and predicament, the ends sought seem laudable, but the disingenuity is somewhat offensive.

Since Israel has been a traditional exporter of soya bean oil, concessional sales of soya beans to this developed country creates serious export control problems. In line with United States policy, Israel, a pre-food aid soya bean oil exporter, has been permitted to both export edible oils and edible oil products (margarine) while receiving food aid soya beans.[65] Most of these exports must be offset by commercial soya bean purchases from the United States.[66] The Netherlands has strongly objected to these arrangements. The Netherlands imports soya beans for use as animal feed and recently through the use of highly efficient extraction processes, obtains soya bean oil for export, in competition with Israel. Under these circumstances, it perceives United States practices as injuring the Netherlands legitimate export possibilities while enriching the United States through tied offset commercial sales to Israel. Thus rather than protecting third countries, United States export "controls" protect only the United States. Israel receives concessionally priced soya beans which facilitate soya bean exports, and the United States is able to make commercial soya bean sales to Israel equal to Israel's oil exports. In response, the United States argues that Israel's soya bean oil exports have been limited to pre-food aid levels and that the United States is entitled to tie the offset purchases to itself because it has been a traditional commercial exporter of soya beans to Israel. It appears that the export limits have not been exceeded. Aside from the ever controversial tying aspect, the problem arises from the difficulty of altering food and patterns in response to changing trade patterns.

Rice Exports. The wheat-rice cross-limitations recently developed in Taiwan and Korea require yet another export control arrangement. Starting from necessity which developed into preference, both these countries have been long-time recipients of concessional wheat from the United States.[67] Gradually they have acquired a taste for wheat products and the demand for commercial wheat has expanded while concessional sales continued.[68] As imports of wheat increased and the two countries developed, some rice became available for export. Since the United States has made large investments in the economic success of both Taiwan and Korea, it is interested in facilitating these increased rice exports.[69] Also there is the distinct possibility that Korea and Taiwan might well follow Japan's example and become substantial commercial wheat customers of the United States.[70] But the United States must also be very sensitive to the impact of additional rice exports on traditional Asian exporters.[71] The problem is further complicated by the chronic instability of the world rice market.[72]

The response to this problem has been an increasingly complex set of rice export limitations combined with mandatory offset wheat purchases. Under the first variation, applicable to calendar 1960, Taiwan could export no more than 150,000 metric tons of rice to those countries which were markets after January 1, 1955.[73] In 1962, Korea was permitted to export a maximum of 60,000 metric tons of rice to Japan and the Ryukyus. Moreover, all exports above 14,000 tons had to be matched by imports of wheat or barley from free world sources.[74] Undoubtedly, the purpose of these restrictions was to keep this rice out of the traditional markets of Burma, Cambodia, Thailand, and Vietnam. Under the next set of agreements for both countries, the restrictions on the destinations of the exports were dropped, but the same quantity limitations retained.[75] The requirement to replace the rice exports with commercial wheat or barley imports remained, but this time, the replacement purchases were tied to the United States.[76] Recent arrangements are still more complex. China agreed to limit exports of rice during calendar 1965 to a maximum of 258,338 metric tons and to purchase with its own resources one ton of wheat (a) for each ton of rice exported between January and September 15 between the levels of 110,000 and 133,338 metric tons; and (b) for each ton of rice exported from September 16 through December 31 between the levels of 198,338 to 258,338 metric tons.[77] Korea was given the unlimited right to export rice provided it matched exports with commercial wheat or barley from the United States.[78]

Justifying Matching and Reimbursement
as Export Control Methods

Upon first glance, matching and reimbursement requirements, particularly the former, seem somehow odd. Indeed, they seem downright pernicious when the matching or offsets are tied to the United States. Take the olive oil-soybean arrangements, for example. As we have seen, the standard pattern is to limit olive oil exports by recipients of concessional edible oils to a given level unless sales above this level are matched on a ton-by-ton basis by commercial purchases of vegetable oils from the United States.[79] Although these restrictions will prevent a country from reducing its total oil consumption in order to facilitate exports of olive oil, they will not prevent a country from augmenting its foreign exchange earnings through using commercially purchased soybean oil from the United States for domestic consumption in lieu of costlier olive oil and exporting the extra olive oil. Under these circumstances, the United States, a huge producer of soybean oil, expands its exports of this product at the expense of third country olive oil exporters.[80] Cotton seems to afford a further example of the United States expanding its own commercial sales through devices ostensibly designed to protect third country exporters. Rather than absolutely barring exports of increased cotton textiles to P.L. 480 cotton importers, such exports are permitted so long as extra cotton is purchased on commercial terms from the United States.[81]

The Case for Matching Requirements. But despite bad appearances, a good case may be made for the matching requirements, if not the United States tying aspect. Developing countries receiving concessional agricultural commodities chronically are short of foreign exchange and therefore strain to capitalize on any possible export opportunities. Moreover, semideveloped countries tend to have fairly complex economies, not always (fortunately) under the full control of their government. In these circumstances, exports of olive oil facilitated by soybean oil imports, exports of rice made possible by the willingness of the populace to eat more imported wheat, and the conversion of cotton to textiles, all may make economic sense, even if the necessary raw materials must be imported on commerical terms. Also in some circumstances, a government may be administratively unable to halt all P.L. 480-related exports while in need of concessional commodities for domestic consumption. Thus, the problem facing food aid administrators is how to simultaneously give food aid for domestic purposes, permit the recipient to develop potential export possibilities, and protect third countries, including the food aid donor from unfair competition from exports subsidized by cut-rate food aid imports.

Neither blanket prohibitions of exports connected to food aid imports nor rigid export quotas provide adequate solutions. Obviously, total prohibition of products economically related to food aid commodities will cut off any chance for export development of these products. Moreover, this might preclude exports which would have made economic sense without concessional sales. Rigid quotas, though, are not much better. Limitation of olive oil exports, for example, to the level prevailing prior to the advent of concessional sales of soybean oil precludes the recipient from importing soybean oil commercially in order to expand olive oil exports. Setting high quotas is no solution either. Under these circumstances, a country could import P.L. 480 soybean oil and substitute it directly for export-bound olive oil. Since the soybean oil was bought on concessional terms, the olive oil could be sold below prevailing market levels and still turn a profit. This would constitute unfair competition to other olive oil exporters not receiving concessional soya beans, many of whom are themselves relatively poor countries (Spain, Portugal, Italy).

Retroactive conversion of sales made on concessional terms to commercial terms in amounts equal to "excess" exports will protect third country producers, but the impact on the recipient may be too severe. Every additional export will in effect reduce the level of concessional sales by that amount. This will ensure that no exports are subsidized by food aid, since for every export there is a matching commercial import. But it is conceivable that a food aid recipient might wish to purchase additional amounts of the food aid commodity on commerical terms for processing into exportable products. For example, a country receiving cotton on concessional terms might wish to purchase more cotton commercially for processing into exportable textiles. But under the conversion to commercial terms restriction, each textile export would mean conversion of an equivalent amount of the original concessionally priced cotton to a commercial basis. The effect would be to reduce the level of concessional sales below that desired by the donor and the recipient.

But, reimbursement may work under certain circumstances. Pakistan provides a good example. Normally, a recipient of concessional wheat, and though a rice producer, not a rice exporter, Pakistan occasionally produces more rice than is required for domestic consumption. The sensible thing is to export the overage. Under these circumstances, reimbursement seems an appropriate remedy. Because of the large crop, the recipient's total food aid needs were overestimated. Reducing the total concessional component by the amount of exports brings the food aid level to where it would have been had needs been correctly computed. The recipient is not harmed since the extra commercial purchases have been offset by an equal amount of exports. In addition, it saves the cost of the food aid commodities, which though lower than commercial levels, is still greater than zero. Third countries cannot complain since the exports may be attributed to commercial imports. Clearly, this is a much better solution than prohibiting exports and forcing a developing country to increase consumption above desirable levels.

Matching and offset arrangements may provide the best possible solutions in situations where food aid recipients are trying to develop exports through commercial imports of raw materials or substitute products. The efforts of Taiwan and Korea are relatively more efficient at growing rice than wheat, to export rice by meeting staple needs through wheat imports provide a good case in point. Initially, we must assume that internal consumption needs and development considerations call for a certain level of concessional wheat sales. Increased rice exports resulting from displacing home-grown rice with concessional wheat may legitimately be criticized by other rice growers. But if for every pound of rice exported, an equivalent amount of wheat were imported commercially, there could be no grounds for complaint. All rice exports may be traced to commercial wheat imports. This transaction could have been accomplished without any food aid imports. Since all exports are matched by commercial imports, we may be sure that all such concessional imports were used solely for domestic consumption. Thus, everyone has been satisfied. The recipient has received its quota of food aid and has been able to increase rice exports. Third country producers have been protected against unfair competition since all exports have stemmed from commercial, note concessional imports.

Tying Matching and Offset Purchases to the Donor. The most controversial aspect of matching and offset arrangements is the United States' practice of tying most such purchase requirements to itself. Clearly, this injures third country exporters, and the protests of other nations against these practices are well founded.

According to an analysis by the CSD of United States food aid agreements signed during 1963-67, the number of offset purchasing requirements in P.L. 480 agreements ranged from 12 to 20 per year, averaging 15 per year. They concerned the supply of wheat, vegetable oil, or cotton. Nearly all were tied to United States procurement; of the 76 such provisions, only a few were global or permitted some degree of procurement from sources other than the United States. Characteristically, they provided that if exports by the recipient country of the same or like commodity exceeded a specified amount, they would have to be offset by commercial purchases from the United States of the commodity supplied. For the bulk commodities, such purchases would normally be on a ton-for-ton basis; where the exported commodity was cotton textiles, offset requirements would reflect the cotton content of such exports and on an oil content basis in the case of margarine.[82] For a variety of reasons, accurate statistics on offset purchases are not available. Although most offset purchases are unplanned, in some cases the United States and the recipient expect offset purchases caused by an expected, though uncertain amount of excess exports. In these cases, the United States estimates that quotas will be exceeded in fifty percent of the cases. The food aid recipient countries subjected to mandatory offset purchases don't really care where they must make the additional commercial purchases. But other exporters of the concessional sale commodity itself or products economically related to that commodity are directly concerned. Indeed, their injury may appear twofold. First, they lose commercial sales through the original concessional transaction. Then, they are precluded from the additional markets for the commodity involved which were created through the offset or matching requirements. Or put another way, the United States in making concessional sales has created the possibility of injury to third countries through increased exports of related or derivative products by food aid recipients. But in curing this ill, it has taken the opportunity further to increase its own *commercial* sales of the original food aid commodity at the expense of third country producers. Since offset and matching purchases are on commercial terms, the United States cannot claim, as it does with respect to the concessional sales themselves, that the transactions are a form of foreign aid.

Although the case against tied offsets is uncomfortably strong, before rendering final judgment, we should examine this variety of tying commodity by commodity. Cotton seems to inspire the United States to its most blatant selfishness. Purchases of raw cotton to offset "excess" textile exports almost always are 100% tied to the United States. Agreements with Korea,[83] Yugoslavia,[84] India,[85] and Tunisia[86] all took this form. Although the United States is the leading exporter of cotton, it only accounts for 27% of total exports, with the remainder shared entirely by underdeveloped countries, including the United Arab Republic, Mexico, Turkey, Brazil, Syria, and Pakistan.[87] But in the countries receiving Food for Peace cotton, the United States has been very successful in increasing both its absolute level and relative share of commercial cotton exports.[88] In Korea, up to fiscal 1965, the United States supplied almost all that country's cotton imports through concessional sales. Thereafter, it increased commercial sales from 49 thousand bales in fiscal 1965 to 168 thousand bales in 1967, the latter representing all Korea's commercial imports for that year. With respect to Tunisia, the United States commercial exports rose from one thousand bales in fiscal 1964 to 12 thousand bales in fiscal 1967, the latter figure again representing all Tunisia's commercial imports. In fiscal 1963, Yugoslavia made less than 1% of its commercial imports (11,000 bales) from the United States, but in fiscal 1967, this figure rose to over 10% (44,000 bales out of about 325 bales). India now imports one-fourth of its commercial requirements from the United States, compared to the one-twelfth share enjoyed by the United States in fiscal 1962. These figures, combined with the tightly United States-tied usual marketing requirements previously discussed, indicate a pattern of determined and successful efforts by the United States to use concessional cotton sales to boost its commercial cotton exports to food aid recipients, apparently at the direct expense of underdeveloped third country cotton exporters.

Soybean oil purchases to offset olive oil exports also are strictly tied to the United States.[89] As with cotton, these follow the pattern established by usual marketing requirements—mandatory purchases are closely tied to the United

States.[90] But given the dominance of this country in soybean production and exportation,[91] relatively little harm can come from this practice, and it may be accepted as window-dressing, designed for the same general public relations purposes as are the practices with respect to usual marketing requirements. But, as noted above, the Netherlands may be injured to some extent.

The treatment of wheat offsets for exports of durum wheat or rice again presents real problems. Similar to both cotton and soybean oils, offset commercial wheat purchases are heavily tied to the United States. True, purchases to compensate for durum wheat exports by concessional wheat recipients are split between global and United States-only requirements. Older agreements with Turkey permit purchase of offsets on a "free world basis."[92] But more recent agreements with Tunisia limit purchases to United States.[93] And wheat purchases to compensate for rice exports by Taiwan and Korea are completely tied to the United States.[94] The arrangements with Taiwan are interesting since in other commodities agreements for wheat signed the same day, wheat flour exports are to be compensated by commercial wheat purchases on a *global* basis.[95] Wheat, as we have already demonstrated, is the most sensitive of the commodities included in concessional transactions. And, under pressure from large exporters such as Canada, Australia, and Argentina, the United States was forced to give up its former practice of tying usual marketing requirements for wheat to the United States in favor of only worldwide (global) requirements. Therefore, tying offset and matching purchases to the United States impinge upon the interests of other nations in a touchy area and is highly inconsistent with practices with respect to the closely related usual marketing requirements.

Boxscore on Matching and
Offset Purchases

Close examination of matching and offset purchase requirements practices precludes easy generalizations. On one level, this technique represents a highly ingenious method for permitting food aid recipients to keep the benefits of concessional sales while developing economically sensible and commercially sound exports. On another, the practice of tying these purchases to the United States seems to be a highly questionable device to use concessional sales to lever up United States commercial exports. The paradox here is that the more a food aid recipient exceeds its export quotas, the more commercial sales the United States makes.

The Impact of Export Limitations on Economic Development. As is the case with usual marketing requirements, it is difficult to evaluate the effectiveness and propriety of the various restrictions imposed upon exports related to the receipt of food aid commodities. The answer depends in considerable part upon one's assumptions about the purpose of food aid programs and the relative foreign aid burden to be shouldered by nations likely to be affected by such transactions. But some things are clear. Exports only sustainable through continued receipt of certain commodities at discount prices should be controlled. Conversely, exports which make or might in the future make economic sense without food aid should be encouraged, even though they require imports of commodities which are also being supplied on concessional terms so long as the exports are attributable to commercial rather than concessional imports. Thus, restrictions on the export of products identical or almost identical in use or form to those provided under food aid sales seems appropriate under most theories of surplus disposal or foreign aid. The same applies to exports of rice made possible by concessional wheat imports. Even then, if the exportable surplus resulted from an unexpectedly good crop, reimbursement arrangements should be available which will permit an economically sensible and useful temporary export opportunity. The anticipated use of commercial imports of commodities also being purchased on concessional terms as substitutes in domestic consumption for exportable commodities may be justified in those cases where the country has a comparative advantage in the production of the exported commodity. Thus, Turkey and Tunisia should be able to import soybean oils for domestic consumption in order to preserve the more valuable and costly olive oil for export. And Korea and Taiwan should export rice, if wheat for domestic consumption can be imported more cheaply. The same applies to augmented cotton textile exports manufactured from imported cotton. Even so, exceptions to export limitations granted under conditions designed to protect or enhance only the donor's interests should be avoided. This would include the arrangements with respect to wheat, cotton and edible oil sales whereby exports of related products are permitted, provided that equivalent commodities are purchased commercially from the food aid donor.

Notes

1. 80 *Stat.* 1527 (1966), 7 U.S.C.A. 1703 (g) (1970).
2. Section 103 (g) states: "[The President shall] obtain commitments from purchasing countries that will prevent resale or transshipment to other countries, or use for other than domestic purposes of agricultural commodities purchased under this title, without specific approval of the President." Ibid.
3. Over time, case law has been developed which resolves most of the recurring export problems. But, after apparently settling this matter, the entire problem seems to have been reopened by certain legislative history accompanying the 1966 extension of the Food for Peace program which might be interpreted to sharply extend the ability of food aid recipients to export commodities similar to or manufactured from agricultural products being imported under food aid.

The House Committee Report states that the statutory language controlling exports was to be read literally; that is, the restrictions only apply to the food aid commodities themselves and not to derivative or similar products. *H.R. Rep.* No. 1558, 89th Cong., 2d sess., 39-40 (1966). However, neither the Senate Report nor the Congressional debates would support a change of this magnitude. See *S. Rep.* No. 1527, 89th Cong., 2d sess. (1966); 112 *Cong. Rec.* 12579, 12581, 25308 (1966). Under these circumstances, the Administration seems unwilling to liberalize restrictions to this extent. The relevant language in post-1966 amendment sales agreements indicates no changes from prior practice. See note 6, infra. Based on conversations with government and food aid officials, I have reason to believe that the legislative history in question was the result of a mistake.

4. See, e.g., Agricultural Commodities Agreement with Ceylon, March 12, 1966, TIAS 5971, 17 UST 190, 194 (1967); Agreement with Tunisia, Feb. 17, 1965, TIAS 5767, 16 UST 97, 101 (1966). Agreements signed after 1967, using the new Standard Form, include substantially the same provisions in Pt. I, Art. III-A-2,3. See, e.g., Agreement with Iceland, June 5, 1967, TIAS 6300, 18 UST 1593 (1967).

5. Agreements with more developed countries such as Israel and Poland which are more likely to export a variety of products, tend to carry particularly complex export restrictions. See Agreement with Poland, Feb. 3, 1964, TIAS 5516, 15 UST 40, 52 (1964); Agreement with Israel, Dec. 6, 1962, TIAS 5220, 13 UST 2550, 2556 (1963).

6. Agreement with the Philippines, April 23, 1965, TIAS 5785, 16 UST 632 (Art. IV) (1966); Agreement with Ethiopia, August 17, 1965, TIAS 5854, 16 UST 1119, 1122 (Art. III) (1966).

7. Syria, Agreement of Nov. 9, 1961, TIAS 14 UST 97, 109 (1962); Cyprus, Agreement of June 18, 1963, TIAS 14 UST 936, 941 (1964). In the Syrian transaction, which authorized wheat sales totaling $6.3 million, export of 70,000 metric tons of durum wheat, worth about $5 million, was permitted. In the immediately prior fiscal years, Syria's exports in metric tons were: 1959—6.82 million; 1960—1 million; 1961—zero. Thereafter, the figures were 1962—2.25 million; 1963—27.4 million; 1964—11.7 million; 1965—19 million. *USDA/FAS, The World Grain Trade* 1963-64/1964-65 at 20 (1966) [hereinafter cited as *World Grain Trade*]. Cyprus was permitted to export 10,000 metric tons of wheat, worth about $700,000 dollars, within a sales agreement authorizing wheat purchases of $11.9 million. Prior to 1958, Cyprus was a net wheat exporter. Id. at 20. The UAR, a traditional rice exporter, was permitted to export rice while receiving concessional imports of this product, provided they were matched by commercial free world purchases. Agreement with UAR of May 5, 1959, TIAS 4223, 10 UST 852, 854 (1960); *International Wheat Council, Trends in Wheat Consumption, Secretariat Paper No. 4*, at 16, A-59 (1964).

8. Agreement with Argentina, June 12, 1959, TIAS 4246, 10 UST 1068, 1072 (1960).

9. Agricultural Commodities Agreement with Jordan, April 5, 1966, TIAS 5985, 17 UST 361, 366 (1967).

10. Agreement with Turkey, Jan. 20, 1958, TIAS 3981, 9 UST 79, 84 (1959).

11. Agreement with Tunisia, Sept. 14, 1962, TIAS 5190, 13 UST 2238, 2246 (1963); Agreement with Tunisia, March 17, 1967, TIAS 6323, Pt. II, Item IV-C, 18 UST 1777, 1784 (1968); *International Wheat Council, 1967 World Wheat Statistics*, 22-23 (1967) [hereinafter cited as *1967 Wheat Statistics*].

12. Agricultural Commodities Agreement with Morocco, Dec. 29, 1964, TIAS 6045, 17 UST 847, 858 (1967); Agreement with Morocco, April 23, Oct. 8, 1965, April 21, 1966, TIAS 6049, 17 UST 873, 884 (1967); *1967 Wheat Statistics*, supra, at 22-23 (1967).

13. Agreement with Pakistan, Nov. 26, 1958, TIAS 4137, 9 UST 1427, 1435 (1959).

14. Agreement with the United Arab Republic, Sept. 17, 1960, TIAS 4575, 11 UST 2136, 2137 (1961).

15. Agricultural Commodities Agreement with India, May 27, 1966, TIAS 6032, 17 UST 778, 780 (1967).

16. In 1966, India exported 200 thousand bales of cotton, while importing 650 thousand bales. *1967 Wheat Statistics*, supra, *USDA/FAS World Production and Trade* 13 (1967) [hereinafter cited as *Production and Trade*].

17. Agreement with UAR, May 5, 1959, TIAS 4223, 10 UST 852, 855 (1960).

18. Agreement with China, August 30, 1960, TIAS 4563, 11 UST 2085, 2082 (1961).

19. In the period 1960-65, tobacco exports rose from $280,000 to 1,760,000.

20. Agreement with Syrian Arab Republic, Nov. 9, 1961, TIAS 4944, 13 UST 97, 109 (1962); Agreement with Cyprus, June 18, 1963, TIAS 5382, 14 UST 936, 941 (1964); Agreement with Turkey, Jan. 20, 1958, TIAS 3981, 9 UST 79, 84 (1959). See pp. 258-60 for a more detailed analysis of matching import requirements.

21. E.G., Agreement with Israel, Aug. 4, 1967, TIAS 6314, Pt. I, Art. III, Pt. II, Item IV, 18 UST 1684, 1687, 1691 (1968).

22. Agricultural Commodities Agreement with Somalia, March 15, 1968, TIAS 6465, 19 UST 4698, 4704-05 (1969). Agreement with Tunisia, March 17, 1967, TIAS 6323, 18 UST 1777, 1780 (1968). Agreement with Afghanistan, July 19, 1967, TIAS 6323, 18 UST 1777, 1780 (1968).

23. Agricultural Commodities Agreement with the Congo, Dec. 11, 1967, TIAS 6396, 18 UST 3065, 3066 (1969); Agreement with Iceland, June 5, 1967, TIAS 6300, 18 UST 1593, 1599 (1968).

24. Agricultural Commodities Agreement with Israel, March 29, 1968, TIAS 6466, 19 UST 4716, 4717 (1969).

25. Agricultural Commodities Agreement with Pakistan, May 26, 1966, TIAS 6052, 17 UST 925, 932 (1967); Agreement with China, Feb. 11, 1966, TIAS 5959, 17 UST 64, 65 (1967); Agreement with Korea, March 18, 1964, TIAS 5547, 15 UST 250, 254 (1964).

26. Agricultural Commodities Agreement with Pakistan, supra, note 25.

27. Op. cit. supra, note 25.

28. See pp. 262-63 infra.

29. Agricultural Commodity Agreement with Ceylon, Oct. 27, 1967, TIAS 6405, Part II, Item IV, 18 UST 3141, 3148 (1969).

30. Agreement with Israel, Aug. 4, 1967, TIAS 6314, Pt. II, Item IV, 18 UST 1684, 1691-92 (1968).

31. In 1969, Turkey produced 54 thousand metric tons of olive oil and in 1970, 125 thousand tons. For the same two years, Tunisia produced 22 thousand and 34 thousand tons, respectively. In 1969, Turkey exported 22.2 thousand tons. Tunisia exported 30.2 thousand tons. UN/FAO, *Monthly Bulletin of Agricultural Economics and Statistics*, vol. 20, no. 4, April 1971 at tables 2, 12.

32. Soybean oil sells for about $314 per metric ton versus $726 per metric ton of olive oil.

33. Spanish olive oil exports in calendar 1967 amounted to 92.0 thousand metric tons, in 1968 44.0 thousand, and in 1969, 90.1 thousand. UN/FAO, *Monthly Bulletin*, supra, at Table 12.

34. UN/FAO, *Uses of Agricultural Surpluses to Finance Economic Development in Underdeveloped Countries—A Pilot Study in India*, Commodity Policy Series No. 6 (June 1955).

35. E.g., Agreement with Afghanistan, May 22, 1965, TIAS 5849, 16 UST 1078, 1080 (1966); Standard P.L. 480 Sales Agreement, Pt. 1, Art. III-A-3, April 20, 1967.

36. *OECD, Food Aid—Its Role in Economic Development* 52 (1963).

37. E.g., Greece, Agreement of Nov. 17, 1964 TIAS 5695, 15 UST, 2132, 2138 (1964). Here, if poultry exports exceed the level of the previous year, Greece must match the overage with commercial poultry purchases from the United States.

38. Agreement with Yugoslavia, June 3, 1960, TIAS 4497, 11 UST 1524, 1528 (1961).

39. In 1965, cotton manufacturers represented the indicated percentages of the total exports of the following countries: Hong Kong—25% ($289.8 millions); India—9% (147.3 millions); Pakistan—10% (53.3 millions); Taiwan—8% ($37.5 millions); Korea—7% ($11.5 millions); UAR—9% ($68 millions). During the same period, the United States' textile exports totalled $671 million, representing only 2% of its total exports.

40. *FAO Commodity Review 1967*, at 192.

41. See, e.g., Agricultural Commodity Agreement with Israel, Jan. 7, 1960, TIAS 5501, 11 UST 8, 13 (1961); Agreement with Israel, June 6, 1966, TIAS

6023, 17 UST 727, 732 (1967); Agreement with Yugoslavia, April 11, 1966, TIAS 6031, 17 UST 771, 775 (1967).

42. Universally, the prohibition begins on the date of the agreement and continues until the final date on which the relevant food aid commodities are being received and utilized. Agreement with India, Feb. 20, 1967, TIAS 6221, Part II, Item IV; 18 UST 217 (1967).

43. Agricultural Commodities Agreement with Morocco, April 23, Oct. 6, 1965, April 21, 1966, TIAS 6049, 17 UST 873, 889 (1967). The last two soybean oil agreements with Morocco have removed all restrictions from olive oil exports.

44. Agricultural Commodities Agreement with Tunisia, July 30, 1966, TIAS 6067, 17 UST 1108, 1114 (1967).

45. Agricultural Commodities Agreement with Poland, Feb. 3, 1964, TIAS 5516, 15 UST 40, 52 (1964).

46. Agricultural Commodities Agreement with China, August 30, 1960, TIAS 4563, 11 UST 2058, 2082 (1961).

47. Agricultural Commodities Agreement with Korea, June 12, 1962, TIAS 5082, 13 UST 1297, 1238 (1963).

48. Understanding with Turkey relating to Agreement of January 20, 1958, TIAS 4160, 10 UST 11 (1960).

49. Agricultural Commodities Agreement with Greece, Jan. 13, 1966, TIAS 6018, 17 UST 679 (1967).

50. Id. at 681.

51. Agricultural Commodities Agreement with Korea, March 6, 1966, TIAS 5978, 17 UST 239, 244-45 (1967).

52. Id. at 245.

53. Agricultural Commodities Agreement with the Congo, July 19, 1965, TIAS 5935, 16 UST 2001, 2010 (1966).

54. Ibid.

55. Agricultural Commodities Agreement with China, Dec. 31, 1964; TIAS 5718, 15 UST 2295 (1965).

56. Id. at 2309.

57. Ibid.

58. Agricultural Commodities Agreement with India, Sept. 12, 1967, TIAS 6342, Part II, Item IV-B, 18 UST 2372, 2373 (1969).

59. E.g., Agreement with Korea, March 2, 1962, TIAS 4969, 13 UST 254, 259 (1962); Agreement with India, Nov. 26, 1962, TIAS 5225, 13 UST 2589, 2594-95 (1963).

60. Agreement with Korea, Dec. 31, 1964, TIAS 5730, 15 UST 2396, 2401 (1965) (100% tied to the U.S.); Agreement with India, Sept. 12, 1967, TIAS 6342, Part II, Item IV-B, 18 UST 2372, 2373 (1969) (100% tied to the U.S.).

61. See discussion of United States food and strategy vis-a-vis Egypt in Ch. 4.

62. Agricultural Commodities Agreement with Tunisia, Sept. 14, 1962, TIAS

5190, 13 UST 2238, 2247 (1963); Agreement with Turkey, Feb. 21, 1963, TIAS 5303, 14 UST 236, 241 (1964); Agreement with Greece, Jan. 13, 1966, TIAS 6018, 17 UST 679, 680 (1967).

63. Agricultural Commodities Agreement with India, May 27, 1966, TIAS 6032, 17 UST 778, 779 (1967) (1966).

64. Agricultural Commodities Agreement with India, June 24, 1967, TIAS 6338, Part II, Item IV.

65. See text at note 30, supra.

66. Agricultural Commodities Agreement with Israel, March 29, 1968, TIAS 6466, Part II, Item IV-C, 19 UST 4716, 4717 (1969).

67. Through December 31, 1967, Korea has received $215.1 million worth of wheat and flour and Taiwan has received $112.3 million (both not including transportation). *Annual Report on Activities Carried Out under Public Law 480, as amended, during the period Jan. 1-Dec. 31, 1967* Table 8 (1968) [hereinafter cited as *1967 Annual Report*].

68. By the fiscal year 1967, commercial exports of wheat to Korea reached $341 million and commercial exports to Taiwan $280 million. During this period, Korea also received $331 millions worth of P.L. 480 wheat, but Taiwan did not receive any. *Hearings on the Extension of P.L. 480 before the Senate Committee on Agriculture and Forestry*, 90th Cong., 2d sess., 160 (1968) [hereinafter cited as *1968 Senate Hearings*].

69. Through fiscal 1966, Taiwan has received economic, military, and food aid totaling almost $4.9 billion. *Agency for International Development Special Report on U.S. Overseas Loans and Grants for the House Foreign Affairs Committee*, 61 (1967). During the same period, Korea has received $6.7 billions. Id. at 66.

70. See Ch. 3, note 29.

71. *OECD*, supra, note 34 at 51-52.

71. *OECD*, supra, note 34 at *Food Aid—Its Role in Economic Development*, 51-52.

72. See analysis of world rice market in Ch. 3.

73. Agreement with China, August 30, 1960, TIAS 4563, 11 UST 2058, 2082 (1961).

74. Agreement with Korea, June 12, 1962, TIAS 5082, 13 UST 1297, 1298 (1953).

75. Agreement with Korea, March 18, 1964, TIAS 5547, 15 UST 250, 254 (1964); Agreement with Taiwan, Dec. 31, 1964, TIAS 5717, 15 UST 2273, 2286 (1964).

76. For Korea, all rice exports between 14,000 tons and the 60,000 ton limit were to be matched by wheat or barley commercial imports from the United States. Id. For Taiwan, all exports between 110,000 tons and the 150,000 ton limit were to be so matched. Id.

77. Agricultural Commodities Agreement with China, Feb. 11, 1966, TIAS 595, 17 UST 64, 65 (1967).

78. Agricultural Commodities Agreement with Korea, March 7, 1966, TIAS 5973, 17 UST 239, 245 (1967).

79. See text and notes at notes 62-66, supra.

80. See analysis of United States edible oil food aid programs, Ch. 8.

81. See text at notes 54-61, supra.

82. UN/FAO, CCP 69/13/3. *Committee on Commodity Problems, Report on Tied Sales*, 9 (17 July 1969).

83. Agricultural Commodities Agreement with Korea, March 7, 1966, TIAS 5973, 17 UST 239, 245 (1967).

84. Agricultural Commodities Agreement with Yugoslavia, April 11, 1966, TIAS 6031, 17 UST 771, 777 (1967).

85. Agricultural Commodities Agreement with India, May 27, 1966, TIAS 6032, 17 UST 778, 780 (1967).

86. Agricultural Commodities Agreement with Tunisia, July 30, 1966, TIAS 6067, 17 UST 1108, 1114 (1966).

87. *Production and Trade*, supra, note 16 at 12-13.

88. The analysis that follows is based upon a comparison of United States commercial and concessional sales to the specified countries with their total imports during comparable periods. The statistics are derived from *Senate Hearings*, 1968, supra, note 68 at 159, and the *Statistical Report on World Agricultural Production and Trade for 1965 and 1967*, as published in the December issues of the United States Department of Agriculture publication of that time. To some extent, the percentages given are estimates, since the United States concessional and commercial sales are given on a fiscal-year basis and those for total imports from all sources are on a calendar-year basis. But since the purpose of the figures is to illustrate a trend, these discrepancies do not effect the conclusions.

89. See, e.g., Agricultural Commodities Agreement with Greece, Jan. 13, 1966, TIAS 6018, 17 UST 679, 681 (1967); Agreement with Tunisia, July 30, 1966, TIAS 6067, 17 UST 1108, 1114-15 (1967); Agreement with Turkey, Feb. 21, 1963, TIAS 5303, 14 UST 236, 241 (1964).

90. See discussion of United States food aid cotton practices in Chapter 8.

91. Ibid.

92. Agricultural Commodities Agreement with Turkey, Jan. 20, 1958, TIAS 3981, 9 UST 79, 85 (1959); Agricultural Agreement, Nov. 21, 1962, TIAS 5235, 13 UST 2738 (1963).

93. Agricultural Commodities Agreement with Tunisia, July 30, 1966, TIAS 6098, 17 UST 1401, 1402 (1967).

94. Agricultural Commodities Agreement with China, Feb. 11, 1966, TIAS 5959, 17 UST 64, 65 (1967); Agreement with Korea, March 7, 1966, TIAS 5973, 17 UST 239, 245 (1967).

95. Agricultural Commodities Agreement with China, Feb. 11, 1966, TIAS 5958, 17 UST 59 (1967).

10 Implementing Control Techniques in a Cold War World

Implementation of internationally accepted standards for the conduct of food aid must proceed at two levels. First, these standards indicate the kind of control devices donors must establish in their food aid transactions to effectuate the conduct norms. Then, methods must be found by the donors to effectively impose these control devices upon food aid recipients. Up to this point, the focus of this book has been upon the acceptability and efficacy of various potential control methods. This chapter will examine means to ensure that food aid recipients will adhere to the limitations which the donors are obliged to impose upon them. This problem is complicated by the pressures upon the principal food aid donor, the United States, to conform its food policies to its current political relationships with permanently or temporarily hostile nations.

Enforcement of International Market Protection Controls

Enforcement of international standards for the protection of normal patterns of production and trade is a two-step process. First, the donating country must recognize and attempt to implement these standards in each food aid transaction it undertakes. Here the noncoercive nature of the FAO control system must be remembered. The only binding aspect of the FAO Principles is the requirement to notify and consult in accordance with the current FAO rules. In this regard, consulting countries need not heed third country protests. Nor is the Consultative Subcommittee on Surplus Disposal (CSD) authorized to make decisions with respect to individual cases of general policies. Thus, the United States is able to continue tying its UMRs and commercial purchase offsets and New Zealand can follow through on its dairy deal with Peru, despite the consensus in the CSD that these actions violate the FAO Principles.

In those cases where the donor is ready to take steps to protect normal trade patterns, it must find ways of assuring that the recipient takes or refrains from those actions deemed dangerous to trade patterns. This is usually accomplished through provisions in an agreement accompanying the food aid transaction. But this still leaves the problem of preventing food aid recipients from violating the crucial terms of the sales agreements. Unlike many international organizations and commodity agreements, no framework exists for enforcing the terms of sales agreement other than the usual diplomatic channels used to resolve international disputes in the absence of specially designed means for this purpose. Even the judicially weak machinery of the CSD is unavailable since the FAO system applies only to donors.

Market Protection Clauses

Both the United States and the European Economic Community have adopted standard language for their sales agreements designed to protect commercial agricultural trade. Article III-A of Part I of the current Standard United States Sales Agreement provides:

World Trade

The two Governments shall take maximum precautions to assure that sales of agricultural commodities pursuant to this agreement will not displace usual marketings of the exporting country in these commodities or unduly disrupt world prices of agricultural commodities or normal patterns of commercial trade with countries the Government of the exporting country considers to be friendly to it (referred to in this agreement as friendly countries). In implementing this provision the Government of the importing country shall:

1. insure that total imports from the exporting country and other friendly countries into the importing country paid for with the resources of the importing country will equal at least the quantities of agricultural commodities as may be specified in the usual marketing table set forth in Part II during each import period specified in the table and during each subsequent comparable period in which commodities financed under this agreement are being delivered. The imports of commodities to satisfy these usual marketing requirements for each import period shall be in addition to purchases financed under this agreement.

2. take all possible measures to prevent the resale, diversion in transit, or transshipment to other countries or the use for other than domestic purposes of the agricultural commodities purchased pursuant to this agreement (except where such resale, diversion in transit, transshipment or use is specifically approved by the Government of the United States of America); and

3. take all possible measures to prevent the export of any commodity of either domestic or foreign origin which is the same as, or like, the commodities financed under this agreement during the export limitation period specified in the export limitation table in Part II (except as may be specified in Part II or where such export is otherwise specifically approved by the Government of the United States of America).

The EEC's standard provisions are quite similar. They provide:

The Contracting Parties will ensure that this transaction does not harmfully affect the usual patterns of world production and trade. To achieve this purpose, they will take appropriate measures to ensure that this aid will be additional to the level of commercial sales which could be reasonably expected in the absence of this aid.

The recipient country will take the appropriate measures to prevent the re-export of the wheat received as well as of the products resulting from the primary processing and from the by-products of this wheat. The same restrictions apply to the commercial or noncommercial exports, within a 6-month period from the date of the last delivery, of the wheat produced locally which would be of the same type, and the products resulting from the primary processing and of the by-products of that local wheat.[1]

Effectiveness of Protective Clauses

Ultimately, usual marketing requirements and export limitations are enforced through the implicit threat of discontinuing future food aid transactions. But in addition, several more specific techniques have been employed. The most common one is to add the shortfalls in meeting usual marketing or matching or offset requirements imposed by prior agreements to the mandatory commercial purchases requirements accompanying subsequent sales.[2] In some instances, a portion of the annual minimum commercial purchase requirements are scheduled for each quarter so that the country will not be faced with an impossibly large backlog at the year's end.[3] This technique was used in Korea where, apparently, requirements had not been met for the prior year.[4] In another variation, shipments of commodities under the current agreement were conditioned upon proportional satisfaction of prior minimum commercial purchase requirements. Thus, shipment of the last 100,000 bales of a 250,000 bale cotton agreement with India was conditioned upon India's having imported half of its global usual marketing requirements and having contracted for purchase of the remainder.[5] Contemporaneously, and certainly not accidentally, Pakistan was required to meet half of its marketing quota of wheat as a condition to shipment of supplemental concessional wheat.[6] Although this technique is rarely formalized by explicitly including appropriate language in the sales agreement, it is widely used by the United States to enforce both usual marketing and offset and matching requirements.

Offset and matching requirements are very difficult to enforce. Most importantly, unlike usual marketing requirements, offset requirements are not preset targets, but represent remedial responses to contingent events. Also, the fact that they are triggered by exports rather than imports complicates enforcement. Although most food aid recipients are deficient to some degree in keeping track of imports, the situation with respect to exports is likely to be worse. Imports into developing countries invariably require licenses and are almost always subject to tariffs, thereby assuring considerable statistical control by the Central Bank. Exports are likely to require less government intervention. Since UMRs constitute a specific precondition to further concessional imports. The recipient is impelled to develop systems which will yield evidence, satisfactory to the donor, of compliance with the requirement. By contrast, the food aid recipient has every reason to conceal its exports in order to avoid offset purchases, thereby throwing the entire burden of enforcement on the donor. Often food aid donors are reduced to surreptitious inquiries by diplomatic personnel based upon personal contacts, a process distasteful to diplomatic representatives anxious to maintain good relationships with their counterparts in the host government. Finally, where the food aid induced exports are not competitive with the donor's own products, the incentives for rigorous enforcement is reduced. Even when the data is available, it usually arrives after the food aid agreement has been completed, making it necessary to attempt to enforce the offset requirements *post hoc*.

Reports and Statements

Compliance with both export and commercial import requirements is monitored through a series of reports and statements. Prior to adoption of the latest standard form sales agreements, the reporting requirements were divided between a general statement in the Sales Agreement's body and a detailed list of reports in the Diplomatic Note transmitting the agreement.[7] These reports included (a) a quarterly statement pertaining to all relevant shipping, loading, and storing information with respect to all commodities received under the Sales Agreement, a quarterly statement of measures taken to prevent the resale or transshipment of commodities furnished; (b) assurances that the program has not resulted in increased availability of the same or like commodities to other nations; and (c) a statement showing progress made toward fulfilling mandatory commercial import requirements, accompanied by statistical data on imports and exports by country of origin and destination of commodities which are the same or like those imported under the agreements.[8] Under the new standard agreement, the same reports are required except that all the terms of the agreement are incorporated in a single document.[9] Generally restrictions apply during the period beginning on the date of the agreement and ending on the final date on which such commodities are being received and utilized.[10] Apparently, utilization ends with the consumption of the products. Since most food aid recipients closely control imports anyway, accurate records are not difficult to maintain.

The Potential Role of The CSD

Perhaps the CSD could play a useful role in the enforcement process. Since this body represents all interested exporters, it would be motivated to help enforce import and export requirements. As an international organ, it should be better able than individual donors to gain access to the necessary statistics. Undoubtedly, the information it gathers for enforcement purposes will be valuable as a basis for evaluating the efficacy of existing control devices and developing more effective ones. Since the CSD is not a party to the food aid transactions, and given the consultative nature of this institution, the CSD could not directly enforce sales agreements. But it could be responsible for gathering the statistics necessary for enforcement. And in so doing, it not only would help insure that the necessary statistics are made available, but it can determine if control devices are being enforced by the donors. Probably, the principal objection to this development would come from large food aid donors anxious to maintain maximum flexibility with respect to enforcement of control devices. The more public the enforcement process, the less room for maneuver.

Cold War Antics

Scattered skirmishes of the cold war are fought over both usual marketing requirements and export limitations. Up till 1966, the P.L. 480 legislation specifically attempted to assure that concessional sales did not indirectly redound to the benefit of "unfriendly nations." Originally, Section 304(a)(2) of the P.L. 480 act, required the President to assure that agricultural commodities sold or transferred under the Act did not result in increased availability of those or like commodities to "unfriendly nations."[11] Although "unfriendly nations" are not directly identified by the Act, friendly countries were defined as all countries except Russia or China and countries supposedly controlled by them.[12] Subsequently, the definition became more complex with Communist countries gradated in accordance with their independence from Moscow or Peking, other countries such as Egypt and Indonesia added and subtracted in accordance with the political tides, and still others punished for trading with whoever happens to be the current chief devil. At the start of 1972, Cuba and North Vietnam are public enemies No. 1.[13]

These provisions were reflected in the sales agreements with respect to both usual marketing requirements and export limitations. Commercial purchases from Communist-bloc nations do not count towards meeting usual marketing requirements. Such purchases must be made from "free world sources"[14] or friendly nations.[15] This precludes, according to current United States practice, all Communist countries except Yugoslavia.[16] With Russia again adhering to the Wheat Trade Convention of the International Wheat Agreement, 1971 these practices might be deemed inconsistent with Article 9(2) of the Convention which authorizes usual marketing requirements for wheat only on a global basis.

Cold war considerations also affect the exports of food aid recipients. Thus, pre-1967 sales agreements routinely included a promise by the recipient to ensure that the particular sale would not result in increased availability of the same or like commodities to nations unfriendly to the United States.[17] Apparently, this was designed to prevent the recipient from using food aid commodities to facilitate exports to Bloc countries. In addition, many agreements contained specific prohibitions or limitations on exports of certain commodities to such countries. For example, an agreement with Morocco limited exports of edible oils to 750 metric tons, none of which could be exported to unfriendly countries.[18] An agreement with Tunisia permitted exports of 40,000 metric tons of olive oil, but exports to unfriendly countries were limited to 4,000 metric tons.[19]

The 1966 extension of the Food for Peace Program dropped the specific language directed at curbing increased availability of food aid products to unfriendly countries.[20] And the post-1966 sales agreements no longer uniformly carry the previous restrictive language.[21] But in certain cases, the old restrictions persist in changed form. Thus, Tunisia, receiving concessional wheat and soybean oil, was permitted to export certain amounts of durum wheat and olive oil.[22] Unlike pre-1966 amendment transactions, no specific limitation was imposed upon exports for "unfriendly countries."[23] But a clause was added incorporating the old and supposedly dead general requirement that the commodities imported under the agreement not result in increased availability of the same or like commodities to countries the United States deems unfriendly to it.[24]

But countries unfriendly for usual marketing requirement purposes may not be so with respect to export limitations. As we have seen, usual marketing requirements may not be satisfied by purchases from any Communist nation but Yugoslavia. But the only unfriendly countries for export purposes are China, Cuba, North Vietnam, and North Korea. This is not quite as weird as it looks. The satisfaction of usual marketing requirements directly affects United States exports. Assuming the use of global requirements, the less eligible sources, the greater the chances for sales by the United States. Losing sales to "friendly" nations is bad enough. Losing them to "enemies" would be outrageous—or so, many in Congress would see it. The impact of exports by recipient countries to the bloc is far more indirect—particularly if the exports are not made to normal United States markets. Although food aid induced exports to "unfriendly countries" may be viewed as tantamount to diverting United States aid to Communist countries, United States commercial interests are not affected. Although Congress and the Administration, to some degree, still likes to strike a firm anti-Communist pose, even if no discernible good can come from it, when no direct commercial interests of the United States are at stake, they are more apt to accept distinctions between terrible Communists and just bad Communists.

Notes

1. FAO/UN, CCP/CSD/71/152, *Implementation of The Food Aid Policy of the EEC* (22 December 1971).

2. See, e.g., Agricultural Commodities Agreement with Yugoslavia, April 11, 1966, TIAS 6031, 17 UST 771, 775 (1967); Agreement with Bolivia April 22, 1967, TIAS 6013, 17 UST 645, 657 (1967).

3. Agricultural Commodities Agreement with Korea, March 7, 1966, TIAS 5973, 17 UST 239, 245 (1967).

4. Ibid.

5. Amendment to Agricultural Commodities Agreement with India, Jan. 28, 1960, TIAS 4426, 11 UST 5, 6 (1961).

6. Supplemental Agricultural Commodities Agreement with Pakistan, Jan. 28, 1960, TIAS 4426, 11 UST 161, 164 (1967).

7. In the Agreement with Ethiopia, August 17, 1965, TIAS 5854, 16 UST 1119 (1966), the General Statement is located in Art. III (4), id. at 1122, and the specific requirements to paragraph 2 of the accompanying note, id. at 1123.

8. Id. at 1123.

9. Standard Sales Agreement of April 20, 1967, Art. III-D; Agricultural Commodities Agreement with Iceland, June 5, 1967, TIAS 6300, Part II, Item III-D, 18 UST 1593 (1968).

10. Id. at Part II, Item IV-A, at 7.

11. 68 *Stat.* 459 (1954).

12. 68 *Stat.* 457 (1954).

13. 80 *Stat.* 1527 (1966), 7 U.S.C.A. 1703 (d) (1970).

14. Agricultural Commodities Agreement with Ryukyu Islands, Dec. 23, 1965 (1966), 16 UST 1932, 1938, TIAS 5927.

15. E.g., Agricultural Commodities Agreement with Chile, July 27, 1965, TIAS 5898, 16 UST 1725, 1737 (1966).

16. See the discussion of the treatment of Communist nations under the International Wheat Agreements in Chapter 4.

17. Agricultural Commodities Agreement with Jordan, April 5, August 25, 1966, TIAS 5985, 17 UST 361, 364 (1967); Agreement with Bolivia, Nov. 15, 1961, TIAS 5064, 13 UST 1197, 1200 (1962).

18. Agricultural Commodities Agreement with Morocco, April 23, Oct. 8, 1965, April 21, 1966, TIAS 6049, 17 UST 873, 889 (1967).

19. Agricultural Commodities Agreement with Tunisia, July 30, 1966, TIAS 6067, 17 UST 1108, 1115 (1967).

20. 80 *Stat.* 1526 (1966).

21. See, e.g., Agricultural Commodities Agreement with Afghanistan, July 19, 1967, TIAS 6322, Part I, Art. III-A, 18 UST 1766, 1769 (1968).

22. Agricultural Commodities Agreement with Tunisia, March 17, 1967, TIAS 6323, Part II, Item I, 18 UST 1777, 1782 (1968).

23. Ibid.

24. Agricultural Commodities Agreement with Tunisia, supra, note 21, Part II, Item IV-D.

Part IV: Conclusions and Recommendations

Part IV consists of a single chapter. In the first section, after a brief recapitulation of the problems attending the availability of food aid and its utility as a tool of economic development assistance, I review and comment upon some of the most important control problems confronting any major food aid effort with respect to food aid/ commercial trade relationships. In the second section, I focus upon the substantive and administrative problems of any control system operating upon the bilaterally managed food aid pro-
grams that still characterize current food aid efforts. In the third section, I consider some alternatives to bilateral, narrowly focused food aid programs and food aid control systems. Finally, I try to assess the overall success of the international community in devising effective methods of conducting large food aid programs without inflicting unacceptable damage on legitimate trade interests. I also briefly consider the relevance of the international experience in food aid control to other intransigent world economic problems.

11 Recapitulation, Recommendations and Radical Alternatives

This study has been based upon a number of implicit assumptions about the characteristics, availability, and organization of food aid. Some exploration of these assumptions is necessary to understand the food aid/commercial trade relationships which have been the focus of this book and to grasp some of the study's principal conclusions. The principal assumptions are: (1) a properly administered food aid program can serve as an effective instrumentality for the relief of hunger and malnutrition and as a useful adjunct of other forms of foreign aid designed to accelerate the economic development of the third world; (2) relatively large quantities of food aid will continue to be available in the foreseeable future; (3) the bulk of food aid will be provided on a bilateral basis; and (4) multilateral institutions for providing food aid or for controlling the impact of food aid on commercial trade will be narrowly focused without direct responsibility for either the overall economic development of potential food aid recipients or the control of domestic and international agricultural prices and production.

The potential utility of food aid as a supplement to more conventional forms of foreign aid has been accepted by both the aid-giving agencies and academic critics. During the early sixties, food aid was severely criticized as a selfish device of the United States to rid itself of politically embarrassing stockpiles of surplus agricultural products which were detrimental both to the commercial agricultural trade and the proper development of the agricultural productive capacity of recipient nations. It is now conceded that properly conceived and administered food aid programs can be made consistent with the overall development needs of the recipient and that although any effective food aid program must have some adverse impact upon the commercial agricultural trade interests of developed and developing countries, these can be reduced to acceptable levels. This can be accomplished, in part, through the control devices discussed in this book.

At various times in the past twenty years, the "experts" have concluded that food aid was but a temporary phenomenon. The latest opinion is to the contrary. The attractiveness of food aid as a form of foreign aid is a function of the status of agricultural surpluses, which, in turn, flow from the basic structure of agriculture in the developed countries, and the availability of conventional foreign aid. In the sixties, it appeared that the surplus problem had been solved by the success of the United States in reducing its agricultural output. This period also was marked by steadily increasing levels of conventional foreign aid by the United States and other developed countries. Therefore, it was concluded that

285

food aid would be unavailable and unnecessary. Both conclusions proved errone-ous. Accompanying its increased military involvement in Southeast Asia, the United States began to reduce its foreign aid. Simultaneously, agricultural sur-pluses reappeared; now concentrated in other developed countries such as Can-ada, Australia, the European Economic Community and Japan and now in-cluding additional products such as rice and dairy products. Although the United States has continued to maintain relatively effective control over its agricultural production, its general balance-of-trade problems has induced it to consider using food aid as a means for expanding its commercial exports. Consequently, the international agencies concerned with agricultural trade and economic devel-opment believe that agricultural surplus problems will continue into the indefi-nite future and that these surpluses can make a valuable contribution to the relief of hunger and malnutrition and can serve as a highly useful adjunct to increasingly scarce conventional foreign aid.

Indeed, it is now perceived that food aid can be used to augment the export potential of some developing countries. Ordinarily, developing countries export-ing products widely used for food aid are likely to be victimized by food aid. Their commercial exports may be undermined by the direct displacement of commercial sales by food aid, and even worse, by food aid practices designed to improve the commercial position of food aid donors. Yet, they do not possess the financial resources to respond by mounting their own food aid programs. The special needs of developing countries has been recognized by the FAO for some time. More recently, the concept of using cash contributions of nonfood-producing countries to purchase food aid commodities for food deficit countries from developing countries has been gaining wide acceptance and has been imple-mented to some extent through the Food Aid Convention and the World Food Program. The Food Aid Convention, 1971 requires that thirty-five percent of the cash contributed under the Convention be used to purchase commodities from developing exporters and the General Regulations of the World Food Pro-gram provide for WFP purchases to be made "insofar as is possible and economic from those developing countries which are exporters of food." Although the WFP has brought 94 percent of its total purchases from developing countries, the amount of cash available under both programs is small. Up to now, total purchases from developing countries represent less than 3 percent of all food aid transactions. Under these circumstances, one developing exporter, Argentina, has proposed a sweeping reorientation of world food aid programs which would drastically improve the utility of food aid to developing agricultural exporters.

Principal Current Food Aid Problems

Food Aid and Economic Development

There are two aspects of the relationship of food aid to the economic develop-ment of the have-not nations that are most relevant to this study. The first is the extent to which food aid supplements or substitutes for conventional foreign aid. Unfortunately, there is no consensus in this issue. On the one hand, countries giving food aid, particularly those without severe surplus problems, may well consider food aid as a full substitute for more conventional forms of foreign aid. While there are circumstances where this attitude is justified—situations in which recipient countries would use untied foreign aid to purchase food—in most circumstances, recipients would prefer to use externally furnished resources for other purposes, thereby rendering food aid an inferior substitute for more conventional aid. On the other hand, countries with surplus problems may find food aid sufficiently useful or inexpensive so that food aid, or some portion of it, may well constitute a net addition to the level of foreign aid otherwise available.

The special reasons inducing the availability of food aid and the unique dangers it presents to commercial agricultural trade has tended to isolate food aid from other forms of foreign aid thereby reducing its effectiveness for this purpose. International efforts to control food aid are centered upon a highly specialized organ of the Food and Agriculture Organization—the Consultative Subcommittee on Surplus Disposal. This body is a subcommittee of the Committee on Commodity Problems which has traditionally been dominated by developed agricultural exporters. These exporters' fear of the potential dangers of food aid to commercial trade has induced them to limit the jurisdiction of the Consultative Subcommittee to this problem, thereby deliberately isolating the Subcommittee from affecting the relationship of food aid to economic development. This deficiency has not been cured through the work of other relevant institutions. Thus, while an increasing number of institutions have been established to coordinate foreign aid: the OECD, the ECOSOC, the U.N. Development Program, the World Bank, Regional Development Banks, and the various World Bank-sponsored Aid Consortia for particular countries—none of these has done much to integrate food aid with the total economic assistance effort. This deficiency also characterizes bilateral, multilateral and international food aid efforts such as the World Food Program, the Food Aid Convention, and other food aid programs related to commodity agreements. It seems that the U.N. has recognized this problem and has been considering a variety of actions to remedy the situation, so far without tangible results.

Additionality

The central organizing concept of the food aid control system is additionality. But, in fact, most food aid does not satisfy its requirements, and strict application of this "principle" would seriously undermine the utility of food aid as an effective adjunct to the economic growth of developing countries. Additionality requires that food aid must result in consumption of agricultural products above and beyond the level that would have pertained without it. Where food aid is used to combat famine or to improve the nutrition of particular segments of the recipient's economy, additionality may be deemed satisfied. With respect to programs to combat malnutrition, it is not hard to demonstrate that the potential food aid recipients are not likely to improve their diets through commercial purchases. Even if a poor country does have some foreign exchange which could be used for food purchases, food aid is beyond criticism so long as the programs are principally directed at increasing food consumption of poor people, since additionality does not condition food aid upon proof that a nation would let its people starve rather than import food commercially.

The case for additionality is much harder to make for food aid designed to agument economic development. Projects based upon the use of food in lieu of cash to purchase services required for the project are justified upon the theory that the food-financed project will induce economic development which ultimately will result in providing increased purchasing power, part of which will be used to increase food purchases. This theory has two glaring weaknesses. The first is that it is very difficult to predict how the expected increase in real income will be distributed throughout the society. Secondly, though increased income will lead to some increased food consumption, not all the increase would be so used. Some, largely unknown, portion will be used for other purposes. It is very seldom that those planning a food based project could predict with any certainty how the additional income will be used. Therefore, the assertion that food-based projects will compensate for initial reduced food purchases by inducing subsequent increases in commercial food purchases is completely unquantifiable and therefore unprovable. It amounts to little more than a pious hope. Even this much is dubious if the food aid is given in large quantities on a program basis. Here, the very purpose of food aid is to substitute for commercial imports in order to free foreign exchange for other purposes. The middle-run and long-run impact of these programs will be distributed throughout the economy, and again, it is impossible to predict the effect on food demand.

To the extent additionality has any meaning or utility, it is as a very general reminder to consider seriously the impact of food aid upon commercial trade. By now, this much is accepted by all participants in the food aid process. Additionality is useless and possibly misleading as a functional guide to measure particular transactions. However, to the extent that the existence of the additionality standards forces food aid donors to analyze the impact of the proposed transaction on commercial trade, it serves the useful purpose of helping to assure that important consequences of food aid for commercial trade are considered and made subject to consultation, under the FAO procedures, with potentially affected third countries.

Projects vs Programs

Closely related to the problems surrounding additionality is the debate over the appropriateness of projects versus programs as the preferred method for giving food aid. A recent review of the role of food aid during the next decade strongly recommended that increased food aid be mainly administered through projects rather than programs. The theory here is that project-oriented food aid is less likely to disturb commercial trade patterns than food aid programs. This may be true only to the extent projects are small and are not designed to promote economic development. As discussed above, economic development-oriented food aid projects always have the initial effect of displacing commercial sales. Although there is the possibility that the resulting economic development ultimately will generate sufficient additional effective demand for food to compensate for the initial loss, this is a very uncertain matter. Also projects are far more expensive to administer than programs which make use of existing commercial channels for distribution of the food aid.

Thus, the preference for projects over programs seems misguided. Upon close analysis, projects, particularly those designed to promote economic development, are not demonstrably less dangerous to commercial trade than programs. They are clearly much more expensive to administer. More importantly, food aid dispensed on a program basis may be closely integrated with the recipient's overall economic development plans. Such coordination is much more difficult to achieve through a series of projects scattered throughout the economy. Probably, much of the public support for projects is ritualistic, designed to allay the fears of agricultural exporters worried about the impact of enlarged food aid upon their commercial exports. In fact, sizeable increases in total food aid levels only can be introduced through the program approach. Specifically targeted feeding programs can absorb some additional food, but the possibilities are limited. Developmentally oriented projects based on food also are relatively difficult to find, develop, and administer. Therefore, if food aid is to serve as an effective partial substitute for increasingly scarce conventional foreign aid, the food will have to be dispensed through the program approach. The decision of the World Food Program to sell considerable quantities of food aid through normal channels as part of its relief efforts in East Pakistan implicitly supports this contention.

Under a realistic view towards displacement of commercial sales, increased reliance upon programs need not threaten legitimate trade interests. Large-scale food aid programs will deprive exporters of some commercial sales. But if the food aid serves as a reasonably adequate substitute for conventional foreign aid, and the lost commercial sales are distributed among agricultural exporters in rough proportion to their economic strength, the lost sales may be viewed as part of the exporter's foreign aid contribution. However, for these losses to be acceptable, measures, of the sort discussed in Part III of this study, must be taken to ensure that food aid is not used by the donor to improve its commercial position vis-a-vis other exporters. Moreover, care must be taken to shield developing exporters from adverse effects on their exports. One way to achieve this might be increased use of the device used in the Food Aid Convention and the World Food Program, whereby food aid commodities are purchased from developing countries with funds provided by nonagricultural contributors.

International Control of Bilaterally Administered Food Aid

Existing concepts and institutions designed to control the impact of food aid upon commercial trade are oriented toward bilateral food aid programs. A basic feature of such programs is the prime concern with donor's own agricultural interests. Agricultural products are made available for food aid where their export will support domestic agricultural policies, and food aid donors are ever on the alert to find ways of using food aid to expand commercial exports. These characteristics have shaped the substantive rules and procedures developed by the international community to moderate the impact of food aid upon commercial trade.

The Jurisprudence of the FAO Control System

The close connection between food aid and the donor's agricultural interests have determined the jurisprudence of the international machinery developed to cope with food aid/commercial trade interrelationships. The system is noncoercive and based upon negotiation and consensus. Actually, these mechanisms do not fall into any known category of international law. The FAO Principles or Surplus Disposal fall short of an international convention because no procedure was established for their ratification by member countries. Yet, they are more than a recommendation by an intergovernmental body because they are subject to formal "acceptance" by adhering governments. The important consideration is that the system has worked; at least up to now. It is likely that some of its success is due to its noncoercive nature. Compliance is based solely upon the recognized common interest in finding workable solutions to the complex and important problems arising from food aid programs imposed upon the highly delicate structure of commercial agricultural trade. It may well be that this approach may serve as a model for effective action in other areas exhibiting similar features.

Unsurprisingly, the operation of the administrative organ of the FAO Control System—the Consultative Subcommittee on Surplus Disposal—follows the same pattern. The basic operating thrust of the CSD is well illustrated by the recommendations of a recent CSD Working Party on tied sales. According to the Working Party Report, the CSD has three tools to apply to this problem. The first is reporting, through notifications of the terms of food aid transactions. The second is consultation in advance of completing transactions to enable third countries to comment upon aspects of programs which may affect their commercial trade. The third is the development of techniques, such as usual marketing requirements to help ensure that food aid are additional to and not in substitution for normal commercial imports.[1] The first two are the traditional CSD weapons. The third, usual marketing requirements, is a departure, involving a more conventional legal approach. However, even here, the ultimate control is based on reporting and consultation. While the FAO Principles may require the imposition of usual marketing requirements, and may set out general standards for setting the level of these requirements, each country retains the right to set its own UMRs subject only to reporting and consultation within the CSD.

The ambit of the FAO Control System is a second central determining feature. It applies only to the impact of food aid upon commercial trade. Jurisdiction over such issues as the level and kind of food aid required for maximum relief of hunger and malnutrition and the most rapid development of the southern hemisphere, the ground rules for international agricultural trade, and the relationship of domestic agricultural policies to the creation of both unwanted surpluses and extra resources for use in international development efforts, is scattered through a host of international agencies or remains with individual nations, beyond effective international control.

United States Attitudes
Toward Food Aid Controls

United States attitudes towards international controls of food aid are deeply influenced by its conviction that many nations, particularly the European Economic Community are grossly unfair in their treatment of United States agricultural exports. This feeling of injury is exacerbated by the reason for EEC restrictions against agricultural imports. These restrictions stem from the policy of subsidizing inefficient farmers through expensive agricultural price support programs, which require, *inter alia*, that lower priced non-EEC imports be barred through use of variable import levies. Thus, it appears to the United States that irrational domestic agricultural policies have deprived the United States of important export markets for its efficiently produced agricultural products. The treatment of agricultural exports assumes greater importance in a period of extraordinary pressures on the United States balance-of-payments and balance-of-trade. Obviously, it is difficult to trace particular actions of the United States with respect to food aid to this general feeling of injury by its trading parties. But it is almost certain to have considerable impact on the willingness of this country to make concessions to other agricultural exporters—particularly those from the EEC. And under an international control system based upon accommodation and compromise, such attitudes pose a very real danger to the system's future effectiveness.

The Need for UMRs and Export Control Devices

The FAO has now adopted the usual marketing requirement mechanism that has been bilaterally employed by the United States from the outset of its food aid efforts. But our analysis indicates that from the food aid recipient's viewpoint, United States type UMRs are inferior to other methods of protecting commercial markets. UMRs, though, have distinct political and administrative advantages which might outweigh their economic defects. General application of global marketing requirements in food aid transactions may well serve to reassure both third country exporters and commercially minded interests in the donor country that a minimum commercial market will be available in every food aid recipient country. Also, it may facilitate advance commercial policy planning by governments interested in estimating their agricultural export potential. These considerations gain importance now that more countries are giving food aid and situations will arise where a country is receiving food aid from more than one source. In these cases, it should be administratively easier to establish a UMR than to induce food aid donors to agree upon the total food aid to be supplied to a recipient from all sources.

The systems of export limitations developed by the United States remain applicable in more or less their present form under the new food aid situation. Like bilateral programs, multilateral food aid giving must cope with potential dangers posed by additional exports by food aid recipient countries attributable to the receipt of food aid. Moreover, the same considerations are relevant to determination of appropriate control devices: how to permit the expansion of economically sound exports by food aid recipients without violently disrupting existing trade patterns and vested interests? For this purpose, the techniques developed by the United States should be transferable en masse. The obvious exception, of course, would be the practice of tying offset and matching purchases to the donor country.

Control Devices as Two-Edged Swords

An interesting and important feature of the devices most commonly employed to protect commercial trade from undue injury from food aid is that with slight variations, the same devices may be employed to protect third countries or to exacerbate their injuries. Usual marketing requirements, designed to ensure a minimum level of commercial imports by food aid recipients, should assist third country exporters. But if the UMR is tied to the food aid donor, third countries may be worse off than if no UMRs were used at all. The same applies to export controls. Offset purchase requirements are effective ways to ensure that third countries are not injured by exports based solely upon underpriced food aid imports. But if the offset purchases are tied to the donor, two groups of exporters may be injured. Exporters of the product shipped under food aid may reduce its commercial imports, and producers of the food and assisted exports must contend with a new competitor. The food aid donor, depending upon the terms of the food aid deal and the nature of its domestic agricultural policies, may benefit from the original food aid sale and certainly benefits from the additional commercial sales compelled by the tied offset requirement. Unrestricted tying presents another ambiguous situation. Under most circumstances, tying food aid to commercial purchases from the donor is highly reprehensible commercial conduct. But if the food aid donor has been the principal historical supplier, as in the New Zealand-Peru dairy arrangement, it may be appropriate for the donor to limit price concessions to purchases made from the donor. There the effect of the transaction was to translate New Zealand's commercial sales into concessional sales; a process that affected only the two countries involved.

In considerable part, it is this two-edgedness which makes formulation of precise rules for food aid conduct so difficult. Usual marketing requirements may be good, bad, or indifferent depending upon the circumstances and the specific terms of the UMR. The same may be said for offset purchase requirements and tying. Therefore, a workable control system must exhibit great flexibility to deal with all the variations that may arise. Fixed rules can neither be formulated nor administered. Under these circumstances, the FAO Control System, as wishy-washy and ineffective as it may sometimes appear, may represent the best available approach. The nature of the problems and the most effective solutions require a system based upon the establishment of general objectives and a forum for finding mutually agreeable ways of applying these objectives to particular situations. And this is just what the FAO system provides.

Developing Coherent Food Aid
Policies and Practices under
Bilateral Programs

General sensitivity to the needs and interests of all parties affected by food aid operations certainly is prerequisite to the formulation and execution of optimum food aid policies and practices. But sensitivity, even coupled with a thorough understanding of the underlying economic processes, does not necessarily provide clear policy guidelines. Since any effective food aid program will deprive someone of potential commercial sales, any policy in this area must be a compromise between the interests of the recipient and all private and national commercial agricultural interests bound up with exports. Moreover, current analytical tools do not permit any precise ordering of alternative compromises in situations requiring the balancing of disparate values held by multiple participants. Therefore, any compromise can be attacked as suboptimum. Under these circumstances, probably the best any given set of food aid policies and practices can achieve is to prevent food aid from causing sharp fluctuations in the nature and direction of commerical transactions, to distribute the commercial losses in a manner which appears reasonably equitable to all affected parties, and, with regard to bilateral programs, to ensure that food aid is not bent to the selfish commercial interests of the aid-giving nation.

From these general objectives, we may be able to extract a set of principles or guidelines with which to measure particular food aid practices. Least controversial would be the proposition that food aid should not be used to directly assist the commercial sales of the aid donor at the expense of third countries. Current international standards and United States practice with respect to the use of food aid as a means to expand the donor's commercial sales are mixed. Such practices clearly are banned with regard to wheat. And although the picture is cloudier regarding other products, the United States has eschewed such tactics with respect to food aid transactions in rice where they might work, and uses them only for oils and feed grains, where it can be demonstrated that United States dominance in the export of these products provides some justification for these practices. Conceivably, indirect impetus to donors' agricultural exports could well result from the impetus towards general economic development of recipient countries provided by food aid or the development of new tastes—wheat in Asia, soybean oil in Spain. Obviously, this kind of benefit is wholly appropriate.

A second possible general criterion for any food aid program might be that the agricultural products should be consumed within the recipient country and not be reexported or lead to directly related exports of other products. Although sophisticated arguments may be made for permitting some types of reexports, the international consensus has run strongly against such practices. They are explicitly condemned by the FAO Principles of Surplus Disposal and United States legislation. By and large, the devices used by the United States to control the exports of countries receiving food aid commodities are elaborate, effective and equitable. Here, the United States has developed instruments of supreme subtlety to deal with delicate and complex economic phenomena. For the most part, these methods seem to have been successful in permitting a high level of food aid, avoiding disruptions in patterns of international trade, yet still permitting developing countries like Tunisia, Turkey, Taiwan and Korea to increase their export potential through simultaneous importation of particular commodities on both commerical and concessional terms.

In descending order of general acceptability, a third possible criterion is that food aid recipients maintain some given level of commercial imports. The most extreme interpretation of this principle would be full additionality—no displacement of commercial sales. But, as we have seen, such a standard is both unattainable and inconsistent with the foreign aid orientation of modern food aid programs. The concept of imposing usual marketing requirement provisions, principally based upon historic levels of commercial imports, in all food aid transactions has been incorporated into the FAO control system. Fortunately, the concept is sufficiently flexible to afford food aid administrators the elbow room necessary to ensure that rigid notions of fixed levels of commercial imports do not interfere with the basic development aims of the program. Thus, usual marketing requirements for poor countries engaged in serious development efforts must take the general economic and foreign exchange position of the recipient into account. The standards for setting UMRs provide considerable flexibility to permit modifications of the UMRs in response to changes in the recipient's economic situation.

A fourth possible ground rule is that food aid should be fashioned to provide maximum possible economic and humanitarian benefit to the recipient. To a palpable degree such a standard may be inconsistent with the desire to assure minimum commercial sales by donors and/or other countries. Indeed, to the extent minimum commercial purchase requirements are effective, they must result in a suboptimum allocation of the recipient's resources.

Food Aid and World Attitudes
towards Agricultural Trade
Practices

I would like to return to the question posed in the first chapter. Why do governments take such pains to insulate commercial trade from the impact of food aid while doing relatively little to moderate the cut-throat competitive measures commonly employed to facilitate the export of agricultural products to commercial markets? I can suggest two types of explanations. One is that the forces that lead to agricultural price-cutting in commercial markets are too powerful and politically important to induce nations to forego the quantum of their unilateral decision-making authority that would be necessary to implement an effective international regulatory system. By contrast, food aid related problems are sufficiently limited to permit the necessary internationalization of domestic political authority. Secondly, food aid related competitive practices are perceived as significantly more dangerous than similar actions in other areas.

Problems stemming from economic imbalances in agriculture are extremely difficult to handle for several reasons. For the most part, they stem from technological advances which permit sharp increases in the production of grains and fibers, which products face highly inelastic demand curves. That is, price decreases do not lead to sufficient increased demand to compensate for the lower prices. Ordinarily, the appropriate economic adjustment would be the withdrawal of resources from the agricultural sector. But, most of these resources like land and otherwise unskilled agricultural labor are highly immobile. Also, agricultural problems are sharply focused upon a politically powerful group of producers. It is also significant that while the developed countries possess excess productive capacity, much of the world remains food short, although without the foreign exchange resources to meet food deficits through commercial imports. Since international action with respect to agriculture is certain to have serious domestic consequences, countries are extremely reluctant to cede any of their autonomy in these areas to international institutions, or to limit their options through international agreements. A major effort to establish comprehensive controls over agriculture was made during the Kennedy Round trade negotiations. There, the United States attempted to establish a commodity agreement encompassing all major food grains, which would combat the causes of agricultural surpluses through limitations upon domestic agricultural subsidies. At this moment, the United States again is attempting to induce the EEC to agree to basic ground rules on the extent of domestic agricultural subsidies in areas likely to affect international trade.

At the same time, agricultural producers recognize the severe disadvantages of a totally unregulated world agricultural economy. Therefore, where nations hesitate to commit themselves to the very extensive international controls necessary to cope with the entire problem, they may be much more willing to agree to controls in limited areas. Food aid related activities may be one such area. The set of problems related to food aid may be sufficiently circumscribed and serious to induce countries unwilling to make general cessions of authority to accept a control system in this particular area. Commodity agreements represent another partial transfer of authority to international structures. Conceivably, this process can be continued even further, but this difficult subject lies beyond the scope of this study.

Food aid programs are not only sufficiently circumscribed to permit international controls, but they are both particularly useful and dangerous. They are useful as a means of disposing of agricultural products that otherwise would constitute a danger to commercial trade or cost more to dispose of through other means. For some nations, they also serve as a relatively painless method for meeting a nation's foreign aid obligations. They are dangerous because they can serve as an effective cloak for aggressive commercial practices. The various methods used to increase agricultural sales outside of food aid are subject to scrutiny, complaint and counteraction by affected nations. Since the purpose of these devices are clearly selfish, other nations are uninhibited in their reactions. But food aid purports to be based upon humanitarian considerations, and undoubtedly is useful to developing recipients. Therefore, it is much more difficult for third countries to voice their complaints, since they risk being accused of insensitivity towards the needs of the recipients.

The combination of these factors may have induced agricultural exporters to develop an effective control system for food aid/commercial trade problems. Food aid is more dangerous to trade interests than other kinds of trade competition because it is much harder to know the extent to which it is being used for selfish ends. Also, food aid may have unintended impacts on trade which can be solved through legal devices with international cooperation. That is, through the use of the kind of control methods discussed in this book, food aid can be sanitized of its most dangerous features and thus be preserved as an effective safety valve for the pressures created by imbalances in domestic agricultural sectors which cannot be solved in the short run. With the problems stemming from highly competitive trade practices excluded from the food aid areas, nations can concentrate their attention upon the specific trade practices requiring their closest attention bilaterally while relying upon effective international controls to permit them to participate in food aid activities with a minimum of risk.

Controlling Food Aid under Internationally Organized Food Aid Programs

Despite the rapid growth of the World Food Program and the inclusion of the Food Aid Convention within the last two International Wheat Agreements, most food aid is conducted bilaterally under programs unrelated to the economic factors responsible for agricultural imbalances. Over the past decade, many proposals have been offered to change this picture to one in which multilateral food aid programs would predominate. Also plans have been suggested to broaden the focus of food aid programs to include direct concern with the overall conditions of agricultural production and trade. These proposals fall into two classes. The first seeks to concentrate food aid efforts or food aid policies into a single international institution. However, the focus of the food aid giving agency would be limited to the traditional objectives of food aid—international relief and economic development. The second class of proposals are designed to combine within one institution responsibility for commercial agricultural trade and the traditional food aid objectives. The concept underlying these plans is that the intimate connection of food aid with commercial trade requires that a single institution be responsible for them both. Also it is believed that if properly handled, food aid is capable of assisting the objectives of international trade rather than thwarting them, as is often the case under the present arrangements.

Concentrating all food aid operations in a single international institution has several clear advantages. These include (1) a relative absence of concern about political motivation and control; (2) convenience for small donors, as well as for donors having only occasional surpluses who may find it uneconomic to set up their own food aid machinery; (3) the possibility of assembling combinations of foodstuffs most suitable for nutritional needs; and (4) convenience for making better use of the food exports of developing countries and those small surpluses which irregularly appear. Also, a multilateral approach enables food aid to be used on a relatively stable and regularly planned basis, even in a situation where supplies and deficiencies in individual countries may fluctuate widely. If the number of food commodity stabilization-cum-food aid agreements increases, the multilateral channel would provide the most efficient way for using such food aid to support development, especially for handling the contributions of small countries or of developing exporting countries. Finally, the multilateral approach where food is channeled into development projects under well-established control procedures minimizes the impact of concessional transactions on commercial trade.

With respect to the problems confronted in this study, food aid channeled through an international institution would be far less likely to directly endanger commercial trade than a set of independent, nationally controlled, bilateral food aid programs. While any sort of unrestricted food aid can do great damage to commercial interests, an international body will not suffer from the multivariate objectives of food aid programs conducted by surplus holding, commercially exporting, individual nations. That is, the international entity only will be interested in maximizing benefits to the food aid recipients. It will harbor no ulterior motives centering about protecting or expanding commercial agricultural exports. Under these circumstances, the task of determining an appropriate level of food aid to each country should be simpler than the analogous problem has been for the United States. It is possible that usual marketing requirements, or something like them, would not be necessary since no single country is making the concessional sales, there is little reason to "protect" anybody's commercial sales. Careful restriction of the food aid level should constitute sufficient control.

Concentrating food aid operations in a single international institution has certain disadvantages. The principal one is that countries might be less willing to contribute resources to such an institution than they would to nationally controlled operations. This, of course, is the same problem faced by efforts to convert all forms of foreign aid to a multilateral basis. To the extent that food aid promotes national interests, donating countries would want the power to conduct food aid with respect to those products, on those terms, and with those conditions pertaining to commercial purchases that would best solve these purposes. In many circumstances, pursuit of these ends will not substantially derrogate from the benefits enjoyed by the food aid recipients. They may well injure other exporters, but, as we have tried to demonstrate, a case may be made for sacrificing the interests of developed exporters to those of developing recipients. A second disadvantage of internationally controlled food aid stems from the nature of food aid and the nature of any international body in today's world order. Given the sensitivity of agriculturally oriented nations to commercial exports, the governing body of any international institution established to conduct all food aid operations would have to include representatives from all these nations as well as those from potential food aid recipients. Almost every decision with respect to the composition and size of food aid transactions with particular recipients is bound to have differential effect upon the group of exporter nations represented on the governing board. And since international institutions can act only in situations exhibiting wide agreement among the countries represented in its governing structure, it is likely that there will be a sizeable dissenting vote on most proposed transactions. The agency might find it very difficult to operate effectively and efficiently. Bilateral programs, which are only subject to general compliance with the FAO Principles and prior consultation with other interested exporters, can be conceived and executed as long as they are consistent with the donor's needs. It may well be that more food aid will be supplied more rapidly under nationally controlled programs than under international ones. Potential food aid recipients, ever sensitive to changes which might reduce their access to food aid, are likely to perceive this and strongly oppose further internationalization.

Controlling The Purchase of Food
Aid Commodities

Large-scale food aid programs, even when conducted under multilateral auspices, must exert considerable impact upon commercial international trade in the same or related commodities. The Argentinian Plan for transforming the World Food Program into a World Food Fund is based on this fact and proposes to use this impact to help cure basic agricultural production and trade problems. Another plan has been proposed which attempts to deal with the potential trade-depressing effects of food aid without integrating food aid operations and commodity stabilization into a single institution. This is the Fisher Plan. This plan is based upon the assumption that the cost to the donor of food aid is well below the market price. Here though, the chief concern is to transfer these agricultural products to underdeveloped countries with minimum impact upon commercial sales of the same commodities. This seems to be related to the abortive World Food Board concept. The latter was supposed to buy and hold reserves of surplus foods and operate as a buffer stock to stabilize world prices and sell the surpluses on easy credit terms to needy countries.

Under the Fisher Plan, an International Food Surplus Disposal Agency would be formed for the purpose of supplying agricultural products to the underdeveloped nations. The Agency would obtain the products from two sources: partly on the world market at prices and in quantities roughly equivalent to those that might have prevailed in the absence of surplus disposal or bilateral food aid activities by food surplus countries and the rest from these countries at rock-bottom prices equivalent to those this country has been accepting under its concessional sale programs. The products would then be sold to the underdeveloped countries at prices permitting the surplus disposal agency to break even on the transaction. Since the surplus products would be cheap, the average price to the consumers should be well below prevailing market rates. And, assuming relatively elastic demands for food in these poor countries, the lower prices should permit sale of a volume considerably above that which would otherwise prevail. The net effect would be that third country exporters would sell the same amount of agricultural products to the underdeveloped countries as they would had no food aid or concessional sales existed. But the underdeveloped countries would receive additional products at less than going prices. Surplus food producers would dispose of its surpluses on roughly the same terms that it now demands, but the intervention of the Food Surplus Agency ensures that the surpluses do not depress the commercial markets.[2]

Theoretically, current arrangements are designed to achieve the same results. Food aid is supposed to be limited to transactions which increase net consumption by the amount of the aid. Safeguards are provided in concessional sales agreements to preserve commercial markets for the United States and other friendly nations. But the current system is far from perfect and relying on one nation to protect the interests of its competitors is not a particularly reassuring arrangement. Thus, the Fisher scheme has its attractions. Practically speaking, though, this plan shares the weaknesses of the World Food Board scheme. Neither the United States nor other potential food aid donors is likely to transfer this much responsibility for its food aid and surplus disposal activities to an international organization. Moreover, it is unlikely that any single nation would undertake the burden of becoming the purchasing agent for all underdeveloped countries and a multination operation is likely to be highly conservative and cumbersome. Probably, the underdeveloped nations themselves would oppose this approach, believing that they can do better bilaterally. In the final analysis, such an elaborate scheme is probably unnecessary. At this point, the world trading community has developed devices under the existing bilateral system which seem to accomplish most of the same objectives.

The World Food Fund

This leads us to the most radical current food aid reform proposal—the Argentina Plan. The objective of this plan is to create a single international institution that would conduct all food aid operations in a manner designed to correct many of the problems now afflicting international agricultural trade. The plan would encompass all countries. These would be divided into four groups: (1) developing countries with food deficits and insufficient spending power;

(2) food-exporting developing countries; (3) developed countries with surplus food production; and (4) food-importing developed countries. The resources of the Fund should consist of contributions in cash and/or in kind depending on the group to which the country in question belongs. The resources of the proposed Fund should have cash and commodity components in as near as possible equal proportions and may be used for donations or long-term loans according to need. The activities of the Fund should be coordinated with those of all international agricultural commodity agreements now in operation or which come into effect. If these agreements result in surplus products, these should be administered by the World Food Fund. The Fund should be operated to correct the imbalances between world supply and demand for agricultural products. It would also seek to end creation of surpluses caused by high domestic price supports and protectionist policies, and promote the expansion of commerce and greater participation in international agricultural trade by efficient developing countries (like Argentina).

The Argentine Plan is based upon Argentina's analysis of current world agricultural policies, which is a mixture of clear truths and more controversial propositions. Thus, the present and potential food deficit in the world requires that the capacity of foodstuffs production in the developing countries be substantially increased. The lack of financial resources in the foodstuffs-producing developing countries should not be a reason for depriving them of market opportunities through their inability to compete in the concessional arena, because this is likely to result in abandoning agricultural production in those countries, instead of increasing it, due to the growing difficulties of finding markets for such production. The increase of trade among the developing countries is one of the elements which could best contribute to closing the gap between developed and developing countries, taking into account the characteristics of the foodstuffs products subject to trade, as well as the need for such products. In the earlier stages of development, foodstuffs and raw materials provide developing countries their best trade prospects. Concessional sales or grants, either from highly industrialized countries or international agencies accumulating foodstuffs produced in the developed countries, interfere with the objectives of expanding trade and economic integration among developing countries. The accumulation of surpluses as it is known up to now in highly industrialized countries has been a consequence of highly protected and subsidized agricultural production resulting in the investment of huge financial resources to produce, quite often at a much higher cost, the amount of commodities which could have been otherwise obtained much more cheaply in areas best suited for agricultural production.

On the basis of this analysis, the World Food Fund would counteract these forces by permitting developing countries to supply the food required by deficit countries under financing provided the fund by the developed nations. The World Food Fund would make available financial resources to the developing countries earmarked for the purchase of foodstuffs and this financial aid should be in addition to the overall aid for development or stabilization programs. It is alleged that under this program, developing recipient countries would not be harmed if food aid was made available under current terms. As their capacity to export foodstuffs increases, they would be helped further by the opportunity to participate in the supply of foodstuffs to even less developed countries. Allegedly, the developed countries supplying the funds necessary to finance exports from the developing countries would not be hurt since these plans would somehow save them some of the costs now incurred in subsidizing domestic agriculture or keeping out agricultural exports. Moreover, it would be appropriate for developed agricultural producers which rely upon import levies to protect domestic markets to direct some of these monies to the World Food Fund for the purchase of food aid commodities since these levies have been responsible for depriving developing exporters of their rightful export possibilities.

Adoption of the Argentine Plan would cure many of the problems plaguing current food aid practices. Concentrating food aid purchases in developing countries would serve two purposes. It would remove all incentives by developed exporters to use food aid as a lever to pry out additional commercial sales from food aid recipients. It also would reverse the disadvantages that developing exporters now suffer under the existing system because of their inability to finance their own food aid programs—which programs to some degree deprive them of potential commercial exports. Similarly, the use of import levies to finance food aid purchases from developing countries is an attractive idea. In fact, this was one of the key concepts of the so-called Pisani-Baumgartner Plan, which was the approach favored by the EEC for dealing with world surplus problems.

The basic, probably fatal, drawback of the Argentine Plan is the certain opposition of the developed countries. They would be required both to supply cash to purchase food aid from developing countries and also to forego the opportunity to move their own surplus products through food aid. Moreover, they would lose any chance to use food aid to increase their commerical sales. At the same time, nothing in the Argentine Plan promises to help the developed countries solve their surplus problems. Actually, the Argentine Plan would require the developed countries to bear the entire brunt of solving surplus problems by voluntarily reducing their output, and accepting the internal economic and political problems that have so far precluded the developing countries from adopting this kind of solution on their own motion. There is also the question of the capacity of the developing countries to supply all the food aid required. Of course, to the extent this is the case, the deficit could be filled by the developed countries.

The most intriguing and controversial aspect of the Argentine Plan is the concept of combining the responsibility for conducting food aid programs and stabilizing international agricultural trade in the same agency. On the surface, this is a very appealing idea. Economically, food aid is inextricably bound up with commercial agricultural trade, since the availability of food aid directly flows from agricultural production and trade imbalances and the dangers of food aid are largely concentrated in its adverse impact on commercial trade. The problem is that the importance, complexity, and political sensitivity of agricultural trade problems precludes delegation of a substantial authority over these issues to an international body. The current international order is too primitive to permit transference of this much power and responsibility from national to international hands. The expert assigned by the World Food Program to study the Argentine proposal reached the same conclusion, but for different reasons.[3] According to him, the stabilization of international commodity prices and food aid are two completely different tasks and it is not desirable to mix them. This is true if food aid is viewed solely from the recipient's viewpoint. From this position, food aid is no more than an equivocal substitute for conventional foreign aid. But when the sources of food aid are considered and the effect of food aid on commercial trade is taken into account, it is clear that food aid and commodity trade stabilization are not separate matters. Although the recommendation against the Plan conforms with existing international political realities, it is still important to fully comprehend the intimate relationship between food aid and commercial trade.

Actually, to some extent, food aid and commodity stabilization problems already are being handled by the same international institutions. The International Wheat Agreement includes a Food Aid Convention designed to assist commodity stabilization through use of food aid. The Food Aid Convention even includes provisions requiring that a minimum portion of the food aid commodities be procured from developing countries. The recently concluded arrangement for dairy products also contemplates use of food aid as part of its overall stabilization efforts. Generally speaking, this kind of integration should be more feasible on the context of a commodity agreement. Here, the member countries already are sufficiently convinced of the need for joint action to establish the commodity arrangement in the first place. The further step of encompassing food aid within the arrangement should cause no additional political difficulties. But, as has been mentioned previously, commodity agreements as the basis for organizing food aid efforts suffer from the particularity of focus upon the commodity concerned. Also, they may unduly restrict healthy competition. While commodity agreements may be effective bodies for considering the trade aspects of food aid, they are all suited to cope with the economic aid aspects.

Progress and Prognostication

A prime objective of this inquiry has been to explore the possibilities of hitching the unruly horsepower of food aid to the creaky foreign aid wagon without upsetting the wagon or crashing into commercial vehicles sharing the same road.

After emerging from the turgid waters of economic theory, and dusty bureaucratic pigeon-holes, we can boast with some confidence that after a long breaking-in period, the marriage will survive. The United States food aid program, for one, does manage to do its job without much damage to innocent bystanders, although performance is uneven in some important quarters.

Whether food aid is the best way of promoting international economic development is another matter. Clearly, foreign aid which can be used to purchase any goods or services from any country, is more useful to the recipient than food aid as a tool of rapid economic development. But, the plain fact is that the two are not equally available, and food aid may be had where other, perhaps superior varieties of foreign assistance, cannot. Also, we must accept the fact that solutions to the problems of agricultural overproduction or overcapacity requiring severe output restrictions or removal of existing controls on international trade in agricultural products are not politically feasible for the foreseeable future. It is often asserted that the poor developing countries would be better off if all existing controls on international agricultural trade were removed. This would reduce the availability of food aid, but this loss would be more than compensated by the reduction of commercial prices for all agricultural goods to their "natural" level. This may make sense, but its achievement would require general dismantling of the protective fences surrounding agricultural trade when, in fact, the trend seems to be towards more rather than less controls over international agricultural transactions. Therefore, no major alternatives to food aid are available.

Whatever the future of the World Food Program and the possibilities for sharply increased food aid activities by individual countries under the Food Aid Convention, up to now and for a while longer, food aid means United States food aid. Undoubtedly, the food aid programs of the United States commenced as rather crude though ingenious devices to rid ourselves of a questionable asset—farm surpluses. They were conducted with minimum sensitivity to the interests of the recipients or third countries. But the complaints of important and allied countries induced reforms, both through the medium of international codes such as the FAO Principles of Surplus Disposal and the institution of effective consultative and dispute-resolving mechanisms. Consequently, during the past ten years, the practices and policies of the United States in conducting the program have evinced a highly responsible international attitude. Conceivably, this might change with the increasing pressure on United States balance-of-payments, but it would appear that the habits and mechanisms of cooperation are too well-established to be easily displaced. The behavior of other donors is too sparse to draw conclusions. Certainly, some of their early efforts frightened the United States into insisting upon a substantial strengthening of the FAO control machinery. The effectiveness of this mechanism under the new circumstances confronting it is yet to be tested.

The Development of Food Aid
Controls as Legal Process

Finally, it is interesting to speculate about the overall configuration of the control mechanisms applied to food aid transactions as an example of a particular variety of the use of law and law-related instruments to resolve intricate economic problems with strong international implications. The history and current status of the international and national legal administrative infrastructure supporting food aid is a paradigm of the process whereby dangerous unilateral actions are gradually transformed into acceptable and useful channels. Thus, the uncontrolled surplus disposal activities of the United States first were made subject to the FAO Principles of Surplus Disposal and then to the consultative and review machinery of the Consultative Subcommittee on Surplus Disposal.

Simultaneously, and undoubtedly partially motivated by the FAO's activities, the United States itself developed increasingly sophisticated control devices designed to achieve the basic objective of food aid programs without inducing unwanted and undesirable side effects. When United States practices neared the peak of technical effectiveness, these standards were applied in part to other potential food aid givers through the Guidelines Relating to Concessional Transactions of the International Wheat Agreements. The cycle became full when the FAO adopted wholesale the United States developed usual marketing requirement techniques. Thus domestic and international law each formed the basis for action by the other. The process may move to the next level if this noncoercive, yet authoritative system may be applied in other areas of economic conduct where reluctance to cede national authority has made adoption of more traditional legal systems unacceptable.

Notes

1. UN/FAO, CCP 69/13/3 (CCP/CSD/69/51); *Report on Tied Sales* 15 (17 July 1969).

2. Fisher, *A Proposal for the Distribution Abroad of the United States' Food Surplus*, 44 *Review of Economics and Statistics* 52 (1962).

3. WFP/IGC 8/15, *Implications of the UNCTAD and Argentina Proposals for The Modification of the World Food Program* (19 Aug. 1965).

Appendixes

Appendix A

The Annex to FAO Council Resolution 1/53 (Nov. 1969) established the following catalog of transactions which are subject to some form of notification and consultation requirements under the FAO Principles of Surplus Disposal.

Catalog of Transactions

1. Gifts or donations of commodities from a government to a government of an importing country, an intergovernmental organization or a private institution for free distribution directly to the final consumers in the importing country;
2. Gifts or donations of commodities from a government to a government of an importing country, or an intergovernmental organization or a private institution for distribution, by means of sale on the open market of the importing country;
3. Monetary grants by the government of an exporting country to an importing country, for the specific purpose of purchasing a commodity from the exporting country;
4. Monetary grants by a government either to a supplying country (or countries) or to a recipient country for the specific purpose of purchasing a commodity from the exporting country (or countries) for delivery to the specific recipient country;
5. Monetary grants by a government to an intergovernmental organization for the specific purpose of purchasing commodities in the open market for delivery to eligible importing countries (developing countries);
6. Transfers of commodities under the rules and established procedures of the World Food Program;
7. Sales for the currency of the importing country which is not transferable and is not convertible into currency or goods and services for use by the contributing country;
8. Sales for the currency of the importing country which is partially convertible into currency or goods and services for use by the contributing country;
9. Government sponsored loans of agricultural commodities repayable in kind[1];
10. Sales[2] on credit in which, as a result of government intervention, or of a centralized marketing scheme, the interest rate, period of repayment (including periods of grace) or other related terms do not conform to the commercial rates, periods or terms prevailing in the world market. In particular, with respect to period of repayment, credit transactions are distinguished as follows:
    a. Ten years or more;
    b. Over three years and under ten years.

11. Sales[2] in which the funds for the purchase of commodities are obtained under a loan from the government of the exporting country tied to the purchase of those commodities, distinguished as follows with respect to period of repayment:
    a. Ten years or more;
    b. Over three years and under ten years;
12. Transactions under categories 1 to 4 and 7 to 11 subject to tied usual marketing requirements or to tied offset purchasing requirements;
13. Transactions under categories 1 to 4 and 7 to 11 tied to purchase of fixed quantities of the same or another commodity from the exporting country.

Notes

1. The delegate of Japan reserved his government's position on the inclusion of this item.

2. The delegate of India reserved his government's position on the inclusion of this item.

Appendix B

Annex to FAO Council Resolution 2/55

[The FAO Council action took the form of adopting the recommendation of the Committee on Commodity Problems, without language changes.]

Procedures for the Establishment of Usual Marketing Requirements (UMRS)

1. The Committee reaffirmed the need for safeguarding usual commercial trade and for this purpose, the need to establish safeguards with the objective that the recipient country maintained at least the usual global commercial imports of the commodity concerned[a] in addition to the imports under the concessional transaction.

2. The Committee agreed that the establishment of tying UMR was a useful and necessary technique in order to ensure observance of the FAO Principle of additionality. The Committee therefore recommended that any transaction undertaken by governments in categories subject to prior consultation (2) of Annex to Council Resolution 1/53 shall be subject to the establishment of a UMR, as appropriate to the specific situation in order to ensure that the transaction resulted in additional consumption and did not harmfully affect normal patterns of production and trade. The UMR should be defined as [the specific agreement by the recipient country to maintain at least a specified level of commercial imports in addition to any imports of the same commodities under the concessional transaction].

3. The Committee noted that the FAO Principles of Surplus Disposal contain provisions aimed at avoiding the danger of displacement of commercial sales of closely related commodities,[b] and it reaffirmed that any interested country should have the opportunity to be consulted in this connection. The Committee therefore agreed that the supplying country should consider whether commercial trade in closely related commodities was likely to be harmfully affected and, if so, it should undertake consultations under the procedures set out in the Annex to Council Resolution 1/53, and take appropriate measures to safeguard such trade. A third party may request consultations with a supplying country on its own initiative.

4. In principle, the UMR should reflect the traditional commercial imports of the recipient country. The determination of a UMR should also take into account the economic and balance-of-payments position of the recipient countries and their development needs, and should not constitute an undue burden on them.

5. If the application of the principles in paragraph 4 leads to a change in UMR

311

levels, wherever they exist, then such changes should take account of the balance-of-payments position of the recipient country and should avoid disruptive effects on its economic development.

6. The following steps will be taken to arrive at a UMR for a particular recipient country for a specified period.[c]

   a. As a point of departure, the supplying country approached will attempt to calculate the statistical figure representing the total commercial imports of the commodity concerned by the requesting country in a representative period of years, which should normally be the preceding five years. To help arrive at an as accurate a statistical basis as possible, the FAO will be prepared to furnish Member Nations with basic trade statistics, including a breakdown according to types of transactions[d] relating to the commodity and country concerned. To this end, Member Nations are requested to extend full cooperation in supplying the data required to facilitate the task of the secretariat.

   b. The Committee recognized that the statistical figure of the total commercial imports of the recipient country in a representative period might need to be modified by special factors such as the following:

      i.   A substantial change in production in relation to consumption of the commodity concerned in the recipient country;

      ii. A substantial change in the balance-of-payments position or general economic situation of the recipient country;

      iii. Evidence of a significant trend in the reference period in the commercial imports of the commodity concerned of the recipient country;

      iv. The level of the relevant UMR negotiated according to the procedures laid down in the present paragraph by the interested countries in the nearest previous period. However, when a UMR is negotiated for the first time under these procedures, note will be taken of the provisions of para. 5 above.

      v.   Any exceptional features affecting the representativeness of the reference period for the recipient country;

      vi. Any other special considerations, including those which the Government of the recipient country may raise in its request or otherwise.[e]

   c. The proposed figure, with appropriate explanation in cases where it differs from the basic statistical figure (which shall also be notified), will be the subject of bilateral consultation with those Member Nations whose normal commercial exports may be affected by the transaction; if there is a suggestion for changing the negotiated UMR, then this should be discussed between the supplying and the recipient country.

   d. The proposed UMR, as determined by the supplying country in the light of the bilateral consultations, will be included in the prior notification to CSD of the main features of the transaction, as provided in para. (2)(b) of Annex to Council Resolution 1/53.

e. The final step in establishing the UMR will be the negotiation between the supplying country and the recipient country.[c]

7. In determining a UMR for a given period, a supplying country would ensure at the stage of bilateral consultations that all the interests concerned were taken fully into account, and use its best endeavours to arrive at a UMR that would be generally acceptable to all the parties concerned.

8. For any given recipient country and commodity, the UMR should be established[e] for a given period of time (e.g., the calendar, fiscal or crop year[e] or any other period of 12 months, according to procedures to be agreed between the supplying country and the recipient), it being understood that during this period of time there can be only one such UMR.

9. In the event of an unforeseen and substantial deterioration in the balance-of-payments and general economic situation of the recipient country during the life of a particular UMR, such UMR may be renegotiated with respect to the same commodity and the same period of time.

10. The Committee agreed that, if the need to improve procedures for establishing the UMR arises, the CSD should study the problems concerned in order to assist any further consideration by the CCP.

Notes

[a]The delegate of the Democratic Republic of the Sudan reserved the position of his Government on the deletion from the original draft of the words "or related commodities."

[b]Especially the Principles in para. 4(2) and that in para. 6(1)(b) (Disposal of Agricultural Surpluses Principles Recommended by FAO, Rome (1967)).

[c]The delegate of France declared that, with respect to the procedures for the establishment of a UMR, France intended to adhere to the undertakings set out in para. 2 of the Annex to Resolution 1/53. [This reservation has now been withdrawn.]

[d]Transactions included in the Annex of the terms of reference of the Consultation Sub-Committee on Surplus Disposal, on the one hand, and all other transactions on the other.

[e]The delegate of Argentina stated: "With respect to this text and with particular reference to paragraph 8, my government understands that since for each period of time there will be only one UMR, both the receiving country and the supplying countries carrying out transactions for those same products during the same period, will be subject to that particular UMR. With this interpretation my delegation agrees to accept the text as proposed by the Working Party and formulates reservations as to the amendments introduced to that text."

Appendix C

A. Reports of food aid transactions subject to prior notification to the FAO Consultative Subcommittee on Surplus Disposal are to be transmitted to the CSD in the following form:

PROFORMA FOR PRIOR NOTIFICATION[1]

Not for publication until
the transaction is officially announced

1. *Types of transaction:* (i.e., identify from those included in Appendix B)
2. *Aid-supplying country:*[2]
3. *Recipient country or international organization:*
4. *Commodity table:*

Commodity[3]	Quantity (M.T.)	World market value f.o.b.[4] $

5. *Supply period:*
6. *Terms of loans or sales on credit, if applicable:* (i.e., for types 9, 10 and 11, indicate interest rate, repayment period, other related terms.)
7. *Provisions to safeguard normal commercial trade, including the usual marketing requirements:*[5]
8. *Tied provisions:*[5] (specify any provisions—usual marketing requirements, export offsets, or any other obligations—that make the concessional transaction conditional on any other commodity or service.)
9. *Other explanatory comments:*
10. Response to bilateral consultations by: (insert date)

Notes

1. This accepts transactions described in paras. 3(a) and (b), 4 and 5 of the Annex to Council Resolution 1/53. (Appendix A).

2. If programmed commodities are a contribution being made in connection with an international program (e.g., FAC), this fact should be specified under this item; if under a monetary grant, a third country or an international organization supplies the commodity, this information should be included.

3. To facilitate consultations on multicommodity transactions, it is suggested that there should be a separate notification for each commodity.

4. I.e., based on prevailing world export market prices excluding insurance and ocean transport; or, if different, value established in this transaction by supplying country. If financing of ocean transport or other service is included in transaction, indicate this cost separately.

5. Basic statistical data used in establishing these provisions and identified as to source should be appended.

315

B. Reports of food aid transactions subject to ex post facto notification to CSD are to be transmitted to the CSD in the following form:

PROFORMA FOR EX POST FACTO NOTIFICATION TO CSD[1]

1. *Type of transaction:* (i.e., identify from those included in Catalog of Transactions attached to Annex to Council Resolution 1/53.)
2. *Aid-supplying country:*[2]
3. *Recipient country or international organization:*
4. *Commodity table:*

Commodity(ies)	Quantity(ies)	World market value f.o.b.[3]

5. *Supply period:*
6. *Terms of loans or sales on credit, if applicable:* (i.e., types 9, 10 and 11—indicate interest rate, repayment period, other related terms.)
7. *Other explanatory comments:*

Notes

1. Transactions described in paras. 3(b) and 4 of the Annex to Council Resolution 1/53 (Appendix B), namely, emergency transactions and government-to-government transactions of relatively small size and not involving sales in the local markets of the recipient country and therefore not likely to result in harmful interference with normal patterns of production and international trade.

2. If programmed commodities are a contribution being made in connection with an international program (e.g., FAC), this fact should be specified under this item; if under a monetary grant, a third country or an international organization supplies the commodity, this information should be included.

3. I.e., based on prevailing world export market prices excluding insurance and ocean transport; or, if different, value established in this transaction by supplying country. If financing of ocean transport or other services in included in transaction, indicate this cost separately.

C. Shipments effected through private charitable institutions must be reported to the CSD annually, in accordance with the following form:

PROFORMA FOR ANNUAL NOTIFICATION OF SHIPMENTS EFFECTED THROUGH PRIVATE CHARITABLE INSTITUTIONS

1. *Notifying country:*
2. *Time period:* (Information available for the latest full year, fiscal or calendar.)
3. *Information to be reported:*

Receiving country	Type of program/project	Name of private Institution	Period[1]	Commodities Type Quantity Value[2]
Algeria	School feeding	CARE	1969	DSM
		CRS		DSM
				Wh/flour
	MCH centers	etc.	1969	DSM
	Refugees, etc.	etc.	1969	Bulgur
Burundi	School feeding	etc.	1969	Cornmeal
	etc.			
	etc.			
Chad	MCH centers	etc.	1969	Wh/flour
Etc.				

[1] If fiscal year, indicate the month beginning the year.

[2] World market value, f.o.b., i.e., based on prevailing world export market prices excluding insurance and ocean transport; or, if different, value established in this transaction by supplying country. If financing of ocean transport or other services is included in transaction, indicate this cost separately.

Index

319

About the Author

Robert L. Bard teaches international law at The University of Connecticut School of Law. His interest in food aid problems stems from his five years' service with the Agency for International Development. He has done graduate work in economics, a particular qualification for agricultural trade problems, which have been the exclusive province of agricultural economists.

Professor Bard is currently beginning work on a study of the efficacy of commodity agreements to regulate agricultural trade for the benefit of developed and developing countries.